WITHDRAWN

Studies in Celtic History XXXI

TOME

STUDIES IN MEDIEVAL CELTIC HISTORY AND LAW IN HONOUR OF THOMAS CHARLES-EDWARDS

STUDIES IN CELTIC HISTORY

ISSN 0261–9865

General editors
Dauvit Broun
Máire Ní Mhaonaigh
Huw Pryce

Studies in Celtic History aims to provide a forum for new research into all aspects of the history of Celtic-speaking peoples throughout the whole of the medieval period. The term 'history' is understood broadly: any study, regardless of discipline, which advances our knowledge and understanding of the history of Celtic-speaking peoples will be considered. Studies of primary sources, and of new methods of exploiting such sources, are encouraged.

Founded by Professor David Dumville, the series was relaunched under new editorship in 1997. Proposals or queries may be sent directly to the editors at the addresses given below; all submissions will receive prompt and informed consideration before being sent to expert readers.

Professor Dauvit Broun, Department of History (Scottish), University of Glasgow, 9 University Gardens, Glasgow G12 8QH

Dr Máire Ní Mhaonaigh, St John's College, Cambridge, CB2 1TP

Professor Huw Pryce, School of History, Welsh History and Archaeology, Bangor University, Gwynedd LL57 2DG

For titles already published in this series
see the end of this volume

Thomas Charles-Edwards addresses the masses at Clonenagh
(Cluain Eidhneach), Co. Laois.

TOME

STUDIES IN MEDIEVAL CELTIC HISTORY AND LAW IN HONOUR OF THOMAS CHARLES-EDWARDS

Edited by

FIONA EDMONDS and PAUL RUSSELL

THE BOYDELL PRESS

First published 2011
The Boydell Press, Woodbridge

ISBN 978–1–84383–661–2

The Boydell Press is an imprint of Boydell & Brewer Ltd
PO Box 9, Woodbridge, Suffolk IP12 3DF, UK
and of Boydell & Brewer Inc.
668 Mount Hope Ave, Rochester, NY 14620, USA
website: www.boydellandbrewer.com

A catalogue record of this publication is available
from the British Library

The publisher has no responsibility for the continued existence or
accuracy of URLs for external or third-party internet websites referred to
in this book, and does not guarantee that any content on such websites
is, or will remain, accurate or appropriate

Papers used by Boydell & Brewer Ltd are natural, recyclable products
made from wood grown in sustainable forests

Printed and bound in the United States of America

CONTENTS

ILLUSTRATIONS

Frontispiece: Thomas Charles-Edwards addresses the masses at Clonenagh (Cluain Eidhneach), Co. Laois.

Figures

Tables

Maps

PREFACE

Fiona Edmonds and Paul Russell

The following collection of essays is offered to Thomas Charles-Edwards on the occasion of his retirement from the Jesus Chair of Celtic in the University of Oxford. Thomas has occupied this position from 1997 until 2011 and before that he was a Fellow and Tutor in History at Corpus Christi College. He has always imparted his knowledge generously, devoting much time to teaching undergraduates and supervising graduate students. Some of the contributors to this volume were supervised by Thomas; others benefited in other ways from his wisdom when they were students; and the work of all, as colleagues in the field, has been shaped by his work. Thomas's research is held in high esteem in the world of Celtic scholarship, and he is renowned for the extraordinary range of his interests and publications. No single volume could reflect the full range of his contribution (strikingly borne out in the difficulty of tracking down all his publications to date, listed in Maredudd ap Huw's contribution), and so it was decided to focus on the areas of Celtic history and law. But even within that it is notable that all the essays here can find a starting point within Thomas's own body of work.

The first half of the volume contains essays which consider historical aspects of Britain and Ireland and often also reflect his interest in archaeology and epigraphy: Sue Youngs discusses some of the Christian symbols found on hanging-bowls from post-Roman Britain; Clare Stancliffe considers aspects of Columbanus's monasticism; Catherine Swift examines the role of priests in early medieval Ireland. Several contributions focus on political or ecclesiastical organisation: David Dumville discusses the political geography of Dál Riata; Oliver Padel considers Asser's *parochia* of Exeter; Thomas Clancy covers succession, jurisdiction and politics in the Columban *familia* in the later tenth century; and Marie Therese Flanagan discusses a twelfth-century indulgence granted by an Irish bishop at Bath Priory. Thomas's archaeological and epigraphical interests are particularly to the fore in Betty O'Brien and Edel Bhreathnach's joint contribution, which examines the physical manifestation and historical context of Irish boundary *ferta* in the light of recent discoveries, and in Nancy Edwards's essay on Viking-age sculpture in north-west Wales. Nor is historiography omitted: Huw Pryce considers Gerald of Wales and his debt to Gildas in the *Descriptio Kambriae*.

Thomas's works on the legal institutions and texts of medieval Ireland and Wales are of fundamental importance. This is reflected in a group of essays which range across the Irish Sea and, indeed, further afield: Roy Flechner seeks the reasons why Patrick left Britain in the legal and political context of post-Roman Britain. Several essays explore aspects of early Irish law: Robin Chapman Stacey discusses how the law might have been learned; Fergus Kelly examines the way in which stolen property might be recovered; Bronagh Ní Chonaill considers some of the more contentious aspects of kinship; and Charlene Eska revisits the question of marriage by purchase. Sara Roberts considers the legal triads in the Iorwerth redaction of the Welsh laws, while Wendy Davies also considers aspects of the law in Wales in a wide-ranging exploration of judicial presidency in Brittany, Wales and Northern Iberia.

Irish and Welsh literature is another area in which Thomas's work has opened up new ways of thinking through his nuanced and subtle readings, which are often informed by his understanding and appreciation of historical and legal context. The final group of essays pays tribute to this. As noted above, Charlene Eska's essay considers marriage by purchase, but does so through a reconsideration of *Tochmarc Étaíne*, a text which formed the subject of an essay by Thomas. Elva Johnston picks up a number of themes addressed elsewhere in this volume in a study of power and the public world in *Longes Mac nUislenn* and, finally, Máire Ní Mhaonaigh offers a reading of a later Mongán tale *Compert Mongáin ocus Serce Duibe Lacha do Mongán*.

Given space and time we could have produced several volumes of essays in honour of Thomas, such was the eagerness of colleagues to contribute. As a result, in order to maximise the number who could contribute, we decided that we ourselves would not offer papers but that our debt to Thomas would be paid in the editing of the volume, a task made far easier by the willingness and indeed eagerness of our contributors to respect our deadlines and tolerate our editorial decisions. We are also grateful to the editorial staff at Boydell, and especially Caroline Palmer, for taking on the volume, and to Ben Russell for the line drawing on the dust jacket. We are also grateful to the various organisations who have kindly allowed images to be reproduced; full acknowledgements appear in the appropriate places.

Finally, the double significance of the title of the volume is in need of explanation. In Thomas's family the current big book in production, and there have been a few, is always known as the 'tome', often prefixed by various disparaging adjectives. The drawing on the cover is of side C of the so-called 'Pillar of Thomas' (Lower Court Farm, Margam, now in the Margam Stones Museum).[1] It shows a carved cross with the word *TO* || *ME*, with two letters either side of the shaft of the cross. *TOME* (a spelling for the Latin genitive singular *Tomae*) means 'of Thomas' and could scarcely be more appropriate as a title for this volume. The work in this volume by colleagues and students is in one sense 'of Thomas', not least because much of it arises from and is stimulated by Thomas's own work. But, of course, *TOME* could also be a dative singular, 'for Thomas', and that is indeed what this volume is, with gratitude and affection.

---

[1] M. Redknap and J. M. Lewis, ed., *A Corpus of the Early Medieval Inscribe Stones and Stones Sculpture in Wales, vol. I South-East Wales and the English Border* (Cardiff, 2007), 445–8 (G89); V. E. Nash-Williams, *The Early Christian Monuments of Wales* (Cardiff, 1950), 168 (item 259) and Plate XXVI.

CONTRIBUTORS

Dr Maredudd ap Huw, National Library of Wales, Aberystwyth

Dr Edel Bhreathnach, Mícheál Ó Cléirigh Institute, University College, Dublin

Professor Thomas Clancy, Celtic and Gaelic, School of Humanities, University of Glasgow

Professor Wendy Davies, Emerita, University College London

Professor David Dumville, Department of History, University of Aberdeen

Dr Fiona Edmonds, Department of Anglo-Saxon, Norse and Celtic, and Clare College, Cambridge

Professor Nancy Edwards, School of History, Welsh History and Archaeology, Bangor University

Dr Charlene Eska, Virginia Tech, Blacksburg, Virginia

Professor Marie Therese Flanagan, School of History and Anthropology, Queen's University, Belfast

Dr Roy Flechner, Trinity College, Cambridge

Dr Elva Johnston, School of History and Archives, University College Dublin

Professor Fergus Kelly, School of Celtic Studies, Dublin Institute for Advanced Studies

Bronagh Ní Chonaill, Celtic and Gaelic, School of Humanities, University of Glasgow

Dr Máire Ní Mhaonaigh, Department of Anglo-Saxon, Norse and Celtic, and St John's College, Cambridge

Dr Betty O'Brien, Míchael Ó Cléirigh Institute, University College Dublin

Dr Oliver Padel, Department of Anglo-Saxon, Norse and Celtic, University of Cambridge

Professor Huw Pryce, School of History, Welsh History and Archaeology, Bangor University

Dr Sara Elin Roberts, School of Law, Bangor University

Dr Paul Russell, Department of Anglo-Saxon, Norse and Celtic, University of Cambridge

Professor Robin Chapman Stacey, Department of History, University of Washington, Seattle

Dr Clare Stancliffe, Department of Theology and Religion, and Department of History, Durham University

Dr Catherine Swift, Mary Immaculate College, University of Limerick

Dr Susan Youngs, School of Archaeology, University of Oxford

ABBREVIATIONS

Irish and Welsh annals are referred to by the year of the entry; editorial dates are in square brackets.

ABoyle   A. M. Freeman, ed., 'The annals in Cotton MS. Titus A. XXV', *Revue Celtique* 41 (1924), 301–30; 42 (1925), 283–305; 43 (1926), 358–84; 44 (1927), 336–61

AC   Annales Cambriae: A Version: E. Phillimore, ed., 'The Annales Cambriae and the Old-Welsh genealogies from Harleian MS. 3859', *Y Cymmrodor*, 9 (1888), 141–83 (repr. in John Morris, *Arthurian Sources*, 6 vols (Chichester, 1995) V.13–55); A, B, and C Versions, ed. J. Williams ab Ithel, *Annales Cambriae* (London, 1860); A, B, and C Versions (682–954): ed. and transl., D. N. Dumville, *Annales Cambriae, A.D. 682–954: Texts A–C in Parallel* (Cambridge, 2002); Paul Martin Remfry, transl., *Annales Cambriae. A translation of Harleian 3859: PRO E.164/1: Cotton Domitian, A 1: Exeter Cathedral Library MS. 3514 and MS Exchequer DB Neath, PRO E.164/1* (Malvern, 2007). References are by year only

AFM   J. O'Donovan, ed. and transl., *Annala Rioghachta Eireann: Annals of the Kingdom of Ireland by the Four Masters, from the Earliest Period to the Year 1616*, 2nd edn, 7 vols (Dublin, 1856)

ALI   W. N. Hancock, *et al.*, ed. and transl., *Ancient Laws of Ireland*, 6 vols (Dublin, 1865–1901)

ALW   A. Owen, ed. and transl., *Ancient Laws and Institutes of Wales*, (London, 1841); published in two forms, a single-volume folio and a two-volume quarto

ARC   Dermot Gleeson and Seán Mac Airt, ed., 'Annals of Roscrea', *PRIA* C, 59 (1958), 145–71

AT   W. Stokes, ed. and transl., 'The Annals of Tigernach', *Revue Celtique* 16 (1895) 374–419; 17 (1896), 6–33, 119–263, 337–420; 18 (1897), 9–59, 150–97, 267–303; reprinted in two vols (Felinfach, 1993)

AU   'The Annals of Ulster' (no particular edition)

AU   W. M. Hennessy and B. MacCarthy, ed. and transl., *Annala Uladh, Annals of Ulster*, 4 vols (Dublin, 1887–1901)

AU²   S. Mac Airt and G. Mac Niocaill, ed. and transl., *The Annals of Ulster (to A.D. 1131)*, Part I. Text and Translation (Dublin, 1983)

BAR   British Archaeological Reports

BBCS   *The Bulletin of the Board of Celtic Studies*

BL   British Library

ByT (Pen. 20)	T. Jones, ed., *Brut y Tywysogyon, Peniarth MS. 20* (Cardiff, 1941); translated in *Brut y Tywysogyon or The Chronicle of the Princes, Peniarth MS. 20 Version* (Cardiff, 1952)
ByT (RB)	T. Jones, ed. and transl., *Brut y Tywysogyon or The Chronicle of the Princes, Red Book of Hergest Version* (Cardiff, 1955)
C	G. Martínez Díez, ed., *Colección documental del monasterio de San Pedro de Cardeña* (Cardeña/Burgos, 1998); charters cited by number
CCIH	L. Breatnach, *Companion to the* Corpus Iuris Hibernici, Studies in Early Irish Law V (Dublin, 2005)
CCSL	Corpus Christianorum, Series Latina
Cel	J. M. Andrade Cernadas, with M. Díaz Tie and F. J. Pérez Rodríguez, ed., *O Tombo de Celanova: Estudio introductorio, edición e índices (ss. ix–xii)*, 2 vols (Santiago de Compostela, 1995); charters cited by number
CIH	D. A. Binchy, ed., *Corpus Iuris Hibernici*, 6 vols (Dublin, 1978)
CIIC	R. A. S. Macalister, ed., *Corpus Inscriptionum Insularum Celticarum*, 2 vols (Dublin, 1945–9)
CKA	*Chronicle of the Kings of Alba*: ed. M. O. Anderson, *Kings and Kingship in Early Scotland* (2nd edn, Edinburgh, 1980), 249–53
CMCS	*Cambridge Medieval Celtic Studies* (vols 1–25); *Cambrian Medieval Celtic Studies* (vol. 26–)
CPDR	*Cethri Prímchenéla Dáil Riata*: ed. D. N. Dumville, '*Cethri Prímchenéla Dáil Riata*', *Scottish Gaelic Studies* 20 (2000), 170–91
CR	A. de Courson, ed., *Cartulaire de l'Abbaye de Redon en Bretagne* (Paris, 1863); charters cited by number
CR A	Appendix to CR; charters cited by number
CS	W. M. Hennessy, ed., *Chronicum Scotorum* (London, 1866)
CSEL	Corpus Scriptorum Ecclesiasticorum Latinorum
CTh	T. Mommsen and P. M. Meyer, ed., *Theodosiani Libri XVI cum Constitutionibus Sirmondianis* (Berlin, 1905); C. Pharr, transl., *The Theodosian Code and Novels and the Sirmondian Constitutions* (Princeton, 1952)
DIL	*Dictionary of the Irish Language, Based Mainly on Old and Middle Irish Materials*, ed. E. G. Quin *et al.* (Dublin, 1913–76); compact edition (Dublin, 1983); electronic edition http://www.dil.ie/
ECMW	V. E. Nash-Williams, *The Early Christian Monuments of Wales* (Cardiff, 1950)
EIWK	T. M. Charles-Edwards, *Early Irish and Welsh Kinship* (Oxford, 1993)
Ep.	Columbanus, *Epistulae*, ed. and transl., G. S. M. Walker, *Sancti Columbani Opera*, SLH 2 (Dublin, 1957), 2–59
GEIL	F. Kelly, *Guide to Early Irish Law*, Studies in Early Irish Law III (Dublin, 1988; repr. with revised bibliography 2009)
HBS	Henry Bradshaw Society

Instr.	Columbanus, *Instructiones*, ed. and transl., G. S. M. Walker, *Sancti Columbani Opera*, SLH 2 (Dublin, 1957), 60–121
JRSAI	*The Journal of the Royal Society of Antiquaries of Ireland*
Li, Lii, Liii	E. Sáez, ed., *Colección documental del archivo de la catedral de León (775–1230)*, vol. 1 (775–952); E. Sáez and C. Sáez, ed., vol. 2 (953–85); J. M. Ruiz Asencio, ed., vol. 3 (986–1031) (León, 1987, 1990, 1987); charters cited by number
LL	J. Gwenogvryn Evans with J. Rhŷs, ed., *The Text of the Book of Llan Dâv* (Oxford, 1893); charters cited by page number of this edition, differentiating those that begin on the same page by a, b, c
LMU	Vernam Hull, ed. and transl., Longes Mac n-Uislenn: *The Exile of the Sons of Uisliu* (New York, 1949)
MGH	Monumenta Germaniae Historica
MIA	S. Ó hInnse, ed. and transl., *Miscellaneous Irish annals, A.D. 1114–1437* (Dublin, 1947)
NLW	National Library of Wales
Nov.	R. Schoell and G. Kroll, ed., *Novellae, Corpus Iuris Civilis*, 3 vols (Berlin, 1877–1895), III
OD	J. A. Fernández Flórez and M. Herrero de la Fuente, ed., *Colección documental del monasterio de Santa María de Otero de las Dueñas*, vol. 1 (León, 1999); charters cited by number
ODNB	*Oxford Dictionary of National Biography*, ed. H. C. G. Matthew and Brian Harrison, 61 vols (Oxford, 2004)
PL	J.-P. Migne, ed., *Patrologia Latina*, 221 vols (Paris, 1844–64)
PMH	A. Herculano de Carvalho e Araujo and J. J. da Silva Mendes Leal, ed., *Portugaliae Monumenta Historica a saeculo octavo post Christum usque ad quintumdecimum, Diplomata et Chartae*, vol. 1 (Lisbon, 1867–73); charters cited by number
PMLA	*Proceedings of the Modern Language Association of America*
PRIA	*Proceedings of the Royal Irish Academy*
RCAHMS	Royal Commission on the Ancient and Historical Monuments of Scotland
RCAHMW	Royal Commission on the Ancient and Historical Monuments of Wales
Reg. Coen.	Columbanus, *Regula Coenobialis*, ed. and transl. G. S. M. Walker, *Sancti Columbani Opera*, SLH 2 (Dublin, 1957), 142–69
Reg. Mon.	Columbanus, *Regula Monachorum*, ed. and transl. G. S. M. Walker, *Sancti Columbani Opera*, SLH 2 (Dublin, 1957), 122–43
RS	Rolls Series: Rerum Britannicarum Medii Aevi Scriptores or Chronicles and Memorials of Great Britain and Ireland during the Middle Ages
S	P. H. Sawyer, *Anglo-Saxon Charters: An Annotated List and Bibliography* (London, 1968) – listed by charter number
Sah	J. M. Mínguez Fernández, ed., *Colección diplomática del monasterio de Sahagún (857–1230)*, vol. 1 (León, 1976); charters cited by number

Sam	M. Lucas Álvarez, ed., *El Tumbo de San Julián de Samos (siglos VIII–XII)* (Santiago de Compostela, 1986); charters cited by number
SC	Sources Chrétiennes
SEIL	R. Thurneysen *et al.*, ed., *Studies in Early Irish Law* (Dublin, 1936)
SH	*Studia Hibernica*
SLH	Scriptores Latini Hiberniae
SM	A. Ubieto Arteta, ed., *Cartulario de San Millán de la Cogolla* (Valencia, 1976); charters cited by number
Sob	P. Loscertales de García de Valdeavellano, ed., *Tumbos del monasterio de Sobrado de los Monjes*, 2 vols (Madrid, 1976); charters cited by number
T	L. Sánchez Belda, ed., *Cartulario de Santo Toribio de Liébana* (Madrid, 1948); charters cited by number
TÉ	Osborn Bergin and R. I. Best, ed. and transl., '*Tochmarc Étaíne*', *Ériu* 12 (1934–8), 137–96
THSC	*Transactions of the Honourable Society of Cymmrodorion*
WML	A. W. Wade-Evans, ed. and transl., *Welsh Medieval Law* (Oxford, 1909)
ZCP	*Zeitschrift für celtische Philologie*

1

CLOUD-CUCKOO LAND?
SOME CHRISTIAN SYMBOLS FROM POST-ROMAN BRITAIN

Susan Youngs

Christian iconography is not so plentiful in the post-Roman states of Britain that we can afford to ignore a varied and interesting range of crosses and other motifs from a period when we are otherwise heavily dependent on epigraphic evidence, a tradition that was largely peculiar to the far west and north. The problem is the source: like Dean Swift's island of Laputa, a substantial body of hanging-bowls floats above the cultural landscape of seventh-century Britain. Often labelled 'Anglo-Saxon' from their usual find-places in furnished burials in eastern England, considerable ingenuity has been expended in the past in arguing for a Germanic context for the manufacture of these distinctive vessels, despite their late Celtic decoration.[1] Most hanging-bowls are demonstrably not made for or by Germanic owners and in their ornament they bear unique witness to the pretensions, changing tastes and religion of the Celtic patrons for whom most of these luxury items were originally manufactured.[2] The tally of early bowls is now well over 150 and steadily rising through metal-detecting and controlled excavations,[3] but is certainly an underestimate because the parts that survive best are the applied mounts, comprising suspension hooks with a decorated plate, separate appliqués or basal plates attached to the inside or outside of the vessel. Otherwise unrecorded bowl-mounts pass through coin fairs and appear on Internet sale sites.

An attractive alternative interpretation, firmly based on shared contemporary artistic traditions and materials, principally the use of enamel and millefiori glass, is to view the enamelled bowls as imports from contemporary Ireland.[4] But this solution is persistently complicated by the continuing lack of evidence for bowls

1   C. Scull, 'Further Evidence from East Anglia for Enamelling on Early Saxon Metalwork', *Anglo-Saxon Studies in Archaeology and History* 4 (1985), 117–24; A. Crone, *The History of a Scottish Lowland Crannog. Excavations at Buiston, Ayrshire 1989–9*, Scottish Trust for Archaeological Research Monograph 4 (Edinburgh, 2000), 157.

2   S. Youngs, 'Anglo-Saxon, Irish and British Relations: Hanging-Bowls Reconsidered', in *Anglo-Saxon/Irish Relations before the Vikings*, ed. J. Graham-Campbell and M. Ryan, Proceedings of the British Academy 157 (London, 2009), 205–30.

3   Assembled in J. Brenan, *Hanging Bowls and their Context*, BAR British Series 220 (Oxford, 1991); R. L. S. Bruce-Mitford with S. Raven, *The Corpus of Late Celtic Hanging-Bowls* (Oxford, 2005), with information up to 1994.

4   Following F. Henry, 'Hanging Bowls', *JRSAI* 66 (1936), 209–46; C. Newman, 'Notes on Some Irish Hanging Bowl Escutcheons', *Journal of Irish Archaeology* 5 (1990), 45–8, where the weakness of suggested Irish comparanda is apparent.

with the distinctive hanging-bowl profile and the absence of additional bowl mounts in the growing corpus of sixth- and seventh-century bronze work from Ireland.[5]

On occasion hanging-bowls appear in the archaeological record in the company of a variety of vessels made in the eastern Mediterranean and, closer to home, of bowls imported from Frankish territories.[6] The rich burials of Sutton Hoo Mound 1 (Suffolk), Kingston Down grave 205 (Kent) and Prittlewell (Essex) have such mixed assemblages of bronze containers.[7] In brief, my contention is that hanging-bowls too should be viewed primarily as imports, prestige items brought in from the independent territories which shared the central, western and northern parts of Britain with the Anglo-Saxon polities in the sixth and seventh centuries; and that the occasional adoption of Germanic motifs reflects proximity and the growing importance of eastern markets as well as local cultural overlap.[8] This is a working hypothesis reached by the elimination of alternatives rather than one based on substantial positive evidence. Nothing could be further from the scholarly analyses of Thomas Charles-Edwards than to pile one hypothesis on another and it is therefore with some trepidation that I propose, first, that we do have a substantial body of fine metalwork from the indigenous peoples of Britain in the sixth and seventh centuries and, secondly, that some of these pieces bear interesting witness to their Christian belief. A small return for so much support and learning so kindly imparted.

It is uncontentious to say that hanging-bowls were luxury items made for wealthy patrons, specialised vessels in an area of the post-Imperial world largely devoid of fine pottery and where glass vessels were rare and valuable items.[9] These fine bowls were designed to be used when suspended from three or four points, rather than to stand on a surface. Unlike handled buckets they are not easy to transport or pour from, and unlike Iron Age and later cauldrons they could not have hung over or stood next to a fire because the great majority of their suspension points were attached by lead solder, which has a low melting point. This demonstrates that, whether these hooked plates were elaborately decorated or simple shapes, these vessels were not intended to be heated. The type of red enamel used on many also discolours irreversibly if heated with oxygen present.

The ancestry of hanging-bowls is unclear and probably complex. There were small native bronze bowls in pre-Roman late Iron Age Britain and Ireland, some with single suspension loops, and it may be that shallow vessels hung in tripods from the Classical world also contributed to the design of the medieval hanging-bowl and brought with them or enhanced an existing association with ritual use.[10]

---

[5] R. L. S. Bruce-Mitford, 'Ireland and the Hanging Bowls: A Review', in *Ireland and Insular Art, A.D. 500–1200*, ed. M. Ryan (Dublin, 1987), 30–9; Youngs, 'Anglo-Saxon, Irish and British Relations', 221–5.

[6] P. Richards, 'Byzantine Bronze Vessels in England and Europe' (unpubl. PhD dissertation, University of Cambridge, 1980); M. Mango *et al.*, 'A 6th-century Mediterranean Bucket from Bromeswell Parish, Suffolk', *Antiquity* 63 no. 259 (1989), 295–311.

[7] R. L. S. Bruce-Mitford, *The Sutton Hoo Ship-Burial Vol. 3* (London, 1983), chs II, X; Bruce-Mitford with Raven, *Corpus*, no. 42; Museum of London Archaeology Service [MOLAS], *The Prittlewell Prince* (London, 2004).

[8] Youngs, 'Anglo-Saxon, Irish and British Relations', 208, 226.

[9] E. Campbell, *Continental and Mediterranean Imports to Atlantic Britain and Ireland, AD 400–800*, Council for British Archaeology Research Report 157 (York, 2007).

[10] E. Fowler, 'Hanging-Bowls', in *Studies in Ancient Europe: Studies Presented to Stuart Piggott,*

Our understanding of the Roman background to the medieval hanging bowl has been clarified by Dr Noel Adams' recent work on late imperial drinking sets and military clubs, her arguments enforced by the recovery of a large British hanging-bowl in a fourth-century vessel hoard from a well in Roman London in 2007.[11] Changes in aristocratic display to suit more intimate surroundings are seen beyond the *limes* too, in the late- and post-Roman period, and there is unique evidence that in the historic period the northern Picts manufactured distinctive hanging-bowl mounts.[12] They were peculiar to Britain and Ireland from the fourth to the ninth centuries.

The functions and purposes of these bowls will have changed through their time above ground; they were probably used in more than one way by more than one owner before burial as an accessory vessel or cremation container. The ornament, however, will remain that created to suit the first owner. This varied widely, beginning with simple leaf-shaped plates in the sixth century; by the seventh century a variety of complex Celtic and classically derived motifs were used, many richly enamelled on complex fine bowls. Practicality was not a key consideration; the rinsing of fingers after a meal or dipping in cups for strong drink are the practices of a class with leisure and aspirations. These pieces were made for people with surplus to invest in or squander (depending on the commentator) on bards, feasts, religious observances and other luxury goods.[13] Such people were themselves, or were close to, the rulers, kings, tyrants and judges of Gildas' day and later.[14] They were also Christians, as were the rulers whose bishops refused to stand up to greet Augustine from Canterbury at their second meeting, the northern Pictish kings being the last native rulers to convert in the 560s or 570s.[15]

Early discussion about the function of the bowls led directly to suggestions that they were equipment seized from British churches where they had served variously as lustral basins, votive pieces or baptismal bowls for children. An interpretation as hanging lamp reflectors, *gabatae*, remains the most long-lived.[16] The presence of crosses on some, and the early-ninth-century description of the gift of bowl lights in the Northumbrian poem *De Abbatibus*, supported this view: *nam plures multi cupiebant pendere caucos limpida qui tribuant quadrato lumina*

---

ed. J. M. Coles and D. D. A. Simpson (Leicester, 1968), 287–309; Bruce-Mitford with Raven, *Corpus*, 459–72. The idea of ritual use in a Classical tripod was developed by H. Vierck, 'Cortina Tripodis: zu Auffrängung und Gebrauch subrömischer Hängebecken aus Britannien und Irland', *Frühmittelalterliche Studien* 4 (1970), 8–52; an interpretation partly demolished on technical grounds by Brenan, *Hanging Bowls*, 31–3.

11 N. Adams, 'Hanging Basins and the Wine-Coloured Sea: The Wider Context of Early Medieval Hanging Bowls', in *Early Medieval Art and Archaeology in the Northern World: Studies in Honour of James Graham-Campbell*, ed. A. Reynolds and L. Webster (Leiden, forthcoming), with thanks to Dr Adams for allowing me access to her paper in advance of publication; J. Hall, 'Archaeological Discovery at Drapers Gardens', *London and Middlesex Archaeological Society Newsletter* 122 (January 2008), 6–8.

12 F. Hunter, *Beyond the Edge of the Empire: Caledonians, Picts and Romans* (Rosemarkie, 2007), 16: 'a personal level of interaction'; Youngs, 'Anglo-Saxon, Irish and British Relations', 209–13.

13 Campbell, *Continental and Mediterranean Imports*.

14 M. Winterbottom, ed. and transl., *Gildas. The Ruin of Britain and other Documents* (London, 1978), 29.

15 This is the traditional account based on Adomnán's *Vita Sancti Columbae*, but conversion may well have occurred earlier, particularly south of the Mounth, see J. E. Fraser, *From Caledonia to Pictland* (Edinburgh, 2009), 99–100, 103–5.

16 All these interpretations are fully documented and analysed in Brenan, *Hanging Bowls*, 36–41.

templo.[17] While hanging lamps are familiar from early illustration, the idea that these metal bowls were reflectors is weakened by a variety of considerations, among them the extreme rarity of glass, which would have been essential for an inner lamp, and other evidence for portable lighting. The large number of hanging-bowls and variations in capacity, form and decoration also speak against this one function. With the passage of time and hunt for alternative uses the interpretation of ornament as specifically Christian has fallen into disfavour.[18] There is a difference between evidence for a Christian social context and specific ecclesiastical functions; the sign of the cross can be prophylactic with no implication of further ritual use.

Hanging-bowls were decorated in a variation of styles, ranging from Roman to native, from Celtic revival to Germanic-influenced, and among the motifs used is the Christian symbol of the cross, represented in different modes. If this is accepted, other appliqué motifs may carry related messages. In order to understand the possible comparanda and contexts some idea of period is essential. The burial contexts of the various bowl forms and almost all types of decoration provide *termini ante quos*. The majority were buried in the course of the seventh century, mainly in the first half and extending into the third quarter; famously, three very different bowls were buried in Mound 1 at Sutton Hoo possibly as late as the 640s or as early as 595, according to the most recent re-assessment of the associated coin hoard.[19] There is, therefore, a broad chronological framework in the search for both the sources and contemporary parallels for motifs used on hanging-bowls, with the usual caveats – that very little early medieval work in Britain and Ireland can be closely dated, whether a manuscript or an inscribed stone, even a barbarous coin with un-named mint or issuer, and that moving from one class of difficult material to another can be hazardous.[20] What we also know is that manufacture may have occurred many years before the burial of what were often incomplete, old and repaired hanging-bowls.

The cross became the most straightforward Christian symbol in early medieval Europe by the seventh century. Eighteen hanging-bowls bear cruciform ornament of five major types (Figs 1–6). Some are based on a curvilinear system also used in the decoration of sacred texts. Some forms are represented by a single mount. Two designs are unambiguously Christian: first, found at Faversham (Kent), a set of hooked mounts with a Latin cross flanked by sea-beasts; the second, excavated at the monastery of Whitby (N. Yorks.), a single hooked-mount carrying

---

17 'Many men wished to hang up numerous bowls which would give soft light in the rectangular church': A. Campbell, ed. and transl., *De Abbatibus* (Oxford, 1967), 50–1; on dating, xxii; F. Henry, 'Hanging-Bowls', *JRSAI* 66 (1936), 209–46, at 211; H. E. Kilbride-Jones, *Celtic Craftsmanship in Bronze* (London, 1980), 236.

18 Brenan, *Hanging Bowls*, 36, on the Latin cross with dolphins from Faversham: 'it would be unwise to be too categorical about interpreting these escutcheons as Christian'.

19 H. Geake, 'When were Hanging Bowls Deposited in Anglo-Saxon Graves?', *Medieval Archaeology* 43 (2001), 1–18; R. Abdy and G. Williams, 'A Catalogue of Hoards and Single Finds from the British Isles, c. AD 410–675', in *Coinage and History in the North Sea World c. 500–1250*, ed. B. Cook and G. Williams, The Northern World 19 (Leiden, 2006), 11–73, at 18: 'the coins could have been deposited at any point in the first four decades of the seventh century'; and see G. Williams, 'The Circulation and Function of Coinage in Conversion-period England, c. AD 580–675', in *Coinage and History*, ed. Cook and Williams, 145–92, at 180: 'a date between c. 595 and c. 640 seems likely'.

20 A programme of refined radiocarbon dating of seventh-century Anglo-Saxon burials now nearing conclusion at the University of Cardiff may well add some helpful new dates.

Figure 1. (a) One of a set of hanging-bowl mounts from an Anglo-Saxon cemetery at Faversham (Kent); (b) mid-sixth-century mosaic with supporting dolphins from the presbytery arch, San Vitale, Ravenna; (c) mount from a bowl buried at Hawnby (N. Yorks.). Scales 1:2 ((b) reduced). Drawn by Alison Wilkins.

an equal-armed cross (Figs 1a and 2a).[21] The Faversham bowl, no longer extant, was carried by openwork discs with fine enamelled lines and spots; the flanking beasts with open jaws are most probably dolphins, here supporting and adoring the cross (Fig. 1a). The hooks themselves are beasts with similar profiles in the round with curled tails and are unique in the series of hanging-bowl mounts. The cross with dolphin iconography is unusual but not unique: it was known in the Byzantine world at the Imperial court, or at least to the artisans commissioned to decorate San Vitale in Ravenna, one of the most important 'small provincial monuments'.[22] On the presbytery arch pairs of naturalistic dolphins linked at the tail surround the central portrait roundel of Christ and support the portrait roun-

---

[21] Bruce-Mitford with Raven, *Corpus*, 79; nos 37 and 101.
[22] Quotation indicating the view from Constantinople: O. Demus, *Byzantine Mosaic Decoration* (4th reprint, London, 1976), 49.

dels to either side (Fig. 1b).[23] The central image has a cross shown on Christ's nimbus, while on a neighbouring arch angels support a roundel framing a Latin cross.[24] This is not to suggest a direct link with Ravenna, but because the city is a unique treasure house of early Christian iconography preserved in one of the power centres of Italy in the sixth century. San Vitale was consecrated in May 548. Other sites in Ravenna, together with nearby Sant'Apollinare in Classe, also provide datable comparanda for motifs that are found on British hanging-bowls.[25]

There has been considerable variation in the dates given to these Faversham mounts; the dating is based on art-historical considerations because we lack knowledge of the grave context and the form of the bowl. Stylised dolphins were, of course, found in Roman Britain, where in the third and fourth centuries some schools of mosaicists favoured lively versions of this sea-beast.[26] This Classical background supports the fifth-century date first suggested by Kendrick; most recently, Bruce-Mitford has agreed with this dating.[27] The broad material evidence from the cemetery and the Classicising influence of the re-introduction of Christianity to Kent have also polarised dating to the seventh century.[28] A gap in the archaeological record for hanging-bowls from ca 400 to at least 550 analysed by Brenan has at last been challenged with radio carbon dates for the cremated bone in an enamelled hanging bowl producing a date of 550 for the burial of an old vessel.[29] This reinforces my reservations on the proposed thirty-year life for old vessels in seventh-century contexts, given their value as high-status pieces and the possibility of the reuse of old mounts on new bowls when in British hands. Nevertheless I support a relatively early period in the sixth century for the manufacture of these mounts because the stylised ambiguity of the dolphins is also found in the early Byzantine tradition.[30]

If the default position of Christian patrons commissioning bowls is accepted, this allows a comparable Christian interpretation of the simple punched ornament on one mount of a bowl buried at Hawnby (N. Yorks.). On a long shield-shaped plate a cross of shallow dots is flanked by sets of triple dots, while a dotted frame splits at the top as though two beasts with open mouths support the tip of the

---

[23] Illustrated by G. Bustacchini, *Ravenna Capital of Mosaic* (Ravenna, no date), 32, 41.

[24] There is a central Latin Cross here in the vault and another, dating between 425 and 443, is held by Christ the Good Shepherd in the mausoleum of Galla Placidia in Ravenna.

[25] A slab from Caher Island, Co. Mayo appears to carry this iconography, with an equal-armed cross in a ring above confronted fish-tailed creatures: C. Swift, *Ogam Stones and the Earliest Irish Christians*, Maynooth Monographs Series Minor 2 (Maynooth, 1997), 80–1.

[26] S. Scott, *Art and Society in Fourth-Century Britain*, Oxford University School of Archaeology Monograph 53 (Oxford, 2000), 45, fig. 18.

[27] Bruce-Mitford with Raven, *Corpus*, 165.

[28] T. D. Kendrick, 'British Hanging-Bowls', *Antiquity* 6 (1932), 161–84, at 168; Bruce-Mitford with Raven, *Corpus*, 163; *'The Work of Angels': Masterpieces of Celtic Metalwork, 6th–9th centuries AD*, ed. S. Youngs (London, 1989), 51.

[29] Pre-publication results from Tranmer House cemetery, Sutton Hoo, courtesy of Dr Chris Fern (ed.).

[30] The lower part of a more realistic dolphin mount was excavated at Whitby, precise context unrecorded, but flat and therefore not from another bowl; as many as nine bowls are represented in the finds from this Northumbrian monastery: C. Peers and C. A. Ralegh Radford, 'The Saxon Monastery at Whitby', *Archaeologia* 89 (1943), 27–88; Bruce-Mitford with Raven, *Corpus*, 435, Group 1, no. 24.

cross (Fig. 1c).[31] The multiple cross bars on another of the Hawnby bowl mount set gives a more ambiguous pattern. A developed bowl profile places this vessel in the mid-seventh century, although the hooked mounts are of archaic shape. Triple dots have a long life on late Roman and early medieval British and Irish metalwork and were a marked characteristic of Insular book production, so that they support both an 'early' or 'late' date for the Hawnby hooked mounts.[32]

The other unambiguously Christian hanging-bowl is represented by one mount. In terms of style and use of enamel the famous Whitby cruciferous mount could not be more different: a simple equal-armed cross with hollow enamelled limbs surrounded by inlaid ribbon knots that play on the numbers three and four, making a pattern against a bed of bright red opaque enamel (Fig. 2a).[33] This is a large mount and the complete bowl would have been brightly and boldly decorated with a set of similar hooks. This ribbon style of enamelling may date from the second half of the seventh century and lasted into the eighth, and has direct parallels in manuscript decoration.[34] This bowl, along with seven others represented by single mounts, belonged to a Northumbrian monastery founded in 657 and is probably the latest in the groups under consideration here. The motifs should be compared with the cruciform decoration on a bowl buried at Manton Warren, North Lincolnshire (formerly Humberside), where bold equal-armed crosses are picked out with millefiori glass, with trefoils between the arms, the cross ringed with a wreath of blue and white glass (Fig. 2b). Further cruciform elements can be read on the basal discs of this bowl.[35]

On a smaller scale, six hanging-bowls were carried on hooked mounts with discs filled by equal-armed crosses built up from eight segments, with four matching triangles at the cardinal points and slightly different panels interpolated. All were enamelled (Fig. 3a–c). This complex cross may reflect a marriage between the Christogram – the Christian symbol widely used in the Empire after the Edict of Milan in 313 – and the early attested cross-of-arcs. The Christogram, with intersecting axes of the chi and rho, gives an equal-armed diagonal cross with additional upright. It forms a six-armed figure with a loop on the vertical arm, a motif well documented in late Roman Britain on metalwork, mosaics, stone and pottery, and on the Continent.[36] These small complex crosses share their panelled construction with some grand Mediterranean examples, including

31 Bruce-Mitford with Raven, *Corpus*, no. 100; Geake, 'Hanging Bowls', 8–9, for a full description of the contents of this grave.

32 S. Youngs, 'From Metalwork to Manuscript: Some Observations on the Use of Celtic Art in Insular Manuscripts', in *Form and Order in the Anglo-Saxon World, AD 600–1100*, ed. S. Crawford, H. Hamerow and L. Webster, Anglo-Saxon Studies in Archaeology and History 16 (2009), 45–64, at 57–60.

33 Bruce-Mitford with Raven, *Corpus*, no. 101; no contrasting yellow enamel was used in the ribboned fields, see 79–80; plate 3e is incorrect in this respect.

34 S. Youngs, 'Medium and Motif: Polychrome Enamelling and Early Manuscript Decoration in Insular Art', in *'From the Isles of the North': Early Medieval Art in Ireland and Britain*, ed. C. Bourke (Belfast, 1995), 37–48. A half disc from Aberdour Castle, Fife, is a later piece in the same tradition, with ribbon interlace and beasts around a central cross set with millefiori; its form mirrors stone cross-heads of the eighth century: Bruce-Mitford with Raven, *Corpus*, no. 111.

35 Bruce-Mitford with Raven, *Corpus*, no. 31, plate 1, a–c.

36 C. Thomas, *Christianity in Roman Britain to AD 500*, 2nd edn (London, 1985), 86–91, 123–33; D. Watts, *Christians and Pagans in Roman Britain* (London and New York, 1991); F. Mawer, *Evidence for Christianity in Roman Britain: The Small Finds*, BAR British Series 242 (Oxford, 1995); D. Petts, *Christianity in Roman* Britain (Stroud, 2008).

Figure 2. (a) enamelled bowl mount from Whitby Monastery (N. Yorks.); (b) mount with enamel, reticella and millefiori glasses from a bowl buried at Manton Warren (north Lincs.). Scales 1:2. Drawn by Alison Wilkins.

the centre-piece of a stone screen from Egypt dated to the sixth century (Fig. 3d) and the roundel of beams radiating from an Alpha in San Vitale, Ravenna.[37] It is the pattern writ small on a complete bowl found in Grave 205 at Kingston (Kent). On this one small bowl some subtle variations were made on the eight-segmented design used on basal discs to create two variant cross patterns.[38] The Prittlewell chamber grave and Faversham cemetery each produced a complete bowl with enamelled bands and hooked mounts with eight simple outlined triangles defining a cross. Four individual hooked discs of this type have been found, one at Coddenham and a pair at Barham (both Suffolk) (Fig. 3b, c), with another set on a damaged band bowl found at Rigsby with Ailby (Lincs.).[39] The Lincolnshire bowl also carries a variant cruciform pattern.

The three surviving bowls hung from these crosses are small, with diameters of 210mm (Prittlewell), 185mm (Faversham) and 140mm (Kingston), and Brenan has suggested that they could share a functional difference, an observa-

---

[37] A. Effenberger and H.-G. Severin, *Das Museum für Spätantike und Byzantinische Kunst* (Berlin, 1992), Kat. 87; Bustacchini, *Ravenna*, 49, 50.

[38] A small bowl found with the great gold Kingston brooch but unfortunately destroyed in 1941. The various pictorial records are of differing reliability and discussed by Bruce-Mitford with Raven, *Corpus*, no. 42.

[39] Rigsby with Ailby bowl, North Lincolnshire Museum 2001.011; my thanks to Dr Kevin Leahy for showing me this bowl.

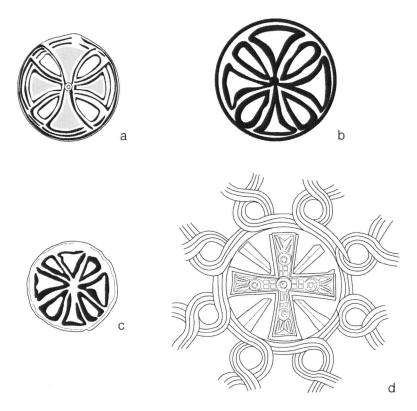

Figure 3. (a) Disc with yellow on red enamel from Camerton (Somerset); (b) hooked disc from a band bowl, Faversham (Kent); (c) incomplete hooked mount from Barham (Suffolk); (d) openwork centre of a sixth-century stone panel from Bawit (Egypt). Scales 3:2 ((d) reduced). Drawn by Alison Wilkins.

tion which has implications for specialist production and a common source.[40] All three bowls were richly decorated with applied enamelled bands, a relatively unusual feature which on the first two creates the effect of a formal wreath on the base. Leaping beasts on the basal discs of the bowl from Prittlewell find a parallel in hares on imported Phocaean red slip ware known from Britain: an early Byzantine context.[41] Bruce-Mitford said of the hooks on the Faversham bowl that 'it is doubtful whether this should be considered as a deliberate representation of a Christian cross'.[42] I do not think, however, that this position is still

---

[40] Brenan, *Hanging-Bowls*, 119, 120, who also commented on the anomalous old form of the Faversham vessel, but this has subsequently proved to be made from brass and was cast, not raised: ibid., 122, 130–1.

[41] S. Youngs, 'The Hanging-Bowl', in MOLAS with Essex Co. Council, *Prittlewell Princely Grave Report* (forthcoming).

[42] Published posthumously and a subject he might have revisited: Bruce-Mitford with Raven, *Corpus*, 167.

tenable in the light of the careful distinction between the vertical and horizontal arms and the intermediate panels, and the placing of the vertical axis in relation to the fixed vertical of the hook, set against what is known of the powerful people in society for whom these bowls were first made. The period of manufacture of this distinctive group of cruciferous bowls is, like their Christian symbolism, largely in the mind of the beholder thanks to the lack of manufacturing evidence. They were certainly made in the first half of the seventh century, possibly earlier. The Prittlewell burial will help with an end-date. This bowl already explains marks from missing elements on the Faversham vessel; the dead man was also buried as a Christian.

A compass was commonly used to construct an equal armed-cross in the early Christian world. A very simple variant was made using four arcs in a circle, each differentiated with a spot of white glass to define the central cross.[43] More elaborately, the arcs intersected to make eight spaces, as can be seen most clearly in contrasting red and yellow enamel on a hanging-bowl disc reused in a neck-lace at Camerton (Somerset) (Fig. 3a).[44] At the centre of a hanging-bowl mount from Thornham (Norfolk) is a simple cross, again made from arcs but tightly compressed to form the arms (Fig. 4a). The pattern made by the metal against the red enamel can also be read as four concave-sided triangles, a motif known in pre-Roman Iron Age Celtic art as a 'tricorne', and which was used in post-Roman decoration in a variety of combinations, of which this is only one.[45] The Thornham pattern may be viewed as iconographically neutral, but such a cross certainly had a Christian role elsewhere in the Celtic world, as on the terminals of six Irish penannular brooches (Fig. 4b).[46] These cross-marked terminals are accepted as signs of Christian belief at some level on the part of the donor and the wearers. In the seventh century the Irish scribe who penned the *Cathach* (Dublin, Royal Irish Academy, MS 12.R.33) and the illuminators who embel-lished the golden Chi and put a small cross at the centre of carpet page 192v in the Book of Durrow (Dublin, Trinity College Library, MS A.4.5.57) used just such a spindly cross with expanded arms built from arcs (Fig. 4c).[47] In the same tradition employed in the scriptoria, a six-petalled marigold pattern was used on the basal disc of an elaborately decorated bowl found at Baginton (Warks.), and others on a complex find of bowl mounts from Old Park, Dover (Kent).[48] Compass-drawn marigolds were incised on the bases of bowls found at Caphe-

[43] Banstead Down, Surrey, bowl: Bruce-Mitford with Raven, *Corpus*, no. 91.

[44] Bruce-Mitford with Raven, *Corpus*, nos 6 and 7 (under Avon). The mosaics of San Vitale, Ravenna, also include a large disc with radiating red and white spokes against eight blue segments, with a central 'Alpha' supported by angels above the apse: Bustacchini, *Ravenna*, 41, 50–1.

[45] J. Joy, 'Reflections on Celtic Art: a Re-examination of the Mirror Style', in *Rethinking Celtic Art*, ed. D. Garrow, C. Gosden and J. D. Hill (Oxford, 2008), 78–99, at 81, 85–6, 89–90, figs 5.1, 5.7.

[46] Dating is always problematic; these brooches may be sixth-century or later: G. Haseloff, *Email im frühen Mittelalter* (Marburg, 1990), upper figs 158 and lower fig. 156 (four in the National Museum of Ireland Dublin and ringed cross in the Ashmolean Museum Oxford, 1886-5819); H. E. Kilbride-Jones, *Zoomorphic Penannular Brooches*, Reports of the Research Committee of the Society of Antiquaries of London 39 (London, 1980), cat. nos 110 (probably Limerick), 121 and 128. A sixth was found in 2009 at Tullahennel, Co. Kerry: report and image in *Irish Times*, 4 February 2010, now in Kerry County Museum.

[47] For the cross in the Cathach and on the 'Chi' on Durrow fo. 23r, see B. Meehan, *The Book of Durrow* (Dublin, 1996), 28, 39.

[48] Bruce-Mitford with Raven, *Corpus*, no. 9; K. Parfitt and T. M. Dickinson, 'The Anglo-Saxon Cemetery at Old Park, near Dover, Revisited', in *Collectanea Antiqua: Essays in Memory of*

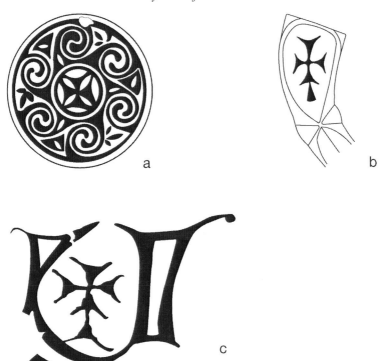

Figure 4. (a) An enamelled disc from Thornham, Suffolk; (b) Irish penannular brooch terminal; (c) cross detail in the earliest Irish psalter, the *Cathach* (Royal Irish Academy, MS12.R.3), fol. 50v. Scales varied. Drawn by Alison Wilkins.

aton (Northumberland) and Basingstoke (Hants).[49] The motif is another symbol familiar from contemporary Christian art Europe-wide, and is widely used in an Insular context in manuscript decoration and, less commonly, incised on stones.[50]

A cross was also built from the curvilinear patterns of the native Celtic tradition. Some hanging-bowls were decorated with richly enamelled crosses formed from extended peltas: on a bowl found at Lighthorne (Warks.) the large vertical cross was filled with blue and white millefiori glass, a material that became more freely available in the seventh century (Fig. 5a).[51] Simpler versions were used on two other bowls (Fig. 5b, c). That this pattern could and did carry Christian

Sonia Chadwick Hawkes, ed. M. Henig and T. J. Smith, BAR International Series 1673 (Oxford, 2007), 111–26, at 119–23.

[49] Bruce-Mitford with Raven, *Corpus*, nos 70 and 22.

[50] Irish examples: P. Lionard, 'Early Irish Grave Slabs', *PRIA* 61C (1961), 110–11; P. M. C. Kermode, *Manx Crosses* (Balgavies, 1994), Maughold 26, 27; Appendix A, 5; D. Craig, 'The Sculptured Stones', in *Whithorn and St Ninian*, ed. D. Hill (Stroud, 1997), 433–41 at 439–41. Welsh examples are given much later dates, it should be noted.

[51] Bruce-Mitford with Raven, *Corpus*, plate X, where the millefiori is shown as patchy and mixed with red, but this is most likely to be the remains of an underlying red layer, a technique seen elsewhere. For millefiori, see J. Carroll, 'Millefiori in the Development of Early Irish Enamelling', in *From the Isles of the North*, ed. Bourke, 49–57.

11

Figure 5. Curvilinear crosses on mounts (a) from Lighthorne (Warks.), with millefiori infill reconstructed; (b) no provenance; (c) Market Rasen (north Lincs.). Scale 1:2. Drawn by Alison Wilkins.

significance is shown by folio 138v in the Lindisfarne Gospels, where a cross was built from the curved elements from the native Celtic repertoire to form the centre-piece of a great carpet page, and there are other eighth-century examples from Insular scriptoria in which Celtic ornament plays just such a central role in Christian manuscripts.[52] This is native Christian art with roots in the sixth and seventh centuries, a tradition to which hanging-bowl ornament also bears witness.

A sub-group in which openwork peltas create a cross pattern when grouped in fours is more difficult to interpret because these are clearly an elaboration of a double-pelta pattern with roots deep in Roman Iron Age ornament. The double-pelta was still being manufactured as a bowl mount at a Pictish site in the sixth or seventh century.[53] A cruciform, four-pelta variant of this design is found at Tummel Bridge (Tayside) and was used on three more bowls, one recovered in Wiltshire and two from the densely settled eastern Germanic territories – one 'outside Ipswich' (Suffolk) and the other at Field Dalling (north Norfolk).[54] It

52 London British Library, Cotton Nero D.iv; J. J. G. Alexander, *Insular Manuscripts 6th to the 9th Century, A Survey of Manuscripts Illuminated in the British Isles 1* (London, 1978), cat. 9.

53 Craig Phadrig, Inverness-shire mould: Bruce-Mitford with Raven, *Corpus*, no. 113.

54 Discussed and illustrated in Youngs, 'Anglo-Saxon, Irish and British Relations', 211, fig. 9.6. Bruce-Mitford included these with other cross-bearing bowls in *Corpus*, 32.

may well be, as Brenan and Bruce-Mitford have argued, that any Christian significance is fortuitous and the design did not necessarily reflect the conversion of
the Pictish ruling class; it is a question of probabilities.

This is the difficulty with interpreting other appliquéd motifs, mostly found
on band bowls. Fish figure in a complex scheme on a bowl from Lullingstone
(Kent), where they are pecked by birds; stags move around this vessel and pairs
of crouching birds face each other, while mounts below the base make a cruciform pattern.[55] Christian parallels can, of course, be found without too much
difficulty, as in the Book of Armagh, written in A.D. 807/8, where the eagle
of St John seizes a fish in his talons, or on a stone ambo from Ravenna, where
three stags walk right and three left without a central healing stream or calyx.[56]
We have no guide to the original contemporary significance of these motifs on
a hanging-bowl in seventh-century Britain; separate bowl-appliqués of fish and
animals may or may not have had a specifically Christian significance. A source
in Celtic heroic tradition and myth has been proposed[57] and all possibilities
should be kept in mind, but they should not exclude a Christian one for which
we have contemporary evidence in other media.

A very different cross-type is seen on the finest and most complex hanging
bowl to survive (Fig. 6a). The patron who commissioned it, or the master smith
who made it, had a programme of new motifs and range of materials and techniques at their disposal. This bowl is the largest of three buried with an East
Anglian ruler in Mound 1 at Sutton Hoo. The inner core is a revolving enamelled
fish in a realistic style. The base and outer decorative panels, in contrast, were
made with curvilinear ornament in the Celtic tradition, but with the most recent
form of stylised animal heads and using niello inlay, something inherited either
directly from the Romano-British world or indirectly, borrowed from contemporary Anglo-Saxon metal working. Colour was important, as demonstrated by a
new palate of four enamel colours including rare blue and a unique pale green.
The deep-relief style of Iron Age repoussé work was picked up on additional
cast animal masks, but these were set with the very latest exotic materials –
garnets imported from Ceylon or India framed with silver beaded wire, another
innovation. Niello, garnet, silver filigree, millefiori glasses, blue glass, green
enamel, casting in the round: the effort was unstinted, but to what end? The three
square panels around the bowl are purely decorative and they are coloured to
make a red equal-armed cross with stubby arms, with an inner cruciform pattern
repeated in blue and white chequered millefiori (Fig. 6a). Such a pattern is seen
in miniature on the Gospel cover held by Christ on an ivory diptych dated to
the mid-sixth century and there are analogous forms on Gospel covers on some
Ravenna mosaics (Figs 6b, c).[58] The stylised zoomorphs in the four 'arms' of the
Sutton Hoo ornament are found again in the cross-carpet pages of the Lindisfarne
Gospels, a coincidence cited to show that such heads were considered appro-

---

[55] Case argued in Vierck, 'Cortina Tripodis', 43, and criticised by Brenan, *Hanging-Bowls*, 36;
Bruce-Mitford with Raven, *Corpus*, 17, 175–9, where the late-seventh-century dating of some
burials needs revision.

[56] Alexander, *Insular Manuscripts*, cat. 53, illus. 230; Bustacchini, *Ravenna*, 67 nos 3, 84, 108.

[57] Andrew Breeze, pers. comm.

[58] Effenberger and Severin, *Das Museum für Spätantike*, Kat. 78. Such a Gospel cover is shown
held by a deacon beside Bishop Maximianus in the apse of San Vitale, Ravenna, an image dating
from 546–7 (C. Weitzman, *Age of Spirituality* no. 65), and the Gospel in the paws of the lion of
St Mark in Ravenna: Bustacchini, *Ravenna*, 53 and 146, respectively.

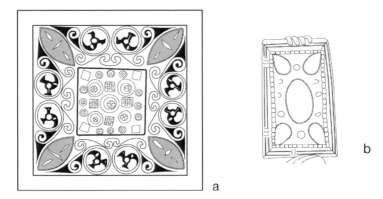

a

b

c

Figure 6. (a) A square plaque with red enamel and green corner panels from the largest hanging-bowl in Mound 1, Sutton Hoo (Suffolk); (b) the book cover held by Christ on a mid-sixth-century ivory diptych from Constantinople; (c) Gospel held by Ursicinus, mosaic in Sant'Apollinare in Classe. Drawn by Alison Wilkins.

priate to a totally Christian context.[59] Five blue rings hold millefiori inlay in a cruciform arrangement on each hook-plate. It seems perverse to exclude a Christian interpretation of the matching cruciform deployment of millefiori glass in the terminal plates of a great composite brooch from Ballinderry crannog 2 (Co. Offaly), given the parallels in Gospel carpet pages and their artists' use of native metalwork.[60]

The scholar Gunther Haseloff read the Sutton Hoo pattern as a cross, and his idea has sat in uncomfortable isolation, but it needs revisiting, whether this bowl is accepted as a prestige British product or argued to represent an Irish smith at work.[61] At a simple level, a cross in the eye of the beholder cannot be denied, but that it was in the mind of the maker is another matter. Given the affluence and overseas contacts demonstrated by the materials used to make this bowl, it

[59] Alexander, *Insular Manuscripts*, cat. 9, illus. 34; Youngs, 'From Metalwork to Manuscript', 56–7.

[60] *Treasures of Ireland Irish Art 3000 B.C.–1500 A.D.*, ed. M. Ryan (Dublin, 1983), cat. 45; Youngs, 'From Metalwork to Manuscript'.

[61] Haseloff, *Email im frühen Mittelalter*, 162–3; M. F. Ryan, 'The Sutton Hoo Ship Burial and Ireland', in *Sutton Hoo: Fifty Years After*, ed. R. Farrell and C. Neuman de Vegvar, American Early Medieval Studies 2 (Hamilton, 1992), 83–95.

was made for one of the most powerful people in contemporary British society somewhere around or shortly after A.D. 600. This person will have been a Christian, even if one living by the standards that Gildas so deplored some sixty or so years before. He or she may well have chosen the imagery of the cross even if largely for prophylactic reasons. This also brings the fish into play, as it swam and turned in an unknown liquid. Here the eye of the viewer could work at different levels, the local bishop seeing more than a prince admiring a novelty. It could, as is now argued for the silver hanging-bowl in the St Ninian's Isle treasure from Shetland, have originally been the property of a British church, as could the Prittlewell group of band bowls discussed above.[62] Uses of the cross in contemporary Christian societies deserve more attention than can be given here. Adomnán, at the end of the seventh century, described how making the sign of the cross was part of the daily life of the monastery of Iona. It was used to purify a wooden pail before it was filled with milk, with untoward consequences when the act was not performed: *Daemonem enim in fundo vacui latitantem vasculi inpresso dominicae crucis signo ante infusionem lactis non effugasti.*[63] Other food stuffs and table equipment were similarly signed with a cross, as in Columbanus's 'Communal Rule of the Brethren', where a spoon was to be *signaverit* ('blessed') before eating, as was a lamp after lighting.[64] The humble pail, like the hanging-bowl, was a vessel for liquid. That this was an early-seventh-century Irish monastic practice is shown by the condemnation of the Columban community of Luxeuil at the synod of Mâcon in A.D. 626–7 for making signs of the cross on common implements.[65] The cross was also physically added to such items, among them a rotary quern found at the royal stronghold of Dunadd: a permanent sign on the most essential equipment for the preparation of bread.[66] This was a simple cross with expanded terminals, here not confined to a special ceremonial or public space on a stone monument. While we cannot be certain that the British churches shared such practices with Irish communities, they were the senior institution and had close connections in the sixth century. The labelling of non-sacred items in this way was certainly not confined to religious communities; finger rings and belt buckles, even an elaborate iron horse-bit from Spain, were cross-inlaid, while the pottery factories of Turkey and north Africa catered for a range of tastes, from religious to erotic, with the motifs applied to vessels and lamps, taking this sign firmly into the lay world.[67]

62 A. Small, C. Thomas and D. M. Wilson, *St Ninian's Isle and its Treasure*, Aberdeen University Studies Series 152, 2 vols (Oxford, 1973), I.108–12; Bruce-Mitford, *Corpus*, no. 114. On aspersion, see C. Farr, 'Bis per chorum hinc et inde: The "Virgin and Child with Angels" in the Book of Kells', in *Text, Image and Interpretation*, ed. A. Minnis and J. Roberts, Studies in the Early Middle Ages 18 (Turnhout, 2007), 117–34 at 122–5.

63 'Before the milk was poured in you did not, by imprinting the sign of the Lord's cross, expel a demon that lurked at the bottom of the empty vessel': A. O. and M. O. Anderson, ed. and transl., *Adomnán's Life of Columba* (London and Edinburgh, 1961), 360–1.

64 *Reg. Coen* 3 (ed. Walker, 146–7).

65 Jonas, *Vita Sancti Columbani*, II.9–10 (MGH Script. rer. Merov. 4, 64–108); P. Riché, 'Columbanus, his Followers and the Merovingian Church', in *Columbanus and Merovingian Monasticism*, ed. H. B. Clarke and M. Brennan, BAR International Series 113 (Oxford, 1981), 59–72, at 63.

66 E. Campbell, 'A Cross-Marked Quern from Dunadd and other Evidence for Relations between Dunadd and Iona', *Proceedings of the Society of Antiquaries of Scotland* 117 (1987), 105–17.

67 J. W. Hayes, *Late Roman Pottery* (London, 1972); J. W. Hayes, *Supplement to Late Roman Pottery* (London, 1980).

We have become very aware of the mobility of prestige items within early medieval societies: 'The movement of fine metal objects between individuals seems to have been an important way in which bonds of obligation and relations of dominance were established and maintained during the Early Historic period.'[68] I propose that some of these fine bowls bear witness in their ornament to a complex and changing Christian heritage beyond the Anglo-Saxon territories. Like Jonathan Swift, however, 'I have now done with all such visionary schemes.'[69]

---

[68] The quotation is from I. Armit, E. Campbell and A. Dunwell, 'Excavations of an Iron Age, Early Historic and Medieval Settlement and Metalworking Site at Eilean Olabhat, North Uist', *Proceedings of the Society of Antiquaries of Scotland* 138 (2008), 27–104, at 99. See also M. Nieke, 'Penannular and Related Brooches: Secular Ornament or Symbol in Action?', in *The Age of Migrating Ideas: Early Medieval Art in Northern Britain and Ireland*, ed. M. Spearman and J. Higgitt (Edinburgh, 1993), 135–42.

[69] Jonathan Swift, *Gulliver's Travels*, Sterling edition (New York and London, 2007), xix.

2

COLUMBANUS'S MONASTICISM AND THE SOURCES OF HIS INSPIRATION: FROM BASIL TO THE MASTER?

Clare Stancliffe

Early medieval Ireland is famed for its monasticism, and the century running from 540 to 640 is that of the major monastic founders, while also being marked by individual ascetic enthusiasm. For the most part, however, contemporary documentation comprises laconic notices in the annals, with just a scattering of more informative texts such as the *Penitential* of Finnian and *The Alphabet of Piety*.[1] Against this background Columbanus stands out as the one figure for whom we have sufficient sources to enable us to discern his monastic vision and to see something of how he put it into practice. From his pen we have six letters, a series of thirteen sermons preached to his monks, a *Regula Monachorum* and *Regula Coenobialis*, a penitential and two poems,[2] while within a generation of his death Jonas produced his *Life of Columbanus and his Disciples*, which, for all its spin-doctoring, was the work of a well-informed author.[3]

There is, however, a problem about taking Columbanus as representative of the formative period of Irish monasticism. Although born in Leinster and trained in Comgall's monastery of Bangor, Columbanus had left Ireland around 591 to go as a *peregrinus* to the Continent. Thereafter he was based in Frankia, where his most important foundation was Luxeuil, until 610, when he was expelled. However, he escaped being sent back to Ireland and instead found his way to the Bregenz area and then over the Alps to northern Italy, where he founded a final monastery at Bobbio, and died in 615.[4] Now, nearly all Columbanus's writings date from his period on the Continent; indeed, this is why and where they have survived. During that time, Columbanus would have encountered existing continental monasteries, and also more texts than had been available to him in

---

[1] Ludwig Bieler, ed. and transl., *Penitentialis Vinniani*, in *idem*, *The Irish Penitentials*, SLH 5 (Dublin, 1963), 74–95; Vernam Hull, 'Apgitir Chrábaid: The Alphabet of Piety', *Celtica* 8 (1968), 44–89.

[2] Letters (henceforth *Ep.*), sermons (*Instr.*), Monks' Rule (*Reg. Mon.*), Communal Rule (*Reg. Coen.*), penitential, and poem *Mundus iste transibit* all ed. G. S. M. Walker, *Sancti Columbani Opera*, SLH 2 (Dublin, 1957); poem *Precamur patrem* ed. F. E. Warren, *The Antiphonary of Bangor*, 2 vols, HBS 4, 10 (London, 1892, 1895), II.5–7.

[3] Jonas, *Vita Columbani discipulique eius*, in Bruno Krusch, ed., *Ionae Vitae Sanctorum Columbani, Vedastis, Iohannis, Scriptores Rerum Germanicarum in usum scholarum ex Monumentis Germaniae Historicis separatim editi* (Hannover, 1905); cf. Clare Stancliffe, 'Jonas's *Life of Columbanus and his Disciples*', in *Studies in Irish Hagiography: Saints and Scholars*, ed. John Carey, Máire Herbert and Pádraig Ó Riain (Dublin, 2001), 189–220.

[4] Donald Bullough, 'The Career of Columbanus', in *Columbanus: Studies on the Latin Writings*, ed. Michael Lapidge (Woodbridge, 1997), 1–28.

Ireland. How far do his extant writings reflect these, rather than his monastic formation in Ireland?

Hitherto, such continental influence has been largely discounted on the inherently plausible grounds that Columbanus was trained at Bangor and that his letters show his explicit loyalty to Irish traditions.[5] Yet these assumptions by most Anglophone scholars[6] ignore the evidence put forward as long ago as 1972 by Adalbert de Vogüé to the effect that Columbanus's *Monks' Rule* reveals his knowledge of *The Rule of Benedict*.[7] We must also acknowledge that Columbanus's letter to Gregory the Great shows his eagerness to read the latest works.[8] On top of this, a liturgical historian has recently questioned whether Columbanus's liturgical usage does not reflect his sojourn in Gaul, rather than his Irish background.[9] The time is ripe, therefore, for investigating whether Columbanus's monasticism was influenced by his lengthy sojourn on the Continent.

In theory, Columbanus's monastic ideals and practices could have changed between his early letters to Gregory and to the Gallic bishops (595×604), and the sermons preached in Italy around 615. Unfortunately, however, the key document, his *Monks' Rule*, cannot be accurately dated.[10] In any case, there is a consistency between the sermons, the *Monks' Rule* and the letters. This also corroborates the attribution of all these works to Columbanus. That of the letters has never been questioned, and that of the sermons has been dealt with elsewhere.[11] As regards the *Monks' Rule*, the final chapter printed in Walker's edition does not occur in two out of the three manuscript families, and should be discarded as inauthentic.[12] In 1956 Laporte also questioned whether Columbanus wrote the first six chapters of the *Monks' Rule*, on account of their 'rough' Latinity; but I accept de Vogüé's vindication of them, as well as chapters seven to nine, as authentic.[13]

Let us begin by outlining Columbanus's understanding and practice of monasticism. In the sermons directed at his monks Columbanus skilfully evoked the mystery and the greatness of the Godhead before turning to the more approachable topic of how the monk should live in order to reach heaven. He developed the theme of this life as but a road (*via*, not *vita*), along which we make our way

---

5   Jane Barbara Stevenson, 'The Monastic Rules of Columbanus', in *Columbanus*, ed. Lapidge, 203–16, at 205; Westley Follett, *Céli Dé in Ireland: Monastic Writing and Identity in the Early Middle Ages* (Woodbridge, 2006), 46.

6   Not, however, all: see Eoin de Bhaldraithe, 'Obedience: The Doctrine of the Irish Monastic Rules', *Monastic Studies* 14 (*Celtic Monasticism*; Montreal, 1983), 63–84, and T. M. Charles-Edwards, *Early Christian Ireland* (Cambridge, 2000), 383–8.

7   *La Règle de saint Benoît* [*RB*] I, SC 181 (Paris, 1972), 163–6; de Vogüé, transl., Saint Colomban, *Règles et pénitentiels monastiques* (Abbaye de Bellefontaine, 1989), 42–3, 47. Despite citing de Vogüé's edition, his argument goes unremarked by Dáibhí Ó Cróinín, 'A Tale of Two Rules: Benedict and Columbanus', in *The Irish Benedictines: A History*, ed. Martin Browne and Colmán Ó Clabaigh (Dublin, 2005), 11–24, at 20 (and cf. 12). Jean Laporte had already noted the parallel with *RB*: 'Etude d'authenticité des œuvres attribuées à saint Colomban. II. La Regula Monachorum', *Revue Mabillon* 46 (1956), 1–14, at 3.

8   *Ep.* 1, 9 (ed. Walker, 16).

9   Peter Jeffery, 'Eastern and Western Elements in the Irish Monastic Prayer of the Hours', in *The Divine Office in the Latin Middle Ages*, ed. Margot E. Fassler and Rebecca A. Baltzer (Oxford, 2000), 99–143, at 110–12.

10   *Reg. Mon.* (ed. Walker, 122–41); cf. de Vogüé, *Règles*, 50–1.

11   Clare Stancliffe, 'The Thirteen Sermons attributed to Columbanus and the Question of their Authorship', in *Columbanus*, ed. Lapidge, 93–202.

12   De Vogüé, *Règles*, 37–8.

13   Laporte, 'Etude d'authenticité'; de Vogüé, *Règles*, 41–7.

as pilgrims. Our true *patria*, or native land, awaits us after our death – *if* we have lived aright. At the Last Judgment,

> *Uniuscuiusque opus quale sit ignis probabit* ... Mortuorum ergo animorum est et desperabilium ista non timere ... Quapropter nihil nobis utilius sciamus, quam ut omnibus diebus vitae nostrae vitam ancipitem retractantes, nosmetipsos cottidie discutiamus, et verborum cogitatuumque nostrorum rationem agentes

– a practice confirmed by the daily confession enjoined by the *Regula Coenobialis*.[14] The high stakes justified the harsh training of the monk, with its mortification of the will.

In these sermons Columbanus brilliantly blends teaching with stimulating a fear of judgment and a longing for heaven, and the last two sermons pass seamlessly into prayer of an almost mystical nature. Crucially, these sermons reveal that Columbanus had fully grasped the vision of ascetic teachers such as Cassian. He did not enjoin monastic discipline for its own sake, but rather as a coherent programme to mould sinful humanity into citizens of heaven.

For more basic monastic teaching we turn to the *Monks' Rule*. This begins with the requirement to love God, and our neighbour as ourselves, followed by six concise chapters on obedience, silence, diet, poverty, overcoming vanity, and chastity, and three longer chapters on the office, discretion and mortification of the will. Since it focuses on the moral formation of the individual monk it is only incidentally that we learn that prayer, work and reading comprised the monks' day.[15] At its heart lies a concise statement that encapsulates Columbanus's monastic teaching:

> *Nuditas et facultatum contemptus* prima perfectio est monachorum, secunda vero purgatio vitiorum, tertia perfectissima dei continuata dilectio ac divinorum iugis amor, qui terrenorum succedit oblivioni.[16]

This chimes with the message of the sermons, and elides the teaching in various places of Cassian's works,[17] thus illustrating Columbanus's deep familiarity with him. It further reveals that Columbanus, for all that he was writing for coenobitic monks, retained Cassian's 'vertical' vision of the monastic life as essentially one of the individual monk under God. For monks in the tradition of Cassian even the round of communal worship had an individual slant to it.[18] Thus, at the end of the psalms Columbanus's monks were to kneel down and repeat three times in silence, *Deus in adiutorium meum intende, domine ad adiuvandum me festina.*

---

14 'Fire shall try each man's work ... Thus not to fear these things is the part of dead and hopeless minds ... Wherefore let us know nothing more profitable for ourselves than to examine ourselves daily, every day of our life reviewing that dubious life, and keeping account of our words and thoughts': *Instr.* 9, 1 and 2, italicising a citation of 1 Cor. 3: 13; *Reg. Coen.* 1 (ed. Walker, 98–101; 144–7).

15 *Reg. Mon.* 3 (ed. Walker, 126–7).

16 'Nakedness and disdain of riches are the first perfection of monks, the second is the purging of vices, the third the most perfect and perpetual love of God and unceasing affection for things divine, which follows on the forgetfulness of earthly things': *Reg. Mon.* 4 (ed. Walker, 126–7), italicising a verbal reminiscence of Cassian (*ibid.*).

17 See Follett, *Céli Dé*, 43–5.

18 For 'monastic' prayer in the tradition of Cassian as 'fundamentally an individual activity', see Paul Bradshaw, *Two Ways of Praying* (London, 1995), 16–21. For the vertical axis of Cassian, see R. A. Markus, *The End of Ancient Christianity* (Cambridge, 1990), 163–8.

They were then expected to return to their cells in silence and continue in prayer there.[19] Most of Columbanus's monastic offices appear to have been modelled on what he read in Cassian's *Institutes*: the daytime offices, with three psalms apiece (together with intercessions), and offices at nightfall and midnight with twelve psalms apiece. Only in the very early morning office, with its psalmody varying between twenty-four psalms in the shorter summer nights on weekdays and seventy-five psalms in the long winter nights of Saturdays and Sundays, do we see a non-Cassianic pattern, this time suggesting the influence of Gaul.[20]

Characteristic of Columbanus's monasticism is language of spiritual warfare: *Inde nunc per* vim et violenti*am* regnum rapi*mus* caelorum ... *Pugnandum ergo hic est et certandum cum vitiis nostris*, ut alibi coronemur.[21] Like his master Faustus, he offers no armchair salvation, no soft options for the hesitant, but rather insists on a literal following of Jesus, even up to death.[22] A letter to his monks reveals that many of them had problems with the strictness of his rule, but he admits of no compromise: strictness is equated with truth and the rebellious are told to depart.[23]

This is the essence of Columbanus's monastic teaching, but two further points should be noted about his own practice: first, he was not only a monk, but a *peregrinus*: one who had left his native Ireland *pro Christo salvatore* as the ultimate renunciation and way of following Christ.[24] Secondly, as he wrote to his monks: *Scis me amare multorum salutem et secretum mihimetipsi, unum pro profectu Domini, id est ecclesiae eius, alterum pro ipsius desiderio.*[25] One might think that neither concern was compatible with being an abbot, but Columbanus, like other Irish *peregrini*, found a way. He preached to the nominal Christians he found when he first entered Gaul, extended repeatable penance to sinners, and evangelised the heathens around Bregenz, while he regularly prepared for major feastdays by withdrawing to a cave in the wilderness for solitary prayer.[26]

As regards his sources of inspiration, Columbanus himself appeals explicitly to the authority of 'St Jerome', Basil and 'St Gregory' of Nazianzus in his letter to the Gallic bishops, while the example of the 'Lord Martin' hovers in the background.[27] In the sermons, citations are generally anonymous, but those from Cassian and a tag from Sulpicius Severus are both introduced as from a

---

19 '"O God make speed to save me, O Lord make haste to help me"': *Reg. Coen.* 9, quoting Ps. 70: 2 (on which see Cassian, *Conlationes* X, 10, ed. Michael Petschenig, CSEL 13 (Vienna, 1886), 297–302); and *Reg. Mon.* 7 (ed. Walker, 158–9, 130–1).

20 *Reg. Mon.* 7 (ed. Walker, 128–33); Jeffery, 'Eastern and Western Elements', 108–12; cf. Stevenson, 'The Monastic Rules', 209–14.

21 'Thence we now force the kingdom of heaven by strength and violence ... So here we must fight and struggle with our vices, that we may be crowned elsewhere': *Instr.* 10, 3 (ed. Walker, 102–5, de-italicising parallels from Matt 11: 12 and Jerome, *Ep.* 22, 3, 1).

22 *Ep.* 4, 6; *Instr.* 10, 2; *Reg. Mon.* 1 and 9 (ed. Walker, 30–1; 102–3; 124–5, 140–1).

23 *Ep.* 4, 4 (ed. Walker, 28–31).

24 'For the sake of Christ our Saviour': *Ep.* 2, 6 (ed. Walker, 16–17); Jonas, *Vita Columbani* I, chs 3–4 (ed. Krusch, 156–60). T. M. Charles-Edwards, 'The Social Background to Irish *peregrinatio*', *Celtica* 11 (1976), 43–59.

25 'You know that I love the salvation of many and seclusion for myself, the one for the progress of the Lord, that is, of his church, the other for my own desire': *Ep.* 4, 4 (ed. Walker, 28–9).

26 Jonas, *Vita Columbani* I, chs 5, 10, 19, 27, and 9 (ed. Krusch, 161, 170, 191–2, 211–17, and 167–8).

27 *Ep.* 2, 8, and cf. 2, 7 (ed. Walker, 18–21); see further Neil Wright, 'Columbanus's *Epistulae*', in *Columbanus*, ed. Lapidge, 29–92, at 66–78.

sapiens or 'wise person': a distinction here given otherwise only to wisdom books of the Bible.[28] Gregory I, although addressed as 'holy pope' and *sapiens* in Columbanus's letter to him, is elsewhere referred to merely as *quidam*, 'a certain person'.[29] The single exception to anonymous citation in the sermons is the explicit reference to *alicuius maioris doctoris auctoritatem quaerentes, sancti scilicet Fausti luculentissimam elegantissimamque doctrinam* at the beginning of sermon two.[30] In the *Monks' Rule*, *seniores nostri*, 'our elders', are referred to in the chapter on the office.[31]

Individual citations of these named authors and, indeed, others, have been identified elsewhere.[32] Here, our concern is rather to tease out the main sources of inspiration for Columbanus's monasticism. We need to recognise that this is complex. On the one hand, he espouses Cassian's 'vertical' axis: he is concerned with the relationship of the individual monk to God (albeit with the abbot as inter-mediary), rather than with the horizontal relationship of the monk to his fellows. Yet at the same time Columbanus is more Gospel-orientated than Cassian, being aware that love of God and love of one's neighbour must go hand in hand. The primary influence of Cassian is widely, and rightly, insisted on.[33] However, right at the beginning of the *Monks' Rule* comes the teaching *deum diligere ex toto corde et ex tota mente et ex totis viribus et proximum tamquam nosmet ipsos*, a biblical text not quoted by Cassian. Its position here suggests the influence of Basil's *Rule*, where it similarly stands at the beginning, being further amplified in the second (and longest) chapter.[34] This suggestion is strengthened by noting that the second chapter of Basil is quoted in Columbanus's eleventh sermon, where, as in Basil, loving God is linked with keeping God's commandment, namely the commandment to love each other.[35] Further, the reference to Basil in Colum-banus's second letter is arguably prompted by this same chapter of Basil's *Rule*, where Basil is recommending the benefit of living apart from society.[36] Whereas both Cassian and Basil were agreed on the primacy of loving God, they differed on the importance of loving one's neighbour. For Basil, the person who loved his neighbour fulfilled, in that act, his love for God; whereas Cassian equated love (*caritas*) with purity of heart, and saw these as enabling divine contemplation, from which good works were a distraction – albeit a necessary one.[37] Colum-

---

28 *Instr.* 4, 2; *Instr.* 3, 4 (ed. Walker, 80, 76).

29 *Ep.* 1, 2 and 1, 4; *Ep.* 4, 6; *Instr.* 12, 1 (ed. Walker, 2, 4–6, 32, 110).

30 'Seeking the authority of a greater teacher, I mean the most perspicuous and polished teaching of St Faustus': *Instr.* 2, 1 (ed. Walker, 68–9); see further Stancliffe, 'The Thirteen Sermons', 194–9.

31 *Reg. Mon.* 7 (ed. Walker, 128–30).

32 In addition to Walker's footnotes and index see Wright, 'Columbanus's *Epistulae*', 66–88; Stancliffe, 'The Thirteen Sermons', 105–27, 200–2; and de Vogüé's footnotes to the texts in his *Règles*.

33 Follett, *Céli Dé*, 40–5; Adalbert de Vogüé, 'L'idéal monastique de saint Colomban', *Studia Monastica* 46 (2004), 253–68.

34 'To love God with the whole heart and mind and strength, and our neighbour as ourselves': *Reg. Mon.* citing Mark 12: 30–1 (ed. Walker, 122–3); Basil, *Regula*, translated into Latin by Rufinus, chs 1–2, ed. Klaus Zelzer, *Basili Regula*, CSEL 86 (Vienna, 1986), 8–25.

35 Columbanus, *Instr.* 11, 1 (ed. Walker, 106–7); Basil, *Regula*, ch. 2, §§63–9 (ed. Zelzer, 17–18); Stancliffe, 'The Thirteen Sermons', 106.

36 Columbanus, *Ep.* 2, 8 (ed. Walker, 20–1); Basil, *Regula*, ch. 2, §§94–105 (ed. Zelzer, 22–3). This would explain Columbanus's reference to Basil, which Wright found 'puzzling' ('Columbanus's *Epistulae*', 69, n. 149).

37 Cf. Basil, *Regula*, ch. 2, §§65–9 (ed. Zelzer, 18) and Cassian, *Conlationes* I, 6–13, ed. Michael Petschenig, CSEL 13 (Vienna, 1886), 12–21.

banus, with his concern for 'the salvation of many' as well as 'seclusion for myself', was the heir to Basil as well as Cassian; and the emotional warmth of Basil's exposition of love also tallies with Columbanus's sermons.[38] In addition, Basil's teaching on obedience has already been recognised as a major source for the first chapter of Columbanus's *Monks' Rule*.[39]

In addition to Cassian and Basil, some of Jerome's letters clearly influenced Columbanus's *Monks' Rule*, particularly the chapter on moderation in eating and drinking.[40] They may also have contributed to the Irish ideal of *peregrinatio* exemplified by Columbanus, and to the frequent use of the sign of the cross that is attested for Luxeuil.[41] Influences from the same letters also appear in a sermon and in Columbanus's second letter, while the latter is also indebted to Jerome's *Commentary on Matthew*.[42]

The influence of sermons by Faustus and Caesarius – Columbanus may not have differentiated between these[43] – is more apparent in Columbanus's sermons, in his rhetorical exhortation, than in identifiable aspects of his monastic practice. Two points make it hard to assess their influence. First, we do not necessarily possess the texts of all Faustus's sermons that influenced Columbanus, and those that we do have may not be in the form that he read them. Thus the editors of the *Collectanea Pseudo-Bedae* draw attention to an excerpt which is virtually identical to a passage in one of Columbanus's sermons, but with an additional sentence, and further note that this passage (without the additional sentence) is cited by Sedulius Scottus as coming from Faustus.[44] The most likely explanation is that this passage did indeed originate with Faustus in a work that has not survived, and that the three later writers all derived it from there, not from each other. Given the extensive loss of manuscripts from early Ireland,[45] this is plausible; but it brings out the difficulty of adequately assessing the influence of Faustus on Columbanus. The second difficulty arises because both Faustus and Caesarius were in the Lérins tradition, which derived primarily from Cassian, while also valuing Basil; and frequently it is impossible to differentiate between the influences.[46] So, for instance, both Faustus and Columbanus echo the same passage of Cassian about how monastic life is not a matter of 'rest and freedom from care', but rather a battle against temptation.[47] Columbanus knew this sermon

---

[38] Cf. Basil, *Regula*, ch. 2, §§14–24 (ed. Zelzer, 11–12) and Columbanus, *Instr.* 12, 2–3 and 13, 3 (ed. Walker, 112–15, 118–20). The example of St Martin – and of Jesus in the Gospels – may have influenced Columbanus in the same direction as Basil, but it is the latter's literary influence that is apparent.

[39] *Reg. Mon.* 1 (ed. Walker, 122–5); Basil, *Regula*, chs 65, 69–71 (ed. Zelzer, 102, 104–7); cf. Adalbert de Vogüé, 'Bourgogne, Angleterre, Alémanie: sur trois étapes du cheminement de la règle', *Regulae Benedicti Studia: Annuarium Internationale* 16 (1987), 123–35, at 123–4.

[40] *Reg. Mon.* 3, and also 6 (virginity) and 9 (obedience) (ed. Walker, 124–9, 138 lines 23–4); Jerome, *Epistulae* 58, §6; 22, §§17 and 38; and 125, §15; ed. Isidore Hilberg, CSEL 54–6 (Vienna, 1910–18), vol. 54, 535, 165, 203; vol. 56, 134.

[41] Jerome, *Ep.* 22, §1 (*peregrinatio*) and §37 (cross) (ed. Hilberg, vol. 54, 144, 202); cf. Columbanus, *Reg. Coen.* 1 and 3 (ed. Walker, 146–7) and Jonas, *Vita Columbani* II, 9 (ed. Krusch, 249–50).

[42] Columbanus, *Instr.* 10, 3 (ed. Walker, 104–5); Wright, 'Columbanus's *Epistulae*', 67–73.

[43] See Stancliffe, 'The Thirteen Sermons', 112–26.

[44] *Collectanea Pseudo-Bedae* §139, ed. Martha Bayless and Michael Lapidge, SLH 14 (Dublin, 1998), 138–9, 232–3.

[45] See Richard Sharpe, 'Books from Ireland, Fifth to Ninth Centuries', *Peritia* 21 (forthcoming).

[46] Cf. de Vogüé, *Règles*, 69 (Cassian/Faustus) and 120 (Basil/Faustus).

[47] Cassian, *De Institutis Coenobiorum* IV, ch. 38, ed. Michael Petschenig, CSEL 17 (Vienna,

of Faustus well, so it may have influenced his predilection for this passage of Cassian; but he quotes the latter directly, in a fuller version. Despite these problems, there are two areas where we may discern the direct influence of Faustus and Caesarius on Columbanus's monasticism. First, there is a greater emphasis in these later writers on the terrible day of judgement, and so on the need to conquer our vices now, and the urgency of action, not just good intentions. In Caesarius this is taken further, with his insistence on the need to examine our consciences daily: something which Columbanus took further again with his requirement for daily confession.[48] Secondly, one of Caesarius's sermons that was used by Columbanus drew the contrast between our exile on this earth and our homeland in heaven, drawing the moral that *non quaeras in via, quod tibi servatur in patria*. This provides the unifying theme for Columbanus's series of sermons, though we should note that one can trace the same theme also in Gregory the Great's *Moralia in Iob*, another work known to Columbanus.[49]

What of the Benedictine Rule? De Vogüé rests his case partly on verbal parallels, which are more extensive than is often assumed;[50] partly on the fact that Columbanus, like Benedict, has a chapter on obedience followed by one on silence; and partly on his suggestion that Benedict furnished Columbanus with a model for producing a rule of this type.[51] This last point is, to me, unimportant: a person of Columbanus's stature could have created his *Monks' Rule* simply on the basis of his knowledge of Basil and, apart from his chapter on the office, he ignored the legislative aspect of the Benedictine Rule. The other points are significant; but did Columbanus draw on Benedict, or on Benedict's source, *The Rule of the Master*?[52] Both have virtually the same verbal parallels in their chapters on obedience, and both follow this with one on silence, like Columbanus.[53] A brief illustration will convey the problem, using **bold** for the Master and Columbanus parallels, *italics* for the Master and Benedict, and <u>underlining</u> for Benedict and Columbanus:

---

48 1888), 74; Faustus, *Homilia ad monachos* 4, §3, ed. F. Glorie, *Eusebius 'Gallicanus', Collectio Homiliarum*, CCSL 101–101B (Turnhout, 1970–1),vol. 101A, 458; Columbanus, *Instr.* 4, 2 (ed. Walker, 80–1).

48 Cf. Faustus, *ibid.* §5 (ed. Glorie, 462–4); Caesarius, *Sermo* 58, §3, ed. Germain Morin, *Sancti Caesarii Arelatensis Sermones*, CCSL 103–4 (Turnhout, 1953), CCSL 103, 256; above, n. 14.

49 'You should not seek on the way what will be kept for you in your homeland': Caesarius, *Sermo* 215, §3 (ed. Morin, CCSL 104, 856–7); Stancliffe, 'The Thirteen Sermons', 110–16; and, for Columbanus's knowledge of Gregory's *Moralia*, see also Clare Stancliffe, 'Creator and Creation: A Preliminary Investigation of Early Irish Views and their Relationship to Biblical and Patristic Traditions', *CMCS* 58 (2009), 9–27, 15.

50 In addition to the sentence quoted below, see de Vogüé, 'Bourgogne, Angleterre', 123–4, and *Regula Magistri* 7, 67–72, ed. Adalbert de Vogüé, *La Règle du Maître*, SC 105–7 (Paris, 1964–5), SC 105, 396.

51 De Vogüé, *Règles*, 42–3, 47–8.

52 Cf. de Vogüé's second thoughts, *Règle Benôit*, SC 181, 494–5.

53 The cento rule attributed to Eugippius also reproduces this chapter on obedience from the Master; but it omits that on silence, that dealing with crumbs (cf. below), and the phrase paralleled in Columbanus's *Ep.* 2, 8 (below), so is less likely to have been Columbanus's source.

Master[54]

*quia oboedientia quae maioribus praebetur **deo** datur, sicut **dic**it **Domin**us doctoribus nostris: '**Qui uos audit me audit.**'*

Benedict[55]

*quia oboedientia quae maioribus praebetur **deo** exhibetur; ipse enim **di**xit: '**Qui uos audit me audit.**'*

Columbanus[56]

*quia oboedientia **deo** exhibetur, **dic**ente **domin**o nostro Iesu Christo: '**Qui uos audit me audit.**'*

Initially, it looks as though Columbanus is closer to Benedict, as both use *exhibetur*, which is more significant than the Master and Columbanus sharing *Dominus*; and it may also be relevant that by 632 Luxeuil had adopted the Benedictine Rule along with that of Columbanus. However, in an earlier chapter, the Master had introduced the same quotation from Luke with the words *dicente ipso Domino*, much as Columbanus does.[57] Further, in the passage immediately preceding that where the verbal parallels start, the Master has two paragraphs which are omitted by Benedict but which tally with Columbanus's teaching on mortification of the will. Both insist that, at the Last Judgment, the monk who has obeyed his superior will have nothing to fear. Secondly, both compare mortification of the will to martyrdom and portray the monk reaching *refrigerium*.[58] Elsewhere, both the Master and Columbanus share a concern for gathering up all the crumbs from the table.[59] All these passages are omitted from Benedict, suggesting that Columbanus may have been using the Rule of the Master rather than (or in addition to?) Benedict.

This suggestion can perhaps be strengthened by considering the earliest manuscript of the Rule of the Master, now Paris, Bibliothèque Nationale, lat. 12205. This was copied in uncials, and assigned by Lowe to 'saec. VI–VII ... origin unknown, probably Italy' – a judgment with which subsequent scholars concur.[60] On fo. 157r there is a pen-trial in the angular type of Luxeuil miniscule which Ganz has identified as that which the first Corbie monks brought with them from Luxeuil to Corbie on the latter's foundation 657×61. He has further opined that this script may date to before 673.[61] I would therefore suggest that this

---

[54] *Regula Magistri* 7, 68.

[55] *RB* 5, 15 (ed. de Vogüé, 468).

[56] *Reg. Mon.* 1 (ed. Walker, 122).

[57] *Reg. Magistri* 1, 89 (ed. de Vogüé SC 105, 348–50); but note that the same quotation is introduced by Basil, *domino dicenti quia 'Qui audit vos me audit'*: *Regula* 70, 3 (ed. Zelzer, 106).

[58] *Reg. Magistri* 7, 53–66 (*ibid.*, 392–4); Columbanus, *Reg. Mon.* 9 (ed. Walker, 138–40). The former point was noted by de Vogüé, *Community and Abbot in the Rule of St Benedict* (Eng. trans. 2 vols Kalamazoo, Michigan, 1979–88), I.198, 212, a reference I owe to de Bhaldraithe, 'Obedience', 70 and n. 21. These parallels between Columbanus and the Master are far closer than those between Columbanus and Cassian which de Vogüé suggests in *Règles*, 45.

[59] *Reg. Magistri* 25 (ed. de Vogüé, SC 106, 132–5 and n. 12); Columbanus, *Reg. Coen.* 2 (ed. Walker, 146–7); Marilyn Dunn, 'Mastering Benedict: Monastic Rules and their Authors in the Early Medieval West', *English Historical Review* 416 (1990), 567–94, at 582 – although I am not persuaded by her general thesis that Benedict preceded the Master.

[60] E. A. Lowe, *Codices Latini Antiquiores*, 11 vols and suppl. (Oxford, 1934–71), V, no. 633; Hubert Vanderhoven and François Masai, *La Règle du Maître: édition diplomatique des manuscrits latins 12205 et 12634 de Paris*, Les Publications de Scriptorium 3 (Brussels–Paris, 1953), 42–67; cf. Dunn, 'Mastering Benedict', 591–2.

[61] David Ganz, *Corbie in the Carolingian Renaissance*, Beihefte der Francia 20 (Sigmaringen,

manuscript might have been acquired in Rome *c.*600 by the bearers of one of Columbanus's letters to the papacy and brought back to Columbanus at Luxeuil. Columbanus's letter to Gregory attests his eagerness to acquire new texts, and the links between Rome and the monasteries to its south-east, where the Rule of the Master is thought to have originated, are well attested for the sixth century, and were probably strengthened by the Lombard depredations which brought refugees flooding into the city.[62] Later, *c.*660, this manuscript would have formed part of Luxeuil's endowment for Corbie, where its presence is amply attested by the pen-trial and subsequent glosses. This hypothesis is strengthened by noting that a second, rather uncommon, work which this manuscript originally contained, *The Sentences of Sextus*, was also known to Columbanus, who cites one of its maxims in his *Monks' Rule*.[63] A final point worth noting is a probable echo of the wording of the Rule of the Master (or Benedict) in Columbanus's second letter of 603×4. His phrase, *iram in corde non tenere*, is reminiscent of their *dolum in corde non tenere*, which follows immediately after their condemnation of *ira* and *iracundia*.[64] Although this does not help us to choose between the Master and Benedict, as the phrase is identical in both, it would confirm that the relevant rule had reached Columbanus at Luxeuil by *c.*603.

Whichever rule Columbanus read, the important thing to grasp is that it is not just a case of his echoing its words. Far more significant is the fact that, whether directly or via Benedict, Columbanus drew his teaching on obedience from the Master. This was suggested in 1983 by Eoin de Bhaldraithe, O. Cist., following a lead previously given by de Vogüé,[65] but has gone unmentioned in de Vogüé's recent work on Columbanus's *Règles*. This is surprising, since it was de Vogüé who first clarified how the Master developed his teaching on obedience in a new way, eliding obedience to God and obedience to superiors.[66] Basil had anticipated this; but he had included a chapter on the need for monks to obey *each other* in love, and, even where he cites the text, 'he who hears you hears me', the context is one of getting a monk to obey rather than the abbot's authority. The Master went further than this, developing the idea that it was through the teacher or abbot that one obeys God, so equating disobedience to monastic superiors with disobedience to God. Now it is precisely this point which both Benedict and Columbanus adopt, as we have seen. This lies at the root of their condemnation of any type of answering back or murmuring. With Columbanus, the teaching on obedience is at its harshest, since he continues (following Basil) to insist that the monk had to obey, whatever the command, even 'up to death', following

1990), 15, 38–40, 126–7; David Ganz, 'Texts and Scripts in Surviving Manuscripts in the Script of Luxeuil', in *Ireland and Europe in the Early Middle Ages: Texts and Transmission*, ed. Próinséas Ní Chatháin and Michael Richter (Dublin, 2002), 186–204, at 201.

62 Above, n. 8; Conrad Leyser, *Authority and Asceticism from Augustine to Gregory the Great* (Oxford, 2000), 101–17. Valentinian, one of Benedict's disciples who had later been in charge of the Lateran monastery, is one example: *ibid.*, 131–2. See also the discussion between P. Meyvaert, F. Prinz and A. de Vogüé in *Grégoire le Grand*, ed. J. Fontaine, R. Gillet and S. Pellistrandi (Paris, 1986), 135–6.

63 Leyser, *Authority and Asceticism*, 114–15; Columbanus, *Reg. Mon.* 9 (ed. Walker, 138, lines 16–17); de Vogüé, *Règles*, 68, n. 7.

64 Columbanus, *Ep.* 2, 8 (ed. Walker, 20); *Reg. Magistri* 3, 26 (ed. de Vogüé, SC 106, 366); *RB* 4, 24 (ed. de Vogüé, 458).

65 'Obedience', esp. 69–70.

66 *The Rule of Saint Benedict: A Doctrinal and Spiritual Commentary* (Eng. trans. Kalamazoo, Michigan, 1983), ch. 5, esp. 100–6.

the example of Christ.[67] The same teaching underlies Columbanus's chapter on mortification of the will, defined as 'the chief part of the monks' rule', where the monk is enjoined to do nothing of his own volition. This mortification, or 'martyrdom', was to be embraced so fully that it would govern not only the monk's tongue and actions, but even his thoughts.[68] Thus the contribution of the Master to Columbanus's monasticism was a significant one.

We have now traced the main sources of inspiration for Columbanus's monasticism, insofar as these were available in texts rather than in oral teaching. It remains to consider how much of this he is likely to have imbibed while in Ireland, and how much he owed to his lengthy continental sojourn. At the outset we should recall that Columbanus was a mature and experienced monk by the time he left Bangor, and that, stylistically, all his writings bear an Insular stamp.[69] When he arrived in Gaul it was precisely his adherence to Irish customs that caused trouble. Encountering hostility from the Gallic bishops because of his insistence on celebrating Easter according to the 84-year cycle traditional in Ireland, he appealed to the pope, pleading *nullas istorum suscipimus regulas Gallorum, sed in desertis sedentes, nulli molesti, cum nostrorum regulis manemus seniorum.*[70] He generally took a dim view of the standards of the church in Gaul and northern Italy in contrast to his native Ireland, *ubi praelia Domini praeliari spiritales duces conspexi.*[71] His ideal of *peregrinatio*, concern to extend repeatable penance to lay people, and attitude to authority in the Church[72] came from Ireland, as, probably, did his simultaneous concern for pastoral care and solitary contemplation and the practice of zoning his monasteries so that only part was accessible to lay people, while the interior was barred to them, thus maintaining monastic seclusion.[73]

One can also make out a case for Columbanus having encountered most of the authors responsible for his monastic inspiration before he left Ireland. Thus his wording about how Faustus *nos viles licet commissos sibi docuit* fits better with Columbanus having encountered Faustus's sermons as a young monk in Ireland rather than as an experienced abbot on the Continent, and transmission

---

67 *Reg. Mon.* 1 (ed. Walker, 124–5); cf. Basil, *Regula* 65 (ed. Zelzer, 102).

68 *Reg. Mon.* 9 (ed. Walker, 138–41).

69 Jonas, *Vita Columbani* I, chs 3–4 (ed. Krusch, 157–60); Bullough, 'The Career ', in *Columbanus*, ed. Lapidge, 2–9; Wright, 'Columbanus's *Epistulae*'; Stancliffe, 'The Thirteen Sermons', 139–74.

70 'We receive no rules of those Gauls, but, dwelling in seclusion, harming no one, we abide with the rules of our elders': *Ep.* 3, 2 (ed. Walker, 24).

71 'Where I have seen spiritual leaders fighting the Lord's battles': *Ep.* 5, 8, from Italy; for Gaul, cf. *Ep.* 2, 2 (ed. Walker, 44–5, 12–13).

72 Clare Stancliffe, 'Columbanus and the Gallic Bishops', in *Auctoritas: Mélanges offerts à Olivier Guillot*, ed. Giles Constable and Michel Rouche (Paris, 2006), 205–15.

73 Clare Stancliffe, 'Cuthbert and the Polarity between Pastor and Solitary', in *St Cuthbert, his Cult and his Community to AD 1200*, ed. Gerald Bonner, David Rollason and Clare Stancliffe (Woodbridge, 1989), 21–44, at 36–42. Jonas, *Vita Columbani* I, ch. 19 (ed. Krusch, 190–1); cf. *Collectio Canonum Hibernensis* XLIV, esp. ch. 5, ed. Hermann Wasserschleben, *Die irische Kanonensammlung*, 2nd edn (Leipzig, 1885), 175, and discussion by Charles-Edwards, *Early Christian Ireland*, 119–20, 358. The Irish background goes unmentioned by Barbara H. Rosenwein, *Negotiating Space: Power, Restraint and Privileges of Immunity in Early Medieval Europe* (Manchester, 1999), 68–73, and Albrecht Diem, 'Monks, Kings, and the Transformation of Sanctity: Jonas of Bobbio and the End of the Holy Man', *Speculum* 82 (2007), 521–59, at 533–7.

of Faustus's sermons to Ireland is plausible.[74] Our main source of information on the works which Columbanus had read in Ireland comes from the evidence of the hymn *Precamur patrem*, which occurs anonymously in the Bangor Antiphonary (Milan, Biblioteca Ambrosiana, C.5.inf.), but has been convincingly attributed to Columbanus; and, given its occurrence in this Irish manuscript, together with Jonas's information that Columbanus as a young man in Ireland had written many things *quae vel ad cantum digna vel ad docendum utilia*, it can reasonably be assigned to his period in Ireland.[75] This hymn contains verbal echoes of Cassian's *Institutes*, of Jerome's famous letter twenty-two to Eustochium on virginity, of an oration of Gregory of Nazianzus, of at least one sermon by Caesarius of Arles (no. 194)[76] and possibly also of a second that was actually used in Columbanus's sermons (no. 58).[77] In addition, knowledge of Cassian in Ireland/Iona is elsewhere attested for *c.*600, most explicitly in the *Amra Choluim Chille*, ascribed to Dallán Forgaill, where the nature of the reference shows that the author actually knew something of Cassian's teaching.[78] The same poem also attests to knowledge of Basil's *Rule*: 'he [Columba] applied the judgments of Basil', which again shows acquaintance with the form of Basil's *Rule*, which comprised Basil's response to specific questions about monasticism.[79] Given how scanty our evidence is on the texts available in sixth-century Ireland, the extent to which our findings tally with the authors who were most influential on Columbanus's monasticism is remarkable: Cassian, Basil, Jerome, Faustus, and Caesarius, with the latter being particularly interesting, as it shows that at least some of Caesarius's sermons had reached Ireland within half a century of their author's death. Whether Columbanus's 'take' on these sources of monastic inspiration was identical to that of Comgall is unknowable; but the verbal echoes in *Precamur patrem* indicate that Columbanus had read most of these sources for himself, in Ireland.

The links with southern Gaul are striking, and should reassure the liturgical scholar who queried the Irishness of Columbanus's monastic office on the grounds of its parallels with Cassian and with sixth-century Gallican practice.[80]

---

74 'Taught us when, though unworthy, we were entrusted to his care': *Instr.* 2, 1 (Walker, 68–9); see Stancliffe, 'The Thirteen Sermons', 194–8.

75 'Which are worthy of singing and useful for teaching': Jonas, *Vita Columbani* I, ch. 3 (Krusch, 158); see Michael Lapidge, '"Precamur patrem": An Easter Hymn by Columbanus?', in *Columbanus*, ed. Lapidge, 255–63. The palaeography, codicology and contents of the Bangor Antiphonary all argue for an Irish (not Bobbio) origin.

76 See *ibid.*, 259–61, and Clare Stancliffe, 'Venantius Fortunatus, Ireland, Jerome: The Evidence of *Precamur patrem*', *Peritia* 10 (1996), 91–7.

77 Cf. stanza 39 of *Precamur patrem* (ed. Warren, *Antiphonary of Bangor*, II.7): *Quem expectamus / Affuturum judicem / Justum cuique / Opus suum reddere*, with Columbanus, *Instr.* 9, 2 (giving citations from Caesarius's sermon 58, 1 in bold, and those from Matt. 16:27 in italics): '**non dixit, secundum misericordiam suam, sed** *secundum opera sua unicuique reddet*; **hic enim misericors,** illic **iustus** iudex.' (Walker, 98; cf. Caesarius, *Sermones*, ed. Morin, CCSL 103, 255). The important thing to note is the stress on 'judex *justus*'. It is further worth noting that some manuscripts, e.g. *Codex Durlacensis* 36, now Karlsruhe, Badische Landesbibliothek MS 340, include all the relevant Caesarius sermons, viz 58, 194, and 215.

78 Stanza 5, ed. Thomas Owen Clancy and Gilbert Márkus, *Iona: The Earliest Poetry of a Celtic Monastery* (Edinburgh, 1995), 106–9, 243 (note).

79 Stanza 4, *ibid.* 106–7.

80 Jeffery, 'Eastern and Western Elements', 110–12. His ideas about the nature of the office in Ireland in the early period, based on his assumption that the 'office of the Three Fifties', (which is not attested before the Culdees), was the original Irish office, appear mistaken. See rather Westley

Given Columbanus's explicit and repeated reference to his agreement with 'our elders' in his liturgical directions, we should take him at his word.[81] Nonetheless, Jeffery was right to raise the question of how 'Irish' Columbanus's monasticism was, since, as we have seen, Columbanus showed himself very ready to take over the Master's teaching on obedience. This is far stronger than the teaching on obedience known to us from contemporary Ireland.[82] Now it is significant that the theme of obedience (and its opposite, rebellion) is particularly prominent in Jonas's *Life of Columbanus and his Disciples*, which is aimed at a monastic audience.[83] What Columbanus's letters reveal, though Jonas does not, is that Columbanus himself experienced divisions within his own monastic community, with some monks clearly unhappy at the strictness of his rule. These were exacerbated by attacks from certain bishops and from the royal family, which would have emboldened the dissident monks.[84] Thus, when Columbanus writes to his successor at Luxeuil that, *quia diversa sensi multorum vota ad firmitatem regulae retinendum, ad radicem ramos ligavi,*[85] we may be glimpsing the problems which led Columbanus to extract from the Italian rule precisely those passages assimilating the abbot's will to Christ's (further strengthened by judicious use of Basil), together with an allusion to his attempted solution. His chapter on obedience in his *Monks' Rule* draws far more extensively on earlier sources than does any other chapter, as though Columbanus was using the authority of others to buttress his call for obedience. It stands as a reminder that we should not glibly assume that Columbanus remained set in his Irish ways. Although what he had witnessed there seems to have served as a 'gold standard' of the heights that monks should scale, his eagerness to read new works and his intelligence in assimilating them enabled him to continue developing his vision of the monk's calling.

Follett, 'The Divine Office and extra-Office Vigils among the Culdees of Tallaght', *The Journal of Celtic Studies* 5 (2005), 81–96.

[81] *Reg. Mon.* 7 (ed. Walker, 128, 130).

[82] Cf. Hull, 'Apgitir Chrábaid'; de Bhaldraithe, 'Obedience', 73–4.

[83] Ian Wood, 'The *Vita Columbani* and Merovingian Hagiography', *Peritia* 1 (1982), 63–80, at 66–8.

[84] Stancliffe, 'Jonas's *Life*', esp. 203–14.

[85] 'Since I have felt the desires of many to differ in respect of maintaining the strictness of the rule, I have bound the branches to the root': *Ep.* 4, 4 (ed. Walker, 28–31).

3

EARLY IRISH PRIESTS WITHIN THEIR OWN LOCALITIES

Catherine Swift

The early-eighth-century collection of canons known as *Collectio Canonum Hibernensis* includes a book entitled *On presbyters and priests*.[1] Chapter twenty-five deals with correct punishment to be meted out to priests who are absent from their locality:

> *Sinodus Hibernensis* decrevit, ut sacerdos una tantum die ab ecclesia defuerit; si duobus, peniteat VII diebus cum pane et aqua; si autem mortuus ad ecclesiam adlatus fuerit et ille absens, penitere debet quia poenae reus illius est. B. *Item*: Si in uno die dominico ab ecclesia defuerit, agat penitentiam XX dierum cum pane et aqua, si autem duobus aut tribus, submovendus honore gradus sui.[2]

This is a relatively rare example of concern about a priest's relationship with his congregation in this particular source. The other twenty-six chapters in the book concern the nature of the priest's role, their Old Testament precursors, the nature of sacrifice, the rituals of ordination and (by far the greatest area of concern, with ten separate chapters) the rules governing clerical income.

The evidence for the duties and functions of priests and their role in Irish society is not limited to *On presbyters and priests*, but can also be found scattered through other books within the *Collectio*.[3] In Book twenty-one, for example, *On judgement*, a priest is identified as a suitable person to be a judge, along with fourteen other characters including a bishop, a king, a legal scholar, a kinsman

---

[1] In 'The Pastoral Role of the Church in the Early Irish Laws', in *Pastoral Care before the Parish*, ed. J. Blair and R. Sharpe (Leicester, 1992), 63–80, at 73, Thomas Charles-Edwards drew attention to the importance of such pastors: 'it remains the priest who is the central figure in the Irish Church as perceived by the laws', but this characteristic insight has not been followed up in more recent studies of Irish Church organisation. I offer this contribution with thanks and appreciation to an erstwhile supervisor, whose patience I often tried but whose level of support never changed. In a world where doctoral studies are becoming ever more constrained by administrative demands and formatting, I remember with deep appreciation that he never tried in any way to impose a particular approach, topic, viewpoint or work ethic and left me free to find my own path.

[2] '*An Irish synod* decreed that a priest should refrain from being away from (his) church for a whole day; if for two days, he must do penance for seven days on bread and water; if however a dead man should be brought to the church and he is absent, he must do penance for he owes compensation to the dead man. *Same source*: If he should be absent one Sunday from church he does penance for twenty days on bread and water; if absent for two or three, he should be removed from the honour of his grade': Hermann Wasserschleben, *Die irische Kanonensammlung* (Darmstadt, 1966), 19 II §25.

[3] Some of this material has been discussed in a forthcoming study of the geographical remit of early Irish priests: 'Early Irish Priests and their Areas of Ministry', in *Parishes in Transition*, ed. E. Duffy (Dublin, 2010).

(on issues concerning his own kin), a craftsman (on matters pertaining to his own craft), the old, the poor and the wise. This role is further underlined in Book twenty-nine, *On theft*, where a priest is also said to be a suitable judge in cases of theft from his church.[4]

The varied responsibilities of a priest as judge are indicated in considerable detail in the Irish penitentials edited and translated by Ludwig Bieler.[5] Within this category of source material we see concern for what might be called the theoretical perspective of priestly judges; the *Bigotian Penitential*, for example, opens with a statement that:

> Hinc procurantibus aliorum sanare uulnera solerter intuendum est cuius aetatis et sexus sit pecans, qua eruditione inbutus, qua fortitudine extstat, quali grauatione conpulsus est peccare, quali pasione inpugnatur, quanto tempore in diliciis remansit, quali lacrimabilitate et labore affligitur et qualiter a mundialibus separatur.[6]

Such concern to include consideration of the specific circumstances in a particular case helps to illustrate the rationale behind the often contradictory nature of the authorities cited in the *Collectio*. As Charles-Edwards has written, it 'may have provided an ecclesiastical judge with authorities for a judgement but it left him with the task of deciding what, in any particular case, was the just solution'.[7]

The author of the *Bigotian Penitential* then cites Pope Gregory on the need for clerical judges to operate with discretion. The idea is taken from a homily on John 20:19–29 and the full text gives us some idea about how seriously such judges were expected to take their responsibilities. Gregory writes that, as God's vicars, the disciples had the right to withhold forgiveness from some while granting it to others, and continues:

> Horum profecto nunc in Ecclesia episcopi locum tenent. Ligandi atque solvendi auctoritatem suscipiunt, qui gradum regiminis sortiuntur. Grandis honor, sed grave pondus istius est honoris. Durum quippe est ut qui nescit tenere moderamina vitae suae judex vitae fiat alienae. Et plerumque contingit ut hic judicii locum teneat, cui ad locum vita minime concordat. Ac saepe agitur, ut vel damnet immeritos, vel alios ipse ligatus solvat. Saepe in solvendis ac ligandis subditis suae voluntatis motus, non autem causarum merita sequitur. Unde fit, ut ipsa hac ligandi et solvendi potestate se privet, qui hanc pro suis voluntatibus, et non pro subjectorum moribus exercet.[8]

---

4   Wasserschleben, *Kanonensammlung*, 62–3 XXI§2, 101 XXIX§6.
5   L. Bieler, ed. and transl., *The Irish Penitentials*, SLH 5 (Dublin, 1963).
6   'Hence those who take care to heal the wounds of others are to observe carefully what is the age and sex of the sinner, what instruction he has received, what is his strength, what trouble he has been driven to sin, with what kind of passion he is assailed, how long he remained in sinful delight, with what sorrow and labour he is afflicted and how much he is detached from worldly things': *ibid.*, Bigotian, 198–9 §2.
7   Charles-Edwards, 'The Pastoral Role', 64.
8   'Their place in the Church is now held by the bishops. Those who obtain the position of governing receive authority to loose and to bind. It is a great honour but the burden is heavy. In truth, it is difficult for one who does not know how to exercise control over his own life to become the judge of someone else's life. And it often happens that someone whose life is hardly in accord with his position holds this place of judgement; it frequently comes about that either he condemns those who do not deserve to be condemned or he looses others who are bound. Often in loosing and binding those subject to him he follows the inclination of his own will and not the merits of the case. Hence it happens that one who exercises this power according to his own inclination and not according to the character of those subject to him deprives himself of this very power

Interestingly, however, while Gregory refers specifically to bishops and, indeed, is cited as doing so in the *Collectio*, the *Bigotian* author in his summary refers to the more inclusive *pastor*:

> Secundum Gregorium magnopere pastoribus procurandum, ne incauti alligauerint quod non alligandum et non soluerint quod non soluendum.[9]

It is possible that the role of clerical judges in Ireland was an evolving or varied one according to either geographical location or legal perspective but the dates of these texts are often debatable and, in fact, what strikes this reader is the broad consistency of the various prescriptions, despite some minor variations.[10] Overall, they suggest that priests were an important part of the local justice system, especially in the overlap between crime and personal responsibility, and that their jurisdiction covered both lay and clerical offenders.

For example, both Finnian and Columbanus' *Penitentials* specify that clerics who commit murder should be exiled from their *patria* for ten years and required the favourable judgement of a priest before they would be received back into the community.[11] At the same time, Finnian specifies that a layman who struck and shed blood should undergo penance for forty days and pay a fine calculated by a priest, while the *First Synod of Patrick* proposes that all Christians accused of murder or adultery or of being a *magus* (sorcerer/druid) should undertake one year's penance and then should go before the priest, accompanied by his (character) witnesses for judgement.[12] On lay adultery, Finnian specifies that, if a layman defiles a woman belonging to someone else, the fruits of his penance are to be paid to the priest. In similar vein, Columbanus says that the penalty for lay adultery is three years (+ the price of chastity to the husband) and the priest will then judge his redemption. Homosexual activity, if it is a long-term practice, qualifies for seven years' penance in Finnian, while Columbanus requires the prayers of a priest and his forgiveness at the end of a similar period. Columbanus adds further that a layman who merely lusts after another woman without taking this further should confess his guilt to a priest and undergo forty days' penance.[13]

On clerical adultery, both authorities identify the case of clerics who beget a son, Finnian adding the further detail that, if he then kills him, the cleric is to be exiled for seven years and deprived of his office for the duration of that time and can then be restored to office on the judgement of a priest or bishop.

---

of binding and loosing': *PL*, LCCVI.1200; D. Hurst, transl., *Gregory the Great: Forty Gospel Homilies* (Kalamazoo, 1990), 204–5 (Homily 26); Wasserschleben, *Kanonensammlung*, 9 I §14.

9   'According to Gregory, great care is to be taken by pastors lest they carelessly bind what ought not to be bound and loose what ought not to be loosed': Bieler, *Penitentials*, Bigotian, 198–9 §3.

10 See discussion of the possible textual relationships of various penitentials by T. M. Charles-Edwards, 'The Penitential of Columbanus', in *Columbanus: Studies on the Latin Writings*, ed. M. Lapidge (Woodbridge, 1997), 217–39. As I am attempting to define the general position of clerical judges in early Ireland, I have not broken down the 'Columbanus' penitential' into the five sub-sections proposed by Charles-Edwards (*ibid.*, 217) nor do I discuss the role of his disciples' teaching in the evolving work. Given the parallels with Finnian's work in the extracts I discuss, I have also avoided attempting to distinguish what might be considered specifically Frankish provisions in the 'Columbanus penitential' (see *ibid.*, 239).

11 Bieler, *Penitentials*, Finnian 80–2 §23; Columbanus 98 §1.

12 *Ibid.*, Finnian 76 §§8–9; First Synod of Patrick 56 §14.

13 *Ibid.*, Finnian 86–8 §36; 74–5 §2 (but the reference to the priest's judgement appears to be an insertion from Cummian X.15); Columbanus 102 §§14–15, 104 §23.

Columbanus, in contrast, prescribes seven years' exile for the begetting of the son (without mentioning the death of the child) but agrees that a priest will make the final judgement and also indicates that in the case of a layman or woman who misuses their child (*infantem suum oppraesserit*), the penalty will be three years.[14]

In these various prescriptions one can see how the specifically religious role of *anamchara* or spiritual confessor has had an impact on social legislation.[15] Other penitential texts, such as Cummian's Penitential or the Bigotian Penitential, drawing on Cassian's eight vices and corresponding virtues, make the link even stronger by indicating a priest's role in judging such sins of personality as arrogance, avarice, anger, envy and bitterness. All of these generally require some form of penance under a priest's supervision.[16] At the same time, these latter texts also include prescriptions about bearing false witness, especially if oaths are sworn 'in the hand of' (a Latin version of the Irish legal phrase *gaib i láim*) bishops, priests and deacons, before the altar or the cross.[17] These are rulings which impact on society in general and echo Finnian's earlier concerns about the swearing of false oaths as well as his dictum on clerics who stir up strife in their neighbourhood.[18]

There is relatively little discussion in the penitentials of sins which could be considered as the specific concerns of priestly ministry.[19] It is clear that baptism was considered a key duty of the clergy: if a child died without having been baptised and the fault lay with the cleric involved, he must do penance on bread and water for six months (if he was not of the same locality) or a year (if he was).[20] Finnian's penitential would seem to indicate that baptism might be undertaken by a deacon if a priest was not available. The *First Synod of Patrick* states that clerics who do not attend matins or vespers should be condemned, while Cummian and the Bigotian Penitential state that those who proclaim heretical views are considered to be guilty of the sins of pride and vainglory.[21] (It seems reasonable to assume that those educated and concerned enough to proclaim such views were predominantly clerical). Cummian also provides a whole section of penances which deal with dropped or lost fragments of the Host or wine from the Chalice – rules which seem to indicate that the floor underneath the altar was often covered with straw and that the altar was covered with a cloth. (Again, similar provisions are found in the penitential section of the *Regula Coeno-*

---

14 *Ibid.* Finnian 76–8 §12; Columbanus 98 §2, 102 §18.
15 Charles-Edwards, 'The Pastoral Role', 74–5.
16 Charles-Edwards, 'Penitential', 218; Bieler, *Penitentials*, Cummian 116 §III.3, 122 §VIII.3, Bigotian 224 §III.1 226 §III.4. See also Finnian 84 §29, where a more oblique reference to Cassian's teaching is made.
17 J. Strachan, *Stories from the Táin*, 2nd edn (Dublin, 1928), 3; Bieler, *Penitentials*, Bigotian 224 §III.3.3; Old Irish Penitential 267 §14 (but see also *id.* §12).
18 Bieler, *Penitentials*, Cummian 118 §12, Bigotian 228–30 §4, Finnian 80 §22, 74–6 §5.
19 The regular duties of such ministry are identified in *Ríagal Phátraic* as baptism, communion, requiem for *manaig*, mass every Sunday and celebration of each canonical hour as well as preaching to the faithful: J. G. O'Keeffe, 'The Rule of Patrick', *Ériu* 1 (1904), 216–24; see Charles-Edwards, 'The Pastoral Role', 70–1; R. Sharpe, 'Churches and Communities in Early Medieval Ireland: Towards a Pastoral Model', in *Pastoral Care*, ed. Blair and Sharpe, 81–109, 81–3.
20 Bieler, *Penitentials*, Finnian 92 §48; Cummian 116 §33; Bigotian 224 §II 11.2.
21 Bieler, *Penitentials*, Finnian 92–3 §49; First Synod of Patrick 54–5 §7; Cummian 12–3 § VIII 1–2; Bigotian 236 §VII 2.

bialis of Columbanus).[22] Cummian further indicates that if the priest stammered during the consecration, perhaps because of a lack of command of Latin, he was to undergo the particular penance of physical beating; specifications for other penances focus instead on fasting and prayer.[23]

It is not clear who might have the authority to administer such a beating; it is stated explicitly that some, but not all, priests had taken monastic vows and were, therefore, presumably living in community with others who might take such responsibility.[24] Binchy translates the Irish phrase *eclais óentad* as 'communal church' and the Old Irish Penitential specifies that a cleric and a *caillech* (veiled one – professional female religious? clerical concubine?) might both live in such a settlement. Other references in the same text are to an *óentu na mbráithre* or 'community of brothers' which included monks – and, taken together, these various references would seem to indicate that an *eclais óentad* would probably be an establishment like Cogitosus's Kildare or the Armagh of *Liber Angeli*, with monks, clerics and female religious all living in such close proximity that they could attend mass together in the one church.[25] There are also references to *fratres* or brothers with whom an excommunicated priest might be living in a single *domus* or house – these may be fellow monks, but it may also imply the existence of episcopal households where priests lived together with their episcopal head, as found in both Merovingian France and the minsters of Anglo-Saxon England.[26] At the same time, however, the *First Synod of Patrick* mentions the possibility that priests might be condemned for building churches and offering the sacraments without permission of their bishop, and this prescription would seem to imply that a priest might be living at some distance from his superior.[27]

At least some priests apparently lived in family groups within the lay community. Famously, the *First Synod of St Patrick* specifies that all clerics up to and including priests must wear a tunic and be tonsured on pain of expulsion from the church. These provisions would seem to accord with the archaeological evidence for ecclesiastical dress.[28] The same canon specified that a priest's *uxor* 'wife'

---

22 Bieler, *Penitentials*, Columbanus 100–3 §12; Cummian 130–3 XI; *Reg. Coen.* 15 (ed. Walker, 162–3).

23 Bieler, *Penitentials*, Cummian 132 §29. See the *Reg. Coen.* of Columbanus (ed. Walker, 142–69) for the use of beating as part of the penance within a monastic house.

24 Bieler, *Penitentials*, Finnian 80–2 §23; First Synod of Patrick 58 §34; Old Irish Penitential 262 §8, Columbanus 100 §4.

25 E. J. Gwynn, 'An Irish Penitential', *Ériu* 7 (1914), 121–95, 154 §6, 156 §10, 158 §20, 168 §14, 172 §3; Bieler, *Penitentials*, Old Irish Penitential, 266 §6 §10, 268 §20, 273 §14, 274 §3. This is a contrasting interpretation to that put forward by Christina Harrington who believes that an *eclais óentad* is a local church of the *túath* – see C. Harrington, *Women in a Celtic Church: Ireland 450–1150* (Oxford, 2002), 116. For descriptions of Armagh, see L. Bieler, ed., *The Patrician Texts in the Book of Armagh*, SLH 10 (Dublin, 1979), 187 §§15–16; for Kildare, see 'Cogitosus: Life of Saint Brigit', transl. S. Connolly and J.-M. Picard, *JRSAI* 119 (1987), 5–27, 25–6 §32.

26 Bieler, *Penitentials*, First Synod of Patrick 58 §28; E. James, 'Review of *Prêtres en Gaul mérovingienne* by R. Godding', *English Historical Review* 120 (2005), 426–8; E. Cambridge, 'The Early Church in County Durham: A Reassessment', *Journal of the British Archaeological Association* 137 (1984), 65–85; C. Cubitt, 'The Clergy in Anglo-Saxon England', *Historical Research* 78 (2001), 273–87.

27 Bieler, *Penitentials*, First Synod of Patrick 56 §23.

28 For examples of early Irish ecclesiastical figures as depicted in sculpture and manuscripts, see F. Henry, *Irish Art in the Early Christian Period to AD 800* (London, 1965), pls 56, 57, 70, 79, 83.

must be veiled – a provision which presumably led to the widespread use of the word *caillech* or 'veiled one' to be used to cover both such individuals and professional female religious in general.[29] The reference to a priest's wife is one of the indicators which led Kathleen Hughes to argue that this text belonged to an earlier phase of Christian activity in Ireland.[30] Two citations from Finnian and Columbanus indicate, however, as she herself noted, the possibility that clerics could be married and that, while it was expected that those above the rank of deacon should be celibate, an individual cleric might continue to live with his family:

> Si quis fuerit clericus diaconis uel alicuius gradus et laicus et ante fuerit cum filiis et filiabus suis et cum clentella habitet et redeat ad carnis desiderium et genuerit filium ex clentella propria sua, ut dicat, sciat se ruina maxima cecidisse et exsurgere debere; non minus peccatum eius est ut esset clericus ex iuuentute sua et ita est ut cum puella aliena peccasset, quia post uotum suum peccauerunt …

> Si quis autem clericus aut diaconus uel alicuius gradus, qui laicus fuit in saeculo cum filiis et filiabus, post conuersionem suam iterum suam cognouerit clientelam et filium iterum de ea genuerit, sciat se adulterium perpetrasse et non minus peccasse quam si ab iuuentute sua clericus fuisset et cum puella aliena peccasset quia post uotum suum peccauit …[31]

Such provisions, which may be earlier versions of arrangements currently in operation in Orthodox Christianity, reflect the instructions of the fifth-century Pope Leo I, who declared that from the level of the subdiaconate, clergy should 'without sending away their wives, live with them as if they did not have them, so that conjugal love be safeguarded and nuptial activity be ended'.[32] They also help to explain the various Irish glosses on the Pauline prescription that a bishop should be a man of one wife; in an eighth-century commentary a revealing addition to this phrase is *renairite gráid iarmbathius*.[33] On the idea that the submissiveness of his sons shows a bishop's ability as a ruler, the Irish author adds the same idea, *manirochoscasom amuntir intain biís cengrád ni uisse toisigecht*

---

29 M. Ní Dhonnchadha, '*Caillech* and Other Terms for Veiled Women in Medieval Irish Texts', *Éigse* 28 (1994–5), 71–96.

30 K. Hughes, *The Church in Early Irish Society* (London, 1966), 47–52.

31 'If anyone is a cleric of the rank of deacon or of any rank and if he formerly was a layman, and if he lives with his sons and daughters and with his mate (*clentella*) and if he returns to carnal desire and begets a son with his own mate, as he might say, let him know that he has fallen to the depths of ruin and ought to rise; his sin is not less than it would be if he had been a cleric from his youth and sinned with a strange girl, since they have sinned after their vow': Bieler, *Penitentials*, Finnian 82 §27; 'If any cleric or deacon or a man in any orders, who in the world was a layman with sons and daughters, after his profession, has again known his mate (*clientela*) and again begotten a child of her, let him know that he has committed adultery and has sinned no less than if he had been a cleric from his youth and had sinned with a strange girl since he sinned after his vow …': *ibid.*, Columbanus 100 §8.

32 W. E. Phipps, *Clerical Celibacy: The Heritage* (New York and London, 2004), 121–5; C. A. Frazee, 'The Origins of Clerical Celibacy in the Western Church', *Church History: Studies in Christianity and Culture* 57 (1988), 108–26. Pope Leo's prescription forms the basis for canons in the Third Council of Orléans in 538 but had extended to all grades of clerics by the Fourth Council of Orléans in 541. See O. Pontel, *Histoire des conciles mérovingiens* (Paris, 1989), 112, 129.

33 'Before receiving orders and after baptism': W. Stokes and J. Strachan, ed., *Thesaurus Palaeohibernicus*, 2 vols (Dublin, 1901), I.682, gloss 28b 21.

sochuide do.[34] An Irish legend on the first bishop of Leinster specifies that the candidate should also be a man of one offspring – *fer óinsétche duna-rructhae act óentuistiu* – while a vernacular text (*Míadšlechtae*?) distinguishes between an *espoc óge* (virgin bishop), an *espoc óinsétche* (bishop of one wife) and an *espoc aithrighe* (penitent bishop).[35] This last appears to reflect the common Late Antique scenario in which established leaders of the lay community were made bishop in their old age, for his equivalent is identified in the *Collectio* as a *grandevus laicus.*[36]

Certainly, the Irish penitentials expend considerable time and effort on the question of clerical celibacy. The basic position appears to be one in which celibacy is considered the norm for all clerics – the word most commonly used is *clericus* and only occasionally are grades such as deacon or priest specified. There is a degree of recognition of human realities, in that there is an escalating series of penances from casual meetings and conversations up to a long-standing affair, for which the participant would be liable for penances of seven years, half of these on bread and water. More austere authorities (or authors writing for a specifically monastic audience), such as Columbanus, sought to enforce the strict letter of Matthew 5:28 (one who looks at a woman lustfully has already committed adultery with her in his heart), with penances of up to a year, while others, such as Finnian or Cummian, allocated such sentiments rather shorter periods of seven or forty days.[37] It is notable that sin with beasts was apparently considered a rather lesser sin than intercourse with a woman but that homosexual relationships between (lay) adult males were considered on a par with heterosexual liaisons by the clergy.[38] There is no specific ruling on homosexually active clerics, although provisions about bathing in Columbanus' penitential suggest that monastic authorities, at least, may have been worried about the possibility.[39]

Interestingly, there is no evidence for the longstanding concern about priestly housekeepers that we see in Merovingian Church canons, where it is expected that female relatives (such as a mother or sister) might live with a priest.[40] A Welsh canon, however, talks about a female servant who could be made a ward of a priest, while the Bigotian penitential refers to the possibility that a pregnant female servant (*glangella*) could contaminate something which the cleric would then drink.[41] The *Collectio* indicates that *ministri* should attend priests and, on the whole, it seems most likely that the norm was that female servants, along with their male counterparts, were considered an integral and necessary part of all Irish clerical households regardless of their overall organisational structure.[42]

---

[34] 'If he cannot correct his household <u>when he is without orders</u>, the leadership of a multitude is not proper for him': *ibid.*, I.682 gloss 28b 28.

[35] R. Thurneysen, ed., *Old Irish Reader* (Dublin, 1949), 33; Bieler, *Patrician Texts*, 179; *CIH* II.588.1–589.32. For the possible distinction of this text from the law tract *Míadšlechtae* which precedes it, see F. Kelly, *GEIL* 267.

[36] Charles-Edwards, 'The Pastoral Role', 68; C. Etchingham, 'Bishops in the Early Irish Church: A Reassessment', *Studia Hibernica* 28 (1994), 35–62, at 43–4; Wasserschleben, *Kanonensammlung*, 8 §I 11; A. H. M. Jones, *The Decline of the Ancient World* (Harlow and New York, 1966), 268–9.

[37] Bieler, *Penitentials*, Columbanus 96 §2; Bigotian 218 §II 5; Finnian 78 §16; Cummian 114 §11–14.

[38] Bieler, *Penitentials*, Old Irish Penitential 263–5, §11–§35; but see Bigotian 218–20, §II 1–§II 3.2.

[39] *Ibid.*, Columbanus 106 §§27–8.

[40] Pontel, *Conciles mérovingiens*, 129.

[41] Bieler, *Penitentials*, Canones Wallici (A), 148–9, §60, Bigotian 216 §I 6.2.

[42] Wasserschleben, *Kanonensammlung*, 15 §II.11

The income that would be required to run such a household was identified in the *Collectio* as being the concern of higher authorities. Ruben and Cú Chuimne cite Old Testament precedent to the effect that, just as Aaron was given his vestments by Moses and others, so too should the necessities required by an Irish priest be provided by his *princeps*, or church superior.[43] The word *princeps* is somewhat ambiguous, as its literal meaning, 'leader', does not allow us to specify whether we are talking about episcopal or monastic superiors and it can, in fact, be used of both, particularly in their role as governors and controllers of economic resources.[44] Those resources came, ultimately, from tithes collected from the congregations, although it is still a matter of debate as to whether those congregations represented the lay population as a whole or merely the tenants of ecclesiastical estates.[45] The list of necessities required by the local priest, living within a *túath* rather than on a larger ecclesiastical settlement, is given in the eighth-century *Ríagail Phátraic*:

> Nach eclais hi mbí fer gráid di minecailsib na túaithe, cenmotát móreclaisi, dligid túarustul a gráid .i. tech 7 airlisi 7 dérgud 7 deigceltaib
> 7 acnámad rod-fera cen turbaid cen díchell do neoch bes hi cumung na eclaisi .i. míach cona indiud 7 bó blicht in cech ráithe 7 biad sollaman.[46]

Other forms of income may have been paid directly from the community. *Ríagal Phátraic* indicates elsewhere that the labour due of a day's ploughing each year was due to each *fer gráid* (ordained man – literally man of rank):

> It é frithfolaidi-seom dond fir gráid .i. lá air n-indraic cech blíadnai cona síl 7 a ithir, 7 lethgabol étaig do brutt nó da léinid nó do inur. Pruind chethruir ar Notlaic 7 Cháisc 7 Chingcís.[47]

---

[43] Wasserschleben, *Kanonensammlung*, 15 §II 11. I am grateful to Dr Jessie Rogers for identifying the source of this statement as Exodus 28: esp. v. 1–3.

[44] Charles-Edwards, 'The Pastoral Role', 67; C. Etchingham, *Church Organisation in Ireland AD 650 to 1000* (Maynooth, 1999), 50–9.

[45] P. J. Corish, *The Christian Mission*, A History of Irish Catholicism 1.3 (Dublin, 1972), 32–41; D. Ó Corráin, 'The Early Irish Churches: some Aspects of Organization', in *Irish Antiquity: Essays and Studies Presented to Professor M. J. O'Kelly*, ed. D. Ó Corráin (Cork, 1981), 327–34, 334; D. Ó Corráin, L. Breatnach and A. Breen, 'The Laws of the Irish', *Peritia* 3 (1984), 382–410, 410; C. Etchingham, 'The Early Irish Church: Some Observations on Pastoral Care and Dues', *Ériu* 42 (1991), 99–118; *idem, Church Organisation*, 239–89; T. M. Charles-Edwards, *Early Irish and Welsh Kinship* (Oxford, 1993), 324–36; Sharpe, 'Churches and Communities', 108–9; T. O. Clancy, 'Annat in Scotland and the Origins of the Parish', *Innes Review* 46 (1995), 91–115, at 93–5.

[46] 'Any church, of the small churches of the *túath* as well as the great churches, in which there is an ordained man owes the stipend of his order i.e. a house (*tech*) and a precinct (*airlise*) and a bed and clothing and food which may suffice him without exemption, without neglect of anything that is in the power of the church i.e. a bushel of corn with its condiment and a milch cow every quarter and food at the festivals': Etchingham, *Church Organisation*, 252–3, translating *CIH* VI.2130.19–23. *Airlise* is identified in Ó Clery's Irish glossary (*DIL* A 226) as a synonym for *garrdha*, a loan from Old Norse *gard*. This has been identified by Patrick Wallace as the word for the house plot (with vegetable gardens) surrounding individual dwellings in Hiberno-Norse cities; see P. Wallace, '*Garrda* and *airbeada*: the Plot Thickens in Viking Dublin', in *Seanchas: Studies in Early and Medieval Irish Archaeology, History and Literature in Honour of Francis J. Byrne*, ed. A. P. Smyth (Dublin, 2000), 261–74, at 261–3.

[47] 'These are their counter-obligations to the ordained man i.e. a standard day's ploughing each year with its seed and its corn-land and a half measure of clothing comprising a mantle or a shirt or

The title *fer gráid* here comes from the usage of Pope Gregory the Great, who, in his work *The Book of Pastoral Rule*, written *c.*590, identifies priests with the Latin word *ordo* 'rank'.[48] In Irish usage, however, the phrase may have been used to translate Latin *clericus* and be relevant to all clerics – this is, at any rate, how it has been understood by modern scholars in their translations.

It has already been mentioned that the *Collectio* shows a particular interest in clerical incomes. Chapters twenty-two to twenty-four of Book two indicate concerns about what are termed *munera/dona iniquorum*, 'gifts of evil men', but conclude that food and clothing, provided they are not in excess, are acceptable. Other canons quote Gregory Nazianzenus to the effect that priests should not involve themselves in trade or agricultural labour, nor should they exploit their congregations for gain, and that excess wealth should be given back to the Church or deployed in Christian endeavours such as the redemption of captives.[49] The *First Synod of Patrick* indicates that a cleric who steals the gifts of the laity to a bishop is to be excommunicated.[50] One can imagine that the process of collecting local tithes on behalf of a *princeps* who then used these goods to pay a priest who himself lived on a self-sufficient agricultural holding within a *túath* was a complicated one and difficult to monitor in detail. It is noteworthy that there are quite a large number of references which, drawing on Old Testament provisions, deal with the possibility of clerics stealing farm animals.[51]

In addition to the general structure of clerical income, priests also earned particular fees for themselves through their local activities in the community. Chapter fourteen of *On presbyters and priests*, for example, states that a priest is entitled to a mortuary due (*sedatium*), while chapter fifteen indicates that this is capped at a maximum of one milch cow.[52] This may be the price of the *viaticum* rather than the price of burial, as Colmán Etchingham has drawn attention to prescriptions in *Córus Bésgnai* for the payment of the deceased's *lóg n-enech* (honour-price) as the fee for burial in consecrated ground, and, for many of the higher ranks in society, this would be considerably more than a single milch cow.[53] On the other hand, perhaps we should see this rule simply as a modification of the *Córus Bésgnai* formulation on burial fees (along the lines of the capping of the honour-price for a *saer* or builder – his *lóg n-enech* increased for every skill he acquired but could never be allowed surpass that of a master poet or academic).[54] Elsewhere the *Collectio* also states that a priest should not seek a *pretium ministrationis*, which one would assume means that they were forbidden to charge for performance of the sacraments. Certainly, in Book forty-two, *On the*

a tunic. A meal for four at Christmas, Easter and Pentecost': Etchingham, *Church Organisation*, 255, translating *CIH* VI.2130.31–3.

[48] Bruno Judic, ed., *Grégoire le Grand: Règle Pastorale*, 2 vols (Paris, 1992), I.68. Gregory is quoted on this in *On presbyters and priests*: see Wasserschleben, *Kanonensammlung*, 13 II §5.

[49] Wasserschleben, *Kanonensammlung*, 15 §II.11, 16 §II.13, 17 §II.17, 18 §II.20, 19 §II.24.

[50] Bieler, *Penitentials*, First Synod of Patrick 58 §§25–6.

[51] Bieler, *Penitentials*, Finnian 82 §25, Columbanus 100 §7; Wasserschleben, *Kanonensammlung*, 99 §XXIX.3; V. Hull, 'Bretha im Gatta', *ZCP* 25 (1956), 21–5.

[52] Wasserschleben, *Kanonensammlung*, 16–17 §II 14 §II 15.

[53] C. Etchingham, 'Pastoral Provision in the First Millennium: A Two-Tier Provision?', in *The Parish in Medieval and Early Modern Ireland*, ed. E. Fitzpatrick and R. Gillespie (Dublin, 2006), 79–90, 86.

[54] *CIH* V.1612.2 –1613.8.

church and the world, it is stated that it is forbidden to charge for either baptism or for 'doctrine'.[55]

Doctrine here may refer to preaching or to education in general. In *Bethu Brigte*, however, Brigit and her community paid a fee to Bishop Mel for preaching during the octave of Easter and they also gave a feast for him.[56] Charles-Edwards draws attention to the fact that Columba, as a young boy, was taught and perhaps fostered by a priest while Tírechán, himself an *alumpnus* of a bishop, refers to Patrick's gifts of *elimenta* and *abgitoria* to young boys.[57] Despite the prohibition on charging for 'doctrine', it seems quite likely that there was normally a fee involved for the priest in payment for their duties as both teachers and fosterers. Martin McNamara has drawn attention to an extract in the *Rule of the Céli Dé* which refers to the fees paid by students at what may be a rather later stage in their education:

> Nach oen tra lasa legait na meic audparthar and do Dia 7 Patraic, dlegait side fochraic 7 dulchinde i n-aimseraib corib .i. loilgech i fochraicc na .lll. cona n-imnaib 7 cantacib 7 liachtanaib 7 co mbaithis 7 comna 7 gabail n-ecnarci 7 co n-eolas a n-ordaigthe olchena co mba tualaing airiten grad. Ag 7 mucc 7 tri meich bracha 7 miach arba bid ina duilchinde cecha bliadna cenmotha gaire 7 algine do étiud 7 biathad il-log mbendachtan. Acht iar taisfenad na salm 7 na n-imond focetoir dorenar in loilgech, iar taisfenad dino in ordusa dlegar in dulchinde 7 in decelt. Dligid imorro in tshui no in t-espoc dia taisfentar na sailm proind coicir de chormaimm 7 biud in oidche sin.[58]

A rather more unexpected stream of income came from the position of clergy as local intercessors with what might be called the supernatural world. We tend to think of their concerns as being entirely with what we recognise as Christian ideology, but the Penitentials of both Finnian and Columbanus indicate that local laity might see them as having rather wider powers:

> Si quis clericus uel si qua mulier malifica uel malificus si aliquem maleficio suo deciperat, inmane peccatum est sed per penitentiam redimi potest … si autem non deciperat aliquem sed pro inlecebroso amore dederat alicui, annum integrum peniteat cum pane et aqua per mensura.

---

55 Wasserschleben, *Kanonensammlung*, 18 §II.21, 167 §XLII.17.

56 D. Ó hAodha, *Bethu Brigte* (Dublin, 1978), 25–6 §24.

57 'Conclusion', in *After Rome*, ed. T. M. Charles-Edwards (Oxford, 2003), 259–70, at 264; Wasserschleben, *Kanonensammlung*, 101 §XXIX.6, 167 §XLII.17; A. O. Anderson and M. O. Anderson, *Adomnán's Life of Columba* (Oxford, 1991), 184 §111.2; D. Ó Cróinín, *Early Medieval Ireland 400–1200* (London and New York), 178–80; Bieler, *Patrician Texts*, 132 §13, 150 §33, 158 §43, 160 §47.

58 'Anyone, moreover, with whom the boys study who are thus offered to God and to Patrick, has a claim to reward and fee at the proper season, namely a milch-cow as remuneration for teaching the psalms with their hymns, canticles and lections and the rites of Baptism and communion and intercession, together with the knowledge of the ritual generally, till the student be capable of receiving Orders. A heifer and a pig and three sacks of malt and a sack of corn are his fee every year besides tendance and a compassionate allowance of raiment and food in return for his blessing. But the milch cow is made over immediately after the student has publicly proved his knowledge of the psalms and hymns and after the public proof of his knowledge of the ritual, the fee and habit are due. Moreover the doctor or bishop before whom proof of the psalms has been made is entitled to a collation of the beer and food for five persons the same night': *Riagail na Céle nDé* §62, in 'The Rule of Tallaght', ed. E. Gwynn, *Hermathena* 44 2nd supplement (1927), 64–87, 83; M. McNamara, *The Psalms in the Early Irish Church* (Sheffield, 2000), 23.

Si autem pro amore quis maleficus sit et neminem perdiderit, annum integrum cum pane et aqua clericus ille paeniteat, laicus dimidium, diaconus duos, sacerdos tres.[59]

As prestigious or individuals of *sóernemed* status within the community, priests were entitled to a high honour price and to larger legal penalties then normal when the victims of crime.[60] If they were refused hospitality, for example, they were entitled to one-eighth of the cost of their *pretium sanguinis* (wergild or blood-price) on the basis that one would die if refused food and drink for eight days. The *Canones Hibernenses* give the blood price of a bishop as fifty *cumals* and implicitly identify the blood price of a priest as approximately forty-two *cumals* (or 126 milch cows).[61] If attacked physically, so that blood poured from a wound onto the ground, a priest was entitled to between three and a half *cumals* (for intentional attacks) and one *cumal* (for unintended injury), whereas the normal fine for such a wound was five *séoit* or five-sixths of a *cumal*.[62] If killed, it was a priest's prerogative to have his *pretium sanguinis* decided upon by either a king or a bishop rather than by judges of lesser rank, and the penalties could go as high as exile for life.[63] On the other hand, it is interesting to note that greater indulgence was felt when keening and/or reciting of bardic poetry took place at the death of a *clericus plebis* (cleric of a *túath*) than when similar behaviour marked the death of a layman or woman; the former attracted a penance of twenty days on bread and water, while the latter deserved over twice that amount, at fifty days.[64] A cleric who composed such laments himself would, however, be liable for double the normal penalty.[65]

To conclude, therefore, what can we deduce from our texts about the role of priests within their local community? It is clear that at least some priests lived on farms not very different from those of their neighbours and in houses which, like their neighbours', had servants and, on occasion at least, other family members in residence. The sustenance for the household came from a mixed agricultural regime with local people doing the ploughing and with a large and varied livestock being kept in the vicinity. Priests themselves were not, however, allowed to labour in the fields, for their contribution to the local economy depended on the gifts of their intellectual calling. The animals which stocked their farms came not from tenancy agreements with local lords but from a contract with their ecclesiastical *princeps*, supplemented by what they raised themselves through their own local activities. Their duties included not just the performance of sacraments for their congregations, for they also had an important role as judges, being respected for their ability to identify suitable penalties with due regard for the

---

59 'If any cleric or woman who practises magic have led astray anyone by their magic, it is a monstrous sin but it can be expiated by penance … If however such a person has not led astray anyone but has given [a potion] for the sake of wanton love to someone, he shall do penance for an entire year on an allowance of bread and water': Bieler, *Penitentials*, Finnian 79 §18; 'If anyone has used magic to excite love and has destroyed no one, let him do penance on bread and water for a whole year if a cleric, for half a year if a layman, if a deacon for two, if a priest for three': *ibid.*, Columbanus 101 §6.

60 For discussion of *sóernemed* status, see Kelly, *A Guide*, 9–10, 183.

61 Bieler, *Penitentials*, Canones Hibernenses 174 §§7–8.

62 *Ibid.*, 170 §§7–8; D. A. Binchy, 'Bretha Déin Chécht', *Ériu* 20 (1966), 1–66, 14, 36 §24, 38 §27.

63 Bieler, *Penitentials*, Bigotian 228 §IV. 1.3, Old Irish Penitential 271 §V.2.

64 *Ibid.*, Canones Hibernenses 162 §26 §28, Bigotian 230 §IV 6.2 §6.4, Old Irish Penitential 273 §17.

65 *Ibid.*, Old Irish Penitential 272 §18.

specific context of a particular case and the true remorse of a perpetrator. They made pronouncements on people's character defects and imposed penalties to help them overcome such faults. They acted as fosterers and educators for young boys who might go on to further study and they could be called upon by the love-lorn for assistance in achieving their heart's desire. They might be interested in writing and proclaiming bardic poetry and laments to commemorate the dead and, when they died, it was expected that appropriate ceremonies would mark their passing. They were respected, high-status individuals who were entitled to hospitality, and crimes against them were punished severely. All in all, local priests can be classified as integral members of the governing classes who controlled early Irish *túatha* while at the same time proclaiming the teaching and values of the Christian Church in a secular world. In this sense, the ongoing debate about what proportion of lay society paid pastoral dues seems to me to largely miss the point: like all tax-collectors, the Church has had perennial difficulties extracting material resources from its subordinate population and ecclesiastical tenantry are, in the nature of things, the most likely to be compliant payers. To deduce that, as a consequence, the early Irish Church was uninterested in the wider question of lay observance would seem, on the face of it, unlikely.

4

POLITICAL ORGANISATION IN DÁL RIATA

David N. Dumville

An examination of the evidence provided by medieval Irish chronicles for political organisation in the Gaelic world before about 1200 has shown that there was an absolute minimum of 600 population groups led by kings in the 750 years of record from the mid-fifth to the late twelfth century.[1] The distribution of these across time and space is interestingly complicated, and detailed discussion of it will have to await publication of the evidence. Suffice it to say, for the moment, that, contrary to what has been stated by some historians over the last generation, the local kingship of local population groups is as visible in Ireland in the twelfth century as it is in the seventh. For what is now Scotland, of course, one could not make any such statement: from the later ninth century at the very latest (and arguably from the mid-eighth) Gaelic North Britain underwent a series of transformations,[2] not the least aspect of which is the dramatic reduction in coverage of its affairs in the extant Irish chronicles – which date, as they stand, from the late eleventh to the mid-seventeenth century.[3]

The external framework of kingly rule in the early medieval Gaelic world – that is, the relations between kings as representatives of their population groups and kingdoms (*tuatha*, in other words)[4] – has, for the last seventy (or perhaps ninety) years, rested on generalisation from the early-eighth-century Irish law tract on status, *Críth Gablach*.[5] On the whole, its evidence has not been tested empirically against bodies of precise and particular data available in other sources, notably the Irish chronicles and the Irish genealogical collections which,

---

1   Katherine Megan McGowan, 'Political Geography and Political Structures in Earlier Mediaeval Ireland: A Chronicle-based Approach' (unpubl. PhD dissertation, University of Cambridge, 2002) and accompanying database.

2   For a preliminary sketch of my views on that subject, see David N. Dumville, *The Churches of North Britain in the First Viking-Age* (Whithorn, 1997), 34–6.

3   On this phenomenon, see Marjorie O. Anderson, *Kings and Kingship in Early Scotland* (Edinburgh, 1973; 2nd edn, 1980), 1–42 *passim*; John Bannerman, *Studies in the History of Dalriada* (Edinburgh, 1974), 9–26, especially 25–6; Daniel P. McCarthy, *The Irish Annals, their Genesis, Evolution and History* (Dublin, 2008), 7.

4   For the word, see *DIL s.v.* 1 túath (where meanings given include 'people', 'petty kingdom', 'territory', 'country', 'laity' ['lay society'], 'lay property').

5   D. A. Binchy, ed., *Críth Gablach* (Dublin, 1941); for the translation and discussion which first brought this text to the centre of discussion of the politics of the Gaelic early Middle Ages, see E. MacNeill, 'Ancient Irish Law. The Law of Status or Franchise', *PRIA* 36 C (1921–4), 265–316, at 265–72, 281–306. Now we have two absolutely fundamental articles by T. M. Charles-Edwards: '*Críth Gablach* and the Law of Status', *Peritia* 5 (1986), 53–73; 'A Contract between King and People in Early Medieval Ireland? *Críth Gablach* on Kingship', *Peritia* 8 (1994), 107–19.

similarly to the chronicles, date as they stand from the mid-twelfth century to the mid-seventeenth.[6] What is clear, nonetheless, is that hierarchies of kingship are variously visible in the precise evidence. These may not always (or even commonly) or perfectly represent the precise pyramid of political relationships among kings, which has long been deduced from *Críth Gablach*.[7] What is clear, however, is that overkingship (indeed, more than one level of overkingship) is an important given of the Gaelic political scene in the early Middle Ages – and henceforth I restrict myself to this period before 800.

The question which must arise in the present context is whether the same is true of Dál Riata. To the extent that Dál Riata – inhabiting territory in both Britain and Ireland – was a population group within the Irish polity,[8] it might seem reasonable to suppose so. But the question has in recent years been raised whether Dál Riata in Ireland arose from a prehistoric migratory movement from Gaelic North Britain.[9] While that seems unlikely to me, in the context of such fundamental doubts as to the place which Dál Riata occupied in the Irish polity it would be wise to return to first principles. In his work of 1964–74 John Bannerman was content to use *Críth Gablach* as a template for his reassessment of the sociopolitical culture of Dál Riata.[10] The reviewers of *Studies in the History of Dalriada*, Thomas Charles-Edwards and Donnchadh Ó Corráin, chewed over this use but did not actively dissent.[11] More recently, explicit challenge has been broached.

On the face of it, the early medieval Gaelic population groups of North Britain were not differently organised at the level of kingly interaction from those of Ireland. However, Richard Sharpe has recently argued,[12] developing a large hint

---

6   The chronicles exist in manuscripts dating from the late eleventh to the later seventeenth century. Different views of their interrelationships have been (partially) articulated by: Kathleen Hughes, *Early Christian Ireland: Introduction to the Sources* (London, 1972), 97–159; Gearóid Mac Niocaill, *The Medieval Irish Annals* (Dublin, 1975); Kathryn Grabowski and D. Dumville, *Chronicles and Annals of Mediaeval Ireland and Wales. The Clonmacnoise-group Texts* (Woodbridge, 1984); T. M. Charles-Edwards, trans., *The Chronicle of Ireland*, 2 vols (Liverpool, 2006); McCarthy, *The Irish Annals*. In giving footnoted references to chronicles, I have resorted to the now customary sigla (which, it should be noted, refer to the chronicles themselves, not to any particular edition or translation): for the present paper, only AU = 'The Annals of Ulster' is needed.

7   *Críth Gablach*, ed. Binchy, 104–5 (*s.v.* rí), 109 (*s.v.* túath). Cf. D. A. Binchy, 'The Passing of the Old Order', in *Proceedings of the [First] International Congress of Celtic Studies held in Dublin, 6–10 July, 1959*, ed. Brian Ó Cuív (Dublin, 1962), 119–32, and *Celtic and Anglo-Saxon Kingship* (Oxford, 1970).

8   On its status, see recent discussion by D. N. Dumville, 'Ireland and North Britain in the Earlier Middle Ages: Contexts for *Míniugud Senchasa Fher nAlban*', in *Rannsachadh na Gàidhlig 2000. Papers read at the Conference* Scottish Gaelic Studies 2000 *held at The University of Aberdeen, 2–4 August, 2000*, ed. Colm Ó Baoill and N. R. McGuire (Aberdeen, 2002), 185–211, especially 195–7, 199, reprinted with minor revisions by David N. Dumville, *Celtic Essays, 2001–2007*, 2 vols (Aberdeen, 2007), II.35–71, especially 49–51, 54–5.

9   E. Campbell, 'Were the Scots Irish?', *Antiquity* 75 (2001), 285–92; cf. R. Sharpe, 'The Thriving of Dalriada', in *Kings, Clerics and Chronicles in Scotland, 500–1297. Essays in Honour of Marjorie Ogilvie Anderson on the Occasion of her Ninetieth Birthday*, ed. Simon Taylor (Dublin, 2000), 47–61, at 50, and Dumville, 'Ireland and North Britain', 194–6 (= *Celtic Essays*, II.47–9).

10 John W. M. Bannerman, 'A Critical Edition of the *Senchus Fer nAlban* with an Assessment of its Historical Value' (unpubl. PhD dissertation, 2 vols, University of Cambridge, 1964); Bannerman, *Studies*, 132–40, 146–8. So too, on the whole, was Anderson, *Kings*, 131–3, 147–8, 162–5.

11 T. M. Charles-Edwards, *Studia Hibernica* 15 (1975), 194–6; D. Ó Corráin, *Celtica* 13 (1980), 168–82.

12 Sharpe, 'The Thriving'.

dropped by Eoin MacNeill,[13] that we should see the political culture of Dál Riata in wholly different terms. He has written of 'the success of [the Dalriadic] dynasty in surviving four hundred years' at least. The singularity implied in this statement is followed up by another, bolder still: 'It is … certain that for a time – already in the late sixth century and at least until the late seventh century – one dynasty ruled' the whole of Dál Riata.[14] That was Cenél nGabráin.[15] It 'produced only one segment, Cenél Comgaill, permanently excluded from the kingship by 650'. 'Neither [Adomnán's] Life [of St Columba] nor the annals mention subordinate kings, and there is nothing that points to the existence of other royal kindreds.' 'Dál Riata in Scotland simply had a king.'[16]

This is indeed too simple. Sharpe has blamed 'that genealogical tract', *Míniugud Senchasa Fher nAlban*, for allowing matters to be made complicated.[17] It presents Cenél Loairn and Cenél nOenguso as the other two principal families of Dál Riata. Sharpe has complained that of these 'we hear nothing until the closing years of the seventh century'. He has taken the ancestral joining of that text's three ruling lineages of Dál Riata in the person of Erc mac Echdach munremair as 'a genealogical fiction, legitimizing two groups in their relationship to the ruling family'.[18] But to describe Cenél nGabráin as 'the ruling family' of Dál Riata is prejudicial.[19] Sharpe has characterised Cenél Loairn as 'local notables in Lorn' and objected that 'Adomnán's recognizing this kindred as the dominant lineage in the north of Dalriada[20] should not be readily equated with regarding it

---

13 Eoin MacNeill, *Phases of Irish History* (Dublin, 1919), 206.

14 Sharpe, 'The Thriving', 49. In a potentially very important essay of interpretation, J. E. Fraser, '*Dux Reuda* and the Corcu Réti', in *Cànan & Cultar/Language & Culture. Rannsachadh na Gàidhlig, 3*, ed. Wilson McLeod *et al.* (Edinburgh, 2006), 1–8, has argued against Sharpe's 'centralist' thesis, but also (*inter alia*) that *Corcu Réti* is the seventh-century name for the descendants of Domangart, father of Comgell and Gabrán, not for the whole of the Gaelic polity of seventh-century North Britain. This will require full discussion elsewhere, but it seems to me that the crucial pieces of evidence have been interpreted in an inappropriately narrow fashion.

15 Adomnán of Iona referred (*Vita Sancti Columbae*, II.22) to a presumably younger contemporary of Columba as *quidam malefactor homo, bonorum persecutor … de regio Gabrani ortus genere*, and wrote (*ibid.*, II.24) further of that man's brothers, sons of Conall mac Domnaill maic Gabráin, as *alios eclesiarum persequutores*: Alan Orr Anderson and M. O. Anderson, ed. and trans., *Adomnán's Life of Columba*, 2nd edn (Oxford, 1991), 124–7, 128/9. We could translate *de regio Gabrani ortus genere* in various ways, but there need be no implication in Adomnán's words that *Gabrani genus*, Cenél nGabráin, was the only royal line in Dál Riata (or even among those claiming descent from Domangart, the father of Gabrán and Comgell, eponyms of their subsequent *cenéla*). See further n. 19, below.

16 Sharpe, 'The Thriving', 52.

17 *Ibid.*, 53.

18 *Ibid.*, 54.

19 See the remarks at n. 15, above, and cf. Bannerman, *Studies*, 107, n. 2. In discussing Adomnán's use of the phrase *genus regium*, Sharpe ('The Thriving', 55) has sought to paint Cenél Loairn as a merely noble lineage, in effect blaming Bannerman (*Studies*, 104, 108–10) for scholars' treatment of that lineage as royal. But Sharpe's argument there is tangled, and his Irish comparison shows that he was unable to grasp how localised royal title and power were in mediaeval Gaeldom.

20 Here, Sharpe was referring to Adomnán, *Vita Sancti Columbae*, II.45 (*Adomnán's Life*, ed. and trans. Anderson and Anderson, 174–9), where, apparently referring to the summer of 697, was narrated an event involving the writer *in plebe generis Loerni*, presumably rendering Old Gaelic *i tuaith ceneoil Loairn*, 'in the kingdom/territory of Cenél Loairn' or 'among the people of Cenél Loairn'. Sharpe ('The Thriving', 55; cf. 54, 'the phrase *genus Loairn* to designate a region') has observed, rather narrowly, that here 'The lineage of Lorn is associated undoubtedly with a territory', thus explaining his wording (quoted above) at this point; 'territory' is not necessarily the first meaning of *tuath* (and certainly not of *plebs*) for which one should reach.

as a royal kindred'. He has gone further: 'If Adomnán was aware of subordinate royal lineages in Dalriada, their royal status was beneath his notice. He regarded the rulers of Dunadd as the only kings of Dalriada ...'.[21]

It is a nice question what Adomnán thought or would have argued. It is certain that he held strong political views, including then modern and outrageous ones about the status of Uí Néill in the Irish polity.[22] What is clear is that *Míniugud Senchasa Fher nAlban* is a presentation of three *cenéla* – (i) of Fergus or Mac Nisse the grandfather of Gabrán and Comgell, (ii) of Loarn, and (iii) of Oengus – as constituting *the* three thirds of Dál Riata.[23] It is also a presentation (in the cases of Cenél nGabráin and Fergus sálach's segment of Cenél Loairn) of their relationships with Uí Néill.[24]

For Sharpe this dated *Míniugud Senchasa Fher nAlban* to the early eighth century, when Cenél Loairn was dominant, holding the overkingship of Dál Riata.[25] He concluded: 'One is left with the thought that there were two locally dominant families in what the rulers of Dunadd may have regarded as the provinces of their kingdom. Neither was a royal segment, though Cenél Loairn for a brief period challenged the royal line, and both enjoyed the genealogical fiction of remote kinship with their masters.'[26] This too is all prejudicial.

This strenuously heroic argument eventually collapses under its own weight when Cenél nOenguso is considered. Here is Sharpe again:[27] 'This argument, unfortunately, will not explain why Cenél nOengusa was similarly attached. Indeed nothing explains their presence in the tract other than their existence on the ground and their relevance to the census rather than the genealogical purpose of the tract.' Again, the last part of this statement is prejudicial: but that does not matter; the argument has just collapsed.

---

21 Sharpe, 'The Thriving', 55. It is not clear from his article why Sharpe regarded the territory of Cenél nGabráin as 'Kintyre and Knapdale with a centre at Dunadd for the royal line of Gabrán' (*ibid.*, 51); he has taken Adomnán's *caput regionis* (*Vita Sancti Columbae*, I.28) as a reference to Dunadd (*ibid.*, 52) rather than as a translation of Kintyre. And of course the logic of these approaches to Dunadd's role is that it was 'the Dalriadic capital' (*ibid.*, 61). The answers are to be found in *Adomnán of Iona, Life of St Columba*, trans. Richard Sharpe (Harmondsworth, 1995), 291, n. 136 (and cf. 288–91, nn. 133 and 135). With these points we may contrast *Early Sources of Scottish History, A.D. 500 to 1286*, trans. Alan Orr Anderson, 2 vols (Edinburgh, 1922), I.233(–4), n. 4, and Bannerman, *Studies*, 112–13 (on Dunadd) and 102–3, 108 (on Kintyre); on the latter, see also W. J. Watson, *The History of the Celtic Place-names of Scotland* (Edinburgh, 1926), 92; Sharpe was agreeing with Anderson and Anderson, *Adomnán's Life*, pp. xxxii–xxxiii, and 55, n. 60. In spite of the important paper by E. Campbell, 'A Cross-marked Quern from Dunadd and Other Evidence for Relations between Dunadd and Iona', *Proceedings of the Society of Antiquaries of Scotland* 117 (1987), 59–71, one must note the studiedly indefinite title of Alan Lane, E. Campbell, *et al.*, *Dunadd, an Early Dalriadic Capital* (Oxford, 2000).
22 On all this, see T. M. Charles-Edwards, *Early Christian Ireland* (Cambridge, 2000), 441–521, with references to earlier scholarship. For my own views, see, for example, D. N. Dumville, 'Anglo-Saxon and Celtic Overkingships: A Discussion of some Shared Historical Problems', *Bulletin of the Institute of Oriental and Occidental Studies, Kansai University* 31 (1998), 81–100, at 88–94, and Pádraig P. Ó Néill and D. N. Dumville, ed. and trans., *Cáin Adomnáin and Canones Adomnani* (2 parts, Cambridge 2003), p. vi.
23 Dumville, 'Ireland and North Britain', 201–3 (= *Celtic Essays*, II.56–8), especially §§38 and 53, and cf. §20 (and, for the detail, §§9–17, 21–30, 39–48).
24 *Ibid.*, §§8 and 45.
25 Sharpe, 'The Thriving', 55–6.
26 *Ibid.*, 56.
27 *Ibid.*, 55–6.

Sharpe's peroration – a paean of praise for monarchy, centralisation and big government – rests on two perceptions of Dalriadic history, early and late, and an argument strung between them.[28] The positive part of the argument is that Cenél nGabráin 'maintained a remarkable hold on the kingship and even succeeded in confining the regnal succession within a significantly narrower range of kinship than was normal in Ireland'.[29] This dynasty 'had derived strength from containing its growth into a single strong stem'.[30] However, the two posts which sustain (and no doubt gave rise to) the argument have no load-bearing capability. The first is that Dál Riata (or at least its North British part) was a colony,[31] even (although he jibbed at Donnchadh Ó Corráin's phrase) 'a conquest society'.[32] The second prop stands in the ninth century. 'The settlement in Argyll … thrived to such an extent that eventually the heirs of its ruling dynasty became kings of Alba. … The progressive Irish takeover of northern Britain represents a more complete success than the English occupation of southern Britain.'[33] The days for those sorts of certainty have passed.

In 2000, I suggested that we might do better to see the gaelicisation of Argyll, Bute and the Inner Hebrides as a thoroughly prehistoric process.[34] This would render any conquest a very distant affair and doubtfully relevant to the circumstances of the period 550–750, when we can see something of the history of Dál Riata. For those two centuries we are dependent variously on Adomnán's Life of St Columba and on *Cáin Adomnáin*,[35] on the genealogical tracts *Míniugud Senchasa Fher nAlban* and *Cethri Prímchenéla Dáil Riata*,[36] on the Columban poetry associated primarily with Iona[37] and on the medieval Irish chronicles, especially in their dependence via 'The Chronicle of Ireland' on a 'Chronicle of Iona'.[38] We need to extract from that corpus a political geography of Dál Riata.

Since Adomnán's evidence has loomed so large in Sharpe's argument, let us begin with the period in which Adomnán wrote and published his *Cáin* and his *Vita Sancti Columbae*. In 'The Annals of Ulster' for 697 the following two entries succeed one another.[39]

3. Adomnanus ad Hiberniam pergit et dedit Legem Inocentium populis.
'Adomnán went to Ireland and gave the Law of the Innocents to the peoples'.

4. Echu nepos Domnaill iugulatur.
'Eochu grandson of Domnall was killed'.

---

[28] *Ibid.*, 61.
[29] *Ibid.*, 60.
[30] *Ibid.*, 61.
[31] *Ibid.*, 48–9.
[32] *Ibid.*, 52–3; cf. Ó Corráin, *Celtica* 13 (1980), 168–82, at 179.
[33] Sharpe, 'The Thriving', 49. It is worth noting Sharpe's inconsistent and generally prejudicial use of the terms 'Gaelic' and 'Irish' in relation to North Britain: it would have been clearer and less controversial to use 'Gaelic' throughout.
[34] Dumville, 'Ireland and North Britain', 185–97 (= *Celtic Essays*, II.35–51).
[35] *Cáin Adomnáin and Canones Adomnani*, ed. and trans. Ó Néill and Dumville.
[36] D. N. Dumville, '*Cethri Prímchenéla Dáil Riata*', *Scottish Gaelic Studies* 20 (2000), 170–91.
[37] Most conveniently assembled and introduced by Thomas Owen Clancy and G. Márkus, ed. and trans., *Iona. The Earliest Poetry of a Celtic Monastery* (Edinburgh, 1995).
[38] For discussion of this, see Thomas F. O'Rahilly, *Early Irish History and Mythology* (Dublin, 1946), 253–7; A. P. Smyth, 'The Earliest Irish Annals: their First Contemporary Entries, and the Earliest Centres of Recording', *PRIA* 72C (1972), 1–48; Bannerman, *Studies*, 9–26; *The Chronicle of Ireland*, trans. Charles-Edwards.
[39] AU 697.3–4.

We meet *Euchu ua Domnaill, rí* as the eighty-fifth guarantor of *Cáin Adomnáin.*[40] He was perhaps the first of the signatories to die. According to the regnal lists for Dál Riata, Eochu was a son of Domangart (who died in 673, according to 'The Annals of Ulster'[41]), son of Domnall brecc.[42]

Seventy-seventh among the royals guaranteeing *Cáin Adomnáin* was *Fiannamuild ua Dúnchatai.*[43] In 'The Annals of Ulster' for 700 we have the following entry pertaining to Dál Riata.[44]

> 4a. Fiannamail nepos Dunchado, rex Dal Riati, et … iugulati sunt.

> 'Fiannamail grandson of Dúnchad, (the) king of Dál Riata, … [was] killed.'

In sum, we have two Dalriadic royals subscribing *Cáin Adomnáin.* On the theory advanced by Máirín Ní Dhonnchadha, who has made the fullest study of the list of guarantors, Eochu would have been the king, Fiannamail a prince and potential heir, a *rígdomnae.*[45] But it is not clear what determined the order of signatories – Fiannamail precedes Eochu. It is also far from clear that overkings and subkings could not sign together as guarantors.

If we are to suppose that both Eochu and Fiannamail were overkings of Dál Riata, we might date their reigns to 697 only, in the case of Eochu, and 698–700 in that of Fiannamail. Eochu's family, as a branch of Cenél nGabráin, is fairly well known. But that of Fiannamail has been marginal in discussion of Dalriadic history.

Nevertheless, we can construct from 'The Annals of Ulster' a six-generation genealogy of Fiannamail's family.[46] We cannot attach its ancestor, one Tuathalán, who would have died by about 640, to any of the principal *cenéla*, and this must serve as a warning to us of the limits of our knowledge. John Bannerman wished to delete from A. O. Anderson's partial reconstruction of this family tree three persons whom 'The Annals of Ulster' name in association with places in Britain – specifically, Kintyre and Skye –, then assigning and restricting the remainder to Dál Riata in Ireland.[47] But this was arbitrary mutilation. We have here a Dalriadic family associated now with Britain, now with Ireland, from 681 to 741, the fourth generation to the sixth. One of its members, Fiannamail ua Dúnchada, is described as '(the) king of Dál Riata'. This was a royal family or an important

---

[40] *Cáin Adomnáin*, §28 (85): ed. and trans. Ó Néill and Dumville, 28/9.

[41] AU 673.2.

[42] Anderson, *Kings*, 239 for comment, and, for texts, 253 and 256 (List E), 265 (List D), 270 (List F, no. 13), 282 (List I), 286 (List K), 290 (List N, as *Etal!*). Cf. n. 63, below. On the relationships of these lists and their consequent evidential status, see Dauvit Broun, *The Irish Identity of the Kingdom of the Scots in the Twelfth and Thirteenth Centuries* (Woodbridge, 1999), 133–74.

[43] *Cáin Adomnáin*, §28 (77): ed. and trans. Ó Néill and Dumville, 26/7.

[44] AU 700.4a.

[45] M. Ní Dhonnchadha, 'The Guarantor List of *Cáin Adomnáin*, 697', *Peritia* 1 (1982), 178–215, at 208–10, 212. On *rígdomnae*, see most recently [K.] M. McGowan, 'Royal Succession in Earlier Medieval Ireland: The Fiction of Tanistry', *Peritia* 17/18 (2003/4), 357–81. To be rejected is the theory that Eochaid belonged exclusively to Dál Riata in Ireland: William M. Hennessy and B. MacCarthy, ed. and trans., *Annala Uladh. Annals of Ulster*, 4 vols (Dublin, 1887–1901), I.148–9, nn. 3–4. There are of course other North British dimensions of *Cáin Adomnáin*, not least the presence of the Pictish overking and a number of bishops.

[46] See Figure 7. For a view, perhaps deriving from the name Ferith in the second recorded generation, that this was a Pictish lineage, see *The Chronicle of Ireland*, trans. Charles-Edwards, I.147, n. 9; I think that consideration of the whole genealogy renders this unlikely.

[47] Bannerman, *Studies*, 8 and n. 2; *Early Sources*, trans. Anderson, I.190, n. 4.

Figure 7: The descendants of Tuathalán, A.D. 653–741

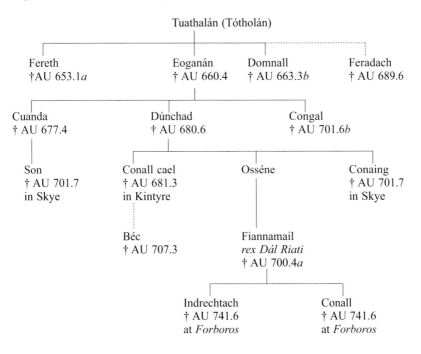

branch of a royal family. And we do not know what its familial and political affiliations were. We should note the geographical range.

Taking the geographical hint, we can enter the text *Cethri Prímchenéla Dáil Riata* and examine the pedigree chosen to represent Cenél nGabráin there.[48] There are possible difficulties (including chronology) with its middle reaches, particularly the relationships of the third generation.[49] It is a line which seems to have had associations with Skye.[50]

An awkward Irish-language entry in 'The Annals of Ulster' for 649 may offer some help: we read *Cocath huae nAedháin ocus Gartnaith maic Accidain.*[51] Gartnait's patronymic is, as far as I am aware, unknown in other texts. I am tempted by a notion that the *-cc-* is a classic transcription error of an Insular Half-uncial **a**,[52] which would allow us (dispensing with the first *A-*) to read *Aidán*, a respectable mid-seventh-century form. Gartnait would then still have

---

48 Dumville, '*Cethri Prímchenéla*', 175–6 (lines 14–21). See Figure 8 here for the genealogical detail.

49 *Ibid.*, 184. Matters have been complicated, perhaps unnecessarily, by trying to read it in association with the recorded line of overkings of Picts: Bannerman, *Studies*, 92–4.

50 Note the 'sons' (*filii*) and the *genus* (*cenél*) of Gartnait in AU 668.3*b* and 670.4.

51 'The war(fare) of the grandsons of Aedán and of Gartnait son of †Accidán†': AU 649.4.

52 For a geographically and culturally proximate example of this process, but with reference to Insular minuscule rather than Insular Half-uncial, see Alan Orr Anderson and M. O. Anderson, ed. and trans., *Adomnan's Life of Columba* (Edinburgh, 1961), 228, n. 6: in *Vita Sancti Columbae*, I.9, for a presumptively original *Miat(h)orum*, two derivative witnesses of a shared exemplar offer *mitithorum* and *micitorum*; the Andersons remarked, 'Here the source … had an open Irish [*sc.*

Figure 8: A lineage of Cenél nGabráin in Cethri Prímchenéla Dáil Riata

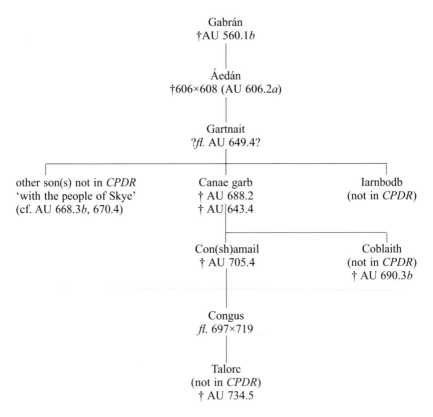

been alive and fighting with his nephews. (However, pause is given by an entry in 'The Annals of Ulster' for 686, possibly displaced by 44 years: *Talorgg mac Acithaen et Domnall brecc mac Echach mortui sunt.*)[53]

This family seems to have had much interaction with the Picts, which might not be surprising if it was based in Skye.[54] It might have come to be there as a result of an exogamous union of a Pictish royal woman with King Aedán mac Gabráin. It was evidently important in the eyes of the author of *Cethri Prímchenéla Dáil Riata*, who was probably an early-eighth-century adherent of Cenél Loairn.[55] It is another warning that a royal lineage not readily identifiable in our other sources had a notable role to play in the Dalriadic politics of the later seventh and early eighth centuries.

Insular] *a*, copied as *ci*'. (We might suspect that the proximity of *mac* bore on the matter too.) Cf. J. Carney, 'The so-called "Lament of Créidhe"', *Éigse* 13 (1969/70), 227–42, at 233–4.

53 'Talorgg, son of Acithaen, and Domnall brecc, son of Eochu, died': AU 686.2. On such displacements, see, for example, Anderson, *Kings*, 30–1. For a more radical example, see [Grabowski and] Dumville, *Chronicles*, 124–7.

54 Bannerman, *Studies*, 92–3, 114 (and map on p. 116), encouraged a generation to think of Skye as straightforwardly Pictish territory. See nn. 47–9, above.

55 Dumville, '*Cethri Prímchenéla*'.

This should perhaps lead us to consider more carefully the nature of the chronicle evidence for the history of Dál Riata. It is worth stressing the difficulties under which we labour, as well as the possible rewards for hard work. Unlike texts derivative of 'The Chronicle of Clonmacnoise' – that seminal text compiled with great labour, learning and ingenuity in 911×954[56] –, 'The Annals of Ulster', presumably in this respect representing 'The Chronicle of Ireland' as it stood in 911,[57] contain notices of many persons whose name and address comprise solely their patronymic.[58] It remains a challenge to scholarship to identify these people and to assign the entries in which they are recorded to the various sources of 'The Chronicle of Ireland'. This is a reminder that those early sources were local and that titles of office seem to have been used minimally.[59]

The point has particular significance in the present context. The general absence of royal titles in the early part of the chronicle record, and in relation to Dál Riata in particular, must inhibit use of that record to argue for the absence of local and regional kingdoms and royal lineages.

It is worth stressing that 'The Annals of Ulster', over the period hypothetically covered by 'The Chronicle of Iona', contains a mere six entries describing persons as '(the) king of Dál Riata' or of some part thereof (Table 1). Of the first four, extending from 616 to 700, none is entirely uncontroversial. The very first, Áedán mac Mongáin, seems indeed to have been rejected altogether by modern scholarship.[60] The fifth and sixth entries speak of parts of Dál Riata. In 721

---

56 Grabowski and Dumville, *Chronicles*, have provided the essential documentation. For another view of the same process, cf. Dumville, 'Ireland and North Britain', 208 (= *Celtic Essays*, II.67–8). This theory has recently been challenged by McCarthy, *The Irish Annals*, 92–111, who deserves (and will receive) a thorough reply; but, for the moment, I must merely say that, in particular, two fundamental differences of approach to the evidence lie at the source of these very different perceptions. It may also be worth remarking here that the various scholarly hypotheses about stages of development of Gaelic chronicling to which McCarthy has given names need some disentangling and refinement: in particular he seems (*ibid.*, 116) to have misdefined the deduced 'Chronicle of Clonmacnoise'.

57 On this reconstructed text, not entirely consistently defined by those who have adopted the relevant hypothesis, see Hughes, *Early Christian Ireland*, 101–15 (the originator); K. Harrison, 'Epacts in Irish Chronicles', *Studia Celtica* 12/13 (1977/8), 17–32; Grabowski and Dumville, *Chronicles*; Charles-Edwards, *Early Christian Ireland*, p. xix; *The Chronicle of Ireland*, trans. Charles-Edwards. Again – and as part and parcel of the same differences of perception, but with some more specific points also at issue – McCarthy, *The Irish Annals*, 92–111, has rejected Hughes's hypothesis. It should also be said that Mac Niocaill, *The Medieval Irish Annals*, 19–20, 21–4, implicitly rejected it too; but his views had been formed well before Hughes's work was published (for example, I heard them – as, I am sure, did Thomas Charles-Edwards – in a lecture given by Mac Niocaill at a Summer School of the School of Celtic Studies, Dublin Institute for Advanced Studies, in 1969), and he was understandably disinclined to withdraw them before scholars had had a chance to assess a printed version.

58 On this matter of identity and identification, see the fundamental paper by H. Meroney, 'Full Name and Address in Early Irish', in *Philologica. The Malone Anniversary Studies*, ed. T. A. Kirby and H. B. Woolf (Baltimore, MD, 1949), 124–31.

59 Compare the comments of Wendy Davies, *Patterns of Power in Early Wales* (Oxford, 1990), 10–15, on a perhaps similar phenomenon in Welsh chronicling of the approximate period 950–1020.

60 AU 616.1*b* (... *et mors Aedháin m. Mongáin regis Dál Riatai* ...). The editors provided no comment on him; but in *The Chronicle of Ireland*, trans. Charles-Edwards, I.129 (*s.a.* 616.2), and n. 2, he has been despatched to Dál nAraidi, on the basis of an interlined variant reading attributed to the main scribe of the principal witness. This entry was not excerpted in *Early Sources*, trans. Anderson. Cf. Bannerman, *Studies*, 4, n. 6.

Table 1: Kings of (part of) Dál Riata in 'The Annals of Ulster'

616.1*b* : et mors Áedháin m. Mongain *regis Dál Riatai* ...

629.1 : Bellum Feda Euin ... Conid cerr, *rex Dál Riati*, cecidit.

673.2 : Iugulatio Domangairt m. Domnaill bricc, *regis Dál Riati*.

700.4 : Fiannamail nepos Dúnchado, *rex Dál Riati*, et ... iugulati sunt.

721.1 : Dúnchad becc, *rex Cinn Tíre*, moritur.

733.2 : Muredach m. Ainfcellaich *regnum generis Loairnd assumit.*

\<then 45-year gap\>

778.7*e* : ... et Áedh finn m. Echdach, *rex Dál Riati* – omnes mortui sunt.

781.3*l* : ... 7 Fergus m. Echach, *rí Dál Riati* – omnes defuncti sunt.

Dúnchad becc, *rex Cinn Tíre*, '(the) king of Kintyre', died;[61] he was of course a member of Cenél nGabráin.[62] If we credit the regnal lists, Selbach mac Ferchair of Cenél Loairn was overking of Dál Riata at that time,[63] in spite of Dúnchad having won a sea battle against him two years earlier.[64] In 733, *Muredach mac Ainfcellaich regnum generis Loairnd assumit*,[65] whereas, if the regnal lists were to be followed, he would now have become overking of Dál Riata.[66]

Essentially the same situation obtains with reference to the *cenéla* of Dál Riata. There are six such notices in 'The Annals of Ulster' for the duration of 'The Chronicle of Iona': they range from 670 to 733 (Table 2). The last is shared with the previous list: it is the notice of accession to (the) kingship of Cenél Loairn.[67] However, the word *cenél* was not employed: instead we find Latin *genus*. This should occasion no surprise, for it is Adomnán's word too, in his 'Life of St Columba', and it has been learnedly and productively discussed by Thomas Charles-Edwards.[68] In general in the chronicle record the word is used for the military representatives of the population group. Cenél Comgaill is mentioned once, at 710, as is Cenél nGabráin, at 719. Cenél Loairn appears three times, at 678 (being killed in Tiree), 719 (being defeated by Cenél nGabráin in a sea-battle), and 733. Cenél Cathboth, a segment of Cenél Loairn, is reported being slaughtered in 701. And *genus Garnaith* from Skye, that lineage of Cenél

---

[61] AU 721.1 (*Dunchad becc, rex Cinn Tíre, moritur*). See *The Chronicle of Ireland*, trans. Charles-Edwards, I.194, n. 1, for interesting but troublesome commentary: 'The title used here is important as showing what kingdom was left to Cenél nGabráin when they did not hold the kingship of all Dál Riata. Their core territory may already have been entirely in Britain.' It is not clear to me that we can be certain that Kintyre was the entirety of the core territory of Cenél nGabráin; and the remark about core territory perhaps *already* being *entirely* in Britain seems to presuppose things which are very controversial.

[62] But it is interesting (cf. n. 61) that he is not described here as 'king of Cenél nGabráin'.

[63] Anderson, *Kings*, 254 (List E), 265 (as *Sealisthant*: List D), 271 (List F: no. 20), 282 (List I), 286 (List K), 290 (List N). Cf. n. 42, above. On interrelationships, see Broun, *The Irish Identity*, 133–74.

[64] AU 719.7.

[65] 'Muiredach mac Ainfchellaig assumed the kingship of Cenél Loairn': AU 733.2. For important commentary, see *The Chronicle of Ireland*, trans. Charles-Edwards, I.205(–6), n. 6.

[66] Charles-Edwards, *ibid.*

[67] Cf. Table 1 and n. 65, above.

[68] T. M. Charles-Edwards, *Early Irish and Welsh Kinship* (Oxford 1993), 138–40. On Adomnán, see nn. 19–20, above.

Table 2: Five Dalriadic cenéla *in 'The Annals of Ulster', A.D. 431–733*

670.4	:	Uenit *genus Garnaith* de Hibernia.
678.3	:	Interfectio *generis Loairnn* i Tírinn.
701.9*a*	:	Iugulatio *generis Cathboth* ...
710.4	:	Imbairecc apud *genus Comghaill* ubi duo filii Nectain m. Doirgarto iugulati sunt.
719.7	:	Bellum maritimum Ardae Nesbi inter Dúnchad mbecc cum *genere Gabráin* et Selbachum cum *genere Loairn*, et uersum est super Selbachum prid. non. Septimbris die .vi. feriẹ, in quo quidam comites conruerunt.
733.2	:	Muredach m. Ainfcellaich regnum *generis Loairnd* assumit.

nGabráin which we met earlier, is recorded at 670.[69] These are thin pickings in terms of absolute record, although the entries no doubt illustrate some of the varieties of conflict in which the forces of a Dalriadic *cenél* might find themselves. It is clear that the extent of such precise political record, which seems generally haphazard, provides no basis for a negative argument about the political importance or royal leadership of the *cenéla*.

In sum, arguments about the relationship of Dál Riata, in so far as they are built up from chronicle evidence, must proceed from analysis of the families attested and from their interactions. It would be unwise in the extreme to suppose that any of the untitled seculars mentioned in the early medieval chronicle record was other than of royal lineage. In those circumstances, Sharpe's vigorous attempt to rewrite the political and constitutional history of Dál Riata must fail. Such explicit evidence as we have indicates a complex and layered polity. When the whole body of prosopographical data has been analysed, that polity will almost certainly be revealed as yet more complex. We shall do well to remember Thomas Charles-Edwards's observation that Insular Celtic, and especially Gaelic, royal lines had an inclusive attitude towards the royal title.[70] There is nothing in the Dalriadic record, it seems to me, to suggest that the model of *tuatha, mórthuatha* and *cóiced* is inappropriate. I reiterate my proposal, made in 2000, that we consider early medieval Dál Riata to be a Gaelic province of its own, not a part (or an extension) of Ulster.[71]

I conclude by taking up briefly another comparative point made by Richard Sharpe in the same paper on 'The thriving of Dalriada'. He wrote that 'The dynastic success of the Dalriadic kings in the ninth century may have been a consequence of mutually complementary succession rules in Dalriada and Pictland'.[72] I do not suppose for a moment that we can any longer speak simply of a Dalriadic takeover of Pictland in the 840s or of someone called 'Cinaed mac Ailpín'. I

---

[69] Cf. pp. 46–8, above. Bannerman, *Studies*, 92–4, 114, seems to me to have misperceived the situation and to have failed to grasp that AU 668.3*b* and 670.4 must be taken together.

[70] T. Charles-Edwards, 'Early Medieval Kingships in the British Isles', in *The Origins of Anglo-Saxon Kingdoms*, ed. Steven Bassett (London, 1989), 28–39, 245–8 (and, in the present context, note his remark on p. 39: 'Dál Riata was as fragmented as any Irish dynasty').

[71] Dumville, 'Ireland and North Britain', 196 (= *Celtic Essays*, II.50). Cf. Anderson, *Kings*, 146–9.

[72] Sharpe, 'The Thriving', 49.

find no indication in contemporary record that Ciniod son of Alpin was anything other than a Pict.[73] If by 'mutually complementary succession rules' Sharpe was summarising the argument of Marjorie Anderson in 1982 that Pictish matriliny and Gaelic patriliny would in their interaction over time produce persons eligible for kingship in both societies,[74] then I find that unexceptionable. But if he was thinking of unitary Pictish as well as unitary Dalriadic kingship – two monarchies, in other words –, then the argument is doubly unacceptable.[75]

---

[73] Dumville, *The Churches of North Britain*, 35–6 (cf. n. 2, above). Cf. D. N. Dumville, 'Gaelic Macro-genealogy and the Development of an Origin-legend for the Kingdom of Alba', *The Journal of Celtic Studies* 8 (2008).

[74] M. O. Anderson, 'Dalriada and the Creation of the Kingdom of the Scots', in *Ireland in Early Mediaeval Europe. Studies in Memory of Kathleen Hughes*, ed. Dorothy Whitelock *et al.* (Cambridge, 1982), 106–32, especially 108–9, 110, 115–16, 121, 124, 131–2.

[75] Cf. David N. Dumville, *Pictish Matriliny Revisited* (Rosemarkie, 2011).

5

IRISH BOUNDARY *FERTA*, THEIR PHYSICAL
MANIFESTATION AND HISTORICAL CONTEXT[1]

Elizabeth O'Brien and Edel Bhreathnach

I

The physical manifestation of Irish boundary ferta
Elizabeth O'Brien

When, in 1976, Thomas Charles-Edwards published his paper 'Boundaries in Irish Law', based on evidence contained in early Irish law tracts,[2] I doubt he envisaged that around thirty years later we would be in a position to corroborate that legal evidence by physically identifying and dating boundary *ferta*. In that paper, and in a subsequent publication,[3] Professor Charles-Edwards describes how the boundary to a territory was marked by a *fert* (a grave mound) or *ferta* (a collection of grave mounds or a collection of burials in one mound). According to the legal procedure *tellach* (legal entry), which is described in the early law tract *Din Techtugad*,[4] a specific process was pursued in order to make a claim to land.

This tract may be summarised as follows: the claimant entered the land in the presence of a witness, taking two yoked horses across the boundary *fert*, the ancestral grave mound. He did not unyoke his horses and only allowed them to graze on half of the land. He then withdrew and waited for five days for a response from the occupant of the land regarding arbitration. If nothing happened, then ten days later the claimant again entered the land, this time with four horses and two witnesses. On this occasion he unyoked the horses and allowed them to graze freely. The occupant now had three days to respond; if he did not, then the claimant entered for the third and last time, ten days after the second entry. This time he brought eight horses and three witnesses with him. If the occupant did not respond immediately, the claimant then went to the house, where he looked

---

1   The genesis of this paper is the research currently being undertaken by the authors as part of the project 'Mapping Death: territories, boundaries and people in Ireland from 1st to 8th centuries AD' funded by the Heritage Council's INSTAR programme. The paper is divided in two parts: part I (Dr E. O'Brien) explores the archaeological evidence and physical manifestation of three *ferta* sites; part II (Dr E. Bhreathnach) details the historical and topographical context of the same sites.
2   T. M. Charles-Edwards, 'Boundaries in Irish Law', in *Medieval Settlement: Continuity and Change*, ed. P. Sawyer (London, 1976), 83–7.
3   T. M. Charles-Edwards, *Early Irish and Welsh Kinship* (Oxford, 1993), 259–61. See also *GEIL* 186–7.
4   *Din Techtugad* 'on legal entry': *CIH* I.205.22–213.37.

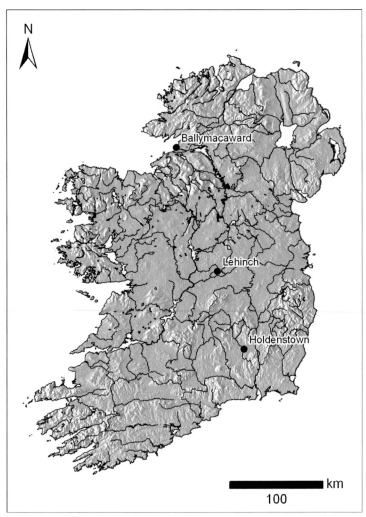

Map 1. Distribution of selected *ferta* sites. We are grateful to Anthony Corns of the Discovery Programme for his assistance in producing the map.

after his animals, kindled a fire and spent the night. The claimant had now established the right to occupy the land as the legal owner.

The ancestral boundary *fert* was an essential part of this process, the perception being that the ancestors who are buried in the *fert* acted as guardians of the disputed land or territory. The permission of these guardians was necessary in order to legitimise the claim and to gain possession legally of the said land. In his 1976 paper Thomas Charles-Edwards refers to ogam stones having a similar legal function, based on the assumption that stones with ogam inscriptions were used to mark graves.[5] However, from an archaeological point of view this cannot

---

5   Charles-Edwards, 'Boundaries', 84.

be proven, because to date no excavated example of a burial marked by an ogam inscribed stone has come to light.

What is a *fert*? A *fert* is an ancestral burial place which often, but not always, involves the reuse of an already existing prehistoric burial monument. The *fert* can be a mound, a ring barrow or a circular ditched enclosure. Bishop Tírecháin, writing his *Collectanea* in the seventh century, when referring to the burial of two daughters of a king, states that they were buried in a *fossam rotundam* after the manner of a *fert*: *et fecerunt fossam rotundam in similitudinem fertae, quia sic faciebant Scotici homines et gentiles, nobiscum autem relic uocatur.*[6] Tírecháin therefore regarded a *fert* as a non-Christian grave.

Recent archaeological investigation at several *ferta* sites has now provided evidence that from time to time during the later Iron Age, and in the period A.D. 400–700, burials were inserted into prehistoric ancestral *ferta*. Such burials were probably inserted either by the legitimate occupants of a territory in order to reinforce their valid title to their land when others sought to make a claim, or by intrusive groups, who by introducing their own 'guardians' into the *ferta* created a contrived form of continuity as a means of legitimising a claim to territory. In either case this is the deliberate incorporation of important individuals into the ancestral landscape somewhat akin to the later literary tradition of inserting new ancestral names into a family genealogy. A further item of interest is the fact that many of the burials inserted during the fifth and sixth centuries were female.[7]

Ferta, when acting as territorial boundary markers, are located in prominent positions, overlooking or close to natural boundaries, which may be represented by a river, the coastline, a bog or, as in at least one case in the Burren, Co. Clare, a ravine. Many *ferta* are reused prehistoric (or ancestral) burial mounds, others are natural hillocks which were probably perceived as ancient burial places and some are primary mounds constructed in the early medieval period as imitations of ancient burial places. For the purpose of this paper we have chosen to describe three examples from a growing list of *ferta* sites (Map 1): Ballymacaward, Bally-shannon, Co. Donegal; Eelweir Hill, Lehinch, Co. Offaly; and Holdenstown, Co. Kilkenny.

The site at Ballymacaward, Ballyshannon, Co. Donegal, which was discovered during land clearance operations in 1997 and was subsequently excavated in 1997/8,[8] is located on the northern shore at the mouth of the River Erne at Ballyshannon Harbour. The River Erne has long been regarded as an important territorial boundary. Excavation revealed a Bronze Age cairn which contained two short cists (both empty) of a type datable to the first half of the second millennium B.C. (*c.*2000–1500 B.C.). The cairn remained undisturbed for over a millennium, but undoubtedly continued to be recognised as an ancestral burial place because in the Iron Age two cremations, in small pits, were inserted into its surface. One of these cremations (an adult, probably female) has produced

6 'And they made a round ditch after the manner of a *ferta*, because this is what the heathen Irish used to do, but we call it *relic*': L. Bieler, ed. and trans., *The Patrician Texts in the Book of Armagh*, SLH 10 (Dublin, 1979), 144–5 §26.

7 E. O'Brien, 'Pagan or Christian? Burial in Ireland during the 5th to 8th Centuries AD', in *The Archaeology of the Early Medieval Celtic Churches*, ed. N. Edwards, Society for Medieval Archaeology Monograph 29, Society for Church Archaeology Monograph 1 (Leeds, 2009), 135–54, at 145.

8 E. O'Brien, 'Excavation of a Multi-Period Burial Site at Ballymacaward, Ballyshannon, Co. Donegal', *Journal of the Co. Donegal Historical Society* 51 (1999), 56–61.

a radiocarbon date placing it in the second or first century B.C.[9] After a further interval of more than a century an extension was added to one side of the cairn into which deposits of charcoal and cremated bone were spread. This material has been radiocarbon dated to between the first and third centuries A.D.[10]

After a further time-lapse, four extended female supine inhumations in slab-lined long cists, orientated west–east and without grave goods, were inserted into the surface of the mound. One of these, a very elderly female who suffered from post-menopausal osteoporosis of the spine, has been dated to the fifth to sixth century A.D.[11] This burial rite of extended inhumation was introduced into Ireland in the late fourth or early fifth centuries A.D., but we have no way of knowing whether these burials were of pagans or Christians.[12]

The final period of use of this monument involved the insertion of a minimum of nine extended inhumations, all female, laid west–east, in unprotected graves. Some of them, at least, were probably Christian, as one of these female burials was dated to the sixth/seventh century A.D.[13] After this, for reasons set out towards the end of this section of the paper, burial at this monument ceased. However, even after the cessation of burial in the seventh century this monument probably continued to act as a prominent feature in the landscape into the medieval period.

The second *fert* site (Map 1) is located at Eelweir Hill, Lehinch, near Clara, Co. Offaly.[14] This site was excavated by Raghnall Ó Floinn in 1978/9 after it had been disturbed by gravel digging. It is located on a natural sand and gravel hillock on the northern bank of the River Brosna. Excavation revealed that the hillock was originally utilised for the deposit of Bronze Age cremations, and also discovered was a small penannular enclosure of a type normally used for burial, but which, because it did not contain any burial, is undated. It could possibly belong in the Iron Age. In the early medieval period this small hillock was regarded as an ancestral burial *fert* because at that time six extended supine inhumations were inserted into the mound (three possible males, two possible females, one unidentified). One further grave contained the remains of several individuals. Two positively identified burials are of interest. Burial III, a female, dated to the fourth to sixth centuries A.D.[15] was accompanied by antler tine and some horse bones. This is of interest because several other burials (predominantly female) from this period in other parts of the country were also accompanied by antler and/or horse bones. Burial V, a male burial dated to the fifth to sixth centuries A.D.,[16] and somewhat later than the female burial, had been decapitated. The head was definitely missing when he was buried. In such cases, the head was either deliberately buried elsewhere, which can happen for various reasons,[17] or had been taken as a trophy at the time of decapitation. It is worth

---

[9]   UB-4196 uncalib 2091±56 BP, cal (at 2 sigma) 230 BC–AD 30.

[10] UB-4425, uncalib 1804±51 BP, cal (at 2 sigma) AD 80–350.

[11] UB-4171, uncalib 1592±20 BP, cal (at 2 sigma) AD 420–540.

[12] O'Brien, 'Pagan or Christian?', 143–5.

[13] UB-4172, uncalib 1448±21 BP, cal (at 2 sigma) AD 570–650.

[14] M. Cahill and M. Sikora, *Mortuary Practice in Early Ireland c 3500BC to 1800AD: A Century of Museum Investigation* (National Museum of Ireland, forthcoming). We thank Mary Cahill, Maeve Sikora and Raghnall Ó Floinn for permission to refer to this site prior to publication.

[15] GrA-24336, uncalib.1625±40 BP, calibrated (at 2 sigma) AD 339–541.

[16] GrA-24350, uncalib. 1550±40 BP, calibrated (at 2 sigma) AD 422–596.

[17] E. O'Brien, *Post-Roman Britain to Anglo-Saxon England: Burial Practices Reviewed*, BAR

noting that this particular ancestral burial mound was not used for the insertion of any further burials after the sixth century A.D, but, here again, it is likely to have continued to act as a territorial boundary marker.

The third *fert* site, at Holdenstown, Co. Kilkenny (Map 1), consists of two sites located in close proximity to each other. They were excavated in 2007 by Irish Archaeological Consultancy Ltd under the direction of Yvonne Whitty.[18] For the purposes of this paper I shall concentrate on Site 1, which is located on the crest of a hill overlooking the valley of the River Nore, with commanding views to the west, north and east. There is intervisibility between Holdenstown 1 and Holdenstown 2. Holdenstown 1 comprises a series of small penannular ring-ditches, none of which have so far been dated. It is postulated, however, that they represent monuments of Iron Age date. Ring-ditches 1 and 2 produced deposits of burnt bone, charcoal and animal bone: twelve antler picks were recovered from ring-ditch 1 and four from ring-ditch 2. Although the excavators suggest that these picks had a utilitarian use and had been used to dig the ditches, it is more likely that they had some symbolic meaning, as antler picks of this type have turned up elsewhere in burials datable to the fifth to sixth centuries A.D. Five extended inhumation burials, two female and three male, were later inserted into part of ring-ditch 2. That they are all contained within the confines of the ditch is an indication that this monument remained visible into the early medieval period. Three further burials, one male and two of unknown sex, were located at some distance from the first group, but are contained within a larger penannular enclosure which encompasses all of the ring-ditches and which on stratigraphical grounds post-dates these features. The male burial (B8) in this latter group has produced a date which places it in the fifth or sixth century A.D.[19] I would suggest, therefore, based on the disposition of the burials and the fact that there is no evidence for shroud wrapping,[20] that all of the burials at Holdenstown 1 pre-date the seventh century.

The cemetery at Holdenstown 2, with ninety-four burials aligned in about five rows, contained a mix of male and female adult burials, with the exception of one baby. One burial in particular, Burial 59, is of interest. This possible male burial, centrally located within the cemetery, was accompanied by an antler pick similar to those recovered in the ditches of Holdenstown 1 and has produced a radiocarbon date also placing it in the fifth or sixth century AD.[21] As in this writer's opinion these antler pick-like objects have some symbolic importance, Burial 59 offers a direct link to the boundary *fert* at Holdenstown 1.

To summarise, I would suggest that Holdenstown 1 is an ancestral boundary *fert* overlooking the valley of the River Nore; into it selected burials were inserted at specific times: (a) possible cremations in the Iron Age; (b) extended

British Series 289 (Oxford, 1999), 54; E. O'Brien, 'Literary Insights into the Basis of some Burial Practices in Ireland and Anglo-Saxon England in the Seventh and Eighth Centuries', in *Aedificia Nova: Studies in Honor of Rosemary Cramp*, ed. C. E. Karkov and H. Damico (Western Michigan University, 2008), 283–99, at 289–92.

18 Y. Whitty and M. Tobin, 'Rites in Transition: The Story told by Holdenstown 1 and 2', *Seanda: NRA Archaeology Magazine* 4 (National Roads Authority, Dublin, 2009), 19–21. We are indebted to Yvonne Whitty, Fintan Walsh and Maeve Tobin for providing details of these sites and for permission to refer to them prior to full publication of their excavation report.

19 Burial 8, UBA-13659, uncalib 1556±23, cal (at 2 sigma) AD 429–558.

20 For a description of shroud-wrapped burials, see O'Brien, 'Pagan or Christian?', 145–6.

21 Burial 59, UBA-13667, uncalib 1569±22, cal (at 2 sigma) AD 427–544.

inhumations in the fifth/sixth centuries and possibly up to the seventh century. Holdenstown 2 is a familial cemetery, founded in the fifth or sixth century A.D. (at the same time that 'ancestors' were being inserted into the nearby boundary *fert*), in which the remainder of the community or family was buried until the late seventh century,[22] after which time burial was in all probability moved to the nearby early church site.

Up until at least the eighth century, and possibly later, burial in Irish monastic cemeteries was reserved for kings, bishops, abbots, clerics and patrons.[23] The laity in general were buried in their familial ancestral cemeteries, which, by their very nature, could contain both pagans and Christians. This practice was tolerated by the Church because of the importance attached by a people to burial among their forebears. It is impossible to differentiate between Christian and pagan supine extended inhumations in Ireland. All graves looked alike, and generally did not contain grave goods. We may of course have some hints that a burial might be pagan when we find it accompanied by objects such as antler, animal bone (especially horse) and burnt grain (this latter practice was outlawed by the Church).[24] But here again we may be looking at Christians who were reluctant to abandon old traditions, and it is evident that some customs lasted well into the medieval period. However, from the eighth century onwards the Church started to legislate regarding acceptable burial practices for Christians. The *Collectio Canonum Hibernensis* ('Collection of Irish Canons'), written in the early eighth century,[25] includes canons urging the faithful to abandon burial among their ancestors in favour of burial in church cemeteries.[26] The Church continued to be conscious of the importance of ancestral graves and had to find ways to accommodate the change. Some canons, for instance, state that it was acceptable to be buried with the forefathers, but alternative canons make it clear that anyone who had become a member of the Christian community had to be buried in a Christian cemetery. Nevertheless, the canons make allowance for the upkeep of ancestral burial places. Finally, one of the dire warnings given by the canons regarding Christians who were still being buried in ancestral cemeteries is that they would be less likely to be visited by angels, because when angels visited such graves they returned sad.[27]

Even though burial in ancestral *ferta*, especially boundary *ferta*, ceased for the most part in the eighth century, these places were not forgotten. The fact that such monuments were included as essential territorial boundary features in the legal procedure of taking possession of land is witness to this. That they are

---

[22] Based on radiocarbon dates received for other burials in this cemetery.

[23] O'Brien, 'Pagan or Christian', 148–50.

[24] O'Brien, 'Post-Roman Britain', 55; O'Brien, 'Literary Insights', 294–5; E. O'Brien, 'Burnt Magic', in *A Grand Gallimaufry, Collected in Honour of Nick Maxwell*, ed. M. Davies, U. MacConville and G. Cooney (Dublin, 2010), 195–8.

[25] H. Wasserschleben, ed, *Die irische Kanonensammlung* (Leipzig, 1885; repr. Darmstadt, 1966). This collection of Canons was compiled by Rubin of Dair-Inis, a monastery near Youghal in the south of Ireland, who died in A.D. 725, and Cú-Chuimne of Iona, who died in A.D. 747; T. Charles-Edwards, 'The Penitential of Theodore and the *Iudicia Theodori*', in *Archbishop Theodore*, ed. M. Lapidge, Cambridge Studies in Anglo-Saxon England 11 (Cambridge, 1995), 141–74, at 142, n. 5.

[26] Wasserschleben, *Kanonensammlung*, 56 XVIII§3(a); 57 XVIII§5; 208 L§1 (a–c); 208–9 L§3 (a, c).

[27] For details and translation of relevant canons, see O'Brien, 'Post-Roman Britain', 53–4, 57–8; O'Brien, 'Literary Insights', 284–2, 289–90.

also remembered as important features in the landscape is evident even from modern place-name evidence.[28] There are at least fifteen recorded instances of place-names throughout the country with the element *fert* or *fertae*, including Ardfert and Clonfert, both of which eventually became the location of major ecclesiastical foundations.

II

On the boundary: history, landscape and myth of three Irish ferta
Edel Bhreathnach

Early medieval Irish sources provide a perspective on different landscapes throughout Ireland as mythical, pseudo-historical landscapes and historical, living landscapes. The mythical and pseudo-historical landscape is primarily reflected in place-names and topographic sources such as the Middle Irish corpus *Dind-shenchas Érenn*[29] and the many onomastic tales that occur in early Irish sagas and saints' Lives. How to disentangle literary composition and etymology from genuine mythical associations with places and monuments – and the consequent possibility that these associations reflect various belief systems and customs – has bedevilled scholarship of this subject for a long time.[30] One successful approach to this discussion is to examine the archaeological and topographical evidence of different landscapes in detail and, by doing so, identify comparable patterns or even the unique features of a particular landscape. Dr Kay Muhr has been to the forefront of such an approach, especially in her study of place-names in *Táin Bó Cúailnge* and other tales of the Ulster Cycle.[31] The historical, living landscape is somewhat easier to depict, as it can be related to more tangible evidence, such as archaeological monuments and features in a landscape superimposed on historical data concerning secular and ecclesiastical settlements, natural and political boundaries, important man-made and natural features (rivers, roads, fords) and local and intrusive dynasties and peoples. This study of the cemeteries at Ballymacaward, Lehinch, and Holdenstown is interdisciplinary insofar as it analyses the landscapes in which they are located from both mythical and historical perspectives. The intention is to decipher the landscape of those buried in the three cemeteries in the hope that we can gain an understanding of the circumstances in which they lived and what their society's beliefs might have been, as reflected in their graves.

Ballymacaward, Co. Donegal

The prominent location of the multi-period site at Ballymacaward on the northern shore of Ballyshannon Bay (the River Erne estuary) in itself suggests that the

---

28 Place-names database of Ireland http://www.logainm.ie.
29 E. Gwynn, *The Metrical Dindshenchas*, 5 vols (Dublin, 1903–35; repr. Dublin, 1991).
30 For relatively recent discussion of aspects of this topic, see J. Carey, 'Time, Memory and the Boyne Necropolis', *Proceedings of the Harvard Colloquium* 10 (1990), 24–36; R. Baumgarten, 'Etymological Aetiology in Irish Tradition', *Ériu* 41 (1990), 115–22.
31 K. Muhr, 'The Location of the Ulster Cycle: Part 1: Tóchustal Ulad', in *Ulidia: Proceedings of the First International Conference on the Ulster Cycle of Tales*, ed. J. P. Mallory and R. Ó hUiginn (Belfast, 1995), 149–58.

site was strategically placed at the entrance to the bay which was re-visited for burial during the Bronze Age, the Iron Age and the early medieval period. That this land was an important border territory is evident from the Lives of Patrick, and especially the *Vita Tripartita*, where the Uí Néill dynasties of Cenél Cairpre (defending their territory north of the Erne) and Cenél Conaill, from further north of Ballyshannon, contended for it probably in the late sixth and seventh centuries.[32] Cenél Conaill ultimately won; Cenél Cairpre lost almost all their lands and what they did not lose was handed over by their enemies to Colum Cille,[33] thus in time-honoured fashion attempting to neutralise the area (as was the case with Fir Chell in the midlands). In *Vita Tripartita*'s description of this contention, Cairpre son of Niall Noígiallach tried to persuade his follower Cúangus to expel Patrick by promising him all the land he could see north of Sliab Cise. This place is probably Sheegy's Hill, just west of the Ballymacaward site, the location of a standing stone. Cúangus's view was reduced by a dark cloud that closed around him and this restricted his claim to extensive lands.[34] Approximately 200m from the cemetery mound is a small freshwater lake, *Loch na mBan Síofróg* (Lough Namansheefroge), 'The lake of the otherworldly women'. This place-name suggests the remnants of a mythological landscape – apparent elsewhere in place-names such as Loch na mBan Fionn, Co. Fermanagh, and Sliabh na mBan Fionn, Co. Tipperary, otherwise *Síd ar Femen*, residence of the goddess of war, Bodb. Finally, while the Patrician Lives and other sources portray this territory as dominated by contending Uí Néill dynasties, Tírechán, as is so often the case, retains the name of an earlier population group, the *gens Lathron*, who left their name on Mag Latrain, subsequently Tír Hugh, the barony in which Ballymacaward is located.[35] Although it is difficult to be absolutely certain, the *gens Lathron* may have been a branch of the Latharna who inhabited areas along the north-eastern coast, their name surviving in Larne, Co. Antrim. They were Cruithni, who lost control to the dynasties who later defined themselves as Uí Néill. A possible theory that might be suggested very tentatively is that the sequence of early medieval burials at Ballymacaward could have involved the insertion of *gens Lathron* women (in the fifth- or sixth-century slab-lined cist graves) and Cenél Coirpre women (in the seventh-century unprotected graves). As most of the burials were females, the Cruithni/Ulaid connection comes even more sharply into focus when we consider that the mothers of the reputed sons of Niall Noígiallach, Coirpre, Conall and Eógan were from the north-eastern dynasty of Dál Fiatach.[36] Cultural contacts between the north-east and north-west were very close and continued to be so throughout the medieval period, and these ties must be reflected to some extent in the archaeological record.

32 B. Lacey, *Cenél Conaill and the Donegal Kingdoms AD 500–800* (Dublin, 2006), 61–5.

33 For a translation of the passage from *Vita Tripartita*, see Lacey, *Cenél Conaill and Donegal Kingdoms*, 64. For the original, K. Mulchrone, ed., *Bethu Phátraic: The Tripartite Life of Patrick* (Dublin and London, 1939), 90–1.

34 Mulchrone, *Bethu Phátraic*, 90: *ro iad néll dorcha im Chuangus conach accai acht co muir síar 7 cusin n-Uinsin tair*; Lacey, *Cenél Conaill and Donegal Kingdoms*, 64: 'a dark cloud closed in around Cuangus so that he only saw as far as the sea westward and as far as the Uinsenn [Abbey/ Twomile River] eastward'.

35 Bieler, *Patrician Texts*, 160–1 §47; Lacey, *Cenél Conaill and Donegal Kingdoms*, 156–7.

36 A. Connon, 'A Prosopography of the Early Queens of Tara', in *The Kingship & Landscape of Tara*, ed. E. Bhreathnach (Dublin, 2005), 254–7.

Lehinch, Co. Offaly

As has been described above, the site at Lehinch is on a natural sand and gravel hillock (Eelweir Hill) overlooking the River Brosna to the south. A clue as to the mythical landscape of this area is found in the place-name Tara, given to a slight rise approximately 3km to the south of Lehinch. According to the Archaeological Inventory of County Offaly there is a low, flat-topped mound with slight evidence of an enclosing fosse on top of the rise. It is classified as a tumulus.[37] In their consideration of the place-name *Temair* (anglicised 'Tara'), Dónall Mac Giolla Easpaig and Nollaig Ó Muraíle identified this site as *Temair Maige Consaitín*, 'Tara of the plain of Consaitín'.[38] Just as the site at Lehinch is located above the River Brosna, so also is *Temair Maige Consaitín*, situated east of a very pronounced bend in the same river. In the genealogies of the Cenél Fiachach, the descendants of Fiachu son of Niall Noígiallach, it is related that Fiachu had three daughters: Finnabar (another female name with mythical connections), from whom was named Finnabar in Máenmag (Finnure, east Galway); Aífe of Uisnech, from whom *Fert Aífe* in Ulaid was named; and Temair Thuathach, the wife of the king of Leinster, who died in Mag Consantín and from whom *Temair Maige Consaitín* was named.[39] Although this text might be dismissed as a medieval genealogical fabrication, it is nonetheless notable that the three women have mythological names and, at least in the case of Temair, are linked to an existing monument. The story of St Mo-Chuta's expulsion from Rahen notes that Mag Co(n)saitín, 'Constantine's plain', is on the River Brosna at *Áth Maigne* (Lismoyny, Co. Westmeath), not far from *Temair Maige Consaitín*.[40] Before dealing with the curious occurrence of the personal name Constantine in the Irish midlands it is important to provide a wider mythical/religious context for this landscape: that of the greater Uisnech region, centred on the prehistoric complex of the Hill of Uisnech, Co. Westmeath. Historically, this region was in the possession of Cenél Fiachach, whose main ceremonial centre was at Uisnech.[41] It is likely that Cenél Fiachach had supplanted Leinster dynasties in this region in the early fifth century. The Patrician literature of the seventh century and later suggests that Uisnech was subjected to the same fate as Tara, Co. Meath, when the Church grappled with the task of Christianising the landscape. Tara and Uisnech were effectively reduced in status as major ceremonial complexes from that period onwards. In Tírechán's *Collectanea*, Fiachu mac Néill and his progeny were cursed by Patrick.[42] In the later Patrician Life, the *Vita Tripartita*, Patrick and bishop Sechnall (Secundinus), who was associated with

37 C. O'Brien and P. D. Sweetman, *Archaeological Inventory of County Offaly* (Dublin, 1997), 12 (no. 68).

38 D. Mac Giolla Easpaig, 'Significance and Etymology of the Placename *Temair*', in Bhreathnach, *The Kingship and Landscape of Tara*, 423–48, at 436–7; N. Ó Muraíle, 'Temair/Tara and Other Places of the Name', in *Kingship and Landscape of Tara*, 449–77, at 461, 471.

39 Dublin, Trinity College MS 1298 (H.2.7), fo.172a13; Ó Muraíle, 'Temair/Tara and Other Places of the Names', 436.

40 C. Plummer, ed., *Bethada Náem nÉrenn*, 2 vols (Oxford, 1922), I.300, I.291.

41 P. Walsh, 'Meath in the Book of Rights', in *Féil-Sgríbhinn Eóin Mhic Néill: Essays and Studies presented to Professor Eoin MacNeill*, ed. J. Ryan (Dublin, 1940; repr. 1995), 508–21, at 510–11 (reprinted in *Irish Leaders and Learning through the Ages*, ed. N. Ó Muraíle (Dublin, 2003), 72–85, at 75); T. M. Charles-Edwards, *Early Christian Ireland* (Cambridge, 2000), 28–9.

42 Bieler, *Patrician Texts*, 136–7 §16 (4).

Dunshaughlin, Co. Meath, travelled from Tara to Uisnech, where they cursed the stones of Uisnech.[43]

One could imagine that people living and dying in the vicinity of Lehinch in the *fifth century* lived under the domination of Cenél Fiachach, although by the sixth century they were losing power to the rising midlands dynasty of Clann Cholmáin.[44] Religious beliefs and ceremonies were performed at places such as *Temair Maige Consaitín* and, more importantly, at Uisnech. Living and dying in the *sixth century* at Lehinch was different: this was the period of the rise of the great midland and northern dynasties of Clann Cholmáin, Cenél Conaill and Cenél nÉogain who pushed the Cenél Fiachach out of contention for dominance of the midlands. Part of their strategy to hold this territory – which was also a border with the provinces of Munster and Connacht – was to hand over much land to the Church, to the extent that this territory became known as Fir Chell, 'the men of churches', or Tír Cell, 'the land of churches'. Durrow, not very far east of Lehinch, was founded by St Columba in the 580s/590s, probably with the support of his distant cousin, the northern Uí Néill king of Tara, Áed mac Ainmirech (d. 598).[45] Raithen (Rahan, Co. Offaly) was reputedly founded by Mo-Chuta (d. 637), a Munsterman, in the late sixth or early seventh century, but there are hints elsewhere of an earlier foundation. Tírechán tells how Patrick sent Camulacus of the *Commienses* from the Hill of Granard to Raithen.[46] This early saint must have been important as a Latin hymn in his honour survives in the late-seventh-century Antiphonary of Bangor.[47] And, as for Co(n)saitín or Constantine, who may also have preceded Mo-Chuta, he appears in *Féilire Óenguso* as *rí Raithen* 'king of Rahan'.[48] He is mentioned in the 'Expulsion of Mo-Chuta from Raithen', where he came to Mo-Chuta's monastery as a holy pilgrim from Alba.[49] In this text he is confused with a king of Scotland of that name and, like his namesakes in Scotland, Cornwall and Brittany, may reflect the local cult of an early royal saint who adopted the name of Emperor Constantine in the fifth century.[50] Cus(t)antin was a personal name used by kings of Alba in the early medieval period but it did not become popular in Ireland.

Such was the domination of the Church in Fir Chell from the late sixth century onwards that one branch of Cenél Fiachach was known as *Síl Conaing ar scaíl*, 'the scattered Síl Conaing': they were scattered on the lands of four saints, namely Colmán Elo of Lynally, the Ua Suanaig of Raithen, Colum Cille of Durrow, Áed

---

[43] Mulchrone, *Bethu Phátraic*, 50–1.

[44] Charles-Edwards, *Early Christian Ireland*, 554–5.

[45] M. Herbert, *Iona, Kells, and Derry: The History and Hagiography of the Monastic Familia of Columba* (Oxford, 1988), 32–3.

[46] Bieler, *Patrician Texts*, 136–7 §16 (7).

[47] J. F. Kenney, *The Sources for the Early History of Ireland: Ecclesiastical* (New York, 1929; repr. Dublin, 1979), 260–1; C. Doherty, 'The Cult of St Patrick and the Politics of Armagh in the Seventh Century', in *Ireland and Northern France AD 600–850*, ed. J.-M. Picard (Dublin, 1991), 53–94, at 60.

[48] W. Stokes, *Félire Óengusso Céli Dé* (London, 1905; repr. 1984), 81 (March 11).

[49] Plummer, *Bethada Náem nÉrenn*, I.300: *conid he ro claidh ⁊ ro thorainn an cill, .i. Rathen, ⁊ ro lesaigh cepaid Consantin fri Rathen andes, ⁊ Magh Constantin for bru Brosnaighe Atha Maighne*; *ibid.*, II.291: 'it is he who marked out the church of Rahen, and dug it, and cultivated "Constantine's Plot" to the south of Rahen, and Magh Constantin (Constantine's Plain) on the bank of the Brosny at Ath Maighne.'

[50] T. O. Clancy, 'Constantine, St (of Govan)', in *Celtic Culture: A Historical Encyclopedia*, ed. J. T. Koch (Santa Barbara, CA, 2006), 479–80.

mac Bric of Killare (near Uisnech and Rahugh, Co. Westmeath) and Ciarán either of Clonmacnoise or Saigir (Seirkieran, Co. Offaly).[51] These people were regarded as subject to their respective saints and their monasteries. The River Brosna acted as a boundary between their different lands, with, for example, the Uí Conaing and Uí Thresacháin living on the northern banks of the river.

If one were to speculate over the identity of the kin-group buried in Lehinch, they either belonged to Síl Conaing, a branch of Cenél Fiachach, or to a group of Leinstermen who were supplanted by the same Síl Conaing in the early fifth century. As for their beliefs: buried as they were in an early mound overlooking the Brosna, they were more likely to have associated themselves with the rituals of *Temair Maige Consaitín* and Uisnech than with those of Raithen or Durrow, but in the fifth and sixth centuries they could not have been ignorant of the increasing influence of Christians such as Camulacus and Constantine on the elite in their midland society.

Holdenstown 1 & 2, Co. Kilkenny

The prehistoric and historic environment of Holdenstown and its surrounding landscape is well researched and has yielded much information to date from both archaeological and historical sources.[52] The parish and barony in which Holdens-town is located (Dunbell and Gowran respectively) occur in the early sources and these references are corroborated by archaeological evidence. Dunbell derives from *Dún Bile*, 'the fort of the ancient tree'. *Bile* 'a tree, tree-trunk' is the term often used for a sacred tree associated with inauguration sites such as Bile Tened and Bile Tortan in Co. Meath. *Bile* is also used in a compound with the settle-ment term *ráith* 'fort', as in Ráith Bil(ig) (Rathvilly, Co. Carlow) and Bile Ráth (near Rathconrath, Co. Meath). The *bile* of Dunbell may have been part of the complex of ringforts and enclosures in Dunbell Big, a site immediately to the west of Holdenstown. Proof of early literacy in this region is evident from the concentration of ogam stones (ten in total) that has been discovered in the barony of Gowran.[53] If the Holdenstown cemeteries date to a period somewhere between A.D. 400 and 700 then these stones and their inscriptions must relate somehow to the identity of some of the people buried at Holdenstown. Two ogam stones were found in one of the ringforts/enclosures at Dunbell Big during nineteenth-century investigations. One stone reads NAVALLO AVVI GENITACC.[54] The patronymic GENITACC might be expected to occur in this area as the Uí Gentig are mentioned among the early genealogies of the Osraige. A version of the name survives in the later cantred of Ogenty, further south around Thomastown, Co. Kilkenny.[55] The genealogies suggest that the Uí Gentig may have not have been of the Osraige, the dominant dynasty of the region, but belonged to the Airgialla, a people from the north (Síl Daimíni) associated with the royal and ecclesiastical

---

51 TCD MS 1298 (H.2.7), fo. 176.6–26; Walsh, in *Irish Leaders and Learning*, 255.

52 R. Ó Floinn, 'Freestone Hill, Co. Kilkenny: A Reassessment', in *Seanchas: Studies in Early and Medieval Irish Archaeology, History and Literature in Honour of Francis J. Byrne*, ed. A. P. Smyth (Dublin, 2000), 12–29. Note in particular p. 13, fig. 1.

53 *CIIC*, I.33–40; C. Manning and F. Moore, 'A Second Ogham Stone at Clara', *Peritia* 11 (1997), 370–2; Ó Floinn, 'Freestone Hill', 27–9.

54 *CIIC*, I, no. 30.

55 C. A. Empey, 'The Cantreds of the Medieval County of Kilkenny', *JRSAI* 101 (1971), 128–34, at 131.

complex of Clogher, Co. Down (known as Clochar meic nDaimíne).[56] Indeed, the death of Daimíne Dam Airgit at the battle of Gabair Liphi in Leinster is recorded in AU 565 and although such an early entry in the annals should be regarded with caution there may be some indication here of an intrusive people from the north settling in the kingdom of Osraige. A saint Tecán of Tír Ua nGentich is listed in the early saints' pedigrees as also belonging to Síl Daimíni.[57] The second ogam stone from Dunbell Big, which reads BRAN[I]TTAS M[A]QI DUCR[I]DDA, has yet to yield any clue as to who is commemorated on the inscription. It may also be significant that the Dunbell Big ringfort from which the ogam stones came yielded other finds dating from the fifth and sixth centuries (and later), including the pin of a zoomorphic penannular brooch.[58] It might be surmised, therefore, that the complex of ringforts at Dunbell and the nearby cemeteries of Holdenstown reflect a chronological horizon that stretches from the fifth century into the medieval period,[59] the later phase relating to the nearby medieval church and graveyard.

Conclusion

This study of three Irish *ferta* sites brings to light the valuable evidence of burials for our understanding of late prehistoric and early medieval Irish society, a period that has been regarded as highly problematic by archaeologists and historians alike. We can begin genuinely to evaluate the process of Irish society converting from one belief system to another – Christianity – and what that entailed with regard to the survival of old traditions. This in turn opens up new avenues in our reading of early Irish literature and its probable reflection of the practices of a non-Christian society. The application of legal procedures such as *tellach* 'legal entry' can actually be related to archaeological monuments. Similarly, the detailed analysis of cemeteries offers the scope to relate kin groups, as described in the laws and elsewhere, to family groups as they are laid out in graves. The influence of the Church and changes in dynastic power, known from historical sources, are now manifesting themselves, along with so much else, in the burial practices of late Iron Age and early medieval Ireland.

---

[56] M. A. O'Brien, ed., *Corpus Genealogiarum Hiberniae Vol. 1* (Dublin, 1976), 129a9 and 130a30.

[57] P. Ó Riain, ed., *Corpus Genealogiarum Sanctorum Hiberniae* (Dublin, 1985), 12.

[58] Ó Floinn, 'Freestone Hill', 24.

[59] Excavations which were undertaken at Dunbell in 1972 (Dunbell 1972:0020; S561528) and in 1990 (Dunbell Ringfort No 5, Dunbel Big 1990:07; S557521) showed uncovered prehistoric burials and early medieval habitation possibly dating up to the tenth century A.D. See www.excavations.ie.

6

ASSER'S *PAROCHIA* OF EXETER

O. J. Padel

... sequentis temporis successu ex improviso dedit mihi Exanceastre, cum omni parochia, quae ad se pertinebat, in Saxonia et in Cornubia ...[1]

This passage in Asser's Life of King Alfred has given rise to discussion owing to the uncertainty of the meaning of the word *parochia*, and particularly with regard to its potential implications for the ecclesiastical assimilation of Cornwall into Wessex, since Cornwall's integration into Wessex advanced considerably during King Alfred's reign.[2] The translation by Keynes and Lapidge, using the non-committal word 'jurisdiction', wisely avoids precision about its implications. My purpose here is to examine some aspects of this clause in closer detail than has been possible in the more general surveys in which it has usually been discussed.[3]

One preliminary aspect to be clarified is the exact meaning of *Saxonia* and *Cornubia*. It has generally been assumed without comment that, in this context, these words mean the later Devon and Cornwall respectively. The interpretation is surely right, but it bears closer examination. At this period such words would normally be understood with an ethnic or linguistic meaning, rather than a political one. In fact the River Tamar was probably, in the late ninth century, the boundary forming not only the administrative division between Devon and Cornwall but also, for much of its course, the linguistic division between speakers of West Saxon and Cornish. Cornwall had emerged into history, by name, in about 700, presumably as a consequence of the loss of much of Devon to the Anglo-Saxons around that date; *Defnas* had been used in the Chronicle under the year 823 specifically to mean '[Saxon] men of Devon', in contrast with the *Walas* of

---

[1] '... with the passage of time he [King Alfred] unexpectedly granted me Exeter with all the jurisdiction pertaining to it in Saxon territory and in Cornwall ...': W. H. Stevenson, ed., *Asser's Life of King Alfred* (Oxford, 1904), 68 (ch. 81); translated in Simon Keynes and Michael Lapidge, *Alfred the Great: Asser's Life of King Alfred and Other Contemporary Sources* (Harmondsworth, 1983), 97.

[2] For example, H. P. R. Finberg, 'Sherborne, Glastonbury, and the Expansion of Wessex', in his *Lucerna: Studies of Some Problems in the Early History of England* (London, 1964), 95–115, at 109–10; Keynes and Lapidge, *Alfred the Great*, 264–5 (n. 193); John Blair, *The Church in Anglo-Saxon Society* (Oxford, 2005), 324–5; most recently Nicholas Orme, *Exeter Cathedral: The First Thousand Years, 400–1550* (Exeter, 2009), 5–6.

[3] I am very grateful to John Blair and Simon Keynes for their helpful comments upon my remarks, and to Thomas himself for discussing the Irish aspect of *parochia*; but none of them is responsible for any infelicities in what follows.

Cornwall;[4] and the anglicisation of Devon by the mid-ninth century is confirmed by the bounds of the South Hams charter (dated 846), where even the smallest details of the landscape all have Old English names, with one possible exception.[5] There is no reason to think that the name which became Middle Cornish *Kernow* ever designated people indigenous to any part of what is now Devon. The jurisdiction to which Asser referred therefore lay partly within Devon (though potentially it could have included lands further north or east as well, in later Somerset or Dorset), and partly in Cornwall, west of the Tamar. Cornwall had been under the rule of Wessex since the reign of King Ecgbert (802–39), but that had been as a colonial territory or client-state, not yet assimilated administratively into Wessex; full administrative assimilation was to follow in the reign of Alfred's grandson, Athelstan (924–39). By the 890s there had probably been some Saxon settlement west of the Tamar, particularly in the far north where Alfred held the estate of Stratton as a personal possession;[6] so Asser's *Saxonia* may have included some areas west of the Tamar; but his *Cornubia* cannot have meant anything to the east of it. In fact Asser's contrasting use of *Saxonia* and *Cornubia* provides further indication that by the late ninth century Cornwall, the land west of the River Tamar, was the only remaining area in the south-west which was not *Saxonia* – that is, which had not been saxonised, linguistically and probably ethnically.

A second preliminary aspect to be considered is King Alfred's role in making the gift. Asser mentioned it in the context of other gifts by the king to himself, both of other churches and of movable goods:

> … tradidit mihi duas epistolas, in quibus erat multiplex supputatio omnium rerum, quae erant in duobus monasteriis, quae Saxonice cognominantur Cungresbyri et Banuwille, et mihi eodem die tradidit illa duo monasteria cum omnibus, quae in eis erant, et sericum pallium valde pretiosum et onus viri fortis de incenso … sequentis temporis successu ex improviso dedit mihi Exanceastre, cum omni parochia, quae ad se pertinebat, in Saxonia et Cornubia, exceptis cotidianis donis innumerabilibus in omni genere terrestris divitiae, quae hoc in loco percensere longum est …[7]

John Blair has alluded to the uncertainty concerning whether Alfred was strictly in a position to make these gifts of churches, inferring that he may have been

---

4 Janet M. Bately, ed., *The Anglo-Saxon Chronicle: A Collaborative Edition*, vol. 3, *MS. A* (Cambridge, 1986), 41: *Her wæs Wala gefeoht and Defna æt Gafulforda* (Galford, in west Devon); also in other manuscripts: Dorothy Whitelock *et al.*, *The Anglo-Saxon Chronicle: a Revised Translation* (London, 1961), 40.

5 S 298; Della Hooke, *Pre-Conquest Charter-Bounds of Devon and Cornwall* (Woodbridge, 1994), 105–12; its date, 26 December '847', means 846 in modern terms.

6 Keynes and Lapidge, *Alfred the Great*, 175 and 317 (n. 18); O. J. Padel, 'Place-Names and the Saxon Conquest of Devon and Cornwall', in *Britons in Anglo-Saxon England*, ed. Nick Higham (Woodbridge, 2007), 215–30, at 223–4.

7 '… he presented me with two documents in which there was a lengthy list of everything in the two monasteries named Congresbury and Banwell in English. On that same day he granted me those two monasteries to me, with all the things which were in them, as well as an extremely valuable silk cloak and a quantity of incense weighing as much as a stout man. … with the passage of time he unexpectedly granted me Exeter with all the jurisdiction pertaining to it in Saxon territory and in Cornwall, not to mention the countless daily gifts of worldly riches of every sort which it would be tedious to recount at this point …': Asser, *Vita Ælfredi regis*, ch. 81 (ed. Stevenson, 67–8; trans. Keynes and Lapidge, 97).

acting in a somewhat heavy-handed manner.[8] It would be unwise to assume from this gift that Exeter was a royal house. The context and wording are also notable for the absence of any mention of an episcopal appointment as such: within the context Exeter's *parochia* appears as something which could be 'given' (*dedit mihi*), similarly to the other prizes, rather than an appointment to a position.

In considering the meaning of *parochia* itself, two aspects need to be distinguished. One is the precise nature of the jurisdiction which Alfred's gift gave to Asser; the other is the area over which the jurisdiction applied. The key question relating to the first aspect is whether *parochia* here implies any episcopal authority. In earlier, continental, use the word meant both 'diocese' and 'parish', since those two concepts were effectively the same thing to begin with; 'parish' is etymologically derived from *parochia*. In writings from Anglo-Saxon England the word is surprisingly rare, in any sense; and Blair has pointed out that the word is nowhere attested signifying the ecclesiastical district belonging to a minster church, as we might have expected.[9] There are some Anglo-Saxon examples, mainly eighth-century, of its use in the sense 'diocese, bishopric';[10] but Asser's use of this rare word might itself suggest that he was writing within a different Latin tradition, in which the word was used more frequently and with broader meaning. Asser's education at St Davids is likely to have included some Irish influence, from teachers educated there or works written there.[11] Little is known, for lack of examples, about the range of meaning of the word in Asser's native Wales; but the usage there could well have been akin to Irish usage as much as to Anglo-Saxon.

In British usage the standard dictionary distinguishes seven meanings of the word in the medieval period, as follows:[12] (1) 'district or territory under ecclesiastical control'; (2) 'ecclesiastical province, archbishopric'; (3) 'diocese, bishopric'; (4) 'parish'; (5) 'inhabitants of a parish, parishioners'; (6) 'parish church'; (7) 'district, territory'. Of particular interest here is the distinction between the first meaning, relating to general ecclesiastical control (illustrated from the tenth-century writings of Abbo of Fleury, and earlier in the broader phrase *parochia catholica*, used by Aldhelm to denote the whole territory of the Christian Church), and the specific sense of episcopal jurisdiction (3); also the even broader (non-ecclesiastical), sense 'district, territory' (7), illustrated from the tenth-century Chronicle of Æthelweard. The modern sense 'parish' is common only from the eleventh century onwards. In Irish writings, by contrast, the word was widely used, and its connotations have dominated twentieth-century historical discussion of the early Church.[13] For present purposes the important conclusion that

---

8 Blair, *Church in Anglo-Saxon Society*, 324–5.
9 *Ibid.*, 427–8.
10 R. E. Latham *et al.*, ed., *Dictionary of Medieval Latin Compiled from British Sources* (Oxford, 1975–), II.2120 (s.v. *paroecia*, 3); Blair, *Church in Anglo-Saxon Society*, 36–8 and 212, n. 127.
11 J. E. Lloyd, *A History of Wales, from the Earliest Times to the Edwardian Conquest*, 3rd edn (London, 1939), I.226–7.
12 *Dictionary of Medieval Latin*, s.v.; some meanings are of course limited in the date-range of their attestations.
13 J. F. Kenney, *The Sources for the Early History of Ireland: Ecclesiastical* (New York, 1929), 291–2; Kathleen Hughes, *The Church in Early Irish Society* (London, 1966), especially 63–4 and 81–90; Richard Sharpe, 'Some Problems Concerning the Organization of the Church in Early Medieval Ireland', *Peritia* 3 (1984), 230–70, especially 239–51; Colmán Etchingham, *Church Organisation in Ireland, A.D. 650 to 1000* (Maynooth, 1999), especially 14–44 and 105–30;

the word there, 'in addition to its episcopal dimension, has connotations of a temporal asset or resource' is particularly relevant.[14]

The question of whether Asser intended to imply episcopal authority by using the word *parochia* is complicated by the fact that he may already have been a bishop at St Davids before coming to England, probably in 885.[15] Exeter lay within the Saxon diocese of Sherborne in Dorset, so in theory there would have been no place for a bishop based at Exeter. However, it was not unknown for an assistant bishop to be allowed to function within a single diocese under special circumstances, and the increasingly unwieldy territory of the diocese of Sherborne, which had grown with the expansion of Wessex into Devon and Cornwall, might have qualified as such.[16] Indeed, the subdivision of Sherborne diocese which took place after Asser himself died as bishop there in 909 suggests that such a need could have been felt a few years earlier, when he came to Exeter at some time in 885×93. However, if Asser did have an episcopal role while he was still at Exeter (before moving to Sherborne) it could have arisen from his status before coming there, if he had already been bishop of St Davids. On the other hand, his wording in the clause concerning the *parochia* clearly implies that the jurisdiction, whatever its nature, was one which had belonged to Exeter before Asser came there in about 890. The *parochia* was Exeter's own, not one created for, or attached to, Asser personally.

At this point the other part of the question, that of the area over which this jurisdiction applied, becomes relevant. If Asser was using *parochia* with episcopal connotations it cannot refer to the whole of Devon and Cornwall, for we know from two tenth-century narrative sources that Sherborne was considered to have had diocesan responsibility for these two regions in the ninth century.[17] If Exeter, before Asser's arrival there, had already had diocesan responsibility for the whole of Devon and Cornwall, then much of what we are told in those two sources about the ecclesiastical development of Wessex would be wrong. Therefore, in terms of the territory implied in Asser's phrase, it is actually irrelevant whether or not he used *parochia* here with diocesan connotations: in either case it must have referred to a territory which formed only part of the later counties of Devon and Cornwall. If we suppose that Asser did use the word here with connotations of episcopal care, and ask how such territories might have been selected or allocated under the overall jurisdiction of the bishop of Sherborne, the natural answer would be that they were lands owned by the minster of Exeter.

Very little is known about the estates belonging to the minster church of Exeter before the late eleventh century, by which time the situation had been complicated by the arrival there of the new combined see of Devon and Cornwall in 1050; but it is easy to envisage that by about 890 the minster had been granted lands to the west of the River Tamar, as well as within Devon: Sherborne minster

---

Thomas Charles-Edwards, *Early Christian Ireland* (Oxford, 2000), 244–5; compare Blair, *Church in Anglo-Saxon Society*, 45–8.

[14] Colmán Etchingham, 'The Implications of *paruchia*', *Ériu* 44 (1993), 139–62, at 162; compare Etchingham, *Church Organisation in Ireland*, 172–7.

[15] Lloyd, *History of Wales*, I.226 and n. 159; Keynes and Lapidge, *Alfred the Great*, 51–2.

[16] Thus Finberg, 'Sherborne, Glastonbury', 109–10.

[17] The 'Plegmund Narrative' concerning the subdivision of the dioceses of Wessex (from Archbishop Plegmund, who presided over it): J. Armitage Robinson, *The Saxon Bishops of Wells* (London, 1918), 18–27; and Archbishop Dunstan's letter, in A. S. Napier and W. H. Stevenson, ed., *The Crawford Collection of Early Charters and Documents* (Oxford, 1895), 18–19 and 102–10.

had been given such estates, both by the Dumnonian king Gerent in about 700 (according to its later cartulary), and by King Ecgbert in 815×39, according to both its cartulary and the tenth-century narratives;[18] and the abbey of Tavistock in western Devon was similarly given estates west of the Tamar when it was founded in 981.[19]

The conclusion is therefore that the phrase used by Asser referred to estates in Devon and Cornwall belonging to the minster at Exeter, whether or not he took any episcopal responsibility under the bishop of Sherborne in those areas. If he did assume any such role he may have done so in a personal capacity, owing to his (probable) episcopal status when he came to England, rather than being appointed to a pre-existing see; and the role would presumably have been limited to estates belonging to the minster of Exeter, leaving Sherborne with the overall jurisdiction which we are told it had in both regions at this period. Asser's use of the word *parochia* might even have been intended ambiguously, referring primarily to the ecclesiastical estate (as in Irish usage, and sense 1 above), but with the advantage that it also carried an implication of an episcopal role (sense 3 above); but that need not be so. This interpretation therefore leaves open the question of whether the minster church at Exeter had any diocesan function over its lands before Asser came there; but at present that seems unlikely, even if Asser himself did take such a role (though that too is uncertain).

Various difficulties which have been raised concerning this conclusion can all be answered.[20] The first is that Exeter is not known to have had any lands in Cornwall before 1066, when the bishop owned twelve estates in the county.[21] These estates had come to Exeter from various sources. Two (Pawton and Lawhitton) had been transferred from Crediton in 1050 along with the diocesan see, and they had a long history of supporting the diocesan work in Cornwall, having originally been given to Sherborne for that purpose by King Ecgbert, transferred to Crediton at the subdivision of the see in about 909, transferred from there to St Germans when Athelstan created that see in about 930,[22] and then back to Crediton and on to Exeter when the two sees were re-amalgamated in the eleventh century. However, the other estates in Cornwall held by the bishop of Exeter in 1066 are of unknown provenance. Some could theoretically have been acquired by Crediton during its brief period as the diocesan church for Cornwall in the period 909–30; others might have belonged to St Germans during its century-long role as the diocesan church there (*c*.930–1027), and have been transferred to Crediton and on to Exeter when the sees were amalgamated. But there is no reason to dismiss the possibility that some of the twelve had belonged to Exeter in its own right as a minster church, before it had any diocesan ambitions. The lands of the bishopric in 1066 also included estates in various distant parts of Devon, some

---

18 Finberg, 'Sherborne, Glastonbury', 100 and 105–6; H. P. R. Finberg, *The Early Charters of Devon and Cornwall*, 2nd edn (Leicester, 1963), 17 (nos 72, 74, 76); Hooke, *Pre-Conquest Charter-Bounds*, 15–16.

19 S 838; H. P. R. Finberg, *Tavistock Abbey*, 2nd edn (Newton Abbot, 1969), 278–83; Hooke, *Pre-Conquest Charter-Bounds*, 19–20; Christopher Holdsworth, 'Tavistock Abbey in its Late Tenth Century Context', *Transactions of the Devonshire Association* 135 (2003), 31–58.

20 Orme, *Exeter Cathedral: The First Thousand Years*, 5–6.

21 C. and F. Thorn, ed., *Domesday Book*, 10, *Cornwall* (Chichester, 1979), 2.1–2.15.

22 'Plegmund Narrative', in Armitage Robinson, *Saxon Bishops of Wells*, 19–23; Dunstan's letter, in Napier and Stevenson, ed., *Crawford Charters*, 102–3; a third estate in Cornwall which accompanied those two, *Cællwic* or *Cællincg*, remains unidentified.

of which may have belonged to the minster before it gained diocesan status.[23] In any case, we have seen that even if Asser did imply an episcopal role by his use of the term *parochia*, it would still probably have operated only on Exeter's own estates, so Asser's phrase makes it necessary to postulate such estates, in Cornwall as well as Devon, however we interpret the administrative role. In fact, the argument that Exeter minster is not known to have owned property in Cornwall before 1066 would rebound upon itself, for it equally is not known to have had any diocesan status before that date. It is simpler to envisage estate ownership having slipped from the historical record than a bishopric having done so.

Two statements dating from the episcopacy of Bishop Leofric (1046–72) are of no help in determining the former landed estates of the minster church. An account of the benefits which Leofric gained for the church claimed that at the time the see was moved to Exeter from Crediton in 1050 all Exeter's former lands (including twenty-six estates given to Exeter by King Athelstan!) had been lost, so that 'scarcely one, very paltry' estate remained ('uix una uilissima [sc. terra] remansit'), and that Leofric had recovered many of the lands;[24] but it is likely that the statement was an exaggeration. An inventory of the cathedral's possessions (both lands and other goods) drawn up by Leofric himself in 1069×72 omitted any mention of the twelve Cornish estates, although they certainly belonged to the bishopric at that date, having been listed in 1066.[25] The structure of the list, first listing alienated lands which Leofric had recovered, and second new lands added by him, seems to preclude mention of lands which had belonged continuously to the minster; and that in turn allows the possibility that the some of Cornish estates which belonged to Exeter in 1066 had been in its possession since before the arrival of the see.

Exeter's *parochia* cannot be explained as those estates in Devon and Cornwall which belonged to Sherborne for the purposes of carrying out its diocesan work in those counties, for such estates could hardly have been described by Asser as 'Exanceastre, cum omni parochia quae ad se pertinebat' at the time when he was given it;[26] moreover, that explanation would also entail, without any supporting evidence, an even more complicated history for the Cornish estates than that which we already know that they had: instead of their known progression from Sherborne to Crediton to St Germans, then to Exeter in 1050, we should be postulating that they went first from Sherborne to Exeter (for Asser), back to Sherborne (with him), then on to Crediton and to St Germans (as above), then to Exeter for a second time in 1050.

The uncertainty over the possible lands of the minster at Exeter is heightened by the merging of its lands with those of the bishopric after 1050. The later distinction made in England, from the twelfth century, between the property of a bishop and that of his cathedral itself (dean and chapter) was not made in Exeter at this date. Thus the sectional heading *Terra episcopi de Exonia* in the Exchequer Domesday corresponds to a heading *Terre Sancti Petri Essecestrensis*

---

23 C. and F. Thorn, ed., *Domesday Book, 9, Devon*, 2 vols (Chichester, 1985), 2.11–12, 2.16, 2.23–4: Bishops Tawton (north Devon), Culmstock (north-east Devon), Salcombe (east Devon), and Dittisham and Slapton (south Devon).

24 Patrick W. Conner, *Anglo-Saxon Exeter* (Woodbridge, 1993), 225; the list of restored properties states that this single estate was at Ide (*ibid.*, 231).

25 Conner, *Anglo-Saxon Exeter*, 226–35; and Domesday Book (see above, n. 21).

26 'Exeter, with all the *parochia* pertaining to it' (see above, n. 1).

ecclesie in the Exeter copy;[27] and in 1086 the five estates in Devon set aside for the maintenance of the canons of the cathedral (*de uictu canonicorum*) were treated under the lands of the bishop of Exeter, being specifically described with the words, *Ipse episcopus tenet*, showing that the bishop was considered to hold the property of the cathedral.[28] The rigid distinction of property did not yet exist, so we cannot exclude the possibility that some of the bishop's Cornish lands in 1086 may have come to the cathedral from the former minster.

Finally, it might be argued that Asser's later appointment as bishop of the whole diocese of Sherborne, at some date before 900, supported the idea that he had previously had an episcopal role at Exeter; but in fact the appointment carries no weight either way, for Asser's background made him an excellent candidate for the bishopric of Sherborne irrespective of his previous role. In the late ninth century the Cornish language and Asser's native Welsh were still close enough to be no more than separating dialects, so he was well qualified to look after Exeter's *parochia* in Devon and Cornwall, whatever the exact nature of the role; and so, too, for later taking the bishopric of Sherborne, with its known episcopal role in Cornwall.

The last aspect to be considered is the choice of Crediton, not Exeter, as the see for Devon and Cornwall when the diocese of Sherborne was subdivided after Asser's death in 909. Exeter, as a former Roman town, was the sort of place that the Anglo-Saxons liked for their bishoprics, and if it had actually had a diocesan role since before Asser's time, either for part or (much less probably) for the whole of Devon and Cornwall, then it might seem strange for Exeter not to have been selected when a new see was needed in the area. John Blair has kindly suggested to me one possible reason, namely that, since Exeter was not a royal minster, it found the prospect of a bishop unattractive and was able to repel the idea.

Another possible reason for Exeter to have been passed over might be that Crediton already belonged to Sherborne, so it already had episcopal connections. Two further possible reasons which have also been suggested are less convincing.[29] The first is a royal reluctance to have a bishop at a minster with close connections to the throne (as evidenced by Alfred's appointment of Asser to take charge of it). However, bishops seem to have fitted well alongside royal estates elsewhere in the Anglo-Saxon period; and in any case, Exeter does not actually seem to have been either a royal minster or a royal *burh* at this time; no property there appears in King Alfred's will, and we have already seen that Alfred seems to have imposed Asser (in whatever role) upon a place where he had, strictly, no right to do so. The other reason suggested is that Crediton, lying slightly further inland, might have been thought safer from Viking attack than Exeter; but in fact when the division took place, in about 909 or shortly thereafter, that was not particularly an issue. There had been no Viking attack in Devon since that of 893, which had been successfully withstood at Exeter,[30] and in fact the division of the diocese occurred during the lull in Viking attacks on England during the first half

---

27 'Land of the bishop of Exeter', *Domesday Book: Devon*, 2.1; 'Lands of St Peter's church of Exeter', Exeter Domesday, fol. 117.

28 'For the maintenance of the canons'; 'The bishop himself holds …': Thorn, ed., *Domesday Book: Devon*, 2.5–8 and 2.22.

29 All three suggestions in Orme, *Exeter Cathedral: The First Thousand Years*, 6.

30 *Anglo-Saxon Chronicle MS A* (ed. Bately, 56–8); Whitelock *et al.*, *Anglo-Saxon Chronicle*, 54–5.

of the tenth century. Moreover, the four places in Devon for which fortification against possible attack was formalised in the Burghal Hidage included one as far inland as Lydford, and Exeter itself, but not Crediton;[31] so for defensive reasons too Exeter might have been thought more appropriate for the new see. Naturally we cannot know what reasons may have influenced the choice of Crediton in 909. If there had been a pre-existing see at Exeter before Asser's appointment there, and continuing under him until his move to Sherborne at some time in the 890s, the choice of Crediton seems curious; but, as we have seen, there is no reason at present to postulate such a see.

All in all, the balance of interpretation is that by Exeter's *parochia ... in Saxonia et in Cornubia* Asser meant estates held by the minster in Devon and Cornwall, whatever the nature of the role given to him. He may have wished to hint at an episcopal role which he himself held there, but (if so) that still would have covered only those estates which belonged to the minster in the two later counties, and which were the primary meaning of his clause. This meaning would also be consistent with the broader context of the phrase in Asser's text, which is of other gifts made by the king to himself, consisting primarily of temporal possessions, of both land and movable goods.

---

[31] *The Defence of Wessex: The Burghal Hidage and Anglo-Saxon Fortifications*, ed. David Hill and Alexander R. Rumble (Manchester, 1996), 138–41, 202–5, 208–9, 213–14.

7

VIKING-AGE SCULPTURE IN NORTH-WEST WALES: WEALTH, POWER, PATRONAGE AND THE CHRISTIAN LANDSCAPE

Nancy Edwards

Early medieval stone sculpture is the most important archaeological evidence we currently have for identifying the process of conversion to Christianity and the development and distribution of ecclesiastical foundations and related sites in Wales before the twelfth century.[1] Moreover, close examination of the sculpture – including quantification, and consideration of its archaeological and historical context, geology, form, function, ornament and inscriptions – also allows us to study it as an important manifestation of material, economic and social invest-ment[2] and consequently to pose other interesting questions concerning cultural contacts, wealth and patronage, the ownership of land and the relationship between secular rulers and the Church.

To date, research on the early medieval sculpture of north-west Wales has tended to focus on the inscribed memorial stones of the fifth to seventh centuries. Though some of the later monuments have been discussed, notably by H. Harold Hughes[3] and C. A. R. Radford,[4] a number were not noted in Nash-Williams's *Early Christian Monuments of Wales* and several others have come to light more recently.[5] The aim of this paper is to focus on the Viking-Age sculpture of north-west Wales, especially Anglesey, which is broadly datable from the tenth to early twelfth centuries, and to examine the complete range of carved stone monu-ments, not just the large-scale, free-standing decorated crosses, particularly those at Penmon,[6] which have tended to receive most attention in the past. After a brief discussion of the problems of dating and chronology, this paper will analyse the various forms of sculpture and their distribution and geology before going on to consider some of the broader questions outlined above.

---

1   This article is offered to Thomas, scholar and friend.
2   Meggen Gondek, 'Investing in Sculpture: Power in Early-historic Scotland', *Medieval Archaeology* 50 (2006), 105–42.
3   Hughes published extensively in *Archaeologia Cambrensis* from the 1890s to the Second World War. The most important articles are: H. Harold Hughes, 'Early Christian Decorative Art on Anglesey', *Archaeologia Cambrensis* 6th ser., 19 (1919), 477–98; 6th ser., 20 (1920), 1–30; 76 (1921), 84–114; 77 (1922), 61–79; 78 (1923), 53–69; 79 (1924), 39–58.
4   Especially his contributions in RCAHMW, *Anglesey* (London, 1937).
5   Of the fifty-five monuments currently known on Anglesey, thirty-seven were noted in *ECMW*, 51–68.
6   For the most recent discussion see Nancy Edwards, 'Viking-influenced Sculpture in North Wales, its Ornament and Context', *Church Archaeology* 3 (1999), 5–16.

Problems of dating and chronology

In contrast to elsewhere in Wales, where cross-carved stones and free-standing crosses with sometimes lengthy inscriptions are comparatively common,[7] only three carved stone monuments in the north-west have inscriptions[8] and these cannot be closely dated. We are therefore dependent upon art-historical dating methods linked to form and ornament, such as the Viking Borre-style ring-chain.[9] Iconography is rare.[10] When we examine less prestigious monuments, such as simple grave-markers carved for the most part with a variety of outline crosses, either incised or sometimes in false relief, one has to admit that at times one is skating on thin ice, though the cross-forms provide a basic framework. It should also be remembered that, although the Normans had invaded and briefly held south-east Anglesey and Arfon at the end of the eleventh century, they were quickly ousted.[11] There was therefore no sharp break resulting from the intro-duction of Norman religious orders and building traditions. Instead a more local form of the Romanesque was introduced into Gwynedd[12] and it is also possible to trace considerable continuity in the sculptural tradition through the twelfth century, especially on Anglesey.

Numbers, forms and distribution

There are thirteen fifth- to seventh-century inscribed memorial stones on Anglesey which are distributed fairly evenly across the island.[13] However, there seems subsequently to have been little or no investment in stone sculpture, as there is only one cross-carved grave-marker with a linear ring-cross of early type.[14] In contrast, there are over forty pieces spanning, approximately, the tenth to earlier

---

[7] See Mark Redknap and John M. Lewis, *A Corpus of Early Medieval Inscribed Stones and Stone Sculpture in Wales: Volume I, Breconshire, Glamorgan, Monmouthshire, Radnorshire and Geographically Contiguous Areas of Herefordshire and Shropshire* (Cardiff, 2007); Nancy Edwards, *A Corpus of Early Medieval Inscribed Stones and Stone Sculpture in Wales: Volume II, South-West Wales* (Cardiff, 2007), 92–106; *eadem*, 'Rethinking the Pillar of Eliseg', *Antiquaries Journal* 89 (2009), 143–77.

[8] *ECMW*, nos 5, 82; *CIIC*, II. no. 1029.

[9] David M. Wilson and Ole Klindt-Jensen, *Viking Art*, 2nd edn (London, 1980), 87–94; Richard N. Bailey, *Viking-Age Sculpture in Northern England* (London, 1980), 54–5.

[10] See *ECMW*, nos 8, 38, 82.

[11] R. R. Davies, *Conquest, Coexistence, and Change. Wales 1063–1415* (Oxford, 1987), 30–6; C. P. Lewis, 'Gruffudd ap Cynan and the Normans', in *Gruffudd ap Cynan: A Collaborative Biography*, ed. K. L. Maund (Woodbridge, 1996), 61–77; Paul Russell, ed. and trans., *Vita Griffini Filii Conani: The Medieval Latin Life of Gruffudd ap Cynan* (Cardiff, 2005), chs 26–31.

[12] Malcolm Thurlby, *Romanesque Architecture and Sculpture in Wales* (Little Logaston, 2006), 189–238.

[13] *ECMW*, nos 6, 9–10, 13, 25–6, 32–5, 39; for Bodedern 1 see Richard B. White, 'Excavations at Arfryn, Bodedern, Long-cist Cemeteries and the Origins of Christianity', *Transactions of the Anglesey Antiquarian Society and Field Club* (1971–2), 10–45, at 34–5, 41, 46–51, pl.; for Llanfihangel Ysgeifiog 1 see Patrick Sims-Williams, 'The DEVORIGI Inscription from Capel Eithin, Llanfihangel Ysceifiog, Anglesey', in Sian Ifor White and George Smith, 'A Funerary and Ceremonial Centre at Capel Eithin, Gaerwen, Anglesey', *Transactions of the Anglesey Antiquarian Society and Field Club* (1999), 9–166, at 146–9, illus.

[14] Llechgynfarwy 1, Nancy Edwards, 'Early Medieval Inscribed Stones and Stone Sculpture in Wales: Context and Function', *Medieval Archaeology* 45 (2001), 15–39, at 30.

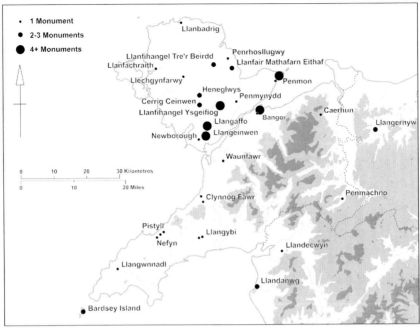

Map 2. Map showing the distribution of stone sculpture (c.600–1150) in north-west Wales (Drawing Charles Green, Crown copyright RCAHMW).

twelfth centuries. These include thirteen free-standing crosses of various sizes, eight of which are decorated, three carved fonts, more than twenty cross-carved stones (which presumably functioned as grave-markers) and one fragment with an incomplete inscription.

The distribution of this later group contrasts with that of the early inscribed stones. With two exceptions,[15] the Viking-Age monuments are confined to the southern and eastern half of the island (Map 2), the majority being concentrated in the *cantref* of Rhosyr.[16] Within this area four foci may be identified. The first is in the south-east of the island at Penmon, which is strategically located at the eastern end of the Menai Strait not far from Llan-faes, later the administrative centre of the commote of Dindaethwy. Both the foundation's Romanesque church (later an Augustinian priory) and associated chapel and hermitage on the adjacent offshore island are dedicated to St Seiriol.[17] The earliest mention of Penmon is in 971, when it was raided by the Vikings led by Maccus Haraldsson.[18] The only early medieval archaeological evidence is the stone sculpture, which is ambitious

---

[15] The cross-carved pillar at Llanbadrig and the cross-head at Llanfachraith, *ECMW*, nos 7–8.

[16] A. D. Carr, *Medieval Anglesey* (Llangefni, 1982), 137, Map 1.

[17] RCAHMW, *Anglesey*, 119–23, 141–4; Richard Gem, 'Gruffudd ap Cynan and the Romanesque Church at Penmon, Anglesey', in *The Archaeology of the Early Medieval Celtic Churches*, ed. Nancy Edwards (Leeds, 2009), 301–12.

[18] *ByT* (Pen. 20) 969 [= 971]; *ByT* (RB) [971]; AC (B) [971]; Colmán Etchingham, 'North Wales, Ireland and the Isles: The Insular Viking Zone', *Peritia* 15 (2001), 145–87, at 168–83.

9. Penmon 1: left, Face A with Borre-style ring-chain ornament. The cross is shown in its earliest known location (Cadw, Welsh Assembly Government. Crown copyright); right, Face C, showing the Temptation of St Anthony and a figure on horseback at the bottom of the shaft (Photograph Jean Williamson, Crown copyright RCAHMW).

and includes three large free-standing crosses,[19] the first of which (Figure 9) has a cross-head with a continuous ring and is carved with Viking Borre-style ring-chain, a representation of the Temptation of St Anthony by beast-headed figures and secular iconography, including a horseman and animals. Another cross-shaft, now lost, also had a Borre ring-chain and interlace. A third, also with a continuous ring on the cross-head, is carved with abstract patterns predominantly in the form of frets but also interlace. In addition, there is a carved stone font[20] which has similar ornament to the third cross and a smaller slab incised with an outline cross in false relief with a sunken ring, which presumably functioned as

---

[19] *ECMW*, nos 37–8; Edwards, 'Viking-influenced Sculpture', fig. 5 left.
[20] *ECMW*, no. 1; H. L. Jones, 'Remarks on Some of the Churches of Anglesey', *Archaeological Journal* 1 (1844), 118–30, at 122.

10. Llanfihangel Tre'r Beirdd, undecorated cross (Photograph Iain Wright, Crown copyright RCAHMW).

an upright grave-marker.[21] A fourth plain free-standing cross, now lost, was noted at Bryn Mawr, about 1km to the south-west.[22] Like the first cross, which originally stood on the hill above Penmon, it may have functioned as an ecclesiastical boundary marker or as an indication of the ownership of land.

The second focus is in eastern Anglesey, straddling the borders of the commotes of Dindaethwy and Twrcelyn north of the landing place at Traeth Coch (Red Wharf Bay) and not far from the Viking-Age and earlier settlement at Llanbedrgoch.[23] A small plain cross and a cross-head have been recorded in the churchyard at Llanfair-Mathafarn-Eithaf[24] and a further plain free-standing cross with expanding arms but, uniquely, without a ring (Figure 10) and a cross-carved

21 J. O. Westwood, *Lapidarium Walliae: The Early Inscribed and Sculptured Stones of Wales* (Oxford, 1876–9), 186, pl. 83(3).

22 Edwards, 'Viking-influenced Sculpture', fig. 5 right.

23 Mark Redknap, 'Viking-Age Settlement in Wales and the Evidence from Llanbedrgoch', in *Land, Sea and Home*, ed. John Hines, Alan Lane and Mark Redknap (Leeds, 2004), 139–75; *idem*, 'Llanbedrgoch: An Early Medieval Settlement and its Significance', *Transactions of the Anglesey Antiquarian Society and Field Club* (2007), 53–72.

24 *ECMW*, no. 11; the second, now exhibited at Stone Science, Llanddyfnan, is unpublished.

11. Fragmentary cross-carved
stone, Llangeinwen (Photograph
Jean Williamson, Crown
copyright RCAHMW).

stone have recently been identified at Llanfihangel Tre'r Beirdd. Finally, there is
a plain cross-base at Capel Lligwy in the parish of Penrhosllugwy.[25]

The third focus is in the south-west of the island at the western end of the Menai
Strait in the commote of Menai. The main concentration here is at Llangaffo, a
foundation first mentioned as *Merthyr Caffo* in the Life of St Cybi *c.*1200.[26] The
sculpture at Llangaffo includes a ringed cross-head carved with interlace, which
was possibly once part of the same monument as the now fragmentary cross-shaft
and base standing in the churchyard.[27] There are also eight grave-stones with
outline crosses of probable eleventh- or twelfth-century date, including at least
four with expanding arms and spikes on the bottom skeuomorphic of wooden or
metal forms.[28] There are also four similar cross-carved stones at the church in
the neighbouring parish of Llangeinwen (Figure 11).[29] To the north-east, at the
church of Llanfihangel Ysgeifiog, there are five probably recumbent grave-slabs,
two of which are now lost, with outline crosses, one with a spike; a small decorated cross-head has also been found.[30] It is also important to note that, to the
south-west of Llangaffo, near Newborough, is the excavated site of Rhosyr, one

---

25 RCAHMW, *Anglesey*, 133.
26 A. W. Wade-Evans, ed. and trans., *Vitae Sanctorum Britanniae et Genealogiae* (Cardiff, 1944),
    ch. 17, 246–7.
27 *ECMW*, nos 14–15.
28 *ECMW*, nos 17–24; RCAHMW, *Anglesey*, xcvi–c; for eleventh- and twelfth-century lead mortuary
    crosses with spikes see Roberta Gilchrist and Barney Sloane, *Requiem: The Medieval Monastic
    Cemetery in Britain* (London, 2005), 89–92.
29 *ECMW*, nos 27–30.
30 *ECMW*, no. 11a; H. L. Jones, 'Mona Mediaeva no. III', *Archaeologia Cambrensis* 1 (1846),
    297–305, at 299; the fifth (unpublished) was found in 2010 and is at Oriel Yays Môn, Llangefni;

12. Font, Cerrig Ceinwen (Photograph Iain Wright, Crown copyright RCAHMW).

of the commotal *llysoedd* ('courts') of the princes of Gwynedd,[31] which is sited close to the landing place at Abermenai. The adjacent church, which must be on the site of the royal estate chapel, has a carved stone font.[32]

Further north, in the commote of Malltraeth, is the final group of monuments, focused on the churches of Cerrig Ceinwen (which may be linked with Llangeinwen because it is dedicated to the same female saint) and Heneglwys, which is dedicated to St Llwydian. Sculpture in the former church includes a font carved with frets and interlace (Figure 12) and a late slab with a decorated cross,[33] while in the latter there is a stone with an incomplete memorial inscription and a fragment incised with a linear cross.[34]

The limited distribution of this sculpture across southern and eastern Anglesey may also be contrasted with that of both the Romanesque churches and sculpture, mainly fonts with a mixture of Romanesque and Insular ornament, which are found throughout Anglesey.[35] The Life of Gruffudd ap Cynan suggests that, in

---

Nancy Edwards, 'St Michael's Church, Llanfihangel Ysgeifiog', *Archaeology in Wales* 33 (1993), 65.

[31] Neil Johnstone, 'Cae Llys, Rhosyr: A Court of the Princes of Gwynedd', *Studia Celtica* 33 (1999), 251–95.

[32] *ECMW*, no. 36.

[33] *ECMW*, nos 3–4.

[34] *ECMW*, no. 5; the second is unpublished.

[35] RCAHMW, pls 58–62; Aimee Pritchard, 'The Early Baptismal Fonts on the Isle of Anglesey' (unpubl. BA dissertation, University of Wales, Bangor, 2001); *eadem*, 'Ideology and Patronage: Romanesque Architecture and Art on the Isle of Anglesey' (unpubl. MA dissertation, University of York, 2002); Thurlby, *Romanesque Architecture and Sculpture in Wales*, 191–238.

all probability, many of these churches were constructed during the later years of that ruler's reign; he died in 1137.[36]

Geology

The geology of all these monuments has recently been identified by Jana Horák of Amgueddfa Cymru – National Museum Wales.[37] In almost every identifiable case a coarse-grained, quartz arenite (sandstone or conglomerate) of Carboniferous age which was well suited to carving had been employed. This was derived from strata interbedded with the Carboniferous Limestone succession, which outcrop in parts of east, south-east and southern Anglesey adjacent to the Menai Strait and on the coast north of Traeth Coch (Red Wharf Bay).[38] The exact sources of the stone within this sequence have, at present, proved difficult to locate. However, the stone of the two surviving crosses at Penmon has distinctive red staining and comes from the vicinity of the limestone quarries still operating nearby. It is important to note that this coarse-grained arenite was also employed for monuments considerably further afield: both for the font decorated with ornament derived from Borre-style ring-chain at Pistyll[39] on the north coast of Llŷn and the cross-shaft carved with a fragmentary figure in a calf-length flared, pleated garment, interlace and an incomplete inscription comprising personal names[40] from the important ecclesiastical foundation on Bardsey Island off the tip of the peninsula (around 50 miles by sea). The latter has red patches, indicating that it is from the Penmon source. Most of the fragments from Bangor Cathedral are also carved from Anglesey Carboniferous quartz arenite.[41]

The Christian landscape

These crosses, cross-carved stones, decorated fonts and other fragments, which are concentrated in southern and eastern Anglesey and carved from the local Carboniferous quartz arenite, comprise by far the largest group of Viking-Age sculpture in north Wales. At the most basic level these monuments, almost all of which are associated with parish churches and often came to light reused as masonry during Victorian restoration and rebuilding, are indicative of a landscape of Christian sites, with or without wooden churches, which had been established

---

36 *Vita Griffini Filii Conani*, ch. 33 (ed. and trans. Russell, 86–7); D. Simon Evans, ed. and trans., *A Mediaeval Prince of Wales: The Life of Gruffudd ap Cynan* (Llanerch, 1990), 49–50, 81–2.

37 Completed as part of the research for: Nancy Edwards (with contributions by Jana Horák, Heather Jackson, Helen McKee, David N. Parsons and Patrick Sims-Williams), *A Corpus of Early Medieval Inscribed Stones and Stone Sculpture in Wales: Volume III, North Wales* (Cardiff, forthcoming).

38 British Geological Survey, *The Rocks of Wales: Geological Map of Wales*, Geological Survey 1:250,000 (1994).

39 RCAHMW, *Caernarvonshire, Volume III: West* (London, 1964), no. 1694, 89–90, pl. 25.

40 Possibly [S]ESILL MAR GUENO ('Seisyll son of Guen'), pers. comm. Patrick Sims-Williams; *ECMW*, no. 82; RCAHMW, *Caernarvonshire III*, no. 1518(i), 19, pl. 7.

41 Nancy Edwards, 'The Early Medieval Sculpture of Bangor Fawr yn Arfon', in *The Modern Traveller to Our Past: Festschrift in Honour of Ann Hamlin*, ed. Marion Meek (Dublin, 2006), 105–11.

by the earlier twelfth century; the sculpture is therefore testimony to the process of parish formation.[42] It is also notable that no fifth- to seventh-century inscribed stone may be closely associated with any of these church sites, which strongly suggests that they were established at a later date, probably during the Viking Age. Both Bede[43] and Gerald of Wales[44] emphasised the agricultural productivity of Anglesey, with soils suitable for cereal cultivation which are concentrated in the southern half of the island; the presence of sculpture likewise testifies to the comparative wealth of this region. The main concentrations of sculpture, which include large free-standing crosses carved with a range of ornament, particularly at Penmon but also at Llangaffo, clearly identify the two most important foundations in the area, which during this period were evolving into mother churches within their commotes and were the centres of local saints' cults. These are the same sites which are mentioned in the documentary record and Penmon was undoubtedly the more important of the two, and was therefore the most influential foundation in the *cantref* of Rhosyr. It was one of the foundations remembered in the will of Gruffudd ap Cynan (d. 1137)[45] and, according to a later medieval genealogical text, his son Idwal was made abbot and subsequently buried there[46] indicating close royal ties with the foundation, which may have been a proprietary church.[47] The rest would appear to be lesser sites which probably originated as estate chapels or local burial grounds and the cross-carved stones which would have functioned as grave-markers at Llangeinwen, for example, have clear links with those on the more important site at Llangaffo, and were in all likelihood produced by the same masons. The presence of the font at the estate chapel of the *llys* at Rhosyr indicates baptismal rights as well and also hints at the role of secular rulers in the patronage of sculpture production.

Landscapes of wealth and patronage

As Derek Craig has shown for the Viking-Age sculpture of Galloway centred upon Whithorn, which has some similarities with the Anglesey material, sculptural production is indicative not only of a Christian landscape but also of areas of comparative wealth, since it is a product of both fashion and display.[48] Meggen Gondek has also recently demonstrated that, in the Whithorn area, where fifth- to seventh-century inscribed stones are also characteristic, there is only modest sculptural investment centred on Whithorn itself in the eighth and ninth centuries,

42 Carr, *Medieval Anglesey*, 37–9; for a recent study of parish formation in Merioneth see Huw Pryce, 'The Medieval Church', in *History of Merioneth: Volume II, The Middle Ages*, ed. J. Beverley Smith and Llinos Beverley Smith (Cardiff, 2001), 254–96, at 257–69.

43 B. Colgrave and R. A. B. Mynors, ed., *Bede's Ecclesiastical History of the English People* (Oxford, 1969), II.9, 162–3.

44 James F. Dimock, ed., *Giraldi Cambrensis Opera, Vol. VI* (London, 1868), 127; Lewis Thorpe, trans., *Gerald of Wales: The Journey through Wales/The Description of Wales* (Harmondsworth, 1978), 187.

45 *Vita Griffini Filii Conani*, ch. 34 (ed. and trans. Russell, 88).

46 P. C. Bartrum, ed., *Early Welsh Genealogical Tracts* (Cardiff, 1966), 99.

47 Huw Pryce, *Native Law and the Church in Medieval Wales* (Oxford, 1993), 244–5; Gem, 'Gruffudd ap Cynan', 307–8; pers. comm. Alex Woolf.

48 Derek Craig, 'Pre-Norman Sculpture in Galloway: A Review of the Evidence', in *Galloway: Land and Lordship*, ed. Richard D. Oram and Geoffrey P. Stell (Edinburgh, 1991), 45–62, at 45.

followed by a dramatic rise in the Viking Age:[49] a pattern broadly comparable with Anglesey. She has also underlined the potential of investment in sculpture to tease out networks of power and patronage, both secular and ecclesiastical.[50] This has also been shown for the area around Govan in Strathclyde.[51] Both these regions, like north-west Wales, were open to waterborne contacts around the Irish Sea as well as further north and were the subject of Viking raids and incursions, though the nature and extent of Viking settlement in these areas, as in north-west Wales, have been the subject of considerable debate.[52]

For north-west Wales, the realisation that the sculpture was fashioned from Carboniferous quartz arenite from southern and eastern Anglesey, some of which was quarried at Penmon, is significant. The quarrying and transportation of the stone, as well as its shaping and decoration, particularly for the more ambitious monuments, would have required considerable resources – not least, access to ships for movement of large pieces over longer distances. This would suggest that sculpture production in north-west Wales is a good indication not just of wealth and display but also of patronage, both secular – centred on rulers and their retinues – and ecclesiastical. Indeed, it may be argued that the virtual restriction of Viking-Age sculpture to the southern and eastern half of Anglesey is significant and may indicate areas of control, while the distribution of sculpture along the mainland coast of Gwynedd highlights further pockets of patronage and influence.

Landscapes of power?

The final question is more controversial. To what extent is it possible to use Viking-Age sculpture in north-west Wales to illuminate the complex and changing networks of political power, both native and Viking, evidenced in the written sources?

Geographical factors undoubtedly played a significant role in the Viking impact on Anglesey in particular because of its pivotal position within the Irish

---

[49] Gondek, 'Investing in Sculpture', 119, 133–7.

[50] *Ibid.*, 108.

[51] Stephen T. Driscoll, Oliver O'Grady and Katherine Forsyth, 'The Govan School Revisited: Searching for Meaning in the Early Medieval Sculpture of Strathclyde', in *Able Minds and Practised Hands: Scotland's Early Medieval Sculpture in the 21st Century*, ed. Sally M. Foster and Morag Cross (Leeds, 2005), 135–58.

[52] For Galloway see Edward J. Cowan, 'The Vikings in Galloway: A Review of the Evidence', in *Galloway: Land and Lordship*, ed. Oram and Stell, 63–75; Gillian Fellows-Jensen, 'Scandinavians in Dumfriesshire and Galloway: The Place-Name Evidence', in *Galloway: Land and Lordship*, ed. Oram and Stell, 77–95; Alex Woolf, *From Pictland to Alba 789–1070* (Edinburgh, 2007), 293–8; James Graham-Campbell and Colleen E. Batey, *Vikings in Scotland: An Archaeological Survey* (Edinburgh, 1998), 202–5. For south-west Scotland see Thomas Owen Clancy, 'The Gall-Ghàidheil and Galloway', *Journal of Scottish Name Studies* 2 (2008), 19–50. For Govan see Stephen T. Driscoll, 'Govan: An Early Medieval Royal Centre on the Clyde', in *The Stone of Destiny, Artefact and Icon*, ed. Richard Welander, David Breeze and Thomas O. Clancy (Edinburgh, 2003), 77–83. For north-west Wales see Henry Loyn, *The Vikings in Wales* (London, 1976); Wendy Davies, *Patterns of Power in Early Wales* (Oxford, 1990), 48–60; Sean Duffy, 'Ostmen, Irish and Welsh in the Eleventh Century', *Peritia* 9 (1995), 378–96; Etchingham, 'North Wales, Ireland and the Isles'; *idem*, 'Viking-age Gwynedd and Ireland: Political Relations', in *Ireland and Wales in the Middle Ages*, ed. Karen Jankulak and Jonathan M. Wooding (Dublin, 2007), 149–67.

Sea zone and on the important route between Dublin and Chester. It is therefore not surprising that it became an important focus of Hiberno-Scandinavian and wider Gaelic-Scandinavian interest. Anglesey itself is a Viking place-name, *Ongullsey*, though the Welsh name, Môn, continued in parallel.[53] The written sources suggest two major phases of Viking incursions.[54] The first spans the second half of the ninth and the earlier tenth centuries. In 853 Anglesey was ravaged by the 'Black Heathens' based in Ireland and in 855 Rhodri Mawr, the ruler of Gwynedd, slew Orm, chief of the 'Dark Foreigners',[55] but in 876/7 he was defeated and forced to flee to Ireland.[56] Then, in 902, the Hiberno-Scandinavian leader Ingimund and his men, having been expelled from Dublin, seized Maes Osfeilion. It is unclear whether they were dislodged or not, but Ingimund went on to make other settlements on the Wirral.[57] Anglesey was ravaged again in 918 by a Hiberno-Scandinavian force from Dublin.[58]

The second phase spans the second half of the tenth, the eleventh and the earlier twelfth centuries. The evidence suggests that the quest to control Anglesey and the coast of mainland Gwynedd at this time was part of a broader claim for overlordship of Ireland, the Isle of Man and western Scotland. This phase began with the ravaging of Holyhead and Llŷn in 961 by the sons of Olaf.[59] Colmán Etchingham has argued that this renewed pressure came from Gaelic-Scandinavians from the Isles and the Isle of Man rather than directly from Ireland and that during the 970s and 980s it was led by two brothers, Godfrey and Maccus Haraldsson, whose ambitions extended to both Ireland and north Wales.[60] In 972 Godfrey Haraldsson reportedly devastated Anglesey and subdued the whole island. In 980 he mounted a further raid on Llŷn and Anglesey, capturing 2000 men who were freed two years later only when tribute was paid.[61] The Life of Gruffudd ap Cynan and other sources suggest that during the earlier eleventh century Gruffudd's grandfather, Olaf Sihtricson of Dublin (d. 1034), also had a major interest in Anglesey and Gwynedd, where he built a castle known as Bon y Dom.[62] Finally, Gruffudd ap Cynan, the ruler of Gwynedd in the earlier twelfth century, who had a Welsh father and a Hiberno-Scandinavian mother, had actually been brought up in Swords in *Dyflinnarskíri* and was supported in his bid for power by Hiberno-Scandinavian men and ships.[63]

53 Gwilym T. Jones and Tomos Roberts, *Place-Names of Anglesey* (Bangor, 1996), 89–90.
54 Loyn, *The Vikings in Wales*. For the most recent discussion of the incursions see Clare Downham, *Viking Kings of Britain and Ireland: The Dynasty of Ívarr to A.D. 1014* (Edinburgh, 2007), 201–30.
55 *AC* (A, B, C) [853]; *AU²* 856.6.
56 *AC* (A, B, C) [877]; *AU²* 877.3.
57 F. T. Wainwright, 'Ingimund's Invasion', *English Historical Review* 63 (1948), 145–69; *AC* (A) [902]; Redknap, 'Viking-Age Settlement in Wales', 140–2.
58 *ByT* (Pen. 20) [918]; *ByT* (RB) [918]; Etchingham, 'North Wales, Ireland and the Isles', 162–7.
59 *ByT* (Pen. 20) 959 [= 961]; *ByT* (RB) [961].
60 Etchingham, 'North Wales, Ireland and the Isles', 168–83.
61 *ByT* (Pen. 20) 979 [= 980]; *ByT* (RB) [980]; K. L. Maund, *Ireland, Wales and England in the Eleventh Century* (Woodbridge, 1991), 57.
62 *Vita Griffini Filii Conani*, ch. 4 (ed. and trans. Russell, 128–30); Etchingham, 'North Wales, Ireland and the Isles', 157–61.
63 Duffy, 'Ostmen', 386–96; David E. Thornton, 'The Genealogy of Gruffudd ap Cynan', in *Gruffudd ap Cynan: A Collaborative Biography*, ed. K. L. Maund (Woodbridge, 1996), 79–108; *Vita Griffini Filii Conani*, chs 1–6, 14, 17–18 (ed. and trans. Russell, 47, 52–9, 64–7, 68–71).

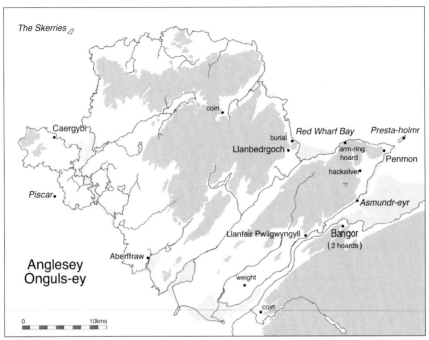

Map 3. Map showing Viking place-names and archaeological evidence on Anglesey and the adjacent mainland in the tenth century (Drawing Tony Daly, Copyright Amgueddfa Cymru – National Museum Wales).

The written sources therefore suggest that Anglesey, which was strategically located, was an integral part of Viking activity in the Irish Sea zone from the mid-ninth century onwards and was repeatedly subjected to the political ambitions of Viking leaders, some of whom seized land and attempted to hold it, however temporarily, from native control. Against such a background the presence of at least some Viking settlers seems certain, though degrees of integration and possible areas of hegemony are more difficult to identify.

We can now bring place-name and archaeological evidence into play. Mark Redknap's recent map (Map 3) shows the locations of Viking place-names, predominantly offshore islands, notably *Presta-holmr* (Priestholm) for Ynys Seiriol at the eastern entrance to the Menai Strait, but also the Skerries and possibly the rock stack known as Maen Piscar.[64] In addition, there is *Asmundr-eyr* (Osmund's Air),[65] which combines a Scandinavian personal name with *eyrr* 'gravel bank' and is located just east of Llan-faes. The increasing amount of archaeological evidence indicates a Viking presence most clearly in eastern and south-eastern Anglesey and at Bangor on the mainland side of the Menai Strait, thereby mirroring the distribution of the sculpture. It includes the settlement at

64 Jones and Roberts, *Place-Names of Anglesey*, 136; Melville Richards, 'Norse Place-Names in Wales', in *The Impact of the Scandinavian Invasions on the Celtic-Speaking Peoples c. 800–1100 A.D.*, ed. Brian Ó Cuív (Dublin, 1975), 51–60, at 55.

65 Bedwyr Lewis Jones and Tomos Roberts, 'Osmund's Air: A Scandinavian Place-Name in Anglesey', *BBCS* 28:4 (1980), 602–3.

Llanbedrgoch which, with its rectangular buildings and typically Viking artefac-tual assemblage, notably hack-silver and lead weights, is indicative of Hiberno-Scandinavian settlement and trading in the later ninth and earlier tenth centuries,[66] as is the Viking grave at Benllech nearby.[67] In addition to the silver hoards from the eastern side of Red Wharf Bay and Bangor[68] and stray finds, such as the ringed pin from the church-yard at Llanfairpwllgwyngyll[69] and the lead weight from Brynsiencyn,[70] fragments of a silver ingot and a Hiberno-Scandinavian silver armband similar to those from Llanbedrgoch have been found north of Llan-faes parish church.[71] The strategic importance of south-east Anglesey, which controlled the eastern approach to the Menai Strait, is also suggested by the fact that Ingimund held Maes Osfeilion, thought to be near Llan-faes,[72] and at the end of the eleventh century the Normans made their unsuccessful bid for control by building their motte at Aberlleiniog near Penmon; it was besieged by Gruffudd ap Cynan, but later captured by Magnus Barelegs of Norway and his fleet.[73] There is also evidence to suggest that from the time of Gruffudd ap Cynan the ruling dynasty of Gwynedd controlled Penmon and its *abadaeth*. As we have seen, Gruffudd's son Idwal was made abbot and in 1237 Llywelyn ap Iorwerth granted the *abadaeth* to Ynys Lannog (Ynys Seiriol).[74]

What can the sculptural evidence tell us about the impact of the Vikings on Anglesey and north-west Wales? Investment in sculpture over a larger number and greater range of sites is a feature of the Viking Age in many areas of Viking settlement, such as parts of northern England,[75] the Isle of Man[76] and southern *Dyflinnarskíri*,[77] where a process of parish formation similar to that on Anglesey and in the area around Whithorn is detectable in the distribution of the sculpture. However, in contrast with the sculpture at Whithorn, which has no overtly Viking features, three of the most ambitious monuments, two of the crosses at Penmon and the font at Pistyll on the Llŷn, are decorated with the distinctive Borre-style

---

66 Mark Redknap, *Vikings in Wales: An Archaeological Quest* (Cardiff, 2000), 65–84; *idem*, 'Viking-Age Settlement'; *idem*, 'Llanbedrgoch'; Etchingham, 'North Wales, Ireland and the Isles', 163. The promontory fort of Porth Trefadog in north-west Anglesey has also been compared with Viking examples on the Isle of Man: see David Longley, 'The Excavation of Castell, Porth Trefadog, A Coastal Promontory Fort in North Wales', *Medieval Archaeology* 35 (1991), 64–85.

67 Nancy Edwards, 'A Possible Viking Grave from Benllech, Anglesey', *Transactions of the Anglesey Antiquarian Society and Field Club* (1985), 19–24.

68 George C. Boon, *Welsh Hoards, 1979–81* (Cardiff, 1986), 92–7. The Red Wharf Bay hoard was formerly known as the Dinorben hoard.

69 Cyril Fox, 'An Irish Bronze Pin from Anglesey', *Archaeologia Cambrensis* 95 (1940), 248, pl. opp. 249.

70 Mark Redknap, 'Anglesey, Brynsiencyn', *Medieval Archaeology* 47 (2003), 214–15, fig. 5(c).

71 Mark Redknap, 'Viking-age Commerce in North Wales', in *The Huxley Viking Hoard: Scandinavian Settlement in the North West*, ed. James Graham-Campbell and Robert Philpott (Liverpool, 2009), 29–41, at 35, pl. 4, 12–13.

72 Downham, *Viking Kings*, 206–7; pers. comm. Thomas Charles-Edwards.

73 *Vita Griffini Filii Conani*, chs 23–9 (ed. and trans. Russell, 74–85); Lewis, 'Gruffudd ap Cynan and the Normans'; Etchingham, 'North Wales, Ireland and the Isles', 148–51.

74 See n. 46; Huw Pryce, ed., *The Acts of Welsh Rulers 1120–1283* (Cardiff, 2005), no. 272.

75 See, for example, Richard N. Bailey and Rosemary Cramp, *Corpus of Anglo-Saxon Stone Sculpture: Vol. II, Cumberland, Westmorland and Lancashire North-of-the Sands* (Oxford, 1988); James Lang, *Corpus of Anglo-Saxon Stone Sculpture: Vol. VI, Northern Yorkshire* (Oxford, 2001).

76 P. M. C. Kermode, *Manx Crosses* (London, 1907, reprinted Balgavies, 1994).

77 Patrick Healy, *Pre-Norman Grave-slabs and Cross-inscribed Stones in the Dublin Region*, ed. Kieran Swords (Tallaght, 2009).

ring-chain or ornament derived from it. The use of the Borre style in Scandinavia and by extension Britain and Ireland can be broadly dated from the later ninth to later tenth centuries.[78] The direction of the ring-chain on the surviving cross from Penmon is comparable with examples on the Isle of Man,[79] where the ornament is characteristic; its *floruit* on the island has been dated to between 925 and 960.[80] A strap-end with Borre-style ring-chain decoration has also been found at Llanbedrgoch.[81] Although the Borre-style ring-chain is rare in Ireland,[82] the Temptation of St Anthony scene has several parallels on Irish crosses[83] and the horseman and animals would have appealed to secular aristocratic taste. Though it has no dedicatory inscription, such an ambitious monument is most likely to have been the product of elite secular patronage of an ecclesiastical site. The form and ornament, particularly the Borre-style ring-chain, on this cross would seem to make it more than simply the product of a Viking Irish Sea zone cultural milieu. Indeed, one might speculate as to whether it is the product of the status, power and patronage of a Viking elite located in the south-eastern part of the island, perhaps even of a ruler such as Godfrey Haraldsson, who, in the third quarter of the tenth century, had a foothold in the Isle of Man and was attempting, with his brother Maccus, to extend his power, however temporarily, into north-west Wales.[84]

The ornament on the other more ambitious sculpture is confined to interlace and frets and, like the simple cross-carved grave-markers, has nothing overtly to suggest a specifically Viking context rather than a more general Insular Viking-Age one. Nevertheless, the overall distribution is concentrated in southern and eastern Anglesey in the *cantref* of Rhosyr and may represent the extent of the influence of the most important ecclesiastical foundation at Penmon. The concentration of sculpture in the vicinity of Traeth Coch is in an area with an increasing amount of evidence for Viking contact and settlement, though whether the sculpture also indicates this is less clear. At the western end of the Menai it may be argued that the concentration around Llangaffo not only represents local elite patronage of the cult of St Caffo but is also linked to the *llys* of the rulers of Gwynedd at Rhosyr, which had been established by the eleventh century. At a broader level such sculpture may simply represent the changing pattern of native and Viking power and influence suggested by the sources.

---

78 Wilson and Jensen, *Viking Art*, 91–3; Neils Bonde and Arne Emil Christensen, 'Dendrochronological Dating of the Viking-Age Ship Burials at Oseberg, Gokstad and Tune, Norway', *Antiquity* 67 (1993), 575–83, at 576, 582; Bailey, *Viking-Age Sculpture*, 54–5; David M. Wilson, *The Vikings in the Isle of Man* (Aarhus, 2008), 62.

79 E.g. Kirk Michael no. 101 (74), Gautr's Cross, *ibid.*, 63–6, fig. 26; see also Kermode, *Manx Crosses*, nos 92 (118), 100 (126), which, like Penmon 1, have double-strand ring-chain running the length of the cross-shaft.

80 Wilson, *Vikings in the Isle of Man*, 67.

81 Redknap, *Vikings in Wales*, 89, illus. 135; *idem*, 'Silver and Commerce', 39.

82 For the Ballinderry 1 gaming-board see Ruth Johnson, 'Ballinderry Crannóg No. 1: A Reinterpretation', *PRIA* 99C (1999), 23–71, at 47–56; see also James T. Lang, *Viking-Age Decorated Wood: A Study of its Ornament and Style* (Dublin, 1988), 11, fig. 12b.

83 Notably, the Market Cross, Kells, Co. Meath: see Peter Harbison, *The High Crosses of Ireland*, 3 vols (Bonn, 1992), I.303–4, III. fig. 949; Edwards, 'Viking-influenced Sculpture', 12, fig. 3.

84 Etchingham, 'North Wales, Ireland and the Isles', 171–83.

The only other monument in the region of possible Viking type was found associated with east–west burials at Ffriddoedd, Bangor, in 1938.[85] The site is located on a prominent ridge with views over the Menai Strait. The stone, which may be of Silurian rather than Carboniferous sandstone,[86] was originally identified as a lintel. However, its context suggests a grave-marker and its shape might identify it as a poorly executed hogback grave-cover. The siting, overlooking the strait, may be compared with the only definite example of a hogback monument in Wales at Llanddewi Aber-arth (Ceredigion.)[87] and was also favoured more generally for Viking pagan burials, including the only known grave in north-west Wales at Benllech in eastern Anglesey.[88] Together with the typically Viking mixed coin and silver hoard containing Islamic dirhams found near Bangor Cathedral, which can be dated to after 921,[89] it is also suggestive of a Viking presence on the adjacent mainland, which would have been consistent with a strategic aspiration to hold both sides of the Menai Strait.

Conclusion

This study has focused upon the largest collection of Viking-Age sculpture in north Wales, concentrated in southern and eastern Anglesey, the monuments of which range from ambitious carved crosses to the simplest of cross-carved grave-markers, carved from local Carboniferous quartz arenite, one source of which was Penmon. Monuments carved from this stone are also found on the adjacent mainland and as far west as Bardsey Island. The aim has been to demonstrate that the form, ornament, context and distribution of the sculpture can be used not only to study the emerging Christian landscape of southern and eastern Anglesey and as evidence of wealth, patronage and display in the tenth to earlier twelfth centuries but also to suggest that in conjunction with other documentary, place-name and archaeological evidence, it may be used to illuminate the complex political landscape of the region in the Viking Age.[90]

---

85   H. Harold Hughes, 'Discovery of Burials at Bangor', *Archaeologia Cambrensis* 93 (1938), 262–4; *ECMW*, no. 80.

86   Pers. comm. Jana Horák.

87   Edwards, *Corpus II*, no. CD7.

88   Edwards, 'Viking Grave from Benllech'; Redknap, *Vikings in Wales*, 98.

89   Boon, *Welsh Hoards*, 92–7.

90   Versions of this paper were delivered at the Early Medieval Wales Archaeology Research Group Colloquium, *The Archaeology of Early Medieval Wales – in Context* (April 2009), and at the 16th Viking Congress in Iceland (August 2009). I benefited greatly on both occasions from questions and discussion which helped me to refine my ideas. I am also pleased to acknowledge financial assistance from the British Academy which enabled me to attend the Congress. I am particularly grateful to Jana Horák (Amgueddfa Cymru – National Museum Wales) for allowing me to draw upon her unpublished research on the geology. Both she and Huw Pryce have read a draft of this article and made valuable corrections and suggestions. I would also like to thank Mark Redknap (Amgueddfa Cymru – National Museum Wales) for allowing me to reproduce Figure 6.

8

IONA V. KELLS:
SUCCESSION, JURISDICTION AND POLITICS IN THE COLUMBAN *FAMILIA* IN THE LATER TENTH CENTURY

Thomas Owen Clancy

In 1988 Máire Herbert's magisterial *Iona, Kells and Derry* laid out a clear map of the progression of the authority within the Columban *familia* along the lines indicated in the title, with the *comarbus* or 'successorship' of the founder saint Columba passing to each of the named major monasteries within the federation from the sixth to the twelfth century.[1] Importantly, she gave careful consideration to the nature of the 'hand-over' periods between the institutions, making it clear, for instance, that despite the construction of the monastery of Kells during the period 807–14, the idea of Iona's abandonment for Kells in the early ninth century owing to Viking raids was simply a modern myth.[2] The *comarbus* of Colum Cille, by her reckoning, arrived in Kells *de facto* only with the accession of the *comarba Pátraic*, Mael Brigte mac Tornáin (891–927).[3] There is no clear evidence that Mael Brigte was based at Kells itself, but his long rule (nearly forty years in Armagh, thirty-six as successor of Colum Cille), apparently spent in Ireland, and the certain fact that by the early eleventh century successors of Columba were based there, made it probable to Herbert that subsequent tenth-century successors were in Kells *de jure*.[4] Its loss of authority came only in the twelfth century, with the rise of Derry under the patronage of the Mac Lochlainn dynasty, 1150 being, in John Bannerman's words, Derry's '*annus mirabilis*'.[5] Bannerman provided some useful correctives and nuances in his important article in 1993,[6] but the basic model of the pattern of succession has remained intact.

Despite the important and persuasive case Herbert made across the full range of her study period, from Iona's foundation through to the mid-twelfth century, this tenth-century phase of the development of the Columban *familia* and its successors, putatively under the domination of Kells, seems open to challenge; it

---

[1] M. Herbert, *Iona, Kells and Derry: The History and Hagiography of the Monastic Familia of Columba* (Oxford, 1988; repr. Dublin, 1996).

[2] *Ibid.*, 68–74. See also T. O. Clancy, 'Diarmait sapientissimus: The Career of Diarmait dalta Daigre, Abbot of Iona, 814×839', *Peritia* 17–18 (2003–4), 215–32.

[3] *Ibid.* 74–9; but see now D. N. Dumville, 'Mael Brigte mac Tornáin, Pluralist Coarb', *Journal of Celtic Studies* 4 (2004), 97–116; reprinted in *idem, Celtic Essays, 2001–2007*, volume 1 (Aberdeen, 2007), 137–58. My references herein are to the pagination in the 2007 reprint.

[4] Herbert, *Iona, Kells and Derry*, 79.

[5] J. Bannerman, 'Comarba Coluim Chille and the Relics of Columba', *Innes Review* 44 (1993), 14–47, at 41.

[6] And a helpful marshalling of the evidence for the period in *ibid.*, 46–7.

has, indeed, already been challenged in part by David Dumville.[7] Here Herbert, although stating her case cautiously, seems to me to have passed too lightly over contradictory evidence. This evidence tends to suggest that, at least during the period 964–86, the headship of the Columban *familia* was in the hands of Iona, and that Kells did not really emerge definitively as the seat of the *comarbus* until 1007, when the renewed strength of Clann Cholmáin patronage under Mael Sechnaill mac Domnaill made it once again a powerful royal monastery.[8]

Important recent work on Irish and Viking politics in the tenth century has strengthened anxieties.[9] Concurrent work by Charles Doherty and Máire Ní Mhaonaigh, and by Edel Bhreathnach, emphasised the complexities of this period.[10] Both Doherty and Ní Mhaonaigh paid particular attention to the figure of Amlaíb Cuarán (†980), stressing the ways in which he can be seen as one of the first truly 'embedded' kings of the Gaill in Ireland, engaging in close co-operation with native dynasts and even accruing the praises of the *príméces* of Ireland, Cinaed ua hArtacáin (†975).[11] Both noted the 'smoking gun' of the relationship suggested by the fact that Cinaed's near-relative, perhaps even his brother, Fiachra, was *airchinnech* of Iona during the 970s. It was, of course, on Iona that Amlaíb Cuarán was to die in pilgrimage in 980.[12] This seemed to them to point to Amlaíb as having a nexus of patronage relationships with local Irish families, particularly those in Brega. Alex Woolf pushed this argument further in an important and careful exploration of the complex and factionalised relationship between Amlaíb and native Irish dynasties, laying down a series of correctives to previous treatments of this figure. He provocatively concluded by suggesting that in light of his embedded status in the politics of eastern Ireland, Amlaíb was 'the first Irishman to rule in Dublin'.[13]

Edel Bhreathnach's arguments have gone even further. In a detailed investigation of the patronage of the churches of St Columba in eastern Ireland she argued persuasively that the church of Scrín Coluim Chille, on the hill of Achall 'which confronts Tara' (as Cinaed ua hArtacáin puts it), was established by

---

7   Dumville, 'Mael Brigte'.

8   See *AU²* 1007.10.

9   There have been several reviews relevant to the period considered here. See especially, but not exclusively, Bart Jaski, 'The Vikings and the Kingship of Tara', *Peritia* 9 (1995), 310–53; C. Etchingham, 'North Wales, Ireland and the Isles: The Insular Viking Zone', *Peritia* 15 (2001), 145–87; Clare Downham, 'The Vikings in Southern Uí Néill to 1014', *Peritia* 17–18 (2003–4), 233–55; *eadem, Viking Kings of Britain and Ireland: The Dynasty of Ívarr to A.D. 1014* (Edinburgh, 2007); and most recently E. Bhreathnach, 'Ireland, c.900–c.1000', in *A Companion to the Early Middle Ages: Britain and Ireland c.500–c.1100*, ed. P. Stafford (Oxford, 2009), 268–84.

10   C. Doherty, 'The Vikings in Ireland: A Review' and M. Ní Mhaonaigh, 'Friend and Foe: Vikings in Ninth- and Tenth-Century Irish Literature', in *Ireland and Scandinavia in the Early Viking Age*, ed. H. B. Clarke, M. Ní Mhaonaigh and R. Ó Floinn (Dublin, 1998), 288–330 and 381–402: see esp. 295–305 and 398–401; E. Bhreathnach, 'Columban Churches in Brega and Leinster: Relations with the Norse and the Anglo-Normans', *JRSAI* 129 (1999), 5–18; see also *eadem*, 'Authority and Supremacy in Tara and its Hinterland, c.950–1200', *Discovery Programme Reports* 5 (1999), 1–23.

11   Doherty, 'Vikings in Ireland', 295–305; Ní Mhaonaigh, 'Friend and Foe', 398–401. On Cinaed see J. Carey, 'Cináed ua hArtacáin', *ODNB*, XI.713; M. Ní Mhaonaigh, 'Cináed ua hArtacáin', in *Medieval Ireland: An Encyclopedia*, ed. Seán Duffy (New York and London, 2005), 87.

12   See *AU²* 978.1, *AFM* 979.5, and *CS* 980.7, *AT* 980.6.

13   A. Woolf, 'Amlaíb Cuarán and the Gael, 941–981', *Medieval Dublin* 3 (Dublin, 2002), 34–43, at 43.

Amlaíb Cuarán as a literal contra-Tara.[14] Other churches in the Dublin hinter-land of Brega and Leinster, such as Sord Coluim Cille (Swords Co. Dublin), may also have been established or at least patronised by Amlaíb.[15] The Dublin king thus emerges from this as a man who had keen patronal interests in St Columba, building up his cult and his churchmen under the aegis of the Viking hegemony. Bhreathnach suggested also, tentatively, that the patronage of such churches may have been 'part of a plan which was intended to undermine the influence of Kells'.[16] Woolf provides an interesting speculation in this regard, airing the possi-bility that among the items plundered from Kells on Amlaíb Cuarán's raid on the monastery in 970 were relics of Columba.[17] While incapable of proof, this idea has its attractions and I shall return to it in due course.

Thus, within a strictly Irish context, Amlaíb Cuarán has emerged in recent scholarship as a figure who, during the years 963–80 at least, may have been developing a cult of Columba for political purposes independent of, and perhaps opposed to, that based in Kells. Missing from these arguments has been the eastern dimension, in particular the situation of Iona within this nexus of Amlaíb's patronage. This contribution explores the hypothesis that Amlaíb attempted to renew the position of Iona as centre of his wider province of power, which stretched far beyond Dublin.[18] I shall be looking both at ecclesiastical and at secular dimensions of the jockeying for power which is evident in these decades, and was most brutally conjoined in the targeting of monasteries for destruction and plunder, monasteries closely allied with particular kings and their interests. I shall begin by examining the status of Iona in the tenth century, and then come to discuss the political background, in particular the alliances between Amlaíb Cuarán and Congalach Cnogba and his descendants. As we shall see, this discus-sion has ramifications in a number of subsidiary arenas, not least the date and analysis of the Middle Irish *Life of Adomnán*.

If Herbert's analysis were correct, Kells would have reached both its earliest height and its earliest nadir under the rule of Mael Brigte mac Tornáin, 891–927. She adduced some indications that this was the main Columban centre during his time; certainly, there is little sign of his interest in Columba's eastern churches, such as Iona. This said, she noted that there was no evidence for where in Ireland Mael Brigte's main residence lay: the choice of Kells is entirely inferential. This problem has been augmented by David Dumville, who has pointed more force-fully towards indications of Mael Brigte's associations with Cenél mBóguine, a Cenél Conaill kindred based around Raphoe, and therefore perhaps for his career originating there, possibly even as a coarb of Adomnán.[19] To this evidence, which dissociates him from Kells, we may add that during his rule Kells became most

---

14 Bhreathnach, 'Columban Churches', esp. 8–11; for Cinaed's poem and its description ('Achall araiccí Temair') see E. Gwynn, *The Metrical Dindshenchas*, vol. I (Dublin, 1903), 46–52. See also her earlier article, 'The Documentary Evidence for pre-Norman Skreen, County Meath', *Ríocht na Midhe* 9.2 (1996), 37–45. The arguments made by Bhreathnach appear to have been missed by Carey in his *ODNB* entry on Cinaed, where he puzzles over his affiliation on the one hand with St Columba and on the other with some of the enemies of Kells.
15 Bhreathnach, 'Columban Churches', 11.
16 *Ibid.*, 8.
17 Woolf, 'Amlaíb Cuarán', 42; see also *AU²* 970.1.
18 For comments on this problem see Woolf, 'Amlaíb Cuarán', 34–5.
19 Dumville, 'Mael Brigte', 141–8, esp. 146.

visibly a 'royal monastery' of the Clann Cholmáin. In 904 Flann Sinna was forced to sack the monastery to oppose his rebellious son Donnchad Donn, and it is in the year that Donnchad first acceded to the kingship of Tara (920) that Kells was first sacked in a clearly political move by the Vikings of Dublin.[20] Although Kells as the site for Mael Brigte's four successors, Dubthach, Robartach, Dub Duin and Dub Scuile, is not an implausible choice, it is worth stressing, as Herbert herself noted, that there is no evidence to prove this.[21] The one notable change in the ascription of the successorship in these years in the chronicles is the addition of Adomnán to the designation of *comarba Coluim Cille* in the cases of Dubthach and Robartach, a feature which caused Reeves to suggest they were based at Raphoe rather than Kells.[22] Herbert dismissed this idea, but it seems to me to have no less in its favour than Kells and, in light of Dumville's work on Mael Brigte and his affiliations, Raphoe may have the edge, at least with respect to the situation up to the death of Robartach in 954.[23] This leaves a bare ten years during which we know nothing of the affiliations of the holders of the *comarbus*: even were they to have been based in Kells this now looks more incidental than anything else. This does not, however, diminish the case that can be made for the importance of Kells itself in the tenth century, if only because of the continued political dominance of Donnchad Donn of Clann Cholmáin, albeit as something of a lame-duck king, from 920 to 944. What I am suggesting, then, is that where we meet Kells in the period between 927 and 964, and indeed afterwards, it is predominantly as a royal monastery of Clann Cholmáin and as a target of hostile political and military adventures. There is nothing in the annalistic record that necessitates, or even suggests, its possession of the successorship of Colum Cille.

By contrast, both with this and with the relative silence of the previous three-quarters of a century, from 963 the annals have a series of important notices of prominent Iona personnel.[24] It is perhaps worth noting these in full.

ARC [963] Fothud m. Brain, scriba optimus et episcopus Innsi Alban, in senili aetate moritur. (cf. *CKA* Fothach episcopus pausauit [during reign of Dub, 962–7])

---

20 AU² 904.2, 920.2, 920.6.
21 Herbert, *Iona, Kells and Derry*, 78–82.
22 W. Reeves, *The Life of St Columba, founder of Hy, written by Adamnan* (Dublin, 1857), 393; Dumville also emphasises the role of Raphoe, 'Mael Brigte'.
23 In light of the discussion below, it might be worth putting into this mix the rise of Cenél Conaill dynasts in parallel with those of Brega in the middle of the tenth century, particularly Ruaidri ua Canannáin.
24 Dumville ('Mael Brigte', 151) has further noted that the evidence of the tenth and eleventh century in general can easily be read as implying continuity of Iona's dominance: 'There is no indication in "The Annals of Ulster" that the coarbs of St Columba recorded from 927 were other than abbots of Iona, and some are specifically so designated.' I would agree with this, and particularly extend it to the period 954–64. The evidence he cites, however, is more complicated than he makes out. *AU²* 1005.1 records the death of an abbot of Iona, but does not note that he was *comarba* (and this is in a year where evidence suggests that Muiredach ua Crichāin was *comarba*); a parallel situation in 947 seemed to Herbert (rightly I suspect) to confirm that Robartach, at any rate, was not abbot of Iona. *AU²* 1025.1 records, unusually, the death of a *comarba Ia*. This suggests both that there was some uncertainty over how to handle designations in the early years of the eleventh century, and that Iona maintained a presence in the Gaelic world in that period (something that has been obscured by Herbert's dropping of the history of Iona for an Irish focus after the tenth century). Either way, it helps to confirm a growing conviction that this period, rather than the earlier one, was when the *comarbus* seems to have shifted towards Kells.

CS 966.4 Fingin, epscop muintire Iae, quieuit. (cf. *AFM*)

AU² 978.1 Fiachra, airchinnech Ia, quieuit.

AFM 976.2 Fiachra Ua hArtacáin, abb Ia Choluim Chille …

ARC [980] Mugron, ab Iae, scriba optimus atque sui-epscop na Tri Rand, obiit. [cf. *AFM* 978.1]

CS 980.6 Mugron ab Iae, scriba et episcopus, quieuit.

AU² 980.3 Mughron, comarba Coluim Cille eter Erinn 7 Albain uitam felicem finiuit.

CS 980.7 Amlaibh mac Sitriucca, ard rí Gall Atha Cliath go hÍ an deoraidhacht iar sanct, iar n-aithrige, mortuus est.

AT 980.6 Amlaim mac Sitriuca, airdrigh ar Gallaibh Atha Cliath, do dul co hÍ a n-aithrighe 7 a n-ailithri iarsin cath, mortuus est. [cf. also *AFM*, *AClon*]

AU² 986.3 Í Coluim Cille do arcain do Danaraibh adhchi Notlaic coro marbsat in apaidh 7 .xu. uiros do sruithibh na cille.

ARC [986] Mael Ciarain ua Máigne, comarba Coluim Cille, do dul deargmartra lasna Danaru in Ath Cliath. (cf. *CS*, *AClon*, *AFM*)

Two of these men, Fothud mac Brain and Mugrón, are described as bishops with putatively wide jurisdictions, while we hear also of a bishop of the community (Fingin in 966) and an *airchinnech* (the already mentioned Fiachra ua hArtacáin in 978). The strange and bloody events of Christmas Eve 986 suggest also not just annalistic but also political attention on Iona, as does the decision of Amlaíb Cuarán to retire there after the battle of Tara in 980.[25] At least for this period, then, Iona seems to have had the limelight among contemporary observers of the fortunes of the Columban *familia*.

Key in any reassessment of this period is the figure of Mugrón, *comarba* from 964 to 980, a span which seems neatly to coincide with Amlaíb Cuarán's sole and stable dominance of Dublin and the Scandinavian settlements of the Irish Sea and Hebrides generally. For Mugrón we have three seemingly separate obits in different annals. Herbert dismissed as generalisation the entry in AU which calls him *comarba Coluim Cille eter Erinn 7 Albain*. However, this is not a formula previously used in AU, or one likely to be simply repeated by a scribe, and should be taken seriously, despite Herbert's assertion that there was no interest among Columba's Irish churches in any of the eastern ones, besides Iona.[26] Equally, she engaged in a rather circular argument in order to dismiss the witness of the *Chronicum Scotorum*, suggesting that they call him abbot of Iona because they misunderstood the sort of entry we have in the Annals of Ulster; while discussing it she noted 'there is no indication that Mugrón lived in Iona'.[27] Colmán Etchingham, however, shed light on this by noting that the probably

---

[25] There is not space here properly to discuss the thorny issue of the identity or otherwise of the abbot of Iona killed in 986, and the *comarba Choluim Chille* also killed that year. In a forthcoming note this will be thoroughly examined: suffice it to say I think these individuals are the same.

[26] Herbert, *Iona, Kells and Derry*, 82–3.

[27] *Ibid.*, 82.

independent witness of the Annals of Roscrea seems to resolve the issue.[28] It calls him not only abbot of Iona but also scribe and 'pre-eminent-bishop of the Three Parts'.

In the context of these three varied witnesses, then, it seems clear that we should accept that Mugrón was both abbot of Iona (not Kells) and also successor of Colum Cille. This is clearly what the evidence suggests to be the case. What, then, of the statement that Mugrón was 'pre-eminent-bishop of the Three Parts'? Etchingham, in a thorough discussion of the still elusive term *suí-epscop*, concludes that this was a bishop who had a pre-eminent position and who, when linked to episcopal territories, claimed quite extensive domains, such as 'Munster' or Mag mBreg. The 'Three Parts' are more difficult. Etchingham tentatively followed John O'Donovan in seeing these as 'Ireland, Scotland and Man', an idea which seems a bit shaky.[29] To understand better Mugrón's possible sphere of jurisdiction we should turn our attention back to another bishop in the same area.

The previous bishop noted, who is likely to have been situated in Iona, Fothud mac Brain, is described as *episcopus Innsi Alban* 'bishop of the Isles of Alba'.[30] This is a term which appears once elsewhere, in *CS* 941.5, where Muirchertach mac Néill plundered these Isles shortly after the death of Olaf Gothfrithson. *AFM* (939.6), recounting the same events, substitutes *Innsi Gall*, and it is notable that when 'the Isles' appear clearly in the annals, at the end of the tenth century, they are rechristened *Innsi Gall*.[31] Fothad's jurisdiction was most likely to be the Hebrides. Etchingham has suggested that we should postulate 'a precursor of the eleventh- and twelfth-century bishopric of the Isles', which then included also the Isle of Man.[32] I would support this in general terms: there is clear evidence in the form of grave-slabs with Runic inscriptions, and also of later Icelandic traditions, that the Scandinavian overlords and inhabitants of the Hebrides were by the tenth century becoming Christian. *Landnámabók* in particular envisages the importation of the cult of Colum Cille to Iceland from the Hebrides in the later ninth century at least.[33]

It is notable, too, that Fothad's period of activity – before 963 – coincides with

---

[28] C. Etchingham, *Church Organisation in Ireland, AD 650 to 1000* (Maynooth, 1999), 186.

[29] Etchingham, *Church Organisation*, 183–6, at 186, citing O'Donovan's note on *AFM* 978.1. See also his earlier discussion, 'Bishops in the Early Irish Church: A Reassessment', *Studia Hibernica* 28 (1994), 35–62.

[30] *ARC* 963; Etchingham, *Church Organisation*, 186 n. 1 notes a possible linguistic difficulty of Innsi as gen. pl. and proposes to amend to Innse. Roughly contemporary forms elsewhere in the Annals of Ulster (e.g. *AU²* 1005.1) do not suggest that emendation is necessary. The absence of nasalisation following the gen. pl. is also shown in contemporary annals. D. N. Dumville, *The Churches of North Britain in the First Viking-Age*, Fifth Whithorn Lecture (Whithorn, 1997), 22 n. 61 worries that the form indicates that it is non-contemporary, but again there is support from roughly contemporary annals elsewhere.

[31] See *AU²* 989.4; for recent discussion and further references see T. O. Clancy, 'The Gall-Ghàidheil and Galloway', *Journal of Scottish Name Studies* 2 (2008), 19–50, at 26–8.

[32] Etchingham, *Church Organisation*, 186; on this diocese and its evolution see A. Woolf, 'The Diocese of Sudreyar', *Ecclesia Nidrosiensis 1153–1537: Søkelys på Nidaroskirkens og Nidarosprovinsens historie*, ed. S. Imsen (Trondheim, 2003), 171–82.

[33] On the conversion of the Hebrides see most recently L. Abrams, 'Conversion and the Church in the Hebrides in the Viking Age: "A very difficult thing indeed"', in *West Over Sea: Studies in Scandinavian Sea-Borne Expansion and Settlement before 1300*, ed. B. Ballin-Smith, S. Taylor and G. Williams (Leiden and Boston, 2007), 169–93.

the 'silent period' of Amlaíb Cuarán.[34] From the time of his second expulsion from York, around 951, until his clear activity as king in Dublin from around 962 or 964, Amlaíb appears only fitfully as a raider alongside others. It is very uncertain where he was during this period. Certainly, as is evident from the annals, he had friends in place among native Irish dynasts;[35] equally it is clear that Dublin could contain multiple factions at some periods.[36] On the other hand, aspects of his subsequent career, and the implication, c.980, that he controlled *Gaill ... na nInnsedh*, 'the foreigners of the Isles',[37] suggest that he may have been consolidating his control over the Hebrides and the Isle of Man.[38] In this context it may be that Fothad's presence as a bishop of 'the Isles of Alba' represents the first phase of a programme of expanding church patronage by Amlaíb in the Isles, to be later developed further in Brega and Leinster.

It is in light of this background that I would suggest, tentatively, that the otherwise unattested *Trí Rainn* mentioned in *ARC* as Mugrón's area of episcopal jurisdiction are the three parts of Amlaíb's dominion: Dublin and its hinterland, the Isles and Man. Episcopal jurisdiction of this politically contingent variety seems to match some of the other 'titles' for bishops given in tenth-century annals.[39] As abbot of Iona, then, and potentially as bishop over Amlaíb's domain, Mugrón emerges as a key figure in the period in question, and his career, 964–80, neatly shadows the period of Amlaíb's greatest dominance.

Before leaving Mugrón, I would like to consider one final piece of evidence relating to him. The description of him as *scriba optimus* in *ARC*, if not purely formulaic, may well be based on his literary endeavours. Mugrón is ascribed several poems of differing quality, some at least of which may actually be his work.[40] One poem in praise of Columba, notably, praises him not only in relation to Aran and Leinster (never Ireland specifically), but first and foremost as *cend Alban*, in sea-based imagery: *grinde im ghargbladh tar gargler; bárc bardlógh gan ordal*.[41] It is not that poem I wish to draw attention to here, however. Another, under-noticed and unedited, poem preserved in one manuscript, London, British Library, Add. 30512, f.40b,[42] is an elegy on the death of Congalach mac Maíle Mithig, attributed to Mugrón, *comarba Coluim Cille*.

---

34 On this period in Amlaíb's career see Woolf, 'Amlaíb Cuarán', 39–40. Downham, *Viking Kings*, 47–9 has accepted the problematic evidence from *AFM* 951.22 (= 953) and 954.7 (= 956), and sees Amlaíb in control of Dublin from the 950s. The evidence is either absent (nothing in the 953 entry necessitates him ruling in Dublin) or inconclusive (the 956 entry names Amlaíb mac Gofraid: see below for another solution to this), and on balance I would favour Woolf's analysis of the period.

35 So, we find him in alliance with the king of northern Leinster in sacking sites in southern Leinster (*AFM* 953); see Downham, *Viking Kings*, 48; and for the identity of the site sacked in 953, M. Ní Dhonnchadha, 'Inis Teimle, between Uí Chennselaig and the Déissi', *Peritia* 16 (2002), 451–8.

36 On the factionalism of the Viking community in Ireland see Woolf, 'Amlaíb Cuarán'.

37 See *AU²* 980.1.

38 See Woolf's description of Man as 'the real Heart of Darkness in the Uí Ímair imperium' ('Amlaíb Cuarán', 37).

39 See Etchingham, *Church Organisation*, 183–6; I have suggested this solution already in print: Clancy, 'Gall-Ghàidheil', 28.

40 For most of the corpus see *The Triumph Tree: Scotland's Earliest Poetry, AD 550–350*, ed. T. O. Clancy (Edinburgh, 1998), 158–63, and sources there cited, 334.

41 'Keen for fierce fame over rough seas, matchless barque of bards' rewards': Clancy, *Triumph Tree*, 158; K. Meyer, 'Mitteilungen aus irische Handschriften', *ZCP* 10 (1915), 340.

42 R. Flower, *Catalogue of Irish Manuscripts in the British Library [formerly British Museum]*, vol. 2 (London 1926; repr. Dublin, 1992), 492, §66. Another poem, also found elsewhere (Oxford,

It is possible that the ascription is a false one, and that it is the sort of 'chronicle' poem which is found in, for example, *AFM* (941.7), where one such piece of verse is also ascribed to Mugrón. However, although it does include some 'dating doggerel' (including a precise day for the battle, nowhere else preserved: 19 July: *quartdecim kl-auguist*), it is nonetheless in other respects a straightforward elegy, and includes at least one detail which is not much noted in the annalistic entries of Congalach's death, at the hands of the Scandinavians of Dublin, in an ambush in 956: his nephew, the son of Aed mac Maíle Mithig, died alongside him.[43] As the poem says:[44]

> Mac a brathar, dirsan dó
> dellig lais i lligi cró;
> Matadán, ba maith a lí,
> mac Aeda co ndubsaigi.

The poem describes Congalach in very complimentary terms: *ardrí Érenn*, 'high king of Ireland', *sluagrí síl Aeda Sláine*, 'the army-king of Sil nAeda Sláine', *Conglach cleithe Gaidhel*, 'Congalach, ridge-pole/roof-tree of the Gaels'. And his death is described in sombre tones: *Duaibsech laithi fri cech toisc*, 'An unlucky day for every business', begins the poem. The day of his death was *satharn serblonn*, 'the full-bitter Saturday'.

On the face of it, there is nothing remarkable about this. However, we should consider that, if this is genuinely a poem by Mugrón, it is written about a figure who seems to have been vilified by segments of the Columban *familia*, particularly those based in Kells. Máire Herbert and Pádraig Ó Riain have made a strong case for seeing in some of the characters, who were subjected to the most negative spin in the tenth-century Kells composition *Betha Adamnáin*, a shadow of the figure of Congalach (though I will return later to other questions concerning this Life). In particular, they see references to the granting of freedom from tribute to non-Columban churches by the king of Tara in the Life as a clear negative reference to Congalach's granting of freedom to Clonard in 951; reference to raids on Kells' hinterland by Saxons in the text as referring to Congalach's putative connivance with Gothfrith mac Sitriuca's sacking of Kells and other monasteries in 951; and the description of the violent and just death of

---

Bodleian Library, Rawlinson B.512, fo. 42ra21), attributed to Mugrón, is preserved in this manuscript without the ascription (*ibid.*, 490, §62), on which see C. Plummer, *Irish Litanies*, HBS 62 (London, 1925, repr. Woodbridge, 1992), pp. xxi, 78–85.

43 *CS* and *AFM* note this detail. For the annals relating this see *AU²* 956.3: Congalach m. Mael Mithidh ... ri Erenn, do marbad do Gallaib Atha Cliath 7 Laignib oc Taigh Giurann i lLaighnibh, 7 Aedh m. Aichidi, ri Tethba 7 alii multi, 'Congalach m. Maíle Mithig ... king of Ireland, was killed by the foreigners of Áth Cliath and by the Laigin at Tech Giurann in Laigin; and Aed son of Aichid, king of Tethba, [and Matudán m. Aeda m. Maíle Mithig *CS*, *AFM*] and many others.' [*AFM* add that ro h-indleadh caithedarnaigh leó fór cind Congalaig, 'Amlaíb m. Gothfrith laid an ambush for Congalach']. The Matudán mac Aeda recorded as dying in *AU²* 950.4 was the king of Ulaid (see *CS* 950.3).

44 'His brother's son, alas for him/he has lain down with him in a bloody bed / Matudán, good was his beauty / mac Aeda, unluckily.' Transcriptions of the poem and translations are my own. I hope to provide an edition of the poem in the near future; the planned revised edition of *The Triumph Tree* will contain a translation. Regarding the date of the battle, 19 July was a Saturday in 956, so these two separate pieces of information in the poem tally.

a disrespectful king of Tara in an expedition to Leinster as a clear reflection of Congalach's own violent death in similar circumstances.[45]

Thus, whether the elegy on Congalach is actually by him, or even if it is only traditionally ascribed to him, it seems to give Mugrón a stance on the issues of the day contrary to those we might expect to be held by a contemporary Kells churchman. It sides Mugrón, abbot of Iona and bishop of the Three Parts, not alongside his Columban brethren in the Clann Cholmáin-dominated monastery of Kells, but alongside the kings of Brega, who, as I will show in more detail below, maintained a close allegiance with Amlaíb Cuarán and his sons over more than half a century. This also helps to make sense of Iona, Mugrón's base by this stage of his career, as the location for Amlaíb Cuarán's final pilgrimage. The probably incorrect information, deriving from one reading of *AFM*, that Amlaíb Cuarán was the king of the Scandinavians of Dublin who connived in Congalach's death in 956 has masked the real durability of the relationship between the kings of Brega and Amlaíb. The annals can be read differently, however, to suggest that, whoever was in charge in Dublin in 956 (and that is far from clear), it was probably not Amlaíb Cuarán.[46]

I wish now to return to the nexus of relationships which can be seen during these years and to situate the developments in the Columban *familia* among them. Chief among these is one I have already alluded to, the alliance between Amlaíb Cuarán and Congalach mac Maíle Mithig, which was continued by their descendants.[47] There are some fairly explicit examples of co-operation between these parties and some that may be inferred. This is not the place for an exhaustive discussion of the issue, but I would like to note that I depart from previous discussions, such as those of Smyth, Jaski and Downham, in my interpretation of several key events and key players of this period. Thus, although Congalach's father had allied himself in 918 with the Scandinavians *quod ei nihil contulit,*[48] we are told, Congalach and his descendants did not ally themselves with just any Scandinavians. It may be of significance in this that Amlaíb was a baptised Christian.[49] So, while Amlaíb during the early part of his career was away trying to rule in York, Congalach consistently opposed Blacaire and ultimately killed him in 948. Woolf has noted that we must refrain from monolithic ethnic constructs in our understanding of the mechanisms of Scandinavian power in the tenth century, and instead think of partisan or factional behaviour. The changeover

---

45 M. Herbert and P. Ó Riain, ed., *Betha Adamnáin: The Irish Life of Adamnán*, Irish Texts Society 54 (London, 1988), 8–20.
46 On this see esp. Woolf, 'Amlaíb Cuarán', 41. Downham appears to accept Amlaíb as Congalach's killer (*Viking Kings*, 48), as has most recently Bhreathnach, 'Ireland', 278. *AFM* 954.7 actually ascribes the deed to 'Amlaoibh mac Gofradha', and it is only one solution to emend this to 'Amlaoibh mac [Sitriuca]'. Another solution to his identity might be to take this as a mistake for the [Gofraid mac] Amlaíb m[ei]c Gofraid who may have been ruling Dublin until his death in 963 (see Woolf, 'Amlaíb Cuarán', 41, on this figure; he does not suggest the emendation I propose here).
47 A. P. Smyth, *Scandinavian York and Dublin*, vol. II (New Jersey / Dublin, 1979), 128–51, details these relationships, *inter alia.*
48 'which availed him not at all': *AU²* 918.7.
49 *The Anglo-Saxon Chronicle: A Collaborative Edition*, gen. ed. D. Dumville and S. Keynes (Cambridge, 1983–), versions ABC and D, at 943; Woolf, 'Amlaíb Cuarán', 37. One might note that Mael Mithig had allied himself with *gente*; by Congalach's time these were viewed as *gaill*, an important change of nomenclature.

between Amlaíb and Blacaire was probably not an amicable one, but rather the edgy exchange of rivals.

Certainly, after Amlaíb's second expulsion from York, in 952 or 951, there is no clarity at all about whether he regained the kingship of Dublin then, and it seems he did not until 963.[50] Thus, rather than Amlaíb Cuarán, it is probably the otherwise shady Gothfrith mac Amlaíb meic Gothfrith who was ruling during the period 954–6, when the Gaill seem to be conniving against Congalach and ultimately ambushed him. Realisation of this helps to pave the way for understanding why Domnall mac Congalaig operated alongside Amlaíb (otherwise his father's killer) in such an effective way. We can see both coming into their own in 964. That year, following the death of Gothfrith mac Amlaíb, Domnall mac Congalaig killed his brother, paving the way for his own achievement of the kingship of Brega, and probably concentrating the mind of his uncle on pilgrimage to far-away St Andrews.[51] Similarly, the plundering of Kildare in 964 by Amlaíb represents the first full action of his new career.

AU² 964.6

Ceall Dara do arcain do Ghall*aib*, sed míserabile pietate misertus est tria Niall H. n-Eruilbh redemptis omnibus clericis pene pro nomine Domini, .i. lan in taighi moir Sanc Brigti & lan in derthaigi iss *ed* do-ruagell Niall diibh dia argat fesin.[52]

Is it coincidence that, soon after the raid, the abbess died and was succeeded by Muirenn, the sister of Domnall mac Congalaig, king of Brega?[53]

Certainly, two actions suggest the strength of the alliance between these two. First, in 970, Amlaíb sacked Kells and Domnall and Amlaíb jointly defeated the king of Tara, Domnall ua Néill. Second, Domnall mac Congalaig was given Ragnailt, daughter of Amlaíb Cuarán, as his wife.[54] It is not clear when this happened, though it is likely to have been after 964. According to the *Banshenchas*, Domnall had three wives. One was Bé Binn, the wife of Fergal ua Ruairc, whom he slew in 966; she may have been a symbolic wife of conquest rather than anything else.[55] Certainly, Ragnailt was the mother of Domnall's son

---

50 Woolf, 'Amlaíb Cuarán', 38–9.
51 *AU²* 964.5, *CS* 964.6, 965.1. Of course, this fratricide might suggest that Domnall was not one to let the little matter of his father's murder stand in the way of a useful alliance!
52 Kildare was plundered by the foreigners [and by Amlaíb m. Sitriucca *CS*], but was spared by miraculous piety through Niall ua Eruilb, almost all the clerics being ransomed for the honour of God: with his own silver Niall ransomed of them as many as would fill Brigit's great house and the oratory.
53 A question also posed by Woolf, 'Amlaíb Cuarán', 41. For Muirenn, Domnall's sister, see *AU²* 967.1; the death of the previous abbess is noted in *CS* 964.2. Niall ua Eruilb, who appears several times in the annals, and from his grandfather's name and other relations looks likely to be Scandinavian (his name derived from ON Herjólfr), seems to have been missed in Downham's prosopography in *Viking Kings*. On this family, with a cautious, though probably correct, suggestion that the family grafted its genealogy onto that of the Uí Néill fictitiously, see D. Thornton, 'Clann Eruilb: Irish or Scandinavian?', *Irish Historical Studies* 30 (1996), 161–6.
54 What follows owes much to the unpublished observations and genealogical tables of Anne Connon, particularly as presented in the *International Congress of Celtic Studies*, Cork, 1999. Woolf, 'Amlaíb Cuarán' presents some of this information also. The data is drawn from M. E. Dobbs, 'The Ban-shenchus', *Revue Celtique* 47 (1930), 312–13, 336–7; *Revue Celtique* 48 (1931), 188.
55 *Ibid.*

Muirchertach, who died as king of Brega in 995.[56] It is Muirchertach who last shows us the alliance in action. The year after the expulsion of Sitriuc, son of Amlaíb Cuarán, from Dublin in 994 we find Muirchertach allied alongside the Dubliners in raiding Domnach Pátraic, a Clann Cholmáin church to judge from other attacks on it. This sequence of revenge attacks also suggests that Swords was still seen as within the ambit of Amlaíb's descendants, as Mael Sechnaill targeted it in 994, just prior to his expulsion of Sitriuc.[57]

Thus the kings of Brega emerge as the partners of Amlaíb Cuarán and his dynasty in his rise to power. In such a context it is less surprising to see other Brega families built into this network, such as the Clann Cernaig Sotail, from whom was descended Cinaed ua hArtacáin, chief poet whom Amlaíb patronised. Cinaed was plausibly linked by the late Mairtín Ó Briain with Monasterboice,[58] and this monastery too seems during this period linked into the Dublin–Brega axis: it was one of the churches sacked by Domnall ua Néill in 970 to avenge his defeat by Amlaíb and Domnall of Brega. So, too, the presence of Cinaed's kinsman Fiachra as *airchinnech* of Iona in 978 fits into a wider context of alliances.

It is within this greater network of alliances that we should situate the development by Amlaíb Cuarán of new and renewed centres of Columban power in Scrín Coluim Cille, perhaps in Sord Coluim Cille and most of all in Iona. And it is within the context of enmity between this alliance and the rulers most closely associated with Kells that we should associate what now looks like the *exclusion* of Kells from the successorship of Colum Cille until 1007. Given John Bannerman's meditations (though they are not entirely persuasive) that it was possession of the corporeal relics of a founding saint which allowed a cleric to claim successorship to that saint,[59] we may well wonder whether Woolf is not correct to see the 970 raid as having extracted the relics of Columba from Kells. Such activity was not unprecedented.[60] And, read in this light, the successive attacks by Domnall ua Néill on the significantly named churches of Scrín Coluim Cille in 976 and Scrín Adomnáin in 978 may indicate that these 'shrines' were less innocuous than they at first appear.[61] Were they seeking to recapture relics of these saints? Continuing in this speculative vein, it is at least worth noting that where we see the presence of relics in Kells in the eleventh century, these are secondary relics: the *flabellum*; the great gospel book; for a time, perhaps, the *Cathach*.[62] Equally, it seems that in the early thirteenth century Iona thought that they had held the body of the saint, and traditions of the visit of Magnus

---

56 *Ibid.* There is some irony in Domnall naming his son after the brother he murdered. Muirchertach had a different mother from Domnall, being the son of Eithne daughter of Fergal mac Domnaill of the Northern Uí Néill, whilst Domnall was the son of Deichter of Southern Brega.

57 *AU²* 994.3, 994.6, 995.2.

58 M. Ó Briain, 'Some Aspects of the Poetry of Cináed Úa hArtacáin', unpublished paper given at International Congress of Celtic Studies, 11th July, 1991. I am grateful to the late Dr Ó Briain for having sent me a copy of this paper.

59 Bannerman, 'Comarba Coluim Chille'.

60 For the phenomenon in a wider European context see P. Geary, *Furta Sacra: Thefts of Relics in the Central Middle Ages* (Princeton, NJ, 1978).

61 *CS* 976.3, 978.1.

62 On Columba's relics generally see R. Ó Floinn, 'Insigniae Columbae I', in *Studies in the Cult of Saint Columba*, ed. C. Bourke (Dublin, 1997), 136–61.

Barelegs to the island in 1098 suggests that perhaps there were corporeal relics there then.[63]

It is worth stressing, finally, that this revision means that the issue of coarbial jurisdiction is left wide open in the monastic *familia* which had hitherto seemed most straightforwardly understood. Abbots continued in place in Iona throughout the tenth and eleventh century, and some of these, it is clear, became coarbs. Equally, in the middle of the tenth century, and even at its opening, while we are presented with individuals who would appear not to be based on Iona, the evidence is very far from suggesting that Kells had emerged to fill its place. Rather, until 1007 we seem to be dealing with a period of factionalism and political contingency in which the heavyweight tradition of Iona as the *familia*'s spiritual hub still had much to offer, and in which the royal monastery of Kells had not yet become sufficiently uncontroversial to carry the title. That sense of the *familia*, and the annalists feeling their way with both jurisdiction and terminology, is reflected well in the early eleventh century, in which terms like *comarba Iae* and *comarba Cenannsa* appear. The details of that period should be revisited in light of the present study, as it looks now as if that was the period of real jurisdictional change.

I would like to finish by reflecting on the historical context of the Middle Irish Life of Adomnán, *Betha Adamnáin*. While I fully agree with the arguments assigning the Life a *terminus post quem* of 956, since the account of the death of the king of Tara Congal seems designed to remind the reader of Congalach's death in Leinster in 956, the *terminus ante quem* of 964 is problematic. Both Caoimhín Breatnach and Mairtín Ó Briain pointed out a series of problems with it in important reviews of the Herbert and Ó Riain edition.[64] As Breatnach noted, several events in the 970s can be seen to be reflected in episodes in the Life which the editors nonetheless argued fixed the text to before 964. For example, Herbert and Ó Riain felt the absence of any reference to the Dál Cais meant that it could not post-date their rise from 964. Breatnach noted, however, that in the mid-970s Mael Muad of the Éoganacht Caisil was a strong resister of Dál Cais claims, and was called king of Caisel on his death in 978. The work might thus belong to this period quite precisely.

In this context we need to ask why Congalach's death should be recalled in the way it is in the first place. Surely the most potent recipient of the messages of his ill fate would be his successors, and in particular his son, Domnall mac Congalaig, king of Brega. But Domnall's rise to power did not really begin until 964. Equally, the editors connected the incident describing the Saxon raid on Brega with the Scandinavian sacking of Kells in 951, as the episode is brought into the hinterland of Kells in the Life. Equally, however, it recalls Amlaíb Cuarán's sacking of Kells in 970, here much more likely to be in cahoots with the king of Brega than was the Scandinavian leader in 951. Most telling of all is the episode which most troubled the editors, in which Adomnán deprived Írgalach ua Conaing and his descendants from the kingship for having killed Niall mac Cernaig. They were unable to find a telling parallel for this, but Breatnach

---

63 Clancy, *Triumph Tree*, 242–6; and on Magnus's visit see RCAHMS, *Argyll 4: Iona* (Edinburgh, 1982), 42.

64 C. Breatnach, 'Review', *Éigse* 26 (1992), 177–87, esp. 180–1; M. Ó Briain, 'Review', *Studia Hibernica* 27 (1993), 155–8, at 158.

provided the clear parallel with the treacherous killing of Fócartach m. Néill uí Tholairg, a descendant of Niall mac Cernaig, in 972. The killer of Fócartach was none other than Domnall mac Congalaig.[65] In other words, although the text looks back to the events of the 950s, it does so by way of reminding the text's political target of the fate of his father, and draws on more recent events in his own life. It thus seems most likely to be partly directed at Domnall mac Congalaig, king of Brega, who, though no king of Tara at the time, was certainly a power to be reckoned with in the early 970s.[66]

The clear opposition displayed in the Life of Adomnán to a key figure in the nexus of alliances outlined above seems to me to support the general thrust of this essay, that far from being at the head of a united *familia* in the period from 956 to 986, Kells was on the other side of a political divide from Iona, and other Columban churches patronised by Amlaíb Cuarán. For much, if not all of this period, the *comarbus* rested with Iona, not Kells, and Kells looks more like a partisan royal monastery than the head of a monastic federation. Returning for one final time to Alex Woolf's speculation about Columba's relics after 970, is it worth wondering why an author based in Kells had to look to Adomnán, rather than Columba himself, for the authority which would allow Kells to oppose the growing powers around them with saintly vigour? Who had the relics which would allow them to claim Columba's authority for their jurisdiction?[67]

---

65 *AU²* 972.4; Breatnach, 'Review', 181.

66 See Ó Briain, 'Review', 158.

67 This contribution has a somewhat extended history. It was presented as a paper to the Irish Conference of Medievalists in Maynooth, 2000; its ideas had been sparked by a sequence of papers whose imprint it bears: Edel Bhreathnach's paper to the 1997 Derry conference (later published as 'Columban Churches'); Alex Woolf's paper to a conference in Stornoway, 2000 (later published in part as 'Amlaíb Cuarán'); Anne Connon's unpublished paper at the 1999 ICCS in Cork on the wives of rulers of Tara in the tenth century. I am very grateful to Edel Bhreathnach and Alex Woolf for their encouragement and advice in the original construction of the paper. Their published work subsequently, and the work of David Dumville, Clare Downham and others, has forced a certain amount of rethinking and redrafting.

9

A TWELFTH-CENTURY INDULGENCE GRANTED BY AN IRISH BISHOP AT BATH PRIORY

Marie Therese Flanagan

A cartulary of the Benedictine cathedral priory of Bath, which on the evidence of its script has been dated to around the mid-twelfth century, contains an indulgence granted by Marcus *Cluanensis episcopus* to the 'truly penitent' who with alms and prayers would visit the church at Bath on the feast of the Exaltation of the Cross (14 September).[1] The text, which is printed in Appendix 1,[2] is preceded in the cartulary by similar indulgences from Theobald, archbishop of Canterbury (1138–61),[3] and Robert, bishop of Bath (1136–66),[4] and followed by one from Nicholas, bishop of Llandaff (1148–83).[5] As is usual in texts of indulgences, none contains a witness-list and this makes dating difficult, with the added consequence in the case of Marcus that his very identity remains obscure. The four indulgences evidently form a series, as in each the period of remission is twenty

---

[1] Cambridge, Corpus Christi College, MS 111, p. 54. For a description of the manuscript, see M. R. James, *A Descriptive Catalogue of the Manuscripts in the Library of Corpus Christi College, Cambridge*, 2 vols (Cambridge, 1912), I.236–47. For its dating to the mid-twelfth century, see also R. H. C. Davis, *Medieval Cartularies of Great Britain: A Short Catalogue* (London, 1958), 5; S. E. Kelly, ed., *Charters of Bath and Wells*, Anglo-Saxon Charters 13 (Oxford 2007), 25–30. The indulgence is printed without the full salutation clause in W. Hunt, ed., *Two Chartularies of the Priory of St Peter at Bath*, Somerset Record Society 7 (London, 1893), 2; cf. p. xlvii, where Marcus is identified as bishop of Clonmacnois.

[2] See below, p. 114.

[3] Printed in Hunt, *Two Chartularies*, 2; A. Saltman, *Theobald, Archbishop of Canterbury* (London, 1956), 241–2. For a tally of at least twenty-four indulgences issued by Theobald, see N. Vincent, 'Some Pardoners' Tales: The Earliest English Indulgences', *Transactions of the Royal Historical Society* 6th series 12 (2002), 23–58, at 39.

[4] Printed in Hunt, *Two Chartularies*, 2; F. M. R. Ramsey, ed., *English Episcopal Acta X: Bath and Wells, 1061–1205* (Oxford, 1995), 13–14.

[5] Printed in A. W. Haddan and W. Stubbs, ed., *Councils and Ecclesiastical Documents Relating to Great Britain and Ireland*, 3 vols (Oxford, 1869–78), I.357; Hunt, *Two Chartularies*, 2–3; calendared in J. Conway Davies, *Episcopal Acts Relating to Welsh Dioceses*, 2 vols, Historical Society of the Church in Wales, 1, 3, 4 ([Cardiff], 1946–8), II.645, where it is dated without explanation to 1148×50; also in D. Crouch, *Llandaff Episcopal Acta* (Cardiff, 1988), 3–4, where a date range 1148×61 is proposed, evidently treating the four indulgences as a series. Conway Davies's narrower date-range appears to have derived from Haddan and Stubbs's unlikely suggestion that Marcus *Cluanensis* could have been 'Maurice of Tuam', alias Muiredach Ua Dubthaig, whose death as *airdespoc Connacht 7 Erenn* is recorded on 16 May 1150 (*AT*, *CS*, *AFM*). Muiredach occurs with the Latinised name of Mauritius in a necrology of the *Schottenkloster* of Würzburg and in a charter issued by Diarmait Mac Carthaig, king of Desmond, 1167×75: M. T. Flanagan, *Irish Royal Charters: Texts and Contexts* (Oxford, 2005), 334–5, 336. For other indulgences granted by Nicholas of Llandaff, see below, notes 11, 13.

days and is linked to the celebration of the same feast.[6] However, there are also differences in the wording of the four texts which may indicate that they were not necessarily issued on the same occasion.[7] The indulgence of Robert, bishop of Bath, recorded that he had consecrated a cross in the cathedral church on the feast of the Exaltation of the Cross, and it was the acquisition of this new cross which appears to have occasioned the indulgences. It is conceivable that Robert may have been assisted at the consecration ceremony by one or more of the other bishops who also granted indulgences.[8]

As a group, the latest date for the four indulgences' issue would be 1161, when Archbishop Theobald died, while the earliest would be the accession of Robert as bishop of Bath in 1136. The date limits would be narrowed to 1148×61 if the consecration of Nicholas as bishop of Llandaff on 14 March 1148[9] by Archbishop Theobald is factored in and the assumption made that none of the indulgences pre-dated Nicholas's consecration. Taking account of the supposition that the compilation of the cartulary may have been preparatory to a request for a papal confirmation that was procured by the priory of Bath from Pope Adrian IV on 21 January 1156 would narrow the date limits to 1148×56.[10]

The indulgence of Archbishop Theobald not only granted twenty days' remission to those visiting the cathedral church of Bath on the feast of the Exaltation of the Cross but also extended to participants the benefits of the prayers and good works of the church of Canterbury. Likewise, Nicholas, bishop of Llandaff, conjoined spiritual benefits from the church of Llandaff to his indulgence.[11] Before his elevation to the episcopate Nicholas, by his own testimony, had been a monk for thirty years in the Benedictine abbey of St Peter's, Gloucester,[12] and this, coupled with the relative proximity of Llandaff, serves to explain his association with the Benedictine priory at Bath.[13] Marcus's indulgence is the

---

[6] The feast of the Exaltation of the Holy Cross is included in the twelfth-century *Félire hÚi Gormáin: The Martyrology of Gorman*; ed. W. Stokes, HBS 9 (London, 1895), 176–7.

[7] That the salutation clause is similar in all four indulgences is obscured by the abbreviated texts in Hunt, *Two Chartularies*.

[8] For rites of dedication of a wooden and a metal crucifix by a bishop in the Romano-Germanic pontifical, the most widely disseminated in this period, see C. Vogel and R. Elze, ed., *Le Pontifical Romano-Germanique du Dixième Siècle*, 3 vols, Studi e Testi 226, 227, 269 (Rome, 1963–72), I.157–61.

[9] W. Stubbs, ed., *The Historical Works of Gervase of Canterbury*, 2 vols, RS (London, 1879–80), II.385; Conway Davies, *Episcopal Acts*, II.645; Saltman, *Theobald*, 105–6.

[10] Kelly, *Charters of Bath and Wells*, 23, 26. For Adrian's privilege, see Hunt, *Two Chartularies*, 68–70; W. Holtzman, *Papsturkunden in England*, 2 vols, Abhandlungen der Akademie der Wissenschaften in Göttingen, Philologisch-Historische Klasse, Neue Folge 25, Dritte Folge 14 (Berlin, 1930–5), II.269–71.

[11] Cf. his grant of remission of twenty days' penance to all who would visit Reading Abbey on the feast of St James the Apostle or who, in the eight days following the feast, would confer any gift for the honour of God and his apostle, and including a clause that recipients would be sharers in the prayers and spiritual benefits of the church of Llandaff: B. Kemp, ed., *Reading Abbey Cartularies*, 2 vols, Camden Society, 4th series 31, 33 (London, 1986–7), I.152–3; Crouch, *Llandaff*, 24.

[12] Conway Davies, *Episcopal Acts*, II.521–2, 655; Saltman, *Theobald*, 106, where it is suggested that Nicholas was the special choice of Archbishop Theobald. Cf. Theobald's mandates to Nicholas describing him as *venerabili fratri et amico*: *ibid.*, 338, 340, 405.

[13] Nicholas, at the request of Prior Peter and the entire convent of Bath, subsequently dedicated a chapel in the suburb of the city of Bath in honour of Saints Werburga, John the Evangelist, and Katherine and granted remission of twenty days' penance to those who confessed in the chapel on the respective feasts of its patron saints: Haddan and Stubbs, *Councils*, I.157. For the probability

exception in not offering a spiritual association with his own cathedral church. That omission, which may be significant, may be linked to the question of the identity of Marcus's diocese and whether he was in possession of his see at the time of granting the indulgence.

The name-form *Cluanensis*[14] is ambiguous in that it might connote a number of Irish dioceses: Cluain moccu Nóis or Clonmacnois, Cluain Uama or Cloyne, Cluain Iraird or Clonard, Cluain Ferta Brénainn or Clonfert. From this list, the first two are *a priori* more likely as *Cluanensis* is attested as a Latin rendering for both Clonmacnois[15] and Cloyne,[16] while *Clunardensis/Cluenardensis*[17] usually occurs as a Latinisation of Clonard and *Cluanfertensis/Clonfertensis*[18] of Clonfert. Additionally, the episcopal succession lists of Clonard and Clonfert, though not indubitably complete, appear to rule out a bishop from either of those two dioceses. Petrus Ua Mórda, previously abbot of the Cistercian community which later settled at Boyle, died as bishop of Clonfert on 27 December 1171[19] and had probably succeeded to that office by the time of the synod of Kells in 1152.[20]

---

that this indulgence was issued during a vacancy in the see of Bath between 1166 and 1173, see Crouch, *Llandaff*, 4.

14 The adjective *Cluanensis* is to be interpreted as designating the place of his origin (in whatever sense); typically such Latin adjectives are formed by adding *-ensis* to a Latinised form of the Irish place-name.

15 M. P. Sheehy, ed., *Pontificia Hibernica*, 2 vols (Dublin, 1962–5), II, nos 232 (*Cluanensi*), 243 (*Cluanensibus*). For *Clonensi, Cloinensis, Clonensis*, see *idem*, nos 220, 222, 355, 470; for *Clonensi, Clunonensi*, see J. T. Gilbert, ed., *Chartularies of St Mary's Abbey, Dublin, 1162–1370*, 2 vols, RS (London, 1884–6) I.154, II.7, 29. For thirteenth-century forms in the cartulary of Reading Abbey, see below, n. 71.

16 For *Cloensis*, see J. T. Gilbert, ed., *Register of the Abbey of St Thomas the Martyr, Dublin*, RS (London, 1889), 319. For *Cluanensem, Clonensi, Clonensibus*, see Sheehy, *Pontificia*, I, no. 68; II, nos 309, 357, 374, 384. For *Cluanensis, Cluenensis* in the *Visio Tnugdali*, see below, p. 106, n. 25. Closer to the Irish is *Episcopatus de cluanuama* in the list of sees endorsed by Cardinal Paparo at the synod of Kells preserved in the *Liber Censuum*, the *provinciale* of Albinus, and a Montpellier manuscript associated with the Cistercian abbey of Pontigny that is dated to the third quarter of the twelfth century: P. Fabre and L. Duchesne, ed., *Liber Censuum de l'Église Romaine*, 3 vols (Paris, 1889–1952), I.234; II.101. H. J. Lawlor, 'A Fresh Authority for the Synod of Kells', *PRIA* 36C (1922), 16–22, at 18; discussion in A. Gwynn, *The Irish Church in the Eleventh and Twelfth Centuries*, ed. G. O'Brien (Blackrock, Co. Dublin, 1992), 223. For the date and provenance of the Pontigny manuscript, see M. Peyrafort-Huin, *La Bibliothèque Médiévale de l'Abbaye de Pontigny (XIIe–XIXe Siècles): Histoire, Inventaires Anciens, Manuscrits, Documents*, Études et Répertoires 60 (Paris [2002]), 541–2. In the list of bishops who swore an oath of loyalty to King Henry II in Ireland, 1171–2 as recorded by Roger of Howden, the form is *Cluanuimensis episcopus*: W. Stubbs, ed., *Gesta Henrici Secundi Benedicti Abbatis*, 2 vols, RS (London, 1867), I.27; *Cluanumensis* in W. Stubbs, ed., *Chronica Rogeri de Houedone*, 4 vols, RS (London, 1868–71), II.31.

17 *Clunardensis*: Gilbert, *Chartularies*, I.91; Gilbert, *Register*, 257–60; *Cluenardensis* in Stubbs, *Gesta*, I.26; *Cluenerardensis* in Stubbs, *Chronica*, II.30.

18 *Cluanferdensi, Cluanfertensi*: Sheehy, *Pontificia*, I, nos 50, 73, 111, 112.

19 He died by drowning in the River Shannon: *ABoyle, AU, ALC, AFM, AI* 1171.6.

20 The date of his accession as bishop of Clonfert is unknown. He is recorded to have been the first abbot of the Cistercian community at Grellach Dá Iach, which subsequently moved to Druim Connaid and then to Bun Finne, before finally settling at Boyle in 1161: *ABoyle*, 1161. The date of foundation of Boyle is given in *ABoyle* and the Cistercian filiation tables as 1148: G. Mac Niocaill, *Na Manaigh Liatha in Éirinn* (Dublin, 1961), 8–9. No bishop of Clonfert is named by Geoffrey Keating as present at the synod of Kells in 1152, although this may be owing to an omission, since the bishopric of Clonfert does occur in the Latin lists of dioceses approved by Cardinal John Paparo at Kells: Fabre and Duchesne, *Liber Censuum*, I.234, II.102; Lawlor, 'A Fresh Authority', 18. Petrus's successors as abbots were Áed Ua Maccain for two years in Druim

Etrú (Eleutherius/Eleuzerius) Ua Miadacháin is attested as bishop of Clonard from no later than his attendance at the synod of Kells in March 1152 until his death in 1173.[21]

Is it possible to identify Marcus as bishop of Cloyne or of Clonmacnois? Unfortunately, there are significant gaps in the episcopal succession lists of both dioceses.[22] Cloyne and Clonmacnois have in common that, although neither was designated as an episcopal see at the synod of Ráith Bressail, 1111, which outlined a territorially delimited diocesan structure for the Irish Church, both had secured that status by the time of the synod of Kells, 1152. Nehemias, bishop of Cloyne, is mentioned in Bernard of Clairvaux's Life of Malachy, composed between Malachy's death on 2 November 1148 and Bernard's own death on 21 August 1153, and in the *Visio Tnugdali* completed in 1149, indicating that Cloyne had achieved episcopal status by that date. Bernard recounted an incident where Malachy performed a miracle at Cloyne at the request of Nehemiah, *episcopus illius civitatis*.[23] In the *Visio Tnugdali* in which a Munster soldier, Tnugdal, experienced a vision of heaven, he saw Nehemias, bishop of Cloyne (*Cluanensis*), as an associate of St Patrick in heaven, alongside Celestinus [Cellach], archbishop of Armagh, St Malachy, and the latter's brother, Christianus [Gilla Críst Ua Morgair], bishop of Louth: in other words, in the company of prominent leaders of the twelfth-century reform movement.[24] Nehemias's death at the advanced age of ninety-five is alluded to in the prologue to the *Visio Tnugdali*, where the year of composition of the text is stated to have been 1149.[25] The death of Gilla na Náem Ua Muirchertaig, 'a noble bishop of the south of Ireland', is recorded in 1149.[26] That this bishop died in the same year as Nehemias, bishop of Cloyne, and that Nehemias is a plausible Latinisation of Gilla na Náem,[27] constitutes the basis on which it has been posited that these two should be identified as one and

Connaid, followed by Mauricius (d. 1174), who was abbot for six years in Druim Connaid, two and a half years in Bunn Finni, and thirteen and a half years in Boyle. Counting back via the length of these abbacies suggests that Petrus became bishop of Clonfert around 1151×2.

21 Etrú is listed as bishop of Clonard at the synod of Kells in 1152: G. Keating, *Foras Feasa ar Éirinn: The History of Ireland*; ed. D. Comyn and P. S. Dinneen, 4 vols, Irish Texts Society 4 (1901); 8 (1905); 9 (1906); 15 (1913) (London, 1902–14), III.316–17. He died *ina seandataibh* ('at an advanced age') in 1173: *AFM*, *AT* (where he is styled *airdespoc na Midhi*). The Latin version of his name, chosen presumably because of its papal resonances, is provided by Roger of Howden: Stubbs, *Gesta*, I.26; Stubbs, *Chronica*, II.30.

22 *A New History of Ireland*, *IX: Maps, Genealogies, Lists*, ed. T. W. Moody, F. X. Martin and F. J. Byrne (Oxford, 1984), 275–6, 293–4; P. MacCotter, *Colmán of Cloyne: A Study* (Dublin, 2004), 100–1.

23 'Bishop of that *civitas*': J. Leclercq, C. H. Talbot and H.-M. Rochais, ed., *Sancti Bernardi Opera*, 8 vols in 9 (Rome 1957–77), III.352 (Cloyne is rendered as *Cluanvania*); R. T. Meyer, trans., *Bernard of Clairvaux: The Life and Death of Saint Malachy the Irishman* (Kalamazoo, MI, 1978), 62.

24 A. Wagner, ed., *Visio Tnugdali: Lateinisch und Altdeutsch* (Erlangen, 1882), 54; B. Pfeil, ed., *Die 'Vision des Tnugdalus' Albers von Windberg: Literatur- und Frömmigkeitsgeschichte im ausgehenden 12. Jahrhundert* (Frankfurt, 1997), *55; J.-M. Picard and Y. de Pontfarcy, trans., *The Vision of Tnugdal* (Dublin, 1989), 155.

25 Wagner, *Visio*, 5; Pfeil, *Die 'Vision'*, *3 (the form is *Cluensis*); Picard and de Pontfarcy, *The Vision*, 110.

26 *AFM* 1149. He is also described as *senoir ogh eccnaidhe cráibhdheach* ('a chaste, wise and pious senior'). Although his obit is the first item listed under that year, the compilers of those annals regularly grouped ecclesiastical death-notices at the beginning of each year.

27 Note, however, that in the case of Gilla na Náem Ua Ruadáin, bishop of Achonry (d. 1214), his forename is latinised as Gelasius: *A New History*, ed. Moody *et al.*, IX.320.

the same person.[28] The death on 7 April of *Nehemias episcopus et monachus Hybernie* is recorded in a necrology of the *Schottenkloster* of Würzburg[29] and in another related calendar, the Wessobrunn fragment, as *Nemias episcopus et monachus nostre congregationis*.[30] It has been suggested that this commemorand should be identified as Bishop Nehemias of Cloyne, with the consequent inference that he had a connection with the Irish Benedictine communities in southern Germany, which would also account for his appearance in the *Visio Tnugdali*. The necrology entries do not make it clear whether Nehemias had been a monk in a *Schottenkloster* before becoming bishop, or whether he had resigned a bishopric to end his days in a *Schottenkloster*. Against the latter assumption is the statement in the *Visio Tnugdali* that Nehemias was still *in propria cathedra* in Cloyne at the time of his death.[31] A Benedictine priory was established at some unknown date at Ros Ailithir – that is, Rosscarbery – as a dependency of Würzburg and it has been suggested 'as a working hypothesis' that Bishop Nehemias of Cloyne may have been responsible for that foundation.[32] However, a secure identification of the Würzburg commemorand with Bishop Nehemias of Cloyne is compromised by the possibility of an alternative candidate in the person of *Gilla na naomh Laighen uasal epscop Glinne dá locha 7 cenn manach iar sin in Uairisburg décc in Idus April*, whose death is recorded as having occurred on 7 April 1160/1.[33] Given that Gilla na Náem Laignech is known to have died on 7 April and to have had a connection with Würzburg, he could have been the individual commemorated in the *Schottenkloster* necrologies, though, unlike in the annalistic death notice in the seventeenth-century Annals of the Four Masters, the entries relating to Bishop Nehemias in the two necrologies do not accord him the title of abbot. An identification with Gilla na Náem Laignech would not, of

---

28 Picard and de Pontfarcy, *The Vision of Tnugdal*, 14; MacCotter, *Colmán of Cloyne*, 109–10. See also D. Ó Riain-Raedel, 'Aspects of the Promotion of Irish Saints' Cults in Medieval Germany', *ZCP* 39 (1982), 220–34, at 228.

29 D. Ó Riain-Raedel, 'Das Nekrolog der irischen Schottenklöster', *Beiträge zur Geschichte des Bistums Regensburg* 26 (1992), 7–119, at 22, 26, 63.

30 A. Dold, 'Wessobrunner Kalendarblätter irischen Ursprungs', *Archivalische Zeitschrift* 58 (1962), 11–33, at 24; Ó Riain-Raedel, 'Aspects of the Promotion of Irish Saints' Cults', 228; *eadem*, 'Irish Kings and Bishops in the *memoria* of the German *Schottenklöster*', in *Irland und Europa/Ireland and Europe: Die Kirche im Frühmittelalter/The Early Church*, ed. P. Ní Chatháin and M. Richter (Stuttgart, 1984), 390–404, at 392–3.

31 Above, n. 25.

32 J. Coombes, 'The Benedictine Priory of Ross', *Journal of the Cork Historical and Archaeological Society* 73 (1968), 152–60, at 154. The earliest documentary references for houses in Ireland affiliated to the *Schottenkongregation* is contained in two papal privileges of 1248 granting the abbot of St James, Regensburg, authority for three years to visit and reform monasteries and priories in Ireland and permitting dependent priories in Ireland to receive suitable novices and perform such other duties which the abbot could not perform because of distance: Sheehy, *Pontificia*, II, nos 307, 308. The earliest documentary evidence for a link between specifically a priory at Roscarbery and Würzburg dates from 1353 when Philip, abbot of Würzburg, visited Ireland and received a profession of obedience from Cornelius, prior of St Mary's, Ross: Coombes, 'The Benedictine Priory of Ross', 155, 159. A connection in the twelfth century between the foundation of Ross and Nehemias, styled, however, bishop of Ross, was made in the mid-seventeenth century by the Würzburg monk, James Brown, who may have been drawing on no longer extant sources: D. Ó Riain, 'New Light on the History of St Mary's Priory, Rosscarbery', *Journal of the Cork Historical and Archaeological Society* 113 (2008), 56–68.

33 'Gilla na Náem Laignech, noble bishop of Glendalough, and afterwards head of the monks of Würzburg on 7 April': *AFM* 1085 (unique entry) among a series of entries that have been misplaced from the years 1159–60, as pointed out in *A New History*, ed. Moody *et al.*, IX.313.

course, preclude Bishop Nehemias of Cloyne from also having had a *Schottenkloster* connection.

One may speculate whether Bishop Nehemias of Cloyne might have introduced Benedictine monks from a south German community to his own cathedral church, a circumstance that would account for the very favourable coverage afforded him in the *Visio Tnugdali*, and, if so, whether Bishop Marcus, who issued the indulgence, could have been his successor in that diocese and might also have been a Benedictine monk, affording a possible explanation for his presence at the Benedictine cathedral priory of Bath. The next attested bishop of Cloyne is Ua Dubcróin, also described as abbot (*ab*), who died in 1159.[34] Since Ua Dubcróin's forename is not recorded it could conceivably have been a vernacular equivalent of Marcus.

Turning to Clonmacnois as the possible cathedral church of Marcus *Cluanensis*, Clonmacnois was not listed as an episcopal see at the synod of Ráith Bressail, which assigned the western half of the kingdom of Mide to the church of Clonard and the eastern half to the church of Duleek.[35] However, later in the same year a local synod held at Uisnech amended those arrangements, allocating the eastern portion of the kingdom of Mide to Clonard at the expense of Duleek, while the western portion was now allocated to Clonmacnois.[36] The implication of the annalistic entry relating to the synod of Uisnech in the Clonmacnois-derived *Chronicum Scotorum* is that pressure had been brought to bear by the abbot (*ab*) of Clonmacnois, Gilla Críst Ua Máel Eóin, who was named as present at Uisnech, alongside Murchad Ua Máel Sechlainn, king of Mide (1106–53).[37] The episcopal succession lists of Clonmacnois are even more lacunose than those of Cloyne. Muirchertach Ua Máel Uidir, whose death is recorded in 1187 as bishop of Clonmacnois,[38] is recorded by Geoffrey Keating to have been present as bishop of Clonmacnois at the synod of Kells in March 1152.[39] His vernacular forename could have been Latinised as Marcus, although Mauricius was the more usual Latin rendering for Muirchertach or Muiredach in sources of Irish provenance.[40] Assuming that Marcus's indulgence was drafted within the priory at Bath, the biblical name of Marcus could, nonetheless, have been chosen as an

---

34 *AI* 1159.1 (unique entry).

35 J. Mac Erlean, 'Synod of Ráith Breasail', *Archivium Hibernicum* 3 (1914), 1–33, at 8.

36 *CS* 1107 = 1111; cf. *AT* 1111 (both Clonmacnoise-derived annals); *ABoyle*.

37 For the view, which has been rejected here, that this entry was elaborated at a later date and that the synod of Uisnech preceded that of Ráith Bressail, see P. I. Maolechlainn, 'Clonmacnois and the XIIth-century Synods', *Teathbha* 1 (1973), 195–201, at 196. The synods of Kells and Brí Mheic Thaidc are conflated in this article. See further below, pp. 109–10.

38 *AFM* 1187, where he is described as bishop of Clonfert and Clonmacnois. The death of Celechair Ua hAirmedaig, bishop of Clonfert, is recorded in 1186: *ALC* (his name has been omitted by homoeoteleuton in *AFM*). That Muirchertach Ua Máel Uidir held both sees for a brief period during 1186–87 is accepted in *A New History*, ed. Moody *et al.*, IX.326. That Muirchertach was also bishop of Clonfert was doubted by Gywnn, *The Irish Church*, 249.

39 Keating, *Foras Feasa*, III.317; *A New History*, ed. Moody *et al.*, IX.277.

40 *Frater* Marcus, author of the *Visio Tnugdali*, may have been an Irish member of a *Schottenkloster* with an otherwise unknown vernacular Irish forename. For Mauritius as a Latin equivalent of Muiredach, see, above n. 5; and as a Latinised version of Muirchertach, see the charter of Muirchertach Mac Lochlainn, king of Cenél nEógain and high-king, to Newry Abbey *c.*1157: Flanagan, *Irish Royal Charters*, 292–3. For other clerics named Mauricius, see n. 20 and below p. 112.

ad hoc Latin rendition.[41] There is a further difficulty in that, although Keating named Muirchertach Ua Máel Uidir as bishop of Clonmacnois at the synod of Kells, the see of Clonmacnois was not apparently included in the list that the papal legate, Cardinal John Paparo, who presided at Kells, took back to the papal curia.[42] Omission from that list may have resulted from an error of transcription: Achonry, for example, is incorrectly represented as two dioceses (*Achad* and *Conaire*). Clonmacnois could have been omitted by haplography with Clonfert.[43] If that interpretation is accepted, it would mean, however, that the synod of Kells had assigned Clonmacnois as a suffragan to the newly created archiepiscopal province of Tuam. A bishop of Clonmacnois was not named among the bishops who swore an oath of loyalty to Henry II during his time in Ireland in 1171–2.[44] This may reflect another change in the diocesan fortunes of Clonmacnois. In 1158 the episcopal status of Clonmacnois appears to have been contested at a synod held at Brí Meic Thaidc in Láegaire: the soldiers of Diarmait Ua Máel Sechlainn, king of Mide, are recorded to have attacked the 'bishop of Connacht' (the archbishop of Tuam) and the bishop of Clonmacnois, 'two *comarbai* of Ciarán', that is, heads of the church of Clonmacnois, because the king did not wish them to attend the synod.[45] Two of the bishops' entourage were killed, whereupon the bishops returned *dia tigib* ('to their dwellings'). The attachment of the diocese of Clonmacnois to the newly created archiepiscopal province of Tuam at the synod of Kells is likely to have been disputed by the king of Mide, not surprisingly if Clonmacnois had been created as a diocese for western Mide. From the standpoint of the king of Mide, it would have been unsatisfactory that one half of his kingdom was in the archdiocese of Armagh and the other half in Tuam. Throughout the twelfth century the kingdom of Mide was partitioned and repartitioned among rival royal candidates, at times by the intervention of Toird-elbach Ua Conchobair, king of Connacht and claimant to the high-kingship,[46] which may also have had repercussions on the disposition of its dioceses. At a subsequent synod held at Birr *fairchi Iarthair Midhi do chur le cathair Cluana Maic Nóis do réir clerech Erenn in bliadain-sin* (1174).[47] This suggests that the

---

41 Cellach of Armagh occurs with different Latinised versions: as Celestinus in the *Visio Tnugdali*, as in n. 24 above, but as Celsus in *Vita Malachiae* in *Sancti Bernardi Opera*, III.328–32, 340, and in *Félire hÚi Gormáin*: 70–1. The form Celsus also occurs in the so-called annals of St Mary's Abbey, Dublin: Gilbert, *Chartularies*, II.254–5, 257. Charters of confirmation issued by Archbishops Gilla an Choimded Ua Caráin (1175–80) and Echdonn mac Gilla Uidir (1202–16) referred to their predecessor, Kellach: *ibid.*, I.142, 147.

42 Fabre and Duchesne, *Liber Censuum*, I.234; II.102; Lawlor, 'A Fresh Authority', 18. Although these Latin lists occur in manuscripts of much earlier date than Keating's seventeenth-century transcript, they also demonstrably contain significant errors.

43 Lawlor, 'A Fresh Authority', 20; Gwynn, *The Irish Church*, 247–8. Unfortunately, Keating did not clearly list the bishops present at Kells according to archiepiscopal province.

44 Stubbs, *Gesta*, I.26–7; *Chronica*, II.30–1. Roger provided only Christian names for Felix, bishop of Lismore as papal legate, for the four archbishops and the bishops in the archiepiscopal province of Armagh. He may have drawn in part on a *provinciale*, or list of Irish sees, so that his list cannot be regarded as a wholly reliable reflection of the bishops who did actually swear loyalty to Henry II.

45 *AT*. For the probable location as Breemount, Co. Meath, see D. Ó Murchadha, *The Annals of Tigernach: Index of Names*, Irish Texts Society, Subsidiary Series 6 (London, 1997), 108.

46 *AU²* 1125; *CS* 1121 [1125], 1143; *AFM* 1125, 1143, 1144, 1150, 1152, 1162, 1163, 1169; *AT* 1125, 1161, 1162, 1163; *ABoyle* 1143.

47 'The diocese of West Mide was put with the *cathair* of Clonmacnois by consent of the clerics of Ireland': *AT*, *AFM* where the location is not named, but it is given as Birr in *ABoyle* and in a note

diocesan area intended to be coterminous with western Mide had been detached from Clonmacnois for a period and was restored to Clonmacnois in 1174. On the same occasion Clonmacnois must have been confirmed to the province of Armagh, to which it was subsequently attached. The allocation of Clonmacnois to the province of Tuam at the synod of Kells, while it would have reflected the dominance of Toirdelbach Ua Conchobair, king of Connacht,[48] would have conflicted with the fact that the remainder of Mide was within the province of Armagh. The fluctuating fortunes of the diocese of Clonmacnois were in part occasioned by the circumstance that it was caught between the competing spheres of influence of the provincial kings of Connacht and of Mide, while, at micropolitical level, it most nearly corresponded to the petty political unit of Delbna Bethra,[49] and its difficulties as a diocese are evidenced by the circumstance that it remained diminutive in extent and impoverished in resources for the remainder of the medieval period, although ironically the Anglo-Norman intrusion into the kingdom of Mide may have ensured its continuity as an *ecclesia inter Hibernicos*. The period between the synod of Kells or perhaps more narrowly between the synods of Brí Meic Thaidc in 1158 and Birr in 1174, therefore, may have been a time when Muirchertach Ua Máel Uidir's possession of the see of Clonmacnois was insecure. It is possible that he, or a predecessor, or even a rival claimant to the see of Clonmacnois, using the Latinised name of Marcus, was the *episcopus Cluanensis* who issued an indulgence at Bath.

The consecration of a new cross for the cathedral church at Bath may have coincided with a rededication of the church, the precise date of which is unknown but which fell within Robert's episcopate (1148–61), following an extensive rebuilding programme undertaken by him as a consequence of fire in 1137 which had engulfed the church, chapter-house, cloister, dormitory, refectory and infirmary.[50] Robert also rebuilt the church at Wells and, on completion, it was consecrated and dedicated by him, assisted by Bishops Jocelin of Salisbury, Simon of Worcester and Robert of Hereford, who joined in conferring an indulgence of remission of one hundred days of penance on the anniversary of the dedication, another example of Robert's assiduity in procuring indulgences from other bishops.[51] From the presence of those bishops, the date of reconsecration of the church at Wells lay between 1142 and 16 April 1148.[52] It is precisely from the 1140s onwards that the first examples survive of multiple indulgences issued for a single beneficiary.[53] The four indulgences associated with the celebration of

---

added in a later hand in *AU*. Birr was located on the borders of the diocese of Killaloe (within the ecclesiastical province of Cashel) and Clonmacnois.

48 For Ua Concobhair patronage of Clonmacnois at the expense of the Ua Máel Sechlainn kings of Mide, see A. Kehnel, *Clonmacnois, the Church and Lands of St Ciaran: Change and Continuity in an Irish Monastic Foundation, 6th to 16th Century*, Vita Regularis 8 (Münster, 1997), 126–32.

49 F. J. Byrne, *Irish Kings and High-Kings* (London, 1972), 92, 169, 171, 220–1, 237. Delbna Bethra was located broadly in the barony of Garrycastle, Co. Offaly: Ó Murchadha, *The Annals of Tigernach*, 133. The Meic Cochláin were kings of Delbna: S. Ó Dubhagáin and G. Ó hUidhrín, *Topographical Poems*; ed. J. Carney, Dublin Institute for Advanced Studies (Dublin, 1943), l. 64. Áed Ua Cochláin died as king of Delbna Bethra in 1134: *AT*.

50 'Historiola de primordii episcopatus Somersetensis', in J. Hunter, ed., *Ecclesiastical Documents*, Camden Society, 1st series 8 (1840), 1–41, at 24–5.

51 *Ibid.*

52 Ramsey, *English Episcopal Acta X*, 202.

53 Vincent, 'Some Pardoners' Tales', 45.

the feast of the Exaltation of the Holy Cross at Bath Priory are in line with that development.

Was Bishop Marcus a passing visitor to Bath, journeying to or from Ireland via the nearby port of Bristol?[54] Or had he failed to establish himself as bishop of the see to which he had been consecrated and, in consequence, sought refuge in England? The fact that, unlike the other bishops, Marcus did not extend the spiritual benefits associated with his cathedral church to the beneficiaries of his indulgence might suggest that he may indeed have been consecrated to a see in which he failed to gain acceptance and thus was to be found exercising episcopal functions in England.[55]

The vicissitudes of the twelfth-century diocese of Clonmacnois may make it more likely that Marcus *Cluanensis* was a bishop of Clonmacnois rather than of Cloyne. The coincidence of the issue of a similar indulgence for Bath cathedral priory by a Welsh and an Irish bishop might even imply that Nicholas, bishop of Llandaff, and Bishop Marcus were found together on the same occasion in the entourage of the archbishop of Canterbury.[56] Might Marcus have sought the support of Canterbury against a rival episcopal candidate, in much the same way as had happened in the case of a disputed episcopal election to the see of Dublin in 1121? A bishop-elect, Gréne (Gregorius), sought consecration from Ralph, archbishop of Canterbury, at the request of the burgesses of Dublin who, if the Canterbury historian, Eadmer, may be believed, wrote to complain that the bishops of Ireland, and especially *ille episcopus qui habitat Archmachae*, was opposed to Gréne's recourse to Canterbury.[57] Another instance is afforded by Patricius, consecrated as bishop of Limerick in 1140 by Theobald, archbishop of Canterbury, but who may never have gained control of his see.[58] In 1145/6 Patricius occurs as a witness to a charter of Alexander, bishop of Lincoln, recording the latter's dedication of the church of Holy Trinity, Markyate, at the petition of Christina and her nuns and by the grant of Ralph, the dean, and the canons of St Paul's London;[59] and in 1148 Patricius was one of four bishops present at the

---

54 The Irish petitioners who in 1096 sought the permission of Walchelin, bishop of Winchester, that one of his monks, Máel Ísu (Malchus) Ua hAinmire be consecrated as bishop of Waterford had ships standing by in the port of Bristol to transport him to Ireland: F. M. Schmitt, ed., *S. Anselmi Cantuariensis Archiepiscopi Opera Omnia*, 6 vols (Rome, 1938–61), IV.93–4; W. Fröhlich, *The Letters of St Anselm of Canterbury*, 3 vols, Cistercian Studies 96, 97, 142 (Kalamazoo MI, 1990–4), II.139. For maritime traffic between Bristol and Ireland, see A. Gwynn, 'Medieval Bristol and Dublin', *Irish Historical Studies* 5 (1947), 275–86.

55 There is a possibility that it may have been considered inappropriate at this early date, when the canon law of indulgences was still being clarified, for a bishop from outside the English province to offer spiritual benefits from his own church; see the request for guidance addressed to Pope Alexander III (1159–81), probably by the archbishop of Canterbury, as to the effect of a bishop's indulgence upon the subjects of other bishops: Vincent, 'Some Pardoners' Tales', 34–5.

56 Marcus *Cluanensis* is not recorded as present at the consecration of Nicholas as bishop of Llandaff on 14 March 1148. See above, n. 9.

57 'That bishop who is in Armagh': Eadmer, *Historia Novorum*, ed. M. Rule, RS (London, 1884), 297–8; M. T. Flanagan, *Irish Society, Anglo-Norman Settlers, Angevin Kingship: Interactions in Ireland in the Late Twelfth Century* (Oxford, 1989), 30–1.

58 *Ibid.*, 30–1; A. Gwynn, 'The Diocese of Limerick in the Twelfth Century', *North Munster Antiquarian Journal* 5 (1946), 35–48, at 39–40.

59 BL Cotton, xi.8, extant original charter of Alexander, bishop of Lincoln; printed in D. M. Smith, ed., *English Episcopal Acta I, Lincoln, 1067–1185* (London, 1980), 31. The charter is dated by the year of incarnation, 1145. Assuming the Annunciation year is being used, the latest possible date

election of Robert, bishop of Lincoln, at Westminster on 13 December, and at the election of David, bishop of St Davids, on the following day at Lambeth, and at the consecration of both bishops on 19 December in Canterbury.[60] No trace of Patrick is found in Irish sources.

On the other hand, one should allow that an Irish bishop could have exercised episcopal functions in England without it necessarily being indicative of difficulties within his own diocese. Gillebertus, bishop of Limerick (d. 1145),[61] who had not been consecrated by an archbishop of Canterbury, is recorded to have dedicated chapels of St Nicholas and Saints Cosmos and Damien in the great Benedictine abbey of St Albans as well as the church of St Stephen in the town of St Albans.[62] The St Albans chronicler even claimed that Gillebertus had issued a charter confirming the dedication of the latter of which he quoted only 'ego etc'. Gillebertus also ordained Roger the Hermit as subdeacon and blessed the large cross that was installed at the south portion of the monastery. No date for those consecrations was given, but they may have occurred around the time when Eadmer, the biographer of Archbishop Anselm of Canterbury, recorded the presence of Gillebertus at the consecration on 19 September 1115 of Bernard, bishop of St Davids, in the church of St Peter, Westminster, by Ralph d'Éscures, archbishop of Canterbury.[63]

The chance notice at some time between 1108 and 1115 of the presence of Mauricius, *quodam episcopo Hiberniae Mauricio*,[64] at a judgement delivered by Richard, bishop of London, alongside Reinhelm, bishop of Hereford, in an assembly at Wistanstow in the diocese of Hereford serves as a cautionary warning. The posited identification of this otherwise unknown Mauricius with Bishop Máel Ísu Ua hAinmire of Waterford is unlikely to be correct, since Máel Ísu's Latinised name of Malchus is well attested in both his own correspondence and in letters addressed to him by Anselm,[65] and he was also known by that name

---

for this document to have been issued would be 25 February, 1146, the date of death of Abbot Geoffrey of St Albans who witnessed the charter. It is reproduced in F. Wormald *et al.*, *The St Albans Psalter (Albani Psalter)*, Studies of the Warburg Institute 25 (London, 1960), plate 169. Cf. plate 172 for the original grant to Markyate Priory from the dean and chapter of St Paul's, London.

60 Stubbs, *The Historical Works*, I.138; Conway Davies, *Episcopal Acts*, I.271.

61 *CS.* For his career, see S. Duffy, 'Gilbert, Bishop of Limerick', *ODNB*, XXII.158–9.

62 Matthew Paris, *Liber Additamentorum*, incorporated into *Gesta Abbatum Monasterii S. Albani a Thoma Walsingham, Regnante Ricardo Secundo, ejusdem Ecclesiae Pracentore, Compilata*, ed. H. T. Riley, 3 vols, RS (London, 1867–69), I.184. I owe this reference to M. Philpott, 'Some Interactions between the English and Irish Churches', *Anglo-Norman Studies* 20 (1998), 187–204, at 202.

63 D. Whitelock, M. Brett and C. N. L. Brooke, ed., *Councils and Synods With Other Documents Relating to the English Church*, I.2 (Oxford, 1981), 715; Conway Davies, *Episcopal Acts*, I.239. It is not necessary to accept Eadmer's insinuation that Gillebertus was present as a suffragan of the archbishop of Canterbury. Eadmer was a passionate partisan of Canterbury's claims to primacy, for which cause he was prepared to stretch evidence to its limits. Gillebertus's position within his own diocese may have been compromised for a time by the serious illness and temporary deposition in 1115 of his patron, Muirchertach Ua Briain, king of Munster and high-king, which may have resulted in his being found in the company of the archbishop of Canterbury.

64 'A former bishop of Ireland': F. Neininger, ed., *English Episcopal Acta, XV: London, 1076–1187* (Oxford, 1999), no. 26.

65 Schmitt, *S. Anselmi Opera*, IV.92–3, 101, 191, nos 201–2, 207, 277, Fröhlich, *Letters*, II, nos 201, 202, 207, 277.

to Bernard of Clairvaux.[66] That an unidentified Irish bishop was to be found in the diocese of Hereford around the time that Bishop Gillebertus of Limerick was consecrating churches in St Albans suggests that only a fraction of the travels in England of Irish bishops has been recorded.[67] As in the case of the indulgence of Bishop Marcus *Cluanensis* transcribed into the Bath cartulary, it is only chance survivals in English records that afford evidence for Irish bishops exercising episcopal functions in twelfth-century England. It may be remarked, in light of criticisms raised by Archbishops Lanfranc[68] and Anselm of Canterbury[69] about episcopal consecration in Ireland that such reservations were evidently not shared by all English churchmen and that Gillebertus of Limerick and Marcus *Cluanensis* were regarded as exercising valid episcopal functions.

Although there is insufficient evidence to rule conclusively on the identity of Marcus *Cluanensis*, the indulgence that he issued in favour of Bath cathedral priory provides evidence for a contact between that community and an Irish bishop around the mid-twelfth century. As is so frustratingly often the case with twelfth-century sources for the Irish Church, there is just enough evidence to postulate a number of hypotheses, but insufficient information to provide conclusive proof. The text constitutes the earliest extant indulgence issued in the name of an Irish bishop. Its diplomatic indicates that it would have been authenticated with a seal which, given the paucity of information on twelfth-century Irish episcopal *acta*, is also worthy of notice.[70] The granting of indulgences was an exclusively episcopal prerogative which heightened awareness of the bishop's pastoral role in the sphere of penance. How such external contacts and experiences may have contributed to episcopal formation and practice in the context of the restructuring and renewal of the Irish Church in the course of the twelfth century and understanding of lay penance and its concomitant of confession, to which was linked the issue of indulgences, can only be conjectured.[71]

---

66 *Vita Malachiae*, in *Sancti Bernardi Opera*, III, 316, l. 16; 318, l. 11; 331, l. 1; Meyer, *Bernard of Clairvaux*, 24–5, 39.

67 As noted by M. Brett, 'Canterbury's Perspective on Church Reform and Ireland, 1070–1115', in *Ireland and Europe in the Twelfth Century: Reform and Renewal*, ed. D. Bracken and D. Ó Riain-Raedel (Dublin, 2006), 13–35, at 30. For numbers of Irish pilgrims and travellers in eleventh- and twelfth-century England, see D. Bethell, 'English Monks and Irish Reform', *Historical Studies* 8 (1971), 111–35, at 122–6.

68 *Quod episcopi ab uno episcopo consecrantur; quod in uillis uel ciuitatibus plures ordinantur* ('bishops are consecrated by a single bishop; many are ordained to *villae* and *civitates*'); *quod sacri ordines per pecuniam ab episcopis dantur* ('holy orders are conferred by bishops for money'): H. Clover and M. Gibson, ed., *The Letters of Lanfranc, Archbishop of Canterbury*, Oxford Medieval Texts (London, 1979), 70–1.

69 Schmitt, *S. Anselmi Opera*, IV.89; V.374, 383; Fröhlich, *Letters*, II, 132, III, 203, 215.

70 The earliest extant original single sheet parchment of an indulgence issued by an Irish bishop is that of Malachias, bishop of Down (1176–1202): H. G. Richardson, 'Some Norman Monastic Foundations in Ireland', in *Medieval Studies Presented to Aubrey Gwynn, S. J.*, ed. J. A. Watt, J. B. Morrall and F. X. Martin (Dublin, 1961), 29–43, at 43.

71 Many more indulgences granted by Irish bishops survive as originals in English repositories and in cartulary copies. A list compiled by Reading Abbey *c.*1258–9 contains indulgences from the archbishops of Armagh, Dublin, Cashel and Tuam and the bishops of Achonry, Annaghdown, Ardfert, Clonmacnois, Elphin, Emly, Ferns, Kildare, Killaloe, Kilmacduagh, Leighlin, Limerick and Waterford: Kemp, *Reading Abbey Cartularies*, I.174–9. The Latinised renderings for Thomas, bishop of Clonmacnois, are *Cluanensis, Cloanensis, Clucensis*. There is an original indulgence in Salisbury cathedral archives issued by David MacCarwell, archbishop of Cashel, on 28 June 1278, remitting forty days' penance to anyone who prayed at the tomb of William Longespée in Salisbury cathedral: J. R. S. Phillips, 'David MacCarwell and the Proposal to Purchase English

Appendix 1

Grant by Marcus, bishop of *Cluain*, of twenty days' indulgence to those penitents visiting Bath Priory on the feast of the Exaltation of the Holy Cross (14
September).

[M]ᵃarcus d*ei* gr*atia* Cluanensis ep*iscopus* omnib*us* s*anctae* eccl*esiae* filiis sal*utem*
7 benedictione*m*. Quia s*anctae* crucis ven*er*atio e*st* cunctor*um* fideli*um* salus &
*pro*tectio, dignum e*st* ei*us*dem s*anctae* crucis venerationi 7 laudi insistere, 7 ad
hoc q*uosque* fideles invitando accende*re*, ut ei*us* muniantur & salvent*ur* signac*u*lo,
cui*us* sunt redempti misterio. Qua devotione accensi, omnib*us* q*ui* ad exaltatione*m*
s*anctae* crucis Bathoniam vere penitentes 7 devoti cu*m* elemosinis & orationib*us*
convenerint xx dierum indulgentia*m* de divina mis*eri*cor*d*ia confisi imp*er*petuum
concedimus. Val*ete*.

Marcus, by the grace of God, bishop of *Cluain*, [sends] to all sons of the holy
church, a greeting and a blessing. Because veneration of the holy cross is the salvation and protection of all the faithful, it is fitting to promote the veneration and
praise of the same holy cross and to inflame by attracting to this purpose those who
are faithful so that they may be protected and saved by its sign, by the mystery
of which they are redeemed. Inflamed by such devotion we grant in perpetuity an
indulgence of twenty days, with confidence in the divine mercy, to all those who
on the feast of the Exaltation of the Holy Cross will visit Bath as true and devoted
penitents with alms and prayers. Farewell.

ᵃ   The initial letter is missing, but the forename cannot be other than Marcus. All the initial letters
of forenames on the page are blank, evidently because the scribe intended that they should be
rubricated or decorated.

Law, *c.* 1273–1280', *Peritia* 10 (1996), 253–73, at 253–4. Salisbury's archives contain other
originals issued during the thirteenth century by three archbishops of Dublin and bishops of
Meath, Kildare and Leighlin.

10

GERALD OF WALES, GILDAS AND
THE *DESCRIPTIO KAMBRIAE*

Huw Pryce

In the first preface to the *Descriptio Kambriae*, completed in 1194, Gerald of Wales makes two related assertions: he had written a work of history, and he had sought to imitate the example of Gildas.[1] Although by no means ignored, both statements have remained at the margins of scholarly discussion, which has tended to concentrate on the *Descriptio*'s novelty as a remarkably detailed, albeit partial, account of a medieval country and people as well as on what it reveals of its author's attitude towards Wales and the Welsh.[2] The emphasis on the work as an original contribution to ethnographic writing strongly coloured by its author's complex relationship with Wales remains highly illuminating. However, this essay will argue that, in order to appreciate the nature of that contribution, Gerald's presentation of the *Descriptio* as a piece of historical writing needs to be taken very seriously, for it was central to his purpose.[3] In particular, it will suggest that, just as Bede's account of the seventh- and eighth-century Britons was informed by a reading of Gildas, so too was Gerald's description of the Welsh.[4] After a brief introduction to the *Descriptio Kambriae* the discussion will consider how Gerald uses the past in the work in general before moving on to explore the implications of his specific identification with Gildas.

Though divided into two books, the *Descriptio Kambriae* effectively falls into four parts.[5] I.1–7 provide a general introduction to Wales that focuses mainly on its topography; I.8–18 describe the 'praiseworthy' and II.1–7 the 'unpraiseworthy' characteristics of the Welsh; while II.8–10 give advice on how to conquer Wales, with Gerald even going so far as to suggest that its native population be

---

1 See below, pp. 116, 118. For the dating and recensions of Gerald's works see Robert Bartlett, *Gerald of Wales 1146–1223* (Oxford, 1982), 213–21. Unless stated otherwise, dates in the present essay refer to a work's first recension.

2 See especially *ibid.*, 15–16, 178–210.

3 Certainly more central than implied in *ibid.*, 182: 'In the absence of an ethnographic tradition, ethnographic writing appeared as a kind of history …'.

4 Cf. T. M. Charles-Edwards, 'Bede, the Irish and the Britons', *Celtica* 15 (1983), 42–52. See also Clare Stancliffe, *Bede and the Britons*, Whithorn Lecture 14 (2007). It is a great pleasure to offer this small acknowledgement of my long-standing debt to Thomas Charles-Edwards, whom I first encountered in 1976 through attending his lectures on Bede's *Historia Ecclesiastica*, which included discussion of Gildas's influence on that text. I remember being particularly impressed that an Oxford historian was able correctly to pronounce Rhiainfellt, the Modern Welsh form of the name of Oswiu's first wife according to the *Historia Brittonum*!

5 Michael Richter, *Giraldus Cambrensis: The Growth of the Welsh Nation*, 2nd edn (Aberystwyth, 1976), 64.

driven out and the country either recolonised or turned into a forest for wild animals, though the final chapter tries to give an appearance of even-handedness by offering advice on how the Welsh might resist.[6] There is, then, a political edge to the text, which exhibits many of the hallmarks of 'applied anthropology' that aimed to disclose valuable intelligence about the enemy to its would-be conquerors.[7] This is hardly surprising, as Gerald not only belonged to a leading Marcher family in south-west Wales but was also a royal clerk in the service of Richard I at the time he composed the work; indeed, as we shall see, its composition was surely in large part a response to very specific circumstances in his career.[8] Yet, in contrast to the harsh condemnation of the Irish in his earlier *Topographia Hibernica*, 'The Topography of Ireland' (1188),[9] the *Descriptio Kambriae* reveals an author who identified himself with the country to some extent; accordingly, rather than merely casting an outsider's disparaging eye on a barbarous and backward people, Gerald presented a quite complex and ambivalent picture that included some sympathy for the Welsh. His sense of belonging is explicable in terms of Gerald's close familiarity with, and strong stake in, the country that resulted from ties of family, locality and career – a familiarity that explains in turn why his observations on Welsh society were unparalleled in their detail and perceptiveness, and why they contrast sharply with his much cruder and more far-fetched depiction of the Irish.[10]

This identification with Wales is made manifest at the beginning of the *Descriptio*.

> Sed quoniam nobiles aliarum regionum historiae, egregiis olim editae scriptoribus, in lucem prodiere, nos, ob patriae favorem et posteritatis, finium nostrorum abdita quidem evolvere, et inclite gesta, necdum tamen in memoriam luculento labore digesta, tenebris exuere, humilemque stilo materiam efferre, nec inutile quidem nec illaudibile reputavimus.[11]

As this statement makes clear, Gerald clearly believed that he had written a work of history. On the face of it this seems misleading, as the book is evidently not a historical narrative comparable to, say, the author's *Expugnatio Hiber-*

---

6 James F. Dimock, ed., *Descriptio Kambriae*, II.8–9, in *Itinerarium Kambriae et Descriptio Kambriae*, Giraldi Cambrensis Opera 6, RS (London, 1868), 218–25, 225, n. 4. The passage was omitted in the second recension of *c*.1215.

7 Bartlett, *Gerald*, 184.

8 See below, pp. 122–3.

9 John J. O'Meara, ed., 'Giraldus Cambrensis in Topographia Hiberniae. Text of the First Recension', *PRIA* 52 C (1948–50), 113–78; trans. John O'Meara, *Gerald of Wales: The History and Topography of Ireland* (Harmondsworth, 1982).

10 For Gerald's career see, for example, Michael Richter, 'Gerald of Wales', *Traditio* 29 (1973), 379–90; Huw Pryce, 'A Cross-border Career: Giraldus Cambrensis between Wales and England', in *Grenzgänger*, ed. Reinhard Schneider, Veröffentlichungen der Kommission für Saarländische Landesgeschichte und Volksforschung 33 (Saarbrücken, 1998), 45–60.

11 'But since noble histories of other countries have been brought into the light, composed by distinguished writers, we, for the sake of the favour of our homeland and of future generations, have considered it neither useless nor unpraiseworthy to disclose the secrets of our country, too, and to uncover from the darkness glorious deeds, which, however, have not yet been recollected in a splendid work, and to set forth the humble subject-matter with our pen': *Descriptio*, 'Praefatio Prima' (ed. Dimock, 157). The duty of writing the history of his own *patria* is further emphasised in *ibid.*, 'Praefatio Secunda' (161). All translations of passages from the *Descriptio Kambriae* are my own.

nica, 'Conquest of Ireland' (1189).[12] However, the *Descriptio* does have a strong historical dimension, for Gerald frequently refers to the Trojan, British or early medieval past in order to explain the characteristics of Wales and Welsh in his own day.[13] More specifically, he draws heavily on the traditions of early British history, including the alleged descent of the Britons from Troy transmitted and elaborated by Geoffrey of Monmouth, albeit studiously avoiding any acknowledgement of his source except when he disagrees with it – as, for example, over the correct derivation of the name *Wallia*, 'Wales'.[14] In other words, a key premise of the *Descriptio* is that the Welsh of the late twelfth century were an ancient people whose distant origins had left a deep and enduring imprint on their character.

The distinctiveness of Gerald's approach here is highlighted by a comparison with his first Welsh book, the *Itinerarium Kambriae*, 'The Journey through Wales' (1191), an account of Archbishop Baldwin of Canterbury's preaching of the Third Crusade in Wales in 1188. While certainly containing references to early British and Welsh history, especially with respect to ecclesiastical traditions, the *Itinerarium* is notable for its numerous flashbacks to events of the late eleventh and twelfth centuries, often assigned to the reigns of particular kings of England, relating to the places through or near which the archbishop's party travelled.[15] By contrast, the *Descriptio* pays little attention to such relatively recent events, though one chapter does note examples of the success of Anglo-Saxon and early Norman kings in subduing Wales.[16] Instead, much greater emphasis is given to the distant past as a point of both contrast and connection with the present, the *Descriptio*'s principal temporal markers consisting either of terms such as *antiquitus* 'in ancient times' and *multis olim temporibus* 'a long time ago', on the one hand, or *modernis diebus* 'in modern days' and *hodie* 'today', on the other. Thus, for example, the first chapter contrasts old and new names for Wales by referring to *Kambria, quae ... modernis diebus Wallia dicitur*, whereas the second opens an account of the country's alleged ancient tripartite division with the words (possibly echoing Caesar's description of Gaul) *Divisa est antiquitus Wallia totalis in tres partes....*[17] This juxtaposition of ancient and modern is also deployed to argue that some characteristics of the Welsh in the

---

12 A. B. Scott and F. X. Martin, ed. and trans., *Expugnatio Hibernica: The Conquest of Ireland, by Giraldus Cambrensis* (Dublin, 1978).

13 This is true of just over two-thirds of the work's chapters, the exceptions being I.9, 12, 13 (though this attributes part-singing in northern England to Scandinavian settlement), 14; II.1, 3, 5, 8–9. Moreover, as argued below, II.7 links the 'unpraiseworthy' characteristics described in I.1–6 to ancient Trojan and British origins.

14 *Descriptio*, I.7 (ed. Dimock, 179); cf. J. C. Crick, 'The British Past and the Welsh Future: Gerald of Wales, Geoffrey of Monmouth and Arthur of Britain', *Celtica* 23 (1999), 60–75, at 64–5; Huw Pryce, 'British or Welsh? National Identity in Twelfth-Century Wales', *English Historical Review* 116 (2001), 775–801, at 784–5.

15 E.g., *Itinerarium Kambriae*, I.1, 4, 9, 11; II.1, 3, 4 (ed. Dimock, 19, 47–8, 78, 88, 103, 118, 121).

16 *Descriptio*, II.7 (ed. Dimock, 217–18).

17 'Kambria, which ... in modern times is called Wallia': *ibid.*, I.1 (ed. Dimock, 165); 'In ancient times the whole of Wales was divided into three parts': *ibid.* I.2 (ed. Dimock, 166). See also *ibid.*, I.4 (*modernis diebus, antiquitus ...*; *antiquitus ... hodie*), 5 (*multis olim temporibus*; *modernis diebus*; *moderno tempore*), 11 (*non de novo, sed ab antiquo*), 17 (*tempora nostra*), 18 (*olim, longeque ante excidium Britannicum ... usque in hodiernum diem*), II.6 (*antiquus in hac gente mos*; *ab antiquo commune*), 7 (*multo jam tempore*), 8 (*hodie*), 10 (*nostris diebus*) (169–70, 171, 176, 185, 202, 214, 215, 227).

late twelfth century had been inherited from their British or even Trojan ancestors. For example, Gerald attributed the dark colouring of the Welsh to their
ancestors' long sojourn in Troy and asserted that the preference of Welshmen for
moustaches was an ancient custom, as Caesar had described a similar practice
among the Britons.[18]

Yet racial inheritance was invoked as an explanation for much more than
external appearances; it also served to underpin Gerald's condemnation of
immoral behaviour. This further aim is flagged up by the other passage in the first
preface of the *Descriptio* mentioned at the beginning of this essay, where Gerald
declares that he is following the sixth-century British writer Gildas, whose critical account of the fall of his fellow Britons, usually known as the *De Excidio
Britanniae*, 'The Ruin of Britain', is praised as an example of true history.[19]

> Prae aliis itaque Britanniae scriptoribus, solus mihi Gildas, quoties eundem mate-
> riae cursus obtulerit, imitabilis esse videtur. Qui ea quae vidit et ipse cognovit
> scripto commendans, excidiumque gentis suae deplorans potius quam describens,
> veram magis historiam texuit quam ornatam. Gildam itaque Giraldus sequitur.
> Quem utinam moribus et vita sequi posset; factus ejusdem plus sapientia quam
> eloquentia, plus animo quam calamo, plus zelo quam stilo, plus vita quam verbis
> imitator.[20]

The wording makes clear that Gerald was referring to the *De Excidio*, which,
after providing a sketch of events in Britain from the Roman occupation to his
own time, proceeds to condemn the native British kings and clergy for their
sinful behaviour and declares that this had led God to punish the Britons by
inflicting foreign conquest on them.[21] Copies of the *De Excidio* were rare in the
twelfth century and Gerald is unusual in showing a direct knowledge of it.[22]
However, though not widely read (indeed, he was often mistaken as the author of
the early ninth-century *Historia Brittonum*, 'History of the Britons'), Gildas was
highly regarded as a historian of the Britons.[23] He had, after all, been described as
such by Bede, whose *Historia Ecclesiastica* enjoyed something of a renaissance
in the twelfth century to judge by the number of surviving manuscripts, as well as
by several Welsh ecclesiastical texts of the early to mid-twelfth century, namely
Caradog of Llancarfan's Life of St Gildas, the Life of St Illtud and the Book of

---

[18] *Ibid.*, I.11, 15 (ed. Dimock, 185, 193).

[19] In his one explicit reference to the work, Gerald gives its title as *De Excidio Britonum*, 'On
the Ruin of the Britons': *ibid.*, II.2 (ed. Dimock, 207). Cf. Karen George, *Gildas's* De Excidio
Britonum *and the Early British Church* (Woodbridge, 2009), 1, n. 1.

[20] 'More than any other British writer, it seems to me that only Gildas, each time the flow of the
subject-matter brings him forward, is worthy of imitation. Committing to writing that which he
saw and understood, and lamenting rather than describing the fall of his people, he composed a
true rather than ornamented history. Thus Gerald follows Gildas. If only he were able to follow
him in his morals and life; and make himself an imitator in wisdom more than eloquence, in spirit
more than writing, in zeal more than style, in life more than words': *Descriptio*, 'Praefatio Prima'
(ed. Dimock, 158).

[21] Michael Winterbottom, ed. and trans., *De Excidio Britanniae*, in *Gildas: The Ruin of Britain and
Other Works* (London and Chichester, 1978).

[22] R. William Leckie, Jr, *The Passage of Dominion: Geoffrey of Monmouth and the Periodization of
Insular History in the Twelfth Century* (Toronto, 1981), 45, 83–4, 95–7; Neil Wright, 'Geoffrey
of Monmouth and Gildas', *Arthurian Literature* 2 (1982), 1–40, at 1–3.

[23] Wright, 'Geoffrey', 1–2.

Llandaf.[24] Above all, Gildas was one of the main sources – along with Bede's *Historia Ecclesiastica* and the *Historia Brittonum* – for Geoffrey of Monmouth's *Historia Regum Britanniae* (*c*.1138), although he is only cited explicitly as an authority in a speech by Caduallo giving a detailed account of the Britons' sins and the divine punishment these provoked.[25] Nevertheless, Gerald differs from Geoffrey in his treatment of Gildas since the *Descriptio* borrowed much less material from the *De Excidio* than did the *Historia*, while, on the other hand, Gerald went further than Geoffrey by explicitly identifying himself with Gildas as an example whose approach to historical writing as well as his holy life were worthy of imitation.[26]

At first sight, this appeal to Gildas is puzzling, since the *Descriptio* lacks any close resemblance to the *De Excidio* and contains very few borrowings from it, the major exception being a chapter discussing the contradictory testimony of Caesar and Gildas regarding the bravery of the Britons. Here, Gerald quotes from chapters six and twenty of the *De Excidio* on the cowardice of the Britons and ends by declaring:

> Et quod omnium istorum validius ignaviae eorum argumentum est, quod Gildas, qui vir sanctus erat et de gente eadem, in cunctis quas de gestis eorum scripsit historiis, nihil unquam egregium de ipsis posteritati reliquit.[27]

In addition, Gildas's description of Britain near the beginning of the *De Excidio* may have influenced Gerald's decision to open his book with chapters describing Wales, including an account of its length and breadth.[28] However, as that description had also been adapted by Bede in the first chapter of his *Historia Ecclesiastica* and thence by Geoffrey of Monmouth in his *Historia Regum Britanniae* (both works that were known to Gerald), any influence may well have been

---

24 Bertram Colgrave and R. A. B. Mynors, ed. and trans., *Bede's Ecclesiastical History of the English People* (Oxford, 1969), I.22 (68–9). See also *ibid.*, p. xxxi; R. H. C. Davis, 'Bede after Bede', in *Studies in Medieval History Presented to R. Allen Brown*, ed. Christopher Harper-Bill, Christopher J. Holdsworth and Janet L. Nelson (Woodbridge, 1989), 103–16. In his 'History of English Affairs' (*c*.1196–8) William of Newburgh implied that he had read Gildas after seeing him referred to in Bede, and added that copies of Gildas's book were rare because of its 'unrefined and tasteless' style: *Historia Rerum Anglicarum*, 'Proœmium', ed. Richard Howlett, *Chronicles of the Reign of Stephen, Henry II., and Richard I.*, 1, RS (London, 1864), p. xi. Welsh texts: Hugh Williams, ed., *Gildas*, 2 parts, Cymmrodorion Record Series 3 (London, 1899–1901), I.7; II.402 and n. 2, 415–20.

25 Wright, 'Geoffrey', esp. 12; Michael D. Reeve, ed. and Neil Wright, trans., *Geoffrey of Monmouth: The History of the Kings of Britain* (Woodbridge, 2007), p. lvii, ch. 195 (268–9).

26 It should be noted, though, that Geoffrey praises the *De Excidio* (*ibid.*, chs 1, 22, 72, 101 (4–5, 30–1, 88–9, 130–1)) and even once refers to Gildas as *beatus* (*ibid.*, ch. 34, line 329 (47)).

27 'And the stronger proof of their cowardice is that Gildas, who was a holy man and of the same people, left nothing distinguished at all about them to future generations in all the histories he wrote of their deeds': *Descriptio*, II.2 (ed. Dimock, 207–8; quotation at 208). In the second recension (*c*.1215) Gerald offered an explanation of this hostility to the Britons by alleging that Gildas had thrown his works on King Arthur and praising the Britons into the sea because Arthur had killed his brother: *ibid.*, II.2 (209). This seems to be a detail added by Gerald to a story that Arthur had killed Gildas's brother found in the mid-twelfth-century Life of St Gildas by Caradog of Llancarfan: Caradog of Llancarfan, *Vita S. Gildae*, ch. 5 (ed. and trans. Williams, *Gildas*, II.400–3); J. S. P. Tatlock, *The Legendary History of Britain* (Berkeley and Los Angeles, CA, 1950), 188–9 and n. 51; O. J. Padel, *Arthur in Medieval Welsh Literature* (Cardiff, 2000), 44.

28 *De Excidio*, ch. 3 (ed. and trans. Winterbottom, 16–17, 89–90).

indirect.[29] Moreover, irrespective of the precise influence on the opening of the *Descriptio*, in his references to early British history Gerald certainly drew far more heavily on Geoffrey than on Gildas.[30]

Given the paucity of borrowings from the *De Excidio* in the *Descriptio*, it is not surprising that scholars have been reluctant to attribute much significance to the comparison with Gildas.[31] Robert Bartlett has offered the fullest explanation. Noting that several of Gerald's writings stressed the need for history to be objective, and that, shortly after the *Descriptio* was first issued, William of Newburgh had likewise praised Gildas's readiness to lament the evils of his fellow Britons, Bartlett suggests that Gerald named Gildas as his only model for the work 'partly because he too wrote about the Britons, but also because of his reputation for historical impartiality'.[32] The argument is convincing, but its implications are more far-reaching than this brief exposition of it may suggest. For one thing, the identification with Gildas served as a rhetorical strategy which enabled Gerald to legitimise and reinforce his negative comments on the Welsh – whose country he had already appropriated a little earlier in the preface by calling it his *patria* – by presenting himself as simply imitating the precedent set by one of the Britons' own writers.[33] However, though claiming Wales as his country, Gerald distanced himself from the Welsh, to whom he referred in the third person: his identification with Gildas was no call to the Welsh to repent by one of their own comparable to the warnings that Alcuin, followed over two centuries later by Wulfstan of York, issued to their compatriots in the wake of Scandinavian attacks on England.[34] Gerald's approach is closer to the way in which he had earlier deployed the Irish *Lebar Gabála Érenn* ('the Book of the Taking of Ireland'), coupled with Geoffrey of Monmouth, to present Henry II's rule in Ireland as the glorious culmination of a pattern of invasions deeply rooted in Irish history; but there the identification is both more superficial (Gerald simply refers to *antiquis-*

---

29 *Descriptio*, I.1 (ed. Dimock, 165–6). Bede and Geoffrey: Wright, 'Geoffrey', 1, 5–7. For detailed analysis of Bede's description of Britain and Ireland see A. H. Merrills, *History and Geography in Late Antiquity* (Cambridge, 2005), ch. 4. See also Brynley F. Roberts, 'Gerald of Wales and Welsh Tradition', in *The Formation of Culture in Medieval Britain: Celtic, Latin, and Norman Influences on English Music, Literature, History, and Art*, ed. Françoise H. M. Le Saux (Lewiston, Queenston and Lampeter, 1995), 129–44, at 135–7.

30 Crick, 'The British Past', 64–8; cf. Roberts, 'Gerald', 135.

31 Richter, *Giraldus*, 62–3, implies that there was little substance to Gerald's claim, and comments (*ibid.*, 63, n. 1) of the phrase *Gildam itaque Giraldus sequitur*: 'It would be typical of Giraldus to include the line mainly to show off with the alliteration.'

32 Bartlett, *Gerald*, 182–3 and n. 21. See also Roberts, 'Gerald', 135, for the suggestion that, as a writer who had recorded 'that which he saw and understood', Gildas provided an example of a contemporary historian.

33 Compare how Gildas declared his sympathy for his *patria*, presumably meaning Britain, at the beginning of the *De Excidio*, although there are no close verbal parallels between that passage and those in the *Descriptio* referred to above at n. 11: *De Excidio*, ch. 1 (ed. and trans. Winterbottom, 87). Hostility to the Welsh (and Breton) descendants of the Britons also informed William of Newburgh's use of Gildas to denounce Geoffrey of Monmouth's *Historia*: Nancy F. Partner, *Serious Entertainments: The Writing of History in Twelfth-Century England* (Chicago, IL, and London, 1977), 64.

34 Cf. Alcuin, *Epistolae*, no. 17, ed. Ernst Dümmler, MGH, *Epistolae Merowingici et Karolini aevi*, 4 (Berlin, 1895), 47; trans. Stephen Allott, *Alcuin of York c. A.D. 732 to 804 – His Life and Letters* (York, 1974), 62; *Sermo Lupi ad Anglos*, ed. Dorothy Whitelock, 2nd edn (London, 1952), 51–2; trans. 'The Sermon of the Wolf to the English', in *English Historical Documents c.500–1042*, ed. Dorothy Whitelock (London, 1955), 854–9, at 859.

simas ... Hibernensium hystorias without praising them or their authors) and less comprehensive than is the case with the use of Gildas in the *Descriptio*.[35]

In addition, the ruin or fall (*excidium*) of the Britons in the post-Roman period is mentioned several times in Book I of the *Descriptio*: for example, their conversion to Christianity is placed *longeque ante excidium Britannicum*.[36] Furthermore, in another of these chapters, Gerald maintained that both Merlin of Celidon and Merlin Ambrosius had prophesied the Britons' fall (*excidium*) after the arrival not only of the Saxons but also of the Normans, and adduces numerous biblical examples to defend the validity of such prophecies.[37] Then, in Book II, he sought to demonstrate that Welsh hopes of recovery in the face of English power were ill-founded by maintaining that the sins, notably sodomy, which had led, first, to the loss of Troy by the Trojan ancestors of the Welsh and, second, to their British ancestors' loss of Britain were no less true of the expansionist, self-confident Welsh of the 1190s whose 'unpraiseworthy' characteristics he had enumerated in the previous six chapters.[38]

The key passage invokes, in Gildasian fashion, the biblical authority of the Old Testament prophet Hosea, who condemned Israel's sinful apostasy from God:

Qualiter etiam poenitentiam egisse, nedum peregisse dicentur, quos tot peccatis vitiorumque voragini datos, perjuriis puta, furtis, latrociniis, rapinis, homicidiis et fratricidiis, adulteriis et incestibus, obstinata de die in diem amplius malitia implicitos videmus et irretitos? Adeo quidem ut verbis Osee prophetae in ipsos uti vere quis possit; 'Non est veritas, et non est misericordia, et non est scientia Domini in

---

35 'The most ancient histories of the Irish': 'Giraldus Cambrensis in Topographia Hiberniae', chs 85–92 (ed. O'Meara, 156–9; quotation at 156); trans. O'Meara, *Gerald of Wales: The History and Topography of Ireland*, 92–100, at 92; summarised in *Expugnatio Hibernica*, II.6 (ed. and trans. Scott and Martin, 148–9). See also *ibid.*, 271–2; Jeanne-Marie Boivin, *L'Irlande au moyen âge: Giraud de Barri et la* Topographia Hibernica *(1188)* (Paris, 1993), 91–7; John Carey, *The Irish National Origin-Legend: Synthetic Pseudohistory*, Quiggin Pamphlets on the Sources of Mediaeval Gaelic History 1 (Cambridge, 1994), esp. 22–3.

36 'Long before the fall of the Britons': *Descriptio*, I.18 (ed. Dimock, 202). See also *ibid.*, I.1 (166 and n. 1), for the third part of the Britons *quae Armoricum ... sinum obtinuit, non post Britannicum excidium, sed long ante a Maximano [sic] tyranno translata est*, 'who gained possesssion of ... the Armorican coast, having been moved there, not after the fall of the Britons, but long before that by the tyrant Maximianus'. The second recension changes the name to Maximus, the name used in the *De Excidio Britanniae*, ch. 13 (ed. and trans. Winterbottom, 20, 93); Maximianus occurs in the *Historia Brittonum*, chs 27, 29, ed. John Morris, *Nennius: The British History and the Welsh Annals* (London and Chichester, 1980), 65, 66 (though Maximus appears in ch. 31, *ibid.*, 67), and the *Historia Regum Britanniae*, chs 81–92, 159, 194 (ed. Reeve and trans. Wright, 98–117, 218–19, 266–7).

37 *Descriptio*, I.16 (ed. Dimock, 196). Biblical examples: *ibid.*, I.16 (197–200). For Gerald's use of prophecy see Ad Putter, 'Gerald of Wales and the Prophet Merlin', *Anglo-Norman Studies* 31 (2008), 90–103.

38 For the campaigns of the Lord Rhys and his sons, 1189–97, see J. E. Lloyd, *A History of Wales from the Earliest Times to the Edwardian Conquest*, 3rd edn (London, 1939), II.573–82; J. Beverley Smith, 'Treftadaeth Deheubarth', in *Yr Arglwydd Rhys*, ed. Nerys Ann Jones and Huw Pryce (Cardiff, 1996), 18–52, at 37–40. The loss of Troy was described, albeit without reference to sodomy, by Geoffrey of Monmouth, greatly elaborating Welsh traditions already found in the early-ninth-century *Historia Brittonum*; that of Britain by Gildas in his *De Excidio*, which accused two of the kings he castigated as being guilty of sodomy, an accusation repeated by Geoffrey – followed by Gerald – with respect to one of these, namely Maelgwn or Malgo. *Historia Regum Britanniae*, chs 6, 183 (ed. Reeve and trans. Wright, 6–7, 184–5); Gildas, *De Excidio Britanniae*, chs 28, 33 (ed. and trans. Winterbottom, 30, 32, 100, 102); *Descriptio*, II.7 (ed. Dimock, 215). See also Tatlock, *The Legendary History*, 354–5; Wright, 'Geoffrey', 10–11.

eis. Maledictum, et mendacium, et homicidium, et furtum, et adulterium inundaverunt; et sanguis sanguinem tetigit. Propter quod lugebit terra eorum, et infirmabitur omnis qui habitat in ea.' 'Et populus non intelligens vapulabit.'[39]

Gerald went on to set out how the conquest of Wales could be completed by the English crown, with crucial assistance from the Marcher lords.[40] In other words, Gerald turned what were essentially native traditions about their distant past against the Welsh in a critique that justified Marcher and royal ambitions. Thus, while observing that the Welsh were inspired by the memory of their former nobility and their glorious Trojan and British origins,[41] as a latter-day Gildas he sought to show that such confidence was mistaken by insisting that their sins, both past and present, should not be forgotten.

If this interpretation is correct it reinforces the case for seeing Gerald's view of the Welsh in the first recension of the *Descriptio* as essentially hostile, and is of a piece with his reliance on Geoffrey of Monmouth's account of early British history, which, though holding out a vague prospect of a British recovery when the time came that Merlin had prophesied to Arthur, nevertheless ended by stressing that the Welsh were unworthy descendants of the Britons and had failed to re-establish their lordship over the island of Britain.[42] Likewise, Gerald ended the *Descriptio* by implying, in the words attributed to the old man of Pencader, that the best the Welsh could hope for was to survive in the 'worst corner' of the island: Wales.[43] Yet the emphasis on the sins of the Britons and their consequent fall was indebted to Gildas (followed by Bede), not Geoffrey, most of whose *Historia*, after all, presented the early Britons in a glorious light and even adopted a largely sympathetic approach to the rulers condemned in the *De Excidio*, recasting them as successors of King Arthur.[44] Moreover, while Gerald affected disdain for Geoffrey and his *Historia*, he had no difficulty in explicitly invoking the authority of Gildas, whom he praised as not only a dispassionate historian but a saint. In other words, Gildas was far better qualified than

---

[39] 'How can it be said that they have performed, let alone finished, penance, when we see them dedicated to so many sins and a deep abyss of vices – namely, to perjuries, thefts, robberies, plunderings, murders and fratricides, adulteries and incests, and are increasingly entangled and ensnared from day to day in stubborn evil? Indeed, one could truly use the words of the prophet Hosea about them: "There is no truth, and there is no mercy, and there is no knowledge of God in them. Cursing, and lying, and killing, and theft, and adultery have overflowed, and blood has touched blood. Therefore their land shall mourn, and everyone that dwells in it shall languish." "And the people that does not understand shall be beaten."': *Descriptio*, II.7 (ed. Dimock, 216–17); Hos. 4:1–3, 14 (slightly amended from the Vulgate in verses 1 and 3). As far as I have been able to ascertain, this is the only place in which Gerald cites these particular verses of Hosea, though he cites Hos. 4:11 in *Gemma Ecclesiastica*, II.19, ed. J. S. Brewer, Giraldi Cambrensis Opera 2, RS (London, 1862), 256 (trans. John J. Hagen, *Gerald of Wales: The Jewel of the Church* (Leiden, 1979), 195 and 323, n. 13). Though it lacks this passage, Gildas's *De Excidio* draws liberally on the Old Testament prophets to condemn the Britons.

[40] *Descriptio*, II.8 (ed. Dimock, 218–22).

[41] *Ibid.*, II.10 (227).

[42] *Historia Regum Britanniae*, chs 205–7 (ed. Reeve and trans. Wright, 278–81).

[43] *Descriptio*, II.10 (ed. Dimock, 226–7); Crick, 'The British Past', 74.

[44] *Historia Regum Britanniae*, chs 179–83 (ed. Reeve and trans. Wright, 252–5); Wright, 'Geoffrey', 10–11. Of course, Bede had already commented that Gildas had described the 'unspeakable crimes' of the Britons, and in one passage Geoffrey refers to Gildas's account of their sins: *Historia Ecclesiastica*, I.22 (ed. and trans. Colgrave and Mynors, 68–9); above, n. 25.

Geoffrey to confer legitimacy on Gerald's argument that, given their early history as Britons, the Welsh of his day 'were merely running true to form'.[45]

A further consideration in assessing why the *Descriptio Kambriae* uses Gildas as a stick to beat the Welsh is Gerald's position as a royal clerk at the time of the work's composition. As with his earlier prose writings on Ireland, Gerald hoped, somewhat naively, that his two books on Wales would bring him personal advancement.[46] One way of looking at the *Descriptio* is to see it as a last-ditch attempt to achieve this goal or, perhaps more accurately, to save his curial career. The *Itinerarium Kambriae* had probably proved less successful than Gerald had hoped in this respect, as its first dedicatee, the justiciar William Longchamp, bishop of Ely, had been driven out of England in October 1191 as a result of manoeuvrings by Prince John during Richard I's absence on crusade.[47] Gerald then appears to have switched his allegiance to John, only to find that he had miscalculated, as Richard, by now a prisoner in Germany, sent Hubert Walter to restore royal authority in England in April 1193; soon elected archbishop of Canterbury and later appointed justiciar, Hubert had ended John's rebellion by Richard's return to the country in March 1194. In the meantime William Wibert, a Cistercian monk who had accompanied Gerald on missions to keep the peace in Wales, accused his companion of plotting with the Welsh princes, to whom he was related, against the English crown.[48] In other words, by the time of Richard's return to England in March 1194 Gerald's position at court had probably become extremely precarious as a result of both his closeness to the rebellious John and the attempts by a rival for royal patronage to exploit his mixed Norman and Welsh ancestry. Small wonder, then, that Gerald, faced with this changed situation, tried to reconcile himself with Richard's regime by dedicating the *Descriptio* to Hubert Walter, the king's right-hand man. Above all, in an implicit rejection of Wibert's aspersions, he sought to demonstrate that his familiarity with the Welsh was fundamental to his loyalty, not only by declaring that their hopes of recovering sovereignty over Britain were contradicted by the very historical tradition invoked to sustain them but by offering practical advice on how Wales could be conquered. Recruiting Gildas to condemn the Welsh helped to serve that self-justifying purpose: his claim to be following in the footsteps of the Britons' greatest historian gave Gerald a uniquely compelling voice in speaking up for Marcher and English ambitions in Wales. However, if he hoped that this display of learning and literary skill would be sufficient to save his career at court, he was mistaken: it is probably no coincidence that Richard's release and return to England in 1194 coincided with Gerald's departure from royal service, a matter about which Gerald was extremely reticent.[49]

What, then, is the significance of the use of the early British past and particularly of Gildas in the *Descriptio Kambriae*? At one level the evidence examined here reflects Gerald's wider interest in the pre-Norman past of Wales, seen

---

45 Charles-Edwards, 'Bede', 48 (apropos of Bede's view of the Britons).

46 Bartlett, *Gerald*, 58–62.

47 Huw Pryce, 'Gerald's Journey through Wales', *Journal of Welsh Ecclesiastical History* 6 (1989), 17–34, esp. 31–4.

48 H. E. Butler, ed. and trans., *The Autobiography of Giraldus Cambrensis* (London, 1937), 111–16, 141–2; Richter, *Giraldus*, 84–5.

49 Richter, 'Gerald', 383; Bartlett, *Gerald*, 64–5; John Gillingham, *The English in the Twelfth Century* (Woodbridge, 2000), 67–8 and n. 57.

also in the *Itinerarium Kambriae* and the autobiographical works focusing on the St Davids struggle, an interest that drew on a variety of written sources, including several that purported to record early British and Welsh traditions.[50] It is worth stressing, though, that Gerald did not attempt to connect that past with the era of Norman conquest from the late eleventh century onwards in a continuous narrative comparable to that achieved by William of Malmesbury, Henry of Huntingdon and several other twelfth-century historians with respect to Anglo-Saxon and Norman England.[51] True, that would have been difficult given the scanty nature of early historical writing in Wales: the *Historia Brittonum* is a poor substitute for Bede's *Historia Ecclesiastica* in terms of coherence and coverage, and early Latin annals from Wales are much sparser than the *Anglo-Saxon Chronicle*. Of course, Gerald drew freely on the elaborate pseudo-history of Geoffrey of Monmouth, but its narrative of the Britons came to an end in the seventh century, and it is by no means clear that Gerald wished to continue it down to his own day. Rather, he used early British and Welsh history in ways that were highly selective and reflected the perspective of a churchman who also identified strongly with the Marcher society of south-west Wales. In part, he furnishes merely another instance of the appropriation by Anglo-Norman churchmen of native Welsh ecclesiastical traditions: witness his tales of Welsh saints and accounts of the early history of St Davids.[52] Above all, though, Gerald sought to turn on their head prevailing Welsh notions of the British past as a source of inspiration and hope for the future. Instead, he discerned in that past deep-rooted patterns of behaviour that gave the lie to Welsh self-confidence and comfort to the Marcher and English conquerors. In short, the first edition of the *Descriptio Kambriae* reveals an ambitious and original approach to the early Welsh past, as Gerald invoked Gildas to imply that the Welsh of his own day were destined to fail as their behaviour was all too similar to that which had caused the ruin of their Trojan and British ancestors.[53]

---

[50] E.g. *Itinerarium Kambriae*, I.2; II.1 (ed. Dimock, 28, 31, 102).

[51] James Campbell, *Essays in Anglo-Saxon History* (London, 1986), 209–28.

[52] E.g. *Itinerarium Kambriae*, I.2, 5; II.1 (ed. Dimock, 28, 31, 56, 101–4).

[53] I am grateful to Nancy Edwards and the editors for their comments on drafts of this essay.

11

PATRICK'S REASONS FOR LEAVING BRITAIN

Roy Flechner

As a foreigner in his adoptive land with no kin to vouch for him, Patrick needed to secure protection from local kings who guaranteed his safety.[1] Such protection, it seems, did not come cheaply. In his *Confessio* Patrick famously describes how he lavished *praemia* 'gifts' on kings and made *mercedes* 'payments' to sons of kings who travelled with him.[2] He also had to grease the palms of judges, to whom he gave *pretium quindecim hominum* 'the price of fifteen men', although we are never told what he received in return.[3] But while Patrick may have given gifts to others, he insists that he never received any himself. Rather, he turned down many gifts and refused to accept so much as *dimidium scriptulae* 'half a scruple', or even *pretium calciamenti mei* 'the price of my shoe' in return for performing baptisms.[4] In an attempt to explain why Patrick should stress his generosity and meekness, Thomas Charles-Edwards proposed that 'in part Patrick emphasised his attitude to gifts because of the accusation that he had gone to Ireland in the hope of enriching himself'.[5] Echoes of this accusation can also be found in Patrick's insistence that he did not go to Ireland of his own free will.[6] Charles-Edwards's comment is the impetus for the present essay, which asks why Patrick was suspected of going to Ireland for financial gain.

The sources

My chief sources will be the *Confessio* and the Letter to the Soldiers of Coroticus, both of which profess to have been written by the saint. Close thematic and textual correspondences confirm that the two were written by the same author. The author, according to the *Confessio*, was based in Ireland. His familiarity with

---

[1]   I am grateful to the editors for their helpful comments on a previous version.

[2]   Patrick's *Confessio* and Letter to the Soldiers of Coroticus were edited by L. Bieler, *Libri Epistolarum Sancti Patricii Episcopi*, 2 vols (Dublin, 1952), I.56–91, 91–102. For the citation, see *Confessio* § 52. A reprint of the editions with translations is A. B. E. Hood, *St Patrick: His Writings and Muirchú's Life* (London, 1978). For more recent translations see D. R. Howlett, *The Book of Letters of Saint Patrick the Bishop* (Dublin, 1994).

[3]   *Confessio* § 53. By the 'price of a man' the author probably meant *lóg n-enech* 'honour-price' (lit: 'price of a face'), which is the Old Irish equivalent of the Frankish *wergeld* (lit: 'man price').

[4]   *Confessio* §§ 37, 50, 57.

[5]   *Early Christian Ireland* (Cambridge, 2000), 220. For this accusation and others see *Confessio* §§ 26–28.

[6]   E.g. *Confessio* § 28.

the Irish landscape is reinforced by his use of an Irish placename, *silua Focluti quae est prope mare occidentale* 'the forest of Voclut by the western sea'.[7] The Letter, in the form that we have it, is said to be the second letter to the soldiers of Coroticus, a British Christian leader who killed some of Patrick's male converts and ignored a previous appeal to free female converts that he had enslaved.[8] However, like many a late antique letter, it is difficult to determine whether the version of the text that has come down to us is faithful to the original that was (or, at least, purports to have been) sent to the soldiers, or whether it is a reworking of the original that was meant to proclaim the author's condemnation of Coroticus and his men to a wider contemporary audience or to posterity.

Neither the Letter nor the *Confessio* can be dated with precision since the internal dating criteria are ambiguous. The problem of dating them is inextricably bound up with the problem of Patrick's own dates, which has attracted considerable scholarly attention over the years but will not be dealt with here at length due to limitations of space.[9] Insofar as the present inquiry is concerned, suffice it to say that although the debate on Patrick's dates is far from being settled, most historians seem to agree that he was active either in the early or late fifth century, corresponding to his contradictory annalistic obits, in 457 and 493, both of which are retrospective.[10] Only rarely has his career, or the bulk thereof, been dated before the fifth century.[11] The strongest objection to a pre-fifth-century date comes from a hypothesis first put forward by Ludwig Bieler and developed by David Dumville. It holds that Patrick must have been writing after 404, but not too soon after, because in this year Jerome completed the Vulgate, which is cited in the *Confessio* and Letter.[12] Dumville rejects the possibility that non-Vulgate readings in Patrick's writings might have been replaced by Vulgate readings in the course of transmission: 'the untidy distribution of Vulgate-readings in the Psalter, Gospels, and Epistles, the absolute dominance of the Vulgate Acts of the Apostles, and the clearly Old Latin nature of the remainder are, in their very inconsistency with one another, as good a guarantee of general authenticity as could be wished for'. However, this common-sense argument is called into question by evidence from early medieval works that exhibit clear, but nevertheless inconsistent, patterns of contamination with variants from alternative biblical

7   *Confessio* § 23.
8   Letter § 21.
9   A critical survey is provided by D. N. Dumville *et al.*, *Saint Patrick, A.D. 493–1993* (Woodbridge, 1993), 13–18.
10 On the annalistic obits see Dumville, *Saint Patrick*, 29–33, 59–64. For the history of the Chronicle of Ireland, whence these entries derive, see T. M. Charles-Edwards, *The Chronicle of Ireland*, 2 vols (Liverpool, 2006), I.7–9.
11 See e.g. M. Esposito, 'The Patrician Problem and a Possible Solution', *Irish Historical Studies* 10 (1956/7), 131–55. Esposito's speculative arguments were followed up by J. T. Koch, who tried to offer linguistic support for them: '*Cothairche*, Esposito's Theory, and Neo-Celtic Lenition', in *Britain 400–600: Language and History*, ed. A. Bammesberger and A. Wollmann (Heidelberg, 1990), 179–202. I am unable to comment on his linguistic analysis, but his historiographical methodology can be seen to suffer from a number of defects, one of which is his tendency to accept or reject the credibility of certain sources when it suits his argument. For instance, Irish words in the seventh-century Patrician hagiography from Armagh (which Koch does not attribute to their source) are accepted as faithful renditions of fourth- or fifth-century utterings (e.g. pp. 180, 182), but later (p. 193) the same sources are dismissed as anachronistic.
12 L. Bieler, 'Der Bibeltext des heiligen Patrick', *Biblica* 28 (1947), 31–58, 236–63. Dumville, *Saint Patrick*, 15–16.

texts. One such work is a recently edited commentary of supposed Irish origin on the Gospel of Matthew dating from *c.*725.[13] The commentary is essentially a compilation of extracts from earlier exegetical works. The redactor of the commentary borrowed biblical citations from a number of these works which cited the Vulgate, such as Ailerán and Frigulus. However, although the redactor replaced some Vulgate readings from these sources with variants from an Irish Bible text, he did not do so consistently, and sometimes chose to retain Vulgate readings.[14] Hence, it would appear that inconsistency in the pattern of biblical texts cited is not an automatic guarantee of authenticity (if it were, then one would have had to pronounce the extracts from Ailerán and Frigulus as authentic, whereas they have clearly been modified).

The implication for Patrick's writings is obvious: there is no compelling argument for dating them (or indeed Patrick) after, rather than before, 404. Indeed, Patrick's writings contain nothing that conflicts with a pre-fifth-century date, but equally they do not contain any distinct pre-fifth-century elements either. Even the reference in the *Confessio* to an imperial administrative office, the decurion-ship, held by Patrick's father, is no proof of an early date.[15] Although one may reasonably infer from this reference that imperial administrative institutions were still extant in the country of Patrick's youth, this does not preclude a fifth-century date for Patrick because we simply do not know when these institutions ceased to exist. The fate of imperial administrative institutions in Britain following the departure of the legions in 410 is among the many puzzles that render this period one of the most obscure in British history. Sadly, our earliest sources for the situation in Britain after 410 are not contemporary, most are foreign, and some – such as Procopius, who argued for continuity of Roman rule into the sixth century – were clearly ill informed.[16]

Patrick in his own words

What do the *Confessio* and Letter tell us about Patrick's life and career? According to the *Confessio* Patrick's family owned a *uillula* near a *uicus* called *Bannauem Taburniae*, which has never been identified. If Patrick's idea of a *uillula* was in any way like the modern catch-all definition of *uilla*, namely 'a site consisting of a rural building of Roman aspect', then his *uillula* is unlikely to have been situated north of the Mersey, where no such site is known to have existed in the west of Britain.[17] Patrick's father, Calpornius, was a deacon and his grandfather, Potitus, a presbyter. Around the age of sixteen Patrick's life changed dramatically when he was taken captive *cum tot milia hominum* 'with so many thousands of people'. After six years of servitude near the Wood of Voclut, Co.

---

13 J. Rittmueller, ed., *Liber Questionum in evangeliis*, CCSL 108F (Turnhout, 2003).

14 Rittmueller, *Liber Questionum*, 25*–29* (Bible-Text Variant List 3).

15 *Confessio* § 1.

16 A. R. Birley, *The Roman Government of Britain* (Oxford, 2005), 461–5.

17 For this definition see D. Mattingly, *An Imperial Possession: Britain in the Roman Empire, 54 BC–AD 409* (London, 2006), 370, and 262, 38–81, 481, for maps showing the distribution of villa sites in Britain. There is no consensus on the location of the *uillula*. A couple of recent suggestions are Southern Dorset or the Cotswolds; see K. R. Dark, 'St Patrick's *Uillula* and the Fifth-Century Occupation of Romano-British Villas', in *Saint Patrick A.D. 493–1993*, 19–24. The account that follows is based on *Confessio* §§ 1, 14, 17, 23, 26, 27, 32, 37, 40–2, 50, 52.

Mayo, during which he grew more steadfast in the Christian faith, he deserted his master and was reunited with his kinsfolk in Britain, who welcomed him with open arms.[18] Although no other sources about slavery in Ireland at this period survive, Patrick's own testimony that a foreigner travelling through Ireland needed to be accompanied by a costly escort and had to secure his protection by paying off kings seems to be at odds with the idea that an unredeemed slave could escape captivity, travel two hundred miles or so from the west to the east coast of Ireland and then cross the Irish Sea to Britain without being captured or harmed. Therefore, even if Patrick was telling the truth, he must have been aware that his contemporaries might find his story fantastic. And even if his readers/hearers believed him, they could nevertheless have considered him to be unfree because he was not formally freed by his master.[19] In this context it is interesting to see what a glossator to Fiacc's Hymn, an eighth-century verse text that drew (directly or indirectly) upon material from the *Confessio*, made of Patrick's captivity. According to the glossator, Patrick's release after six years in captivity was *fo intamail na hiubile Ebreorum* 'after the manner of the little jubilee of the Hebrews', a reference to Exod. 21:2 or Jer. 34:14: 'he shall serve you six years, and you shall let him go free from you'.[20] This comment should make us wonder whether Patrick was consciously alluding to the Bible. Indeed, in recent years scholarship has grown more aware of Patrick's sophisticated use of biblical allusions and metaphors.[21] Perhaps what we have before us is a case in which Patrick 'titivated' (or even made up) the facts in order to legitimise his status as a free person by appealing to Old Testament law. Curiously, Irish canon law of the late seventh or early eighth century codified a modified version of the Old Testament jubilee laws, which may already have been practised in Ireland from an earlier date.[22]

Following his release, Patrick remained in Britain for a number of years and was ordained deacon. However, the *Confessio* goes on to say that a vision he

---

18 On Voclut, mentioned by Patrick himself, see Charles-Edwards, *Early Christian Ireland*, 217.

19 Roman law, though allowing slaves to be released through manumission, imposed a series of restrictions on freedmen, who continued to owe certain services to their former masters; see A. Borkowski and P. du Plessis, *Textbook on Roman Law*, 3rd edn (Oxford, 2005), 104–7. Although Irish law acknowledged that slaves could be freed, it strongly discouraged masters from freeing them; see *GEIL* 96–7. That Patrick's status as a free man was of concern to the early medieval followers of his cult is confirmed by the episode in Muirchú's Life of Patrick, I.11, in which the saint, upon returning from Britain, attempts to redeem himself from his former master with a *geminum seruitutis praetium terrenum utique et caeleste* 'a double price for his servitude, both earthly and heavenly'. See L. Bieler, ed., *The Patrician Texts in the Book of Armagh* (Dublin, 1979), 78, lines 3–4.

20 An edition and translation of Fiacc's Hymn is W. Stokes and J. Strachan, *Thesaurus Palaeohibernicus*, 2 vols (Dublin, 1901–1903), II.307–21. The gloss is on p. 309 lines 13–14. For the dating of the text see J. F. Kenney, *The Sources for the Early History of Ireland: Ecclesiastical* (New York, 1929), 340.

21 For studies that consider Patrick's literary background and rhetorical ingenuity see, for example, P. Dronke, 'St. Patrick's Reading', *CMCS* 1 (1981), 21–38; E. MacLuhan, ' "*Ministerium seruitutis meae*": The Metaphor and Reality of Slavery in Saint Patrick's *Epistola* and *Confessio*', in *Studies in Irish Hagiography: Saints and Scholars*, ed. J. Carey, M. Herbert and P. Ó Riain (Dublin, 2001), 63–71; Howlett, *Book of Letters*, 11. For a short discussion of literary antecedents of the *Confessio* see C. Stancliffe, 'Patrick', in *ODNB* XLIII.69–80, http://www.oxforddnb.com/view/article/21562 (accessed 26 June 2010).

22 *Collectio Canonum Hibernensis*, ed. H. Wasserschleben, *Die irische Kanonensammlung*, 2nd edn (Leipzig, 1885), 128–31.

had had persuaded him to return to Ireland, which he did, taking with him sufficient funds to enable him to pay Irish kings and judges. He devoted himself to the missionary life, baptised thousands, converted nobles and sons of kings and trained clerics to succeed him. He also endured many hardships, including a two-week imprisonment, during which his property was taken away from him and then restored. At no point does he say what his property consisted of, nor does he say how it could have been of value in Ireland's non-monetary economy, where wealth was based primarily on the ownership of land and cattle, neither of which Patrick could transport across the Irish Sea from Britain.[23]

Patrick was to return again to Britain later in his life, when he was already a bishop. During that visit he was put on trial by his *seniores* 'elders' on a charge that is not specified. According to Patrick, the trial was only an *occasio* 'pretext' that his elders used to settle an open score with him. The offence for which he was charged had been committed thirty years earlier, before Patrick reached the age of fifteen, and he admits he had confessed it to a friend. We are not told what punishment he was given, if any. He subsequently returned to Ireland, where he wrote his *Confessio*.

Thus far the *Confessio*. What does the Letter to the Soldiers of Coroticus add to this picture? At the outset we learn that Patrick was already a bishop when he wrote the letter.[24] As such, he was in a position to excommunicate the soldiers, who are understood to be Christian. From the fact that he refuses to address them as his 'fellow citizens' or 'citizens of the holy Romans' because of their wickedness, one may surmise that they were in fact Roman citizens, or at least self-proclaimed citizens.[25] Alternatively, as suggested by Dumville, one can interpret this passage metaphorically, and take 'citizens of the holy Romans' to mean 'Christians'.[26] Later in the Letter we learn that Patrick was *ingenuus* 'free-born' and that his father was a decurion, and not just a deacon as he was styled in the *Confessio*. In the same sentence he says that he sold his nobility and declares that he is not ashamed of that.[27] Patrick was eventually stripped of his freedom when he was abducted from Britain. His captors, we are told, *deuastauerunt seruos et ancillas domus patris mei*.[28] This is yet another phrase that can be interpreted metaphorically by taking *seruos et ancillas domus patris mei* to mean 'fellow Christians'. Metaphors of this kind, that portray Christian believers as slaves of the Father, were used by other late antique authors; for instance, in his commentary on Paul's letter to Titus, Jerome says that *apostolus igitur, qui peccati non fuit seruus, recte Dei patris uocatur seruus et Christi.*[29] This is not

---

23 B. Raftery, 'Iron-Age Ireland', in *A New History of Ireland I: Prehistoric and Early Ireland*, ed. D. Ó Cróinín (Oxford, 2005), 134–81, at 153.

24 The account that follows is based on Letter §§ 1, 2, 10, 21.

25 Letter § 2: *non dico ciuibus meis neque ciuibus sanctorum Romanorum* 'I do not say to my fellow citizens, nor to the citizens of the holy Romans'.

26 Dumville, *Saint Patrick*, 108: 'it is unwise to press the word *ciues* to a specific association with Roman citizenship; the clue is provided by the *sancti romani*, the Roman saints'. R. P. C. Hanson, *Saint Patrick: His Origins and Career* (Oxford, 1968), 114, offers a similar hypothesis, which he reaches via a more complicated route.

27 Letter § 10: *uendidi enim nobilitatem meam, non erubesco* 'for I have sold my nobility, I am not ashamed [of it]'.

28 'harried the male and female slaves of my father's house'.

29 'the apostle, who was not a slave to sin, is rightly called the slave of God the Father and Christ': *Commentarii in iv epistulas Paulinas*, PL XXVI, cols 307–618, at col. 592.

to say that Patrick has read his Jerome, but that such slavery metaphors were not unheard of in late antiquity.[30]

Patrick and imperial administration

We may assume that Patrick would not have mentioned his father's decurion-ship unless that position still carried authority when his father held it and unless he believed that his contemporaries knew what a decurion was. Although these assumptions do not bring us any closer to placing any absolute dates on Patrick's career, they suggest at least that Patrick was active either at a time when decu-rions still held authority, or not long after. Richard Hanson believed that Patrick's father, Calpornius, was a decurion in the council of a *ciuitas* within whose juris-diction fell the *uicus* of *Bannauem Taburniae*.[31] To date, twenty to twenty-four towns that could be considered important enough to have had a council by the standards that obtained elsewhere in the empire have been identified in Roman Britain.[32] Like other members of the rural aristocracy, Patrick's father would presumably have held both a country estate, his *uillula*, and an urban residence in the town where he discharged his obligations as a decurion on the town coun-cil.[33] Since there is no reason to assume that the decurionship in Britain was fundamentally different from the decurionship elsewhere in the empire, there are a few general observations that can be made about Calpornius's office. Decu-rions, also known as *curiales* after the local administrative councils, *curiae*, of which they were members, made up the great bulk of aristocratic landowners in the late empire.[34] Any individual who possessed enough property to qualify as a decurion was obliged to serve on the council if nominated.[35] What counted as property for the purpose of being appointed to a council was normally land, but from 383 those whose wealth was invested primarily in slaves could also enrol in the councils.[36] Membership of the *curia* was not only obligatory but also *de facto* hereditary, because the heirs of decurions possessed the necessary property quali-fication by default. From 390 the hereditary aspect was also enshrined in Roman law.[37] Sons of decurions were nominated as soon as they came of age, in their eighteenth year, but in practice children as young as seven or eight are known to have been nominated.[38] Certain wealthy individuals could claim exemption from serving on the council, for instance if they held senatorial rank or, from 313, if they joined the clergy.[39]

---

[30] See also MacLuhan, 'Metaphor and Reality', 63–71.
[31] Hanson, *Saint Patrick*, 118.
[32] Mattingly, *Imperial Possession*, 260–3.
[33] On villas and the rural aristocracy of Roman Britain see Mattingly, *Imperial Possession*, 369–75, 453–71.
[34] C. Wickham, *Framing the Early Middle Ages* (Oxford, 2005), 167.
[35] A. H. M. Jones, *The Later Roman Empire 284–602: A Social Economic and Administrative Survey*, 2 vols (Oxford, 1964), 738 (page numbering is continuous from one volume to the next).
[36] *CTh* XII.1.96 (AD 383).
[37] *CTh* XIII.5.19: *manebit uero in ordine curiali et ei filius in officium curiale succedat* 'he shall remain in the curial order and let his son succeed him in the curial office' (my translation).
[38] Jones, *Later Roman Empire*, 739.
[39] *Ibid.*, 745.

Decurions were expected to fulfil a variety of roles which included collecting taxes, seeing to the maintenance of roads, administering the public post and recruiting soldiers for the army. Of these, the most onerous obligation was tax collecting, because a decurion was expected to make up for any shortfall in tax revenues from his own pocket. This inconvenience was believed to have contributed to a surge in *curiales* seeking to escape their position on councils. During the fourth and fifth centuries emperors show a growing concern with what has come to be known as the 'flight of the *curiales*'.[40] The exact scale of the phenomenon is difficult to assess due to imprecise and rhetorically exaggerated figures provided by contemporary sources. For instance, the fourth-century Antiochene master of rhetoric, Libanius, says in one oration that numbers decreased locally from 1200 to 12, but in a different oration the decrease is said to be slightly less extreme: from 600 to 60.[41]

From 313 a favourite escape route for *curiales* was to join the clergy (which also accounts for their predominance in the episcopate).[42] But approximately fifteen years later, when it became evident that many decurions adopted the religious life only to avoid the councils, Constantine restricted the clergy's immunity from curial charges.[43] However, the restrictions were soon relaxed, and *curiales* were allowed to take orders provided that they proved their sincerity by surrendering either all or two-thirds of their property to their sons or, if they had no sons, to other relatives who would replace them on the *curia*. Between 361 and 452 emperors sometimes tightened and sometimes relaxed the restrictions they imposed on *curiales* who wanted to take orders.[44]

A disgruntled decurion?

Arbitrary lawsuits against decurions were a persistent menace, and decurions in Britain seem to have been just as susceptible to them as were their colleagues elsewhere in the empire. Indeed, in 319 a Roman governor of Britain found it necessary to seek a rescript from the emperor restricting the circumstances under which a decurion could be sued.[45] The decurions' discontent with the obligations of their office and the refuge that many of them sought in the clergy provide the background for the dual career that Patrick's father had as decurion and deacon. It has already been suggested that Calpornius sought relief from certain burdens associated with the decurionship by swapping his place on the council for a deaconate.[46] What seems to have escaped notice, however, is that Calpornius's tenure of the imperial office would also have affected his heir. The heir, as we have seen, was obliged by his property ranking to enter the council, but he was also obliged to do so by law if his father took clerical orders.

---

40 C. Rapp, 'The Elite Status of Bishops in Late Antiquity in Ecclesiastical, Spiritual, and Social Contexts', *Arethusa* 33.3 (2000), 379–99, at 390.
41 Wickham, *Framing the Early Middle Ages*, 68.
42 Rapp, 'Elite Status', 390.
43 Jones, *Later Roman Empire*, 745.
44 *Ibid.*, 746, n. 79.
45 *CTh* II.7.2.
46 J. B. Bury, *The Life of St. Patrick and his Place in History* (London, 1905), 20; E. MacNeill, *St Patrick: Apostle of Ireland* (London, 1934); Hanson, *Saint Patrick*, 176–78; Howlett, *Book of Letters*, 116; M. B. De Paor, *Patrick: The Pilgrim Apostle of Ireland* (Dublin, 1998), 127.

That Patrick was heir to his father is a reasonable inference from the fact that he was a wealthy man. Since he was not a soldier or merchant, the only legitimate path open before him to become rich was to inherit the family fortune. The hypothesis that Patrick held an imperial office gains further support from his own admission that he sold his nobility.[47] Nobility in post-republican Rome was conferred through wealth and the participation in government by holding an office.[48] Therefore, if Patrick was speaking of nobility in the Roman sense then he must have held an imperial office. He adds that he was not ashamed to admit that he sold his nobility, and nor should he have been, because trafficking in imperial offices was ubiquitous and a thriving business in the fourth century.[49]

The selling of noble status was one way in which Patrick could raise funds to sustain his operations in Ireland, but there might have been other ways. For instance, he could, hypothetically, have sold the family land, or parts of it. But he could only do this while Britain still had an active land market. From what we know of the land market in Roman Britain, it owed its existence primarily to major absentee landowners like the famous Melania the younger.[50] But once the legions left no imperial armed forces remained to protect the landed estates of the absentee landowners. Consequently, it is difficult to imagine that Britain could continue to attract new investors from outside. In all likelihood, then, the land market would have collapsed around 410 if not before, during the long years of political unrest. Hence, if Patrick did in fact sell land, he is likely to have done so before 410.

Another way in which Patrick could have secured the funding he needed was by selling the family slaves or by bringing them with him to Ireland. Even if we take the expression 'slaves of my father's house' to be a metaphor, as suggested above, his family may still be assumed to have owned slaves, like any other aristocratic family of its day. Patrick is not known to have objected to slave trafficking nor to slavery as an institution. He was only incensed by the fact that Coroticus killed free-born newly converted Christians whom he captured and sold others to non-Christian Pictish masters.[51] Patrick's ecclesiastical status would not have debarred him from possessing slaves either, for the Church's ownership of slaves in late antiquity and the early Middle Ages is well documented, and clerics themselves were not always free men.[52] It is not until Justinian that one finds legislation granting manumission to slaves joining the clergy, and then only with their masters' permission.[53] A later settlement, allowing slaves owned by monasteries to be freed once they have take monastic vows, was severely limited by Pope Gregory the Great in 595.[54] Slaves were in fact a convenient form of 'movable' property for wealthy travellers like Patrick. Not only could they have been ferried across the Irish Sea, but there would certainly have been a market

---

[47] Letter § 10: *uendidi enim nobilitatem meam* 'for I have sold my nobility'.

[48] G. Mousourakis, *The Historical and Institutional Context of Roman Law* (Aldershot, 2003), 65.

[49] C. Kelly, *Ruling the Later Roman Empire* (Cambridge, MA, 2004), 160–3.

[50] Mattingly, *Imperial Possession*, 353–5.

[51] Letter §§ 13, 15.

[52] On the manner in which the papacy concerned itself with slaves owned by churches see Gregory the Great's letters, *Sancti Gregorii Magni Registrum Epistularum Libri I–XIV*, ed. D. Norberg, CCSL 140–140A (Turnhout, 1982), letters 1.39a (pp. 1092–1094), 6.36 (pp. 410–11), 9.30 (p. 549).

[53] *Nov.* CXXIII.17 (ed. Mommsen, III.607).

[54] Roman council of 595. MGH epp. I, 362–7.

for them in Ireland's non-monetary economy. Their importance as a commodity is attested by the use of the Old Irish term *cumal* 'slave woman' to denote a unit of value, roughly the worth of three milch cows.[55]

Was there another commodity that Patrick could have traded? One might guess silver, which is also known to have been used as a unit of value from the seventh century. Although there are hardly any silver finds from pre-Viking Ireland, it has been suggested that silver and other precious metal objects were exchanged between members of the elite in early medieval times.[56] Textual references to ounces of silver (like references to *cumal*s, for that matter) are not necessarily references to the actual metal, but to its value.[57]

The question of Patrick's sources of wealth brings to an end my discussion of the background to Patrick's departure to Ireland. At this point it will be useful to paraphrase the problem with which I opened this essay in the following way: there were (at least) two distinct contemporary narratives for the events that Patrick described and alluded to in the *Confessio*: one was Patrick's and the other was a rival narrative that discredited Patrick. But can the evidence reviewed here shed any light on the rival narrative? I believe the evidence can – at the very least – allow us to sketch a hypothetical background for that narrative, which would read as follows: when Patrick's father took holy orders he would have been legally obliged as a decurion to install his son in his place at the *curia* and surrender much of his property to him. But Patrick, like his father, would have been loathe to serve on the *curia* in the decades leading up to or immediately following 400, a period characterised by social, economic and political unrest. At such times curial obligations such as collecting and underwriting taxes would have been extremely difficult, and even risky, to discharge. Patrick might then have decided, perhaps with his father's consent and encouragement, that the best escape route open before him would be to set himself up in Ireland and by so doing to ensure that the family wealth would not be depleted through the under-writing of taxes or malicious lawsuits. All this, of course, contradicts Patrick's version that he did not leave Britain willingly and that he legitimately sold his nobility rather than relinquished it as a means of avoiding curial obligations. If we are to choose between Patrick's version and the rival one, then the latter can at least be said to offer a more plausible narrative which better suits the historical context.

---

55 On the *cumal* see Kelly, *Guide*, 112–13; *idem*, *Early Irish Farming* (Dublin, 2000), 592–3.

56 Prominent among the rare finds is the famous 'Coleraine Hoard' from Co. Derry, which was brought together not before *c.*410. The name *Patricius* on one of the silver ingots is believed to belong to the owner of a private workshop that produced it. See H. Mattingly and J. W. E. Pearce, 'The Coleraine Hoard', *Antiquity* 11 (1937), 39–45. On the use of precious metal objects as a form of currency in seventh- and eighth-century Ireland see C. Etchingham and C. Swift, 'English and Pictish Terms for Brooch in an 8th-Century Irish Law Text', *Medieval Archaeology* 48 (2004), 31–50.

57 E.g. *lóg leith ungae di muccib* 'the value of half an ounce of silver in pigs', for which see the *Additamenta* to Tírechán's *Collectanea*, ed. L. Bieler, *Patrician Texts*, 174, line 10.

12

LEARNING LAW IN MEDIEVAL IRELAND

Robin Chapman Stacey

One of the many subjects on which Thomas Charles-Edwards has immeasurably broadened our understanding over the years is that of early Irish legal education.[1] Through his work we have been invited to contemplate not merely what, but how, budding lawyers were being taught in the schools. No tract addresses the issue of instructional method specifically; however, given the traditional understanding of the extant law tracts as textbooks for junior jurists, it seems only reasonable to imagine that one might be able to infer something about this from the texts that remain. Particularly difficult to reconstruct from this distance are the oral aspects of early legal instruction, though one tract in the corpus has always seemed to me especially promising in this respect. *Berrad Airechta*, an early-eighth-century tract on suretyship and contract (and the first text I ever read with Professor Charles-Edwards thirty years ago at Oxford), is well known among specialists for the large amount of purportedly oral material it contains. Not only is it one of our most important sources for sayings attributed to the traditional oral law known as *Fénechas*, but at the core of the tract are replicated what purport to be the ritualised oral exchanges used by creditor and debtor in contracting obligations. Equally intriguing are the ten quotations not ascribed to *Fénechas* but introduced in the text by expressions such as *is de asberr*, 'it is regarding this that this is said', or *cid dia nepir*, 'why is this said?'[2] If ever an extant text had the potential to shed light on the oral curriculum of an early Irish law school, it should be this one.[3]

As will soon become apparent, however, what this text suggests about legal education is more complex than its apparently oral contents would lead us to anticipate. Our first step must be to establish that *Berrad Airechta* actually was intended to function within an instructional and judicial context. As David Dumville has pointed out, it may not be wise simply to presume that the *raison d'etre* for every legal text was to serve as a textbook for educating practising judges – as opposed to, for example, functioning as a venue for learned analysis

---

1   T. M. Charles-Edwards, 'The Context and Uses of Literacy in Early Christian Ireland', in *Literacy in Medieval Celtic Societies*, ed. Huw Pryce (Cambridge, 1998), 62–86; Charles-Edwards, *The Early Mediaeval Gaelic Lawyer*, Quiggin Pamphlets on the Sources of Mediaeval Gaelic History 4 (Cambridge, 1999); Charles-Edwards, Review of the *Corpus Iuris Hibernici*, *Studia Hibernica* 20 (1980), 141–62.
2   Full references in n. 39 below.
3   Robin Chapman Stacey, *Dark Speech: The Performance of Law in Early Ireland* (Philadelphia, PA, 2007), 194.

having little to do with the judicial world outside.[4] Some texts in the corpus do explicitly enjoin their own use as instructional tools for real-life practitioners through phrases such as *dia mbe brithem*, 'if you would be a judge'.[5] However, phrases such as this may well have been, or become over time, rhetorical tropes rather than genuine statements of intent, and there is in any case no *a priori* reason why all texts must have the same origins and purpose. Patrick Wormald's study of the Anglo-Saxon legal texts revealed a wide diversity of genres amongst the legal writings of early England and demonstrated convincingly that a learned tradition of law can exist entirely separate from the deciding of cases in real life.[6] His work must surely sound a cautionary note for early Irish specialists: a direct connection between the intellectualised world of the jurists, and the world of legal practice outside the schools, needs to be demonstrated rather than assumed, probably text by text.

In the case of *Berrad Airechta* the evidence does suggest that we are dealing with a text composed directly in response to the concerns of real-life legal practitioners. Earlier I described this text as centring on suretyship and contract. However, close examination of the tract suggests that the compiler's primary intention was to articulate guidelines by which disputes over debts arising out of a wide variety of relationships might be anticipated, avoided or resolved. Because contractual sureties constituted the most definitive means of guaranteeing that payments owed would ultimately be made, they occupy the largest portion of the tract. However, the text is at least as concerned with those circumstances in which no sureties existed,[7] or in which multiple parties claimed the right to intervene regardless of whether they had been officially designated as surety,[8] or in which a failure by one party or another in the relationship threatened to abrogate the agreement altogether.[9] In early Ireland disputes of this type that came to court (many would probably have been settled privately with or without the assistance of a judge) would have been prosecuted on the judicial path known as *dliged*, 'entitlement';[10] it is, I would suggest, with the various questions of status, mutual obligation, concession and performance relating to cases of *dliged* that the tract is primarily concerned.[11] If this is right, then *Berrad Airechta* enlarges our sense

---

4   David Dumville, Review of *Progress in Medieval Irish Studies*, *Peritia* 11 (1997), 451–68, at 457.
5   The phrase is particularly common in *Bretha Nemed* tracts; e.g. *CIH* VI.2221.8, 12, 17; VI.2222.34, 39; VI.2223.18, etc.; see also *Bechbretha: An Old Irish Law-tract on Bee-keeping*, ed. Thomas Charles-Edwards and Fergus Kelly (Dublin, 1983, rev. edn. 2008), §36; and the rhetorical text on horses edited and translated by Fergus Kelly, *Early Irish Farming: A Study Based Mainly on the Law-Texts of the 7th and 8th Centuries AD* (Dublin, 1998), 555, §1; see further *GEIL* 242–63.
6   Patrick Wormald, *The Making of English Law: King Alfred to the Twelfth Century* (Oxford and Malden, MA, 1999); and see further R. H. Helmholz, *The Canon Law and Ecclesiastical Jurisdiction from 597 to the 1640s*, Oxford History of the Laws of England, 1 (Oxford, 2004); and *GEIL* 253, n. 52.
7   *CIH* II.591.9–592.21; II.593.24–5.
8   *CIH* II.592.26–593.2; II.593.10–12, 20–21, 24–40.
9   *CIH* II.591.9–592.21; II.593.8–40.
10 Richard Sharpe, 'Dispute Settlement in Medieval Ireland: A Preliminary Enquiry', in *The Settlement of Disputes in Early Medieval Europe*, ed. W. Davies and P. Fouracre (Cambridge, 1986), 169–89; and Robin Chapman Stacey, *The Road to Judgment: From Custom to Court in Medieval Ireland and Wales* (Philadelphia, PA, 1994), 119–21.
11 *Berrad Airechta* states directly that *dliged* validates payments made in the course of long-term social, legal or service relationships, many of which did not involve sureties: *CIH* II.593.22–3 and II.594.1–7. A possible objection to *dliged* as the focus of this text is inclusion of the *aitire*, a surety usually associated with the path known as *coir n-athcomairc* rather than with *dliged*.

of how this path was conceptualised: not as uniquely focused on contract, as the procedural tract *Cóic Conara Fugill* implies, but rather as concerned with payments made in the context of a variety of relationships, temporary and long-term, in which sureties may or may not have been involved.[12]

Indeed, a focus on *dliged* may even explain the mysterious title of this tract, assuming it to be one contemporary with the compiler. *Berrad Airechta* means, literally, 'shearing of the (or a) court'; Liam Breatnach and Fergus Kelly have argued that *berrad* here should be taken in the sense of 'abridgment' or 'synopsis', and hence 'a synopsis of court procedure'.[13] This may well be right; however, the word *airecht*, 'court' occurs only once in the text, and that in a very general and rhetorical clause in the very last sentence.[14] Given the tract's specific focus on debt and obligation it would be difficult to regard it as a synopsis of court procedure generally speaking. Perhaps 'shearing' here is, like the more frequently used 'path' or 'road', a metaphor for one of several judicial options open to parties in dispute – in this case *dliged*.[15] Just as roads can be selected one day and ignored the next, sheep can be shorn more than once and in more than one way; such a metaphor would make reasonable sense in such a context.

The link between this text and the real-life world of justice would seem in any case to be fairly solid, and it thus seems reasonable to hope that the tract might shed light on the manner in which aspiring practitioners were educated. Of course, speculating about oral instruction on the basis of a written source is inevitably problematic. Recent research has made it clear that we cannot simply presume that instruction consisted of the verbatim memorisation of oral tradition. Rather, jurists seem actively to have reconceptualised 'traditional' lore in accordance with the political, rhetorical or artistic needs of the moment. Certainly, *Berrad Airechta* provides evidence of the idea of memory as a creative rather than a passively reiterative process.[16] We may also catch a glimpse of oral instructional techniques in the quotations attributed in the text to *Fénechas*. *Berrad Airechta* is one of only two tracts in the corpus to make frequent and explicit appeal by name to *Fénechas* as a body of traditional oral legal lore.[17] Charles-Edwards suggested that memorised quotations from the tradition might have formed the nucleus around which less formal oral instruction would then proceed;[18] *Berrad Airechta*

However, the *aitire* may also have functioned in private obligations: *Críth Gablach*, ed. D. A. Binchy (Dublin, 1979), 74–5 (= *CIH* III.777.6–783.38; II. 563.1–570.32); Stacey, *The Road to Judgment*, 87–98, 124–34.

12 *CIH* VI.2200.34–2201.5 = *Cóic Conara Fugill: Die fünf Wege zum Urteil*, ed. R. Thurneysen, Abhandlungen der preussischen Akademie der Wissenschaften 7, Phil.-Hist. Klasse, Jahrgang 1925 (Berlin, 1926), §§ 8–9 (p. 18,); *GEIL* 192; Stacey, *The Road to Judgment*, 119–21, and note 32 (pp. 271–2). For a recent discussion of this text, see Christophe Archan, *Les Chemins du Jugement. Procédure et science du droit dans l'Irlande médiévale* (Paris, 2007).

13 *GEIL* 278; *CCIH* 170; Howard Meroney, 'The Titles of Some Early Law-Tracts', *The Journal of Celtic Studies* 2 (1958), 189–206; Michael O'Brien, 'Varia 5. *Berrad Airechta*', *Ériu* 11 (1932), 88–9.

14 *CIH* II.599.37–8: *nibi forranach dalae, arnapat huidech airechtae*, 'thou shouldst not be violent in an assembly, lest thou be a delayer of the court'.

15 *Cóic Conara Fugill* (literally 'the five paths of judgment') uses both *conar*, 'path' and *raite*, 'road' (*CIH* VI.2202.33–34).

16 Robin Chapman Stacey, 'Law and Memory in Early Ireland', *Journal of Celtic Studies* 4 (2004) 43–69, at 59.

17 The other being *Críth Gablach*, on which see discussion below (pp. 140–1) and Stacey, *Dark Speech*, 189–97.

18 Charles-Edwards, Review of *CIH*, 153.

supports this idea in its structure and phrasing (questions of whether *Fénechas* actually is traditional oral lore aside). All five of the instances in which a passage ascribed to *Fénechas* is quoted in the text occur in the context of a plain prose discussion of the same issue, where they reiterate or enlarge upon the point just made.[19] The following example is typical:

> Doathbongatar no forlinaiter manibet ogha folaith; air arachan fenechus: Scuirith dochiall deimnigthiu; dororben fosair firnadmen ...[20]

Similarly, sayings not attributed to *Fénechas* but introduced by expressions such as 'why is it said' or 'therefore it is said' seem also to serve as pillars around which discussion of the legal point at issue is structured:

> Cach cend for a memru corai ... as de ata: segar a nad aic[d]ither.[21]

There is a visible difference between the passages ascribed to *Fénechas*, which are frequently allusive, rhetorical and seemingly archaic in their phrasing, and those not so ascribed, which are often couched in plain or alliterative prose. The impression is created that, while the former are regarded as in some sense validating what has just been said, the latter are functioning either as prompts for explication (where the passage precedes the main discussion) or as references to a familiar phrase relating to the point just discussed (where it follows it). In the following excerpt from *Córus Fíadnaise*, for example, the *Fénechas*-style excerpt justifying the inadmissibility of hearsay evidence displays archaic diction and syntax, alliteration, and the old conjunction *sceo*:

> Ni fiadnaise mani taisilbter do bes fiado dognether; arachan fenechas: ... Tromdith dia medamain messathar ar noillib ciall; gle cluine sin saeraibh sceo daeraib.[22]

By contrast, the syntax of the clause quoted above on lords enforcing obligations on their dependents, while proverbial in aspect, displays no such rhetorical qualities.

Other insights into oral instruction in this school are visible elsewhere. Commands in the imperative or second person jussive subjunctive are well represented throughout; Charles-Edwards has already suggested that the ultimate venue of origin for these is the relationship between teacher and pupil.[23] The fact

---

19 In one instance the quotation is missing: *CIH* II.591.34–35.

20 '[Discrepancies in the value of the goods or services exchanged] are "cut away" or "filled up" if the goods or services be not complete [in value], for as the native law recites: "Defective understanding dissolves confirmations. A [proper] foundation promotes just bindings" ...': *CIH* II.599.16–18. On the reading *manibet ogha*, see *Lawyers and Laymen. Studies in the History of Law presented to Dafydd Jenkins on his seventy-fifth birthday Gŵyl Dewi 1986*, ed. T. M. Charles-Edwards et al. (Cardiff, 1986), pp. 228, n.4, and 233, n.98.

21 'Each "head" for his proper "limbs" ... therefore is it said: "[A claim] is enforced and [a *naidm*-surety] is not appointed"': *CIH* II.592.35–36.

22 'It is not [valid] witnessing unless it is ascribed to him in whose presence the action be done. As the native law recites: ... "[It is] a grievous ruin for the judge in a case [literally: its judge] who judges according to oaths [made on the basis] of opinions – that type of oath is a "clarification of deception", [whether offered] by free persons or unfree persons"': *CIH* II.596.19, 23–4.

23 Charles-Edwards, Review of *CIH*, 146–7. We may compare the use of second person verbs in some of the Latin versions of the Welsh laws; cf., for example, the imperatives *tolle tecum* and *relinque* in the section on jetsam in Latin B (H. D. Emanuel, ed., *The Latin Texts of the Welsh Laws* (Cardiff, 1967), 208.21–3).

that the ritualised statements between contracting parties are presented within the text as actual verbal exchanges raises the possibility that these might have been learned and perhaps even performed by students intent on familiarising themselves with the syntactical and alliterative patterns characteristic of contractual speech.[24] There are also indications that oral or written riddling may have played a role in fixing legal norms in the minds of students. This is a device best known from *Gúbretha Caratniad*, where the hapless king requests explanations from the wise jurist Caratnia as to the judgments he has delivered, all of which seem contrary to standard practice but in fact constitute legally sound exceptions to the normal rule.[25] *Berrad Airechta* preserves no riddles of the Caratnia type; however, it does make use of deliberately paradoxical rhetorical statements that seem designed to encourage precisely this sort of reflection on rules and the exceptions to them.[26]

But while *Berrad Airechta* may thus afford some insight into oral legal training in this period, what is most striking about it is the role it implies for texts and textuality, defying expectations generated by the seemingly oral nature of its contents. Charles-Edwards has underscored the influence of Latin instructional grammars on the early Irish laws; such influence is very evident in *Berrad Airechta*, the first and third sections of which particularly are phrased in a manner similar to that of Donatus' *Ars Minor*.[27] The compiler's textual knowledge is clearly not limited to Latin grammatical works, however: he also displays a good knowledge of the vernacular legal tradition as manifested in texts from a variety of regions of Ireland. He refers to one tract by name, *Macslechta* – presumably the text known as *Bretha for Macslechtaib* that eventually became part of the *Senchas Már*, a compilation generally associated with the northern midlands.[28] He alludes to and quotes (albeit not by name) the status tract *Críth Gablach*, the provenance of which is uncertain, but which may derive from Munster.[29] He incorporates into his tract an originally independent written text entitled *Córus Fíadnaise* which, to judge from its style, probably originated in

---

24 *CIH* II.595.2–596.2; II.597.6–25; II.598.16–599.14. Mnemonic devices such as alliteration and rhyme also abound, although of course these are not limited to oral venues. On similar activities in a Welsh legal context, see Robin Chapman Stacey, 'Learning to Plead in Medieval Welsh Law', *Studia Celtica* 38 (2004), 107–24.

25 Rudolf Thurneysen, 'Aus dem irischen Recht III, [4. Die falschen Urteilssprüche Caratnia's; 5. Zur Überlieferung und zur Ausgabe der Texte über das Unfrei-Lehen und das Frei-Lehen]', *ZCP* 15 (1925), 302–76, at 302–70 (= *CIH* VI.2192–9).

26 For example, *CIH* II.593.20–21 and II.592.36: *atguidter na seghar, seagar na aic[d]ither*, '[A *naidm*-surety] is appointed and [a claim] is not enforced; [a claim] is enforced and [a *naidm*-surety] is not appointed'.

27 Charles-Edwards, Review of *CIH*, 147–52. Forms found both in Donatus and in *Berrad Airechta* include rhetorical questions, enumeration, lists and the occasional interjection of the compiler into his text via the use of the first person plural. For examples, see *Donat et la tradition de l'enseignement grammatical: etude sur L'Ars Donati et sa diffusion (ive–ixe siècle) et edition critique*, ed. Louis Holtz (Paris, 1981), §2 (p. 585, lines 8–13); §3 (p. 588, lines 2–8 and 11–17); § 4 (p. 591, line 11–p. 592, line 15); § 5 (p. 596, line 17); § 8 (p. 600, line 13), and so on; for English translations, see *The Ars Minor of Donatus*, ed. Wayland Johnson Chase (Madison, 1926), 28, 30, 32, 34, 38; 46, 52–64, etc.

28 *CIH* II.592.9. Breatnach cites two other instances in which *Bretha for Macslechtaib* is referred to as *Macslechta*: *CCIH* 300; see also *GEIL* 242–3.

29 *CIH* II.594.1–2 and discussion below.

the *Bretha Nemed* school, also thought to have been located in Munster.[30] (In fact, two phrases in *Córus Fíadnaise* appear also in *Bretha Nemed Toísech*, although they are used in these tracts in totally different ways and applied to completely different subjects.[31]) Another possibly independent written work, *Córus Aitire*, may similarly have been his source for the oral exchanges that form the backbone of the tract.[32] And other phrases incorporated into *Berrad Airechta* appear elsewhere in the written legal tradition, although of course it is difficult to tell who got this material from whom.[33]

Moreover, and more to the point for understanding the educational aspects of this text, the *Berrad Airechta* compiler clearly expects those for whom he is writing already either to have access to, or be familiar with, the texts from which he cites. Fosterage fees returned by the foster-father are noted as *dosgni hi macslechtaib*;[34] no further explanation is forthcoming: the presumption is that the audience already knows or would be able to find out what the *Macslechta* author had said. Another passage addresses the circumstances in which kin members acted as enforcing sureties for debts due from their relatives. The *Berrad Airechta* compiler provides a single example of an occasion on which this would be viewed as appropriate and then concludes with 'and so on' – a reference, presumably, to a longer list he assumes his audience will know (perhaps the one the scribes have in front of them but cannot be bothered to copy).[35] In one case, the compiler actually refers back to his own work in what I would suggest is a separate tract authored by him:

> Atait d[ano] ruidilsi gona duine hi tuaith, amail isindubartamar .i. fer [dosaig] do cenn fort.[36]

The wounding of men in ways that do not invite retaliation or damages has not appeared as a subject for discussion previous to this point in *Berrad Airechta*. It is, however, a topic discussed in *Críth Gablach*, which is also the tract from which the quotation reproduced in the gloss is taken.[37] If the gloss is an old one, an explanatory note by the compiler rather than the work of a later commentator

---

30 *CIH* II.596.3–597.3, and see *GEIL* 246; and Stacey, *Dark Speech*, 184–5. The question of whether the titles *Córus Fíadnaise* and *Córus Aitire* are the work of the *Berrad Airechta* compiler remains open.

31 Compare *CIH* II.596.20 and 596.24 with *CIH* VI.2218.5–6, VI.2224.26–7.

32 On which see discussion below, p. 142.

33 Parallels include the three types of *macslabra*: compare *CIH* II.591.32–4 with *Bretha Éitgid* (*CIH* I.294.1–3) and *Findsruth Fithail* (*CIH* VI.2139.25–6), both of which texts display stylistic similarities to *Bretha Nemed* texts. The phrase *da mbaegal naltrama* (*CIH* II.591.37) is paralleled in a passage in the *Senchas Már* text *Cáin Íarraith* (*CIH* V.1766.19). *Berrad Airechta*'s passage on the three drunken contracts is similar in content, but not in phrasing, to a passage in *Di Astud Chor*: compare *CIH* II.592.16–17 with *Early Irish Contract Law* (ed. McLeod), §21. Both McLeod and Breatnach think *Di Astud Chor* borrowed here from *Berrad Airechta* (*Early Irish Contract Law* (ed. McLeod), 112, 242; *CCIH* 245–6). The *naidms* of *Berrad Airechta* who bind what they cannot enforce appear as the 'four *naidms* who do not enforce though they have been appointed' in the *Senchas Már* text *Recholl Breth*; the persons listed are the same in both texts (compare *CIH* II.592.2–4 with I.220.1–2).

34 'he (presumably another compiler) sets them out in *Macslechta*': *CIH* II.592.9.

35 One version of this larger list is preserved elsewhere in heptad form: compare *CIH* II.592.32–3 with III.795.25–31.

36 'There are, moreover, [situations where], within the tribe, wounding a man is immune from claim, as we have said it, i.e. [wounding] a person who seeks to kill you': *CIH* II.594.1–2.

37 *Críth Gablach* (ed. Binchy), 142–4 (= *CIH* III.779.19 (the A version of the text)).

– which is certainly how the sentence would seem most naturally to read – this would seem to suggest that both texts were redacted by the same man.[38] In any case, the lack of subsequent discussion again suggests that the compiler presumes that those for whom he is writing are not only already familiar with these texts and passages, but could find them again if memory failed.

Of course, one can learn a text by hearing as well as by reading. Asides of this sort need not necessarily evoke visions of trainee jurists poring tirelessly over legal manuscripts in order to learn their craft. They do, however, suggest that written texts, whether learned by ear or by eye, lay very much at the centre of the instruction taking place in this school. This possibility is, ironically, underscored by the non-*Fénechas* quotations that I had at one time taken as constituting traces of an oral curriculum.[39] As can be seen from the following examples, these passages vary enormously in character and phrasing, though all are introduced by some variation of the phrase 'why is it said?'

C[eist], cid dia nepir: ni crie ni ria de doraith? Naidm son for doeru …[40]

… adsuidetar tra frisnadmann-so 7 ni diuprat; is de ata: adsuidet nadmen 7 ni diuprat.[41]

In tan im[murgu] is creicc iter da slan, is comsruithiu naidm fri dliged hi suidiu, ar is 'co sasar? Co foastar?' ann.[42]

Some exhibit the sort of rhetorical style usually associated with *Fénechas*, but some do not. There are second person jussive subjunctive commands, instances of the paradox riddles mentioned earlier, plain prose statements of law, syntactically marked statements of law and rhetorical questions. Perhaps the most interesting is *tresgata mac dliged*, 'a contractual surety pierces entitlement'.[43] This is the earliest example known to me of the legal proverb 'a contract breaks law', variants of which appeared both in Latin and in the vernacular in a variety of lawbooks from Britain and the Continent in the high and late Middle Ages. Its widespread circulation in such a variety of languages and legal traditions suggests an ultimate origin in Roman law, although no convincing parallel has yet been found.[44]

---

38 Compare *Berrad Airechta* in *CIH* II 594.1–2 with *CIH* III.779.18–19. Reasons to think these were written by the same man are summarised in Stacey, *Dark Speech*, 301, n. 106. To this one can add that neither evokes legal personalities like Sencha, neither is heavily glossed and both possess imaginatively evocative early titles. Both may also be affiliated with the *Bretha Nemed* school of Munster: the witnessing tract incorporated into *Berrad Airechta* has clear affiliations with this school, and *Crith Gablach* may once have ended with a type of *roscad* widely associated with the *Bretha Nemed* style (cf. *CCIH* 242–3).

39 Stacey, *Dark Speech*, 194 and note 125. The complete list is as follows: *CIH* II.592.22, 26, 36, 39; II.593.5–6, 14, 14–15, 15–16, 20–1, 28–9; II.594.6–7.

40 'A question: why is it said: "thou shouldst not buy from, thou shouldst not sell to, a legal incompetent"? That refers to *naidm*-binding on unfree-persons …': *CIH* II.592.26.

41 '[contracts] are then made fast through these *naidm*-sureties and they do not defraud; therefore is it said: "*naidm*-sureties make fast and they do not defraud"': *CIH* II.38–9.

42 'When, however, it is a transaction between two competent people, a *naidm*-surety is as much to be respected in that case as is entitlement, for then is it [asked]: "How may it be enforced? How may it be violated"?': *CIH* II.593.13–14.

43 *CIH* II.593.15–16.

44 The earliest datable appearance outside the Irish and Welsh is in the *Leges Henrici Primi*: Dafydd Jenkins, 'The Medieval Welsh Idea of Law', *Tijdschrift voor Rechtsgeschiedenis/Revue d'Histoire du Droit/The Legal History Review*, 49, numbers 3–4 (1981), 323–48, at 340–2.

The varied nature of these phrases makes it difficult to see them as part of a unified oral curriculum. Their phrasing and placement in the text may, however, provide some clues as to their nature and function. In *Berrad Airechta* they occur generally as partial phrases rather than as complete sentences – as fragments, in other words, of a larger whole that the audience was expected to recognise. Significantly, all of them centre on a particular legal issue (oral contracts) and, more importantly, occur in one section only of *Berrad Airechta*, within two pages of one another in Binchy's edition. We know already that the compiler of *Berrad Airechta* made use of a variety of written texts of proximate, though not identical, dates in composing his tract. *Córus Fíadnaise* was probably an independent text of the *Bretha Nemed* tradition incorporated virtually wholesale into *Berrad Airechta*, for example. And the compiler's principal written source must surely have been *Córus Aitire*, the other text to which a separate title is given in the tract. The similarities in phrasing between the oral exchanges found in *Córus Aitire* and those found in the earlier contractual section of *Berrad Airechta* leave little doubt but that they ultimately derived from the same source.[45] Presumably the *Berrad Airechta* compiler separated *Córus Aitire*'s discussion of the *aitire nadma* from its discussion of the other two types of *aitire* and reconfigured it as the core of his earlier discussion of oral contracts.

The implications of this are significant. First, it confirms the very deliberate nature of *Berrad Airechta* as a compilation – the fact that the compiler did not simply reproduce the written sources from which he was working, but actively reworked them in ways that suited his own purposes. It also suggests that *Córus Fíadnaise* and *Córus Aitire* were probably not the only written texts he had in front of him. The fact that all of the non-*Fénechas* quotations occur in close proximity to one another, and that almost all of them are visibly fragmentary or allusive, presuming a knowledge of the greater whole from which they were abstracted, suggests that what we probably have here are sentences excerpted from another unnamed text or texts known to, and perhaps even being studied simultaneously by, students in the school in which *Berrad Airechta* originated. Phrases like 'therefore is it [said]' may be less an indicator of oral origins or application than a reflection of teacher and students working together from a particular text and making frequent reference to it. If this is right, then it is likely that the plain prose discussion accompanying these brief citations reflects the teacher's commentary on this unnamed text or texts – which commentary could, of course, have been communicated orally, in writing, or both.[46]

As important as the processes by which apprentice jurists were learning is the content of what they were being taught, and it would be remiss not to comment on this subject as well. *Berrad Airechta* makes clear that what was going on in the schools was not merely the passive transfer of knowledge. As has been argued already for *Críth Gablach*, which may have been written by the same

---

45 Compare, for example *CIH* II.595.13–14 with II.598.26 and II.599.11.

46 No single text of this sort, combining all of the passages alluded to, has survived to us. However, two passages do occur together in a later digest on the virtues of seniority, which may imply the existence of a text like the one I am suggesting – unless, of course, the digest's compiler was himself drawing on *Berrad Airechta*. It is worth noting that the two passages in question are not sequential in *Berrad Airechta* as they are in the digest and are joined in the digest to another clause *Berrad Airechta* does not contain: *CIH* IV.1290.20–1.

author, analysis rather than mere description is the true focus.[47] The phrase *dosgni hi macslechtaib*, 'he sets them out in *Macslechta*'[48] seems implicitly to acknowledge that there might be other ways that a person would choose to 'set them out', and implies a qualitative value judgment on the *Macslechta* compiler's work (in that the *Berrad Airechta* compiler chooses to refer to it). Moreover, within *Berrad Airechta* itself there are several instances in which the compiler's way of categorising legal personalities and practices is if not unique to himself then surely not the only possible way to perceive or present those things. The idea that contractual sureties might be regarded as forms of *aitire* is not replicated elsewhere in the literature, for example, with the possible exception (again) of *Crith Gablach*.[49] And whereas a modern historian would almost certainly treat the *aitire*, a form of hostage surety, together with the *giall*, the hostage per se, this text pointedly does not. Indeed, the *giall* does not even appear in this text as a subject for discussion – a sure sign that, for the compiler, the high status associated with the *aitire* mattered more than any functional similarity between *aitire* and *giall*.[50] Students are, in other words, being exposed not merely to what legal practice is, but to how one thinks about law and legal categories – and to the fact that compilers do not always agree.

Thus, despite being the most visibly 'oral' of the extant Irish legal texts, *Berrad Airechta* underscores the important role played by the written word in legal composition and instruction. Already by the year 700, and presumably even earlier, there existed in Ireland a sophisticated and self-reflective tradition of law in which both texts and the analyses of texts (of which *Berrad Airechta* might arguably be counted an example) were being traded back and forth, drawn on in oral and written instruction, and commented on. It is worth reflecting on the role textuality might have played in the development of a professional legal identity in Ireland. Native law undoubtedly existed before the wide-scale dissemination of written texts. However, it was presumably intensely localised and, in any case, the commitment of law to writing and subsequent development of a textual community around the written lawbooks must surely have changed whatever class or tradition was already in place almost beyond recognition. Regardless of one's views on the extent of ecclesiastical involvement in the composition of the early Irish law tracts – and *Berrad Airechta* shows little signs of having originated in clerical circles – the days of seeing the jurists of the law tracts as uncomplicatedly direct descendants of Caesar's druids are numbered. Patrick's famous passage testifying to the early existence in Ireland of a professional judicial class cannot bear the weight traditionally placed upon it.[51] What we are

---

47 T. M. Charles-Edwards, '*Crith Gablach* and the Law of Status', *Peritia* 5 (1986), 53–73, at 72–3 especially.

48 *CIH* II.592.9.

49 *Crith Gablach* (ed. Binchy), 52–62 (with p. 26, n. 59). Binchy sees a discrepancy here, but it is worth noting that *Berrad Airechta* treats the *ráth* as a form of *aitire*: *CIH* II.597.5–6, 30–4.

50 Stacey, *The Road to Judgment*, 82–111.

51 Not only does the circumlocution he uses, *illis qui iudicabant*, admit of the possibility of a wide variety of persons being involved in the judicial process (on which see Stacey, *The Road to Judgment*, 126–9) but it may also derive as a phrase from the deuterocanonical Book of Baruch; cf. Patrick's *Confessio* §53 (ed. R. P. C. Hanson with Cécile Blanc, *Saint Patrick: Confession et lettre à Coroticus* (Paris, 1978), §53 (pp. 126–7), *illis qui iudicabant per omnes regiones* with Baruch 2:1, *iudices nostros qui iudicabant Israel* (*Nova Vulgata*).

seeing in the jurists' exaltation of poets as the ancient custodians of native law may be an awareness of the historical limits of their identity as a professional class – an identity created and perpetuated through the study of written texts.

13

HOLDING COURT: JUDICIAL PRESIDENCY IN BRITTANY, WALES AND NORTHERN IBERIA IN THE EARLY MIDDLE AGES

Wendy Davies

The capacity to hold court can be a key to the distribution and exercise of political power; to the existence of public or of private power; and to the interplay both between local community and landlords and between local community and rulers' agents. Of course, the phrase 'holding court' in modern English offers a multiplicity of meanings, just as the notion of holding court in the early Middle Ages covers a multiplicity of occasions: there were kings' courts, bishops' courts, secular lords' courts, monastic lords' courts – where business was done, celebrations held, visitors received, dues paid, gifts exchanged, plans made. My concern in this paper is with the court as judicial court – the place where disputes were heard, in accordance with fixed procedures and in the knowledge of such law as pertained, and where disputes were sometimes settled, sometimes judged, and unsuccessful litigants were sometimes sentenced.

My particular concern is with the presidency of the court.[1] Did someone always preside, and was the presidency always held by a single individual? Can we always identify a president? Could someone preside *in absentia* – in other words, be notionally but not physically present? Was presiding separable from judging? Determining who presided in court is much more difficult to fathom than one might initially think. There are issues concerning both the normal actions, powers and obligations of court holders and also the meaning of words: it might be supposed, for example, that use of the Latin word *ante* 'before' would clearly identify a president, but that certainly was not always the case. The use and the semantic range of the word *iudicium* in early medieval charters makes the point that words did not have simple meanings: the term can mean court, judgment, panel of judges, case, hearing, sentence, fine, at the least. The issues are worth addressing, however, for our perception of court-holder power bears upon the deeper issues of the line between presiding and judging, of the distribution of the capacity to punish and constrain, and of the shift, if such there be, from public to private jurisdiction – issues whose solution is fundamental to our understanding of social and political change in the central Middle Ages.

There is a particularly rich set of material from early medieval Brittany which allows us to see much of the practical operation of judicial assemblies, espe-

[1] I use the word 'court' in this paper because no other word satisfactorily conveys the sense of the place for doing explicit judicial business in accordance with standard procedures.

cially in some very local, rural contexts; there is a little relevant material from early medieval Wales; and there is a large and rich corpus of case material from northern Iberia which is full of detail of practice. In what follows I want to compare presiding in court in these three regions to the west of Francia. My focus is on the ninth and tenth centuries, since the tenth is the first well-documented century in Spain and Portugal and the ninth is the best-documented in Brittany. Welsh contemporary evidence for settlement procedure in the early Middle Ages is very limited, although there are relevant texts in the Llandaff collection, especially of the tenth and eleventh centuries, and there is a little hagiographic material.[2] The Breton contemporary evidence, which occurs in charters, focuses on the ninth century, since there are few tenth- and early-eleventh-century charters and not many post-ninth-century court cases. The charters come from eastern Brittany and most are preserved in a single late-eleventh-century cartulary from the monastery of Redon;[3] the others are known from early modern transcripts, whose originals appear to have been collected by the same source.[4]

The Iberian material comes from the north of Spain and Portugal (at that time part of Galicia), since it was the north that produced the texts (southern Iberia was Muslim-controlled and its – doubtless rich – documentation does not survive). These texts begin in the late eighth century but become very numerous in the tenth century and thereafter; some are preserved in eleventh- and twelfth-century cartularies but significant numbers survive on single sheets, especially in the great collections of the *meseta*, the high central plateau of Spain.[5] The biggest collections are from the monasteries of Celanova and Sobrado in Galicia; the bishopric of León and monastery of Sahagún on the *meseta*, León material coming from several different original sources; the monastery of Cardeña in Castile; and that of San Millán de la Cogolla in the Rioja. There are also important smaller collections, from Otero de las Dueñas on the northern edge of the *meseta*, which includes a lay archive with a high proportion of single sheets; from the monastery of Santo Toribio, to the far north in the Liébana; and from San Juan de la Peña, a monastery well to the east in Aragón. There is, in addition, significant material from different sources in northern Portugal. The corpus is much more varied in range than the Breton and there is vastly more of it: more than 2000 tenth-century charters (excluding Catalan material) and in the order of

---

[2] *LL*; *Vita Sancti Cadoci*: A. W. Wade-Evans, ed. and trans., *Vitae Sanctorum Britanniae et Genealogiae* (Cardiff, 1944).

[3] CR; A.D. dates, in brackets, follow charter numbers. See also the facsimile edition: *Cartulaire de l'abbaye Saint-Sauveur de Redon*, 2 vols (Rennes, 1998–2004), and the fundamental comments therein of Guillotel, 'Le manuscrit' and 'Répertoire chronologique', I.9–25, 71–8. The few eleventh-century court records in this collection are procedurally very different from the ninth-century cases. Other collections do not include records of court cases; remarkably, the Landévennec cartulary, which is the largest alternative source of the period, includes none among its tenth- and early-eleventh-century charters; the closest is a thirteenth-century marginal note of a property dispute that went to court (A. de la Borderie, ed., *Cartulaire de l'abbaye de Landévennec* (Rennes, 1888), 176).

[4] Fifty-five such charters are published as an Appendix to de Courson's edition. For further detail, see my 'The Composition of the Redon Cartulary', *Francia: Forschungen zur westeuropäischen Geschichte, Mittelalter* 17/1 (1990), 69–90 (repr. in W. Davies, *Brittany in the Early Middle Ages: Texts and Societies* (Farnham, 2009)).

[5] Many, although not all, of the charters on single sheets are originals. Their texts are in Latin, but deviate significantly from classical Latin; irregular case endings are particularly common. For the abbreviations of the charter collections, see above, pp. xiv–xvii.

250 recorded dispute cases in that century. Comparative figures for ninth-century Brittany are 283 charters and 49 dispute cases.

Brittany

When I wrote about early medieval Breton dispute settlement a generation ago I made a point of differentiating the function of presiding from that of judging.[6] My purpose initially was to counter assumptions that all presidents were judges in early medieval courts, but some serious implications for the nature and distribution of political power in that world became evident: the relationship between presidency and judgment varied in accordance with social status, and practice in aristocratic cases was different from that of village courts. Looking back at that material, the distinction between those functions still seems to hold good and can be taken further.

Firstly, let us look at words. There are two types of phrasing which appear to indicate presidency of a court in these Breton charters: *ante N* and *coram N*, [this was done] 'before N' or 'in the presence of N', in Latin; there are no recorded vernacular equivalents. Neither phrase is used exclusively of a president and *coram*, especially, can be used of the whole (or a large section) of the assembled court. Some charters use both expressions interchangeably and preference for one word or the other does not appear to be determined by charter type, place or date; in fact, most of the dispute records were written in local diplomatic style and it seems that both expressions were freely used by the scribes who wrote for local villages and local churches.[7] Despite this, the identity of the president is nearly always clear from the content of the texts, for the president is usually differentiated in some way both from witnesses and from judges. So, an abbot came *ante* Count Rivilin to raise a case, which was finally settled in Peillac *ante* the count and *coram* many witnesses; a brother and sister came to court *ante* the machtiern Iarnhitin and his two sons, where judgment was found by twelve named *scabini* 'judgment finders'; a case was determined in Ruffiac church *coram* two machtierns and a representative of the ruler and *coram* (repeated) many named witnesses; and when the ruler Salomon gave the troublesome machtiern Ratfred ten days to gather evidence and appear before him in his own court at his residence, the record uses first-person speech to emphasise the distinctive role of the ruler.[8] Presidency is also clearly indicated by such circumstances as: agreements and confessions that took place before the ruler; cases (occasionally) raised before a count; cases that were brought to a public court before the ruler's representative (*missus*); people who came to a machtiern and asked him to do

---

6 'Disputes, their Conduct and their Settlement in the Village Communities of Eastern Brittany in the Ninth Century', *History and Anthropology* 1 pt 2 (1985), 289–312; 'People and Places in Dispute in Ninth-Century Brittany', in *The Settlement of Disputes in Early Medieval Europe*, ed. W. Davies and P. Fouracre (Cambridge, 1986), 65–84 (both repr. in Davies, *Brittany in the Early Middle Ages*).

7 For local diplomatic, see Davies, 'Composition of the Redon Cartulary', 78–80; for scribes, Davies, 'People and Places in Dispute', 68–70.

8 Respectively CR 96 (867); CR 147 (821×6); CR 139 (860); CR 105 (857×8). A machtiern was a local petty aristocrat, who presided over the public performance of transactions in village communities.

justice; the many people who came before machtierns to testify.[9] Indeed, transactions of sale were performed before machtierns too: both disputes and sales were concluded before him in his *lis*, his machtiernly residence.[10] Although *coram* more often refers to a larger group 'this was done *coram multis testibus*, whose names are …', such lists of witnesses can be headed by machtiern or *missus* or ruler, thereby indicating a pre-eminence in the context of the assembled crowd.[11] So, while the words *ante* and *coram* do not necessarily designate presidents, they clearly do so in many contexts; some assessment of what happened in court, however, is essential in order to determine who, if anyone, presided.

Secondly, we turn to the functions of presidents. The president could be a single individual – a machtiern or a ruler, for example – but there could also be a pair of them, or more: a machtiern and his sons; two machtierns and a *missus*; and, exceptionally, five machtierns and a *missus*.[12] How, in practice, they shared this job we do not know, although presumably, as in any tribunal, one of them took the lead. What they did as presidents was ask questions and conduct enquiries; and they sometimes launched a case as a consequence of a petition to do so. Machtierns never took part in the judging, which was done by panels of locals; by contrast, the ruler did judge, and would characteristically preside, make a judgment and pass sentence himself.[13] What is implied is that most presidents were – literally – chair persons; so literally that we have a description of a machtiern sitting on a special bench, the *trifocalium*, glossed *iscomid*, in front of the church at Cléguerec, instructing that a charter be drawn up, as well as another description of the ruler sitting *in scamno*, together with his wife.[14]

---

[9]   For example, CR 47 (893), CR 21 (868); CR 96; CR 124 (843×4); CR 162 (854); CR 180 (843×9), again respectively.

[10]   For example, CR 112 (844), CR 172 (856), CR 147. *Lis* is usually conveyed in Latin by *aula*; cf. Modern Welsh *llys*, which has as wide a semantic range as 'court'.

[11]   CR 180, CR 191 (801×12), CR 258 (865), for example; position in a witness list certainly does not signify status in charters from some regions, but practice is so consistent in this corpus that it seems to do so here.

[12]   CR 147, CR 139, CR 180.

[13]   Davies, 'Disputes, their Conduct and their Settlement', 300–4.

[14]   CR A 4 (833) – only known from an early modern transcript, CR 176 (843×50). I am extremely grateful to Paul Russell for supplying the following note, which shows that both the Latin word and its Breton gloss referred to a large block of wood or bench. '*Trifocalium* seems not to be attested elsewhere. However, a French reflex seems to have survived in Normandy as a lexical item and also as a surname elsewhere as *Trefouel, Trefoueil, Trifoueil*. As a lexical item it refers to the Yule log, a large block of wood lit on Christmas Eve and intended to last for three feast days; see M.-T. Morlet, *Le Dictionnaire étymologique des noms de famille*, 2nd edn (Paris, 1997), s.n. *Trefouel, Trefeu*. It is likely that the *tri-* of the Latin form is not to be interpreted as "three" but as a reflex of Latin *trans*; thus a *trifocalium* is that which lies across the hearth. *Iscomid* (emended from *istomid*) means literally "something hewn, stool"; see L. Fleuriot and C. Evans, *A Dictionary of Old Breton/Dictionnaire du vieux Breton: Historical and Comparative*, 2 vols (Toronto, 1985), I.231, II.496–7, following I. Williams, "*istomid, ysgymydd*", *BBCS* 16 (1954–6), 191–2. The Welsh forms, *ysgymydd* and *ysgemydd*, seem to mean "block of wood, chopping block" in the medieval period, although seventeenth-century lexicographers also give it the sense of "bench". The reference to a *scamnum* offers a more common word for stool or seat.'

Wales

The search for comparable Welsh material from the early Middle Ages is much less successful because there are few relevant contemporary written sources; further, what there is tends to assume that a bishop was in charge. Most of the potentially relevant texts are Llandaff charters; these were heavily edited in the eleventh and twelfth centuries, specifically in order to enhance the role and standing of bishops of Llandaff.[15] Where these texts indicate a president it is almost invariably the bishop, who takes initiatives, calls synods and sometimes imprisons; this could well have been the case, particularly in contexts from the late ninth century onwards, but the records are clearly not impartial and this is hardly a view of the entire judicial system.[16]

Beyond the Llandaff material, the late-eleventh-century Life of Cadog has some chapters relating dispute resolution;[17] although, like Llandaff charters, they refer to assembled judges (*iudices*), they do not identify presidents.[18] There is, however, one chapter which attributes judgment, sentencing and *de facto* presidency to a petty king (*regulus*) who heard a theft case (*actio*) in his court (*curia*); and another which claims immunity for the church of Llancarfan from the judgment of any king, bishop or *optimas* – which must imply that it was envisaged that kings, bishops and aristocrats could hold courts at the time of writing.[19]

In fact, by far the most useful Welsh text is that known as 'Braint Teilo', another Llandaff text but one with a distinctive character, dealing explicitly with issues of jurisdiction; it occurs both in Latin and in Welsh.[20] It is basically an elaborate immunity claim for the church of Llandaff, mostly drawn up in the early twelfth century. However, it has an earlier section – not precisely dated but probably from the late tenth or early eleventh century – which claims explicitly that the bishop of Llandaff shall have every law (*lex/cyfraith*) in his court (*curia/llys*) that the king of Morgannwg has in his court; in other words, the claim is that bishop and king shall have comparable powers of jurisdiction, a clear acknowledgment that in principle persons other than the ruler could hold judicial courts, whether or not in fact they did so. Though the twelfth-century document elaborates this, it is a text whose origin lies squarely in the particular local

---

15 See W. Davies, *The Llandaff Charters* (Aberystwyth, 1979), for a guide to suspect charters. I do not share the scepticism of K. L. Maund, *Ireland, Wales, and England in the Eleventh Century* (Woodbridge, 1991), 183–206, or of J. R. Davies, '*Liber Landavensis*: its Date and the Identity of its Editor', *CMCS* 35 (1998), 1–11.

16 For example, *LL* 214 (*c.*862), *LL* 217 (*c.*960), *LL* 249b (*c.*1015), *LL* 263 (*c.*1040); much less credibly *LL* 144 (*c.*650), *LL* 152 (*c.*670), *LL* 180b (*c.*710), *LL* 167 (*c.*750).

17 See my 'Property Rights and Property Claims in Welsh *Vitae* of the Eleventh Century', in *Hagiographie, cultures et sociétés, IV–XII siècles*, ed. E. Patlagean and P. Riché (Paris, 1981), 515–33, at 517–20 (repr. in W. Davies, *Welsh History in the Early Middle Ages: Texts and Societies* (Farnham, 2009)), for references and critical comment on the text and date of *Vita Sancti Cadoci*.

18 *Vita Sancti Cadoci*, cc. 22, 37; and ch. 69, a twelfth-century addition to the main text, which probably derives from earlier material.

19 *Vita Sancti Cadoci*, cc. 33, 37.

20 *LL* 118–21; for critical comment see my 'Braint Teilo', *BBCS* 26 (1974–6), 123–37 (repr. in Davies, *Welsh History*).

circumstances of the early twelfth century, and it cannot credibly be projected backwards.[21]

Looking at the contemporary evidence of Welsh sources before 1100, we cannot say much beyond the following: texts that deal with court cases, while providing useful information about matters such as scales of worth or family responsibility, and while tending to emphasise the importance of judgment, are extremely vague about presidency; such indications as there are give a presiding role to those with political power – kings, petty kings, bishops, some aristocrats – as emphasised by the very notion of the Law of Hywel, but there is little about their functions as presidents beyond calling meetings.

Northern Iberia

Although there are plenty of records of court cases in northern Iberia, charters that detail disputes do not always indicate who presided. Standard procedures were clearly employed across a wide area, with a dedicated law officer – the *saio* – carrying out practical functions such as calling people to court.[22] Some words that might be thought to indicate presidency are commonly used in these texts, but understanding the import of the words is tricky: neither *ante N* 'before N' nor *in presentia N* 'in the presence of N' in themselves specifically indicate presidency. Rather, they indicate the important person or persons at a hearing, whose presence gave authority to proceedings whatever their other functions in the court. So, while the statement of those before whom, or in the presence of whom, a case was heard can indeed include a president, and sometimes such a statement names only the president, it may not include him or her at all and it can include others too. That a case was heard *ante iudigum* 'before judges' is a point made three times in the long record of a court in the far north in 953; another case was heard in León *ante iudices* in 946, with the oath to be taken before the aforesaid judges.[23] Before a judge, or judges, is common enough; so too is *in*

---

21 The judges by privilege of land of thirteenth-century Deheubarth may appear projectable backwards too, but J. Beverley Smith has demonstrated that they do not derive from ancient custom: 'Judgement under the Law of Wales', *Studia Celtica* 39 (2005), 63–103, at 75–82. Note also the problems of characterising judicial practice identified by R. R. Davies, 'The Administration of Law in Medieval Wales: The Role of the *ynad cwmwd* (*judex patrie*)', in *Lawyers and Laymen: Studies in the History of Law presented to Professor Dafydd Jenkins on his seventy-fifth birthday, Gŵyl Ddewi 1986*, ed. T. M. Charles-Edwards, M. E. Owen and D. B. Walters (Cardiff, 1986), 258–73.

22 There is a large Spanish historiography; see, for example, the following recent papers: I. Alfonso Antón, 'Resolución de disputas y prácticas judiciales en el Burgos medieval', in *Burgos en la plena edad media*, ed. J. J. García González, F. J. Peña Perez and L. Martínez García (Burgos, 1994), 211–43; J. M. Salrach, 'Prácticas judiciales, transformación social y acción política en Cataluña (siglos IX–XIII)', *Hispania* 57/3 (1997), 1009–48; G. Martínez Díez, 'Terminología jurídica en la documentación del reino de León. Siglos IX–XI', in *Orígenes de las Lenguas Romances en el Reino de León, Siglos IX–XII*, 2 vols (León, 2004), I.229–72; P. Martínez Sopena, 'La justicia en la época asturleonesa: entre el *Liber* y los mediadores sociales', in *El Lugar del Campesino. En Torno a la Obra de Reyna Pastor*, ed. A. Rodríguez (Valencia, 2007), 239–60; or, for a guide in English, my 'Settling Disputes in Early Medieval Spain and Portugal: a Contrast with Wales and Brittany?', in *Wales and the Welsh in the Middle Ages*, ed. R. Griffiths and P. Schofield (Cardiff, 2011), forthcoming.

23 S. García Larragueta, ed., *Colección de documentos de la catedral de Oviedo* (Oviedo, 1962), no. 26, a charter on a single sheet; Li 191.

presencia iudicum 'in the presence of judges', and sometimes of magnates too.[24] A panel of judges often made necessary decisions, especially in respect of what should happen next in the conduct of the case – who should, for example, be permitted to take the oath – but this happened whether a president was specified or not; these decisions are commonly attributed to the judges, even when someone else clearly presided.[25]

By contrast, these same expressions are sometimes used in contexts where presidency is quite clear: *in presentia principis* 'in the presence of the ruler', where a case between a bishop and an abbot was made before the king of León, who explicitly gave orders to both parties to present their documents and, only then, together with judges and magnates, concluded the case; *in presentia regis/ imperatoris* 'in the presence of the king' is used in the same text as *ante pontificem* 'before the bishop', and both indicate presidency, for a case was made in Simancas before the ruler, who ordered Velasco Hánniz to appear before him some days later in León, or, if he were delayed, to appear before the bishop, as in fact happened; *in presentia comitis* 'in the presence of the count', in which an appeal was made to Count Gutier, who then took action; or *ante domino meo* 'before my lord', in which a request was made to the secular lord Assur to help a priest who had committed homicide, with the intercession of local elders; and *ad rege Garcia* 'to King García' of a case in Aragón heard before this Navarre king, who subsequently judged.[26] Occasions when an appeal was made to a specific person, often king or count, who then directed others to seek evidence, are particularly clear. That is especially striking in two cases where the president personally led an investigation, having received an appeal: in northern Portugal, in 936, disputants over a boundary arrived in the presence of the count to make their complaints; the count ordered them to take him to the disputed area, which they did; then the count, together with those 'who saw', decided on the right boundary line.[27] The case of Count Gutier, in nearby southern Galicia in 940, is similar: when a boundary case was made to him he then sent out *previsores*, 'seers', to sort it out.[28] So, presidency can be clearly indicated when there is sufficient detail about the actions taken. Presidents are also sometimes named alongside others: *in presentia comitis* and of five others, in a Castile case where the count clearly (from the context) presided; *in presentia vestra et iudicum* 'in the presence of yourself and judges', where 'yourself' was clearly in charge (and received the fine); *ante episcopum et iudicum regis* 'before the bishop and king's judges', where it is in practice unthinkable that the bishop did other than preside.[29]

---

24 Li 144 (941).

25 I have dealt with the functions of judges at greater length in 'Judges and Judging. Truth and Justice in Northern Iberia on the Eve of the Millennium', *Journal of Medieval History*, 36 (2010), 193–203.

26 Sam 126 (960); Li 256 (952); Cel 502 (940) – see further below, this page; *PMH* 53 (943), a charter on a single sheet; a charter on a single sheet from the cathedral archive of Jaca (958), for text of which see R. Collins, 'Visigothic Law and Regional Custom in Disputes in Early Medieval Spain', in *Settlement of Disputes*, ed. Davies and Fouracre, 85–104, 252–7, at 98, 255–6.

27 *PMH* 42: *previdimus*.

28 Cel 502. Cf. *previsores*, in Sob 129 (942), where the word is explicitly synonymous with judges; one might see an analogy with Irish druid and *fili* – pagan priest and poet-seer – both with some legal functions in the immediately pre-Christian period: see T. M. Charles-Edwards, 'Early Irish law', in *A New History of Ireland, 1, Prehistoric and Early Ireland*, ed. D. Ó Cróinín (Oxford, 2005), 331–70, at 350–4.

29 C 22 (932); Sob 103 (952); Sah 159 (958).

It is not these expressions in themselves, then, that indicate presidency, but the whole context, and the accompanying detail of the course of the case and of who did what. *In vestra presencia ante Iuliano iudicum* 'in your [= the count's] presence before Judge Juliano', in a record in which the count received a fine, must identify the count as president because of the fine; *antem gomite vel suos iudizes*, but the count again received the fine; or *ante comite et ante abba*, where it was the count who ordered action (*per mandato de comite*); and there is the extremely interesting case of the powerful monastic official Cresconio, member of the Celanova community, who heard cases between lay parties within the monastery (*ante vos* and also *in presentia iudices*) and subsequently received fines (*in vestro iudicato* 'your fine').[30]

Where presidency is clear the president was usually an authority figure – king, count, bishop or, very occasionally, a private lord. As in the example above, the king of León sometimes delegated presidency to the bishop of León; the particular relationship between this king and bishop is very explicitly evidenced, but the principle of delegation must have applied elsewhere as well. Presidents were not necessarily male, for we know of women who could take the chair: Queen Elvira did in 968, and together with the whole council gave the oath to one party and endorsed what was sworn; the secular lord Dona Domitria, at whose feet the priest Sagulfu fell while elders interceded for him, also appears to have presided in northern Portugal in 991.[31] Sometimes a pair of, or even more, individuals may have presided together (like the two brothers who shared countship in the Verín valley): in records in which no prominence is attributed to any one individual *in presencia abbas et sagoni* may indicate such a pairing (in the Liébana in 962) and *in presencia iudicum et saioni* and *ante udice et saione* another (in Valdoré in 946).[32] Reference to *saiones* here raises the possibility that these officers also took the chair alone, particularly at local and at preliminary meetings: people with a grievance often went to the *saio* in the first instance; it was the *saio* who frequently heard initial statements and sometimes witness evidence; it was the *saio* who got people to court and who formally transferred property; and *saiones* sometimes explicitly acted on behalf of kings.[33]

The functions of presidents in court in northern Iberia are not so very different from those found in eastern Brittany, although we have more detail of their actions, there are many more cases and the social contexts are much wider – from great kings, such as the king of León, to minor secular lords. They received complaints and initiated proceedings; they ordered investigations, particularly in the case of boundary disputes – where they often sent representatives to inspect the land and make an assessment – but also in relation to issues over water rights.[34] They gave orders: for example, for a party to take the oath, as the Navarre king once did

---

[30] Liii 556 (993); OD 43 (997) – single sheet; C 90 (957); Cel 197 and Cel 368 (975–1011). The latter are inventories of property accumulated by Cresconio and include summaries of how the property was acquired; much was acquired by gift and sale, but some came as a result of judicial process.

[31] Lii 410; *PMH* 163; both on single sheets.

[32] Cel 95 (950, 951); T66 – cf. in the same record *in iure de abbati nostro Hopila et Allorito* [the *saio*]; OD4 – another single sheet.

[33] Li 34 (915); Sam 44 (975) – single sheet, *PMH* 183 (999); Sob 129 (942), OD 39 (995) – single sheet. Acting for kings: Li 144 (941), Li 191 (946).

[34] Kings: Li 89 (931) – single sheet, Li 128 (938); counts: *PMH* 42 (936), Cel 502 (940); bishop: Sob 129 (942).

(and as judges more often did too), or for a party to appear before him or herself on a specified date, perhaps with evidence or witnesses, or to the count to put a judgment into effect, as the Navarre king did in Aragón, or for the restoration of property.[35] They also could take part in judging, alongside other judges, although they did not invariably do so; and sometimes they made final decisions, as the count of Castile did when he decided between two monasteries in a case over salt rights.[36] And they took fines, particularly well evidenced in the case of counts, though by no means confined to them.[37]

Some reflections

Our perceptions of presidency depend very much on the wording of the available texts, and therefore on the training and perspectives of the scribes who made the records, which have both formulaic and free narrative aspects, the formulas sometimes carefully chosen, sometimes not. Further, the Latin records from these three regions had different relationships with local vernaculars, for a form of Latin was the spoken language in Iberia whereas in Wales and Brittany the main spoken languages were Brittonic. The Iberian record was close to the language of speech; the Welsh and Breton were in a language of learning; there are therefore differences in the windows through which we now view this material. Systematic comparison nevertheless makes it clear that we cannot be certain what apparently straightforward words mean, and hence that it is extremely important to take all the reported action into account.

Presidents can often be identified in Breton and Iberian records, although by no means always. In Brittany they are usually identifiable and their functions are clear. In Wales this is rarely the case. In Iberia presidents are not as frequently identifiable as in Brittany, although many can be identified and there is much more detail about their functions. In Brittany, Spain and Portugal, presidents did not always act alone: they could act in pairs and sometimes in larger groups; and presidency *in absentia* looks possible. On the whole those who presided let others deal with evidence, but they did sometimes join in the judging in Iberia, presumably depending on local circumstances and the level of their political interest. That they did not always do so makes it clear that presidency was separable from judging.[38]

There are two significant differences between regions: in Spain and Portugal presidents clearly joined in the judging on many occasions, although apparently not all; and they equally clearly took fines. In eastern Brittany most court presidents do not appear to have done either, although rulers judged. The machtiern neither judged nor took a fine – presumably a comment on the low level of his or her political interest in these cases.[39]

---

35 SM 98 (984), Sah 356 (998); C 90 (957), Sam 126 (960); A. Ubieto Arteta, ed., *Cartulario de San Juan de la Peña*, 2 vols (Valencia, 1962, 1963), no. 18 (948); Sob 130 (992).

36 Joining with judges: *PMH* 42 (936), Sob 103 (952), Jaca (958) – see n. 26 above, Sam 126 (960). Final decisions: SM 50 (948); cf. C 59 (947), [*comes*] *qui iudicavit isto iudicio*.

37 For example, Sob 21 (931); C 151 (972); OD 34 (993) – single sheet; Liii 556 (993).

38 Susan Reynolds makes essentially the same point for other parts of western Europe in *Kingdoms and Communities in Western Europe 900–1300* (Oxford, 1984), 26–9.

39 Compare, perhaps, the fees of Welsh judges cited in the (later) Laws of Court, J. B. Smith, '*Ynad*

Comparison emphasises the absence of fines in Brittany and the level of political interest in many recorded court proceedings in Iberia. That we do not see much of punishment in Brittany is partly because we see only the free peasant population – the servile population had no voice – but only partly so.[40] The capacity to punish in Spain and Portugal – the fines for small-scale theft, especially in Galicia, are particularly notable – may have a bearing on the relative social status of the peasantry. This contrast serves to emphasise the freedom of the Breton free peasant and it raises interesting questions about the place of a dependent peasantry in the construction of political power. In all areas, Wales too, there are ruler interests in the judicial process, including at village level in Brittany: a representative of the ruler or count (*missus*) frequently joined machtierns when cases were heard (in 56% of recorded cases); when machtierns chaired exchange transactions they did so without such higher-level representatives. In Iberia we see vastly more of rulers' and counts' courts than those of others and therefore less, though something, of the interaction between ruler and the smallest-scale localities. Ruler or someone else, those who presided were the people with political power; they acted as authority figures in court, commanding that this or that be done; and they joined in the judging when it suited them. To take the chair in a judicial court was to make a statement about power and was thereby a mechanism for enhancing it.[41]

---

llys, iudex curie', in *The Welsh King and his Court*, ed. T. M. Charles-Edwards, M. E. Owen, P. Russell (Cardiff, 2000, 94–115, at 100–1.

[40] It might be objected that many Breton cases were property disputes, but there were some 'criminal' cases, for which penalties of mutilation and death are specified: CR 202 (858).

[41] I am very grateful to Isabel Alfonso, Paul Fouracre, John Hudson, Paul Russell, and Chris Wickham for their extremely helpful comments on drafts of this paper.

14

THE IORWERTH TRIADS

Sara Elin Roberts

Cyfraith Hywel, the law of Hywel, was the system of law followed in Wales throughout the Middle Ages; attributed to Hywel ap Cadell (Hywel Dda), d. 949 or 950, it survives in some forty manuscripts dating from the mid-thirteenth century to the fifteenth century.[1] It was a native legal system, distinct from both English law and Canon Law; had the system survived to this day, it would be a third class of law in the United Kingdom, a *Volksrecht*-system to join the Scottish civil law tradition and the English common law.[2]

The manuscripts of Welsh law divide into three Welsh groups or redactions, named after eminent lawyers noted in the prologues of each redaction: Iorwerth, Blegywryd and Cyfnerth.[3] The Latin manuscripts form a separate group.[4] There are eight manuscripts in the Iorwerth redaction, and they take up the first letters of the alphabet in the sigla assigned to them by Aneurin Owen. They are: Aberystwyth, National Library of Wales, Peniarth 29 (The Black Book of Chirk, Owen's *A*); London, British Library, Cotton Titus D.ii (*B*); BL Cotton Caligula A.iii (*C*); NLW Peniarth 32 (*D*); BL Additional MS. 14931 (*E*); NLW Peniarth 35 (*G*); NLW Peniarth 40 (*K*); and NLW Peniarth 39 (named *Lew* by William Maurice, it was not known to Owen).[5] Llyfr Colan, NLW Peniarth MS

---

[1] D. Jenkins, ed. and trans., *The Law of Hywel Dda: Law Texts from Medieval Wales* (Llandysul, 1986), xxi.

[2] T. Jones Pierce, 'The Law of Wales – the Last Phase', *THSC* (1963), 7–32, at 20 (reprinted in *Medieval Welsh Society: Selected Essays by T. Jones Pierce*, ed. J. B. Smith (Cardiff, 1972), 369–89, at 379).

[3] T. M. Charles-Edwards, *The Welsh Laws* (Writers of Wales; Cardiff, 1989), 17–21. *ALW* presents edited texts for each of the four redactions, but more recent studies of individual redactions are available: for Blegywryd, M. Richards, ed., *Cyfreithiau Hywel Dda yn Ôl Llawysgrif Coleg yr Iesu LVII*, rev. edn (Cardiff, 1990), and see also S. J. Williams and J. E. Powell, ed., *Llyfr Blegywryd* (Cardiff, 1942); for Iorwerth, A. Rh. Wiliam, ed., *Llyfr Iorwerth* (Cardiff, 1960); for Cyfnerth, *WML*.

[4] H. D. Emanuel, ed., *The Latin Texts of the Welsh Laws* (Cardiff, 1967). The Latin texts were treated as one redaction by Aneurin Owen, but in fact there are five Latin redactions, labelled Latin A–E by Emanuel; cf. Charles-Edwards, *The Welsh Laws*, 31–5.

[5] *ALW* vol. I xxv–xxxii (x–xiii in the folio version). Welsh law manuscripts are commonly referred to using the siglum designated to each manuscript by Aneurin Owen. A more up-to-date list can be found in Charles-Edwards, *The Welsh Laws*, 100–2; the Iorwerth manuscripts are discussed separately in *Llyfr Iorwerth* (Wiliam, ed.), xix–xx. For William Maurice and his use of the Welsh law manuscripts, see D. Jenkins, 'Deddfgrawn William Maurice', *National Library of Wales Journal* 2 (1941), 33–6. A facsimile copy of Iorwerth *A* is available in J. G. Evans, *The Chirk Codex of the Welsh Laws* (Llanbedrog, 1921), and the main printed text for the redaction is *Llyfr Iorwerth* (Wiliam, ed.), an edition of Iorwerth *B*. Aneurin Owen's main text for Iorwerth was from

30, is a revised version of the Iorwerth redaction.[6] The Iorwerth redaction is from north Wales and includes some of the earliest manuscripts of Welsh law; the text itself can be linked to the kingdom of Gwynedd during the time of Llywelyn ap Iorwerth and Llywelyn ap Gruffudd.[7] Of the Welsh redactions, this is perhaps the only one that was accurately located by Aneurin Owen, who named it the 'Venedotian Code'. The first – and to date, only – full study of the Iorwerth redaction was undertaken by Aled Rhys William and was published as *Llyfr Iorwerth* in 1960.[8] Iorwerth contains many of the same tractates as Cyfnerth and Blegywryd, and may be derived at least in part from an early version of Cyfnerth; the third part of *Llyfr Iorwerth*, named *Llyfr Prawf* 'the Test Book', is a section unique to this redaction which may have been the outcome of reworking and reordering of legal matter by Iorwerth ap Madog.[9]

Legal triads are a common feature in all Welsh law manuscripts.[10] The basic form is a simple sentence consisting of a heading, and with three 'limbs' giving the three items in the triad;[11] for example, *Teyr ford y serheyr y urenhynes: vn ev o torry y navd; eyl ev o tarav dyrnavt arney; trydyd yv o grypdeyllav peth o'y llav.*[12] The original purpose of the triad form may have been as a mnemonic, although it developed to become a literary convention;[13] they usually set out legal rules or parts of a legal discussion in sets of three, and can either summarise a section of legal text or add detail to it.[14] Of the forty or more manuscripts of medieval Welsh law, every single one of them includes triads at some point. However, a distinction needs to be made between the triads which are found within the tractates, which are inserted at relevant points or on the same topic as the surrounding text, and triads found in the main triad collection. The triad collection could be classified as a tractate, and it was seen as a separate entity at least by some redactors.[15] Manuscripts of the Blegywryd and Cyfnerth redactions usually have one large triad collection – the triad-tractate – and also have thematically linked triads included as one element within a tractate on a certain topic. The editions presented in *The Legal Triads of Medieval Wales* were an attempt to present all of the triads within the law manuscripts, and, while the study did consider all legal triads, the editions presented the triads found in the Blegywryd and Cyfnerth redaction manuscripts only, with a focus on the triad-tractate.[16] The triads in the Iorwerth redaction and also in NLW Peniarth 164 (Owen's *H*) were

---

Iorwerth *A*. Diplomatic texts of Iorwerth *A*, *B*, *C*, *E* and *Colan* are available in *Rhyddiaith Gymraeg o Lawysgrifau'r 13eg ganrif*, ed. S. Rodway and Graham R. Isaac (CD-ROM, Aberystwyth, Bangor, Swansea and Cardiff, 2003).

6   D. Jenkins, ed., *Llyfr Colan* (Cardiff, 1963), xxvi; Jenkins, *The Law of Hywel Dda*, xxvi.
7   D. Jenkins, 'The Significance of the Law of Hywel', *THSC* (1977), 54–76.
8   Charles-Edwards, *The Welsh Laws*, 16–28.
9   *Ibid.*, 29–30.
10 S. E. Roberts, ed. and trans., *The Legal Triads of Medieval Wales* (Cardiff, 2007).
11 *Ibid.*, 7–9.
12 'In three ways *sarhaed* is done to the queen: one is to break her protection; a second is to strike her a blow; a third is to snatch something from her hand': *Llyfr Iorwerth*, §3/6 (ed. Wiliam, 2). (References are in the format § section/sentence.)
13 Triads also occur in other Welsh genres: see Roberts, *Legal Triads*, 4–5.
14 *Ibid.*, 7–9.
15 Emanuel, *Latin Texts*, 369: the section is labelled *De Trinis* in Latin D.
16 See, for example, the discussion on the triads in Iorwerth in Roberts, *Legal Triads*, 12–13; the triad collection in manuscript *K* is also discussed, 13–14.

not presented, although they were discussed.[17] For the purposes of the edition, in the case of manuscript *H* space was an issue; for the Iorwerth triads the problem was fitting the material in with the Blegywryd and Cyfnerth material. This study will examine the Iorwerth triads separately and is an attempt to complete the picture of the legal triads in the Iorwerth redaction.

While all law manuscripts include triads, it has been seen as striking that the Iorwerth redaction has so few triads. Aled Rhys Wiliam noted that Iorwerth *B* contains 'about thirty-five legal triads', and he attributed this low number to the fact that it is an earlier manuscript and 'accretions are most numerous and detailed in the latest MSS'.[18] He did not see triads as a part of the basic texts of Welsh law, but as later additions; he then noted that Iorwerth *K*, which he dated to 1469, has fifty-seven triads. It turns out, however, that Iorwerth *K* is a special case, as it has a tail of additional material, including a southern triad collection witnessed in two other (Blegywryd) manuscripts.[19] Wiliam's comment on the number of triads in Iorwerth *B* is correct but, rather than attributing this to the fact that Iorwerth *B* is an earlier manuscript, it may be more accurate to say that this is a phenomenon of the basic Iorwerth texts, and in fact Iorwerth *B* has the highest number of triads in any complete Iorwerth manuscript: Iorwerth *D* has thirty-two triads, and Iorwerth *E* has thirty. Iorwerth *A* has twenty-six but is missing a section of text including land law; the Iorwerth main-text sections in Iorwerth *G* include fourteen triads, and Iorwerth *C*, which is fragmentary, has five triads. *Lew* is also incomplete but the Iorwerth sections which survive include seven triads. So, while Iorwerth *B*, with its thirty-five triads, may have a low number for a law manuscript, it is not because it is an early manuscript; the number is low only when compared with the other redactions. By contrast, BL Cotton Cleopatra B. v (Cyfnerth *X*) has a total of seventy-six triads, and basic Blegywryd texts have a total of 156.[20] The Latin texts have more variety – Latin A has fifty, Latin B seventy-two and Latin E ninety-two, and there is a large collection of forty or more triads in each; Latin D has 155 with a collection which becomes the main Blegywryd collection, but Latin C, which is the closest of the Latin texts to Iorwerth, is fragmentary and the surviving sections include only four triads.[21] While it is true that later manuscripts have higher numbers of triads (for example, Blegywryd *Q*, NLW Wynnstay 36 has 262), the explanation for the low number of triads in total in the Iorwerth manuscripts reflects a difference in the structure and arrangement of the redaction. The crucial factor is that the Iorwerth redaction does not include a large triad collection.

The Iorwerth manuscripts, in fact, show reasonable uniformity in their numbers of triads (see Table 3). Iorwerth *B* has more triads than the other manuscripts,

17 C. James, Review of Roberts, *Legal Triads*, *Studia Celtica* 42 (2008), 176–8. The triads in *H* have been examined elsewhere, and a complete text of the manuscript is found in G. A. Elias's thorough work: 'Golygiad ac Astudiaeth Destunol o'r Llyfr Cyfraith yn LlGC Llawysgrif Peniarth 164 (H), Ynghyd â'r Copïau Ohoni yn Llawysgrifau Peniarth 278 a Llanstephan 121' (unpubl. PhD dissertation, Bangor University, 2007); see also S. E. Roberts, 'Law Texts and Their Sources in Medieval Wales: The Case of *H* and Tails of Other Legal Manuscripts', *Welsh History Review* 24 (2008), 41–59.

18 *Llyfr Iorwerth* (ed. Wiliam), xxi.

19 Roberts, *Legal Triads*, 32–4.

20 *Ibid.*; see the Blegywryd collections; the combined text in *Llyfr Blegywryd* (ed. Williams and Powell) represents a Blegywryd text without a tail of additional material.

21 Roberts, *Legal Triads*, 421–7, 414–18, and 24–9; Emanuel, *Latin Texts*, 276–90.

Table 3: The triads in the manuscripts of the Iorwerth redaction.[22]

No.	Iorwerth triads	B	A	C	D	E	G	K	Lew	Col
1	O teir ffordd y gwneir sarhad i'r brenin	3/2	2	—	1v	2	—	—	—	
2	O teir ffordd y sarheir y frenhines	3/6	3	—	2r	2	—	—	—	
3	Tri anhebcor brenin	42/2	29	—	80v	22	—	—	—	
4	Tri anhebcor breyr	42/3	29	—	80v	22	—	—	—	
5	Tri anhebcor taeog	42/4	29	—	80v	22	—	—	—	
6	Tri pheth ni dele y brenin cyfran a neb	42/5	29	—	80v	22	—	—	—	
7	Tri rhwyd brenin	42/6	29	—	81r	22	—	—	—	
8	Tri rhwyd breyr	42/7	29	—	81r	22	—	—	—	
9	Tri rhwyd taeog	42/8	29	—	81r	22	—	—	—	
10	Tri chorn cyweithas	42/9	29	—	81r	22	—	—	—	
11	Tair telyn cyfreithiol	42/10,11	29	—	81r	22	—	—	—	
12	Tri pheth ni eill taeog y gwerthu	42/12	29	—	81r	22	—	—	—	
13	Tair celfyddyd ni eill taeog	42/13	29	—	81r	22	—	—	—	
14	Tri pheth ni dyly y brenin rhannu ac arall	43/8	30	—	81v	23	—	—	—	
15	Tair agweddi cyfreithiol	48/9	36	—	21v	27	93v	—	—	
16	Tri prifurey gwreic	51/1	27	—	22v	28	94r	—	—	
17	Tri gorsaf gwreic	51/11	38	—	23r		94v	—	—	6
18	O tri modd y dylyir amobr i wraig	51/12	38	—	23r	29	95r	—	—	7
19	Teir gwragedd a dele y meybyon vamwys	53/5	39	—		30	96r	—	—	
20	Tri anghyfarch gwr	55/14		—	26r		98v	—	—	40
21	Tri anghyfarch gwraig	55/15		—	26r		98v	—	—	[40]
22	Tair ofer fechni	65	47	160rb	30r	38	26r	76	19v	111
23	Tri pheth ni dylyir nawdd rhagddunt	71/1	51	164rb	33v	42	29v	84	26r	
24	Try gorsedauc esyd	83/10	—	—	43v	54	43r	103	—	
25	Tri ryw dadannudd	84/1	—	—	43v	54	43r	103	55r	566

[22] References to *B* are to section/sentence in the printed edition (*Llyfr Iorwerth*, ed. Wiliam), references to *A* are to page numbers in the printed facsimile, and references to *Colan* are to sentences in the printed edition (ed. Jenkins). Other manuscripts are referred to by folio or page in the manuscript. — denotes a hiatus in the manuscript, whereas blank cells show missing triads where the surrounding text is in that manuscript. For the division between tractates, see below, p. 159.

26	Tair gwragedd a dyly eu meibion tir o fam	86/5	—	171vb	45r	55	44v	106	57v	
27	Tri thlws cenedyl	88/2	—	—	46r	57	46r	108	60v	
28	Tri dygyngoll	101	—	179va	54r	67	—	123	65r	
29	O teir ffordd y serheir y frenhines	110/6	—				—			
30	O teir ffordd y serheir bob dyn	110/10	—				—			
31	Try than ny diwygir	118/1	62	185va	65r	78	—	38	39r	430
32	Tryded hele ryd	135/7	71	—	71r	83	107r	48	—	
33	Tri gwaed ni diwygir	147/1	82	—	75r	89	—	57	—	
34	Tri arberigyl dyn	147/3	81	—	75r	88	—	56	—	
35	Tair craith gogyfarch	147/10	82	—	75r	89	—	57	—	

but in each Iorwerth manuscript the same triads are found at the same point in the text. In other words, we have the same triads in all the texts but with omissions, and additions in Iorwerth *B* only. This classification makes a distinction between triads which are not included in the text and triads which are in a text hiatus in a manuscript: where a manuscript is missing text, such as the law of women in Iorwerth *C*, for example, it will necessarily be lacking the triads within that section.

The triads in Iorwerth are a pair of triads on the *sarhaed* (insult value) of the king and the queen (numbers 1–2 in the table) found in the first part of the Laws of Court, then eleven triads (3–14) in a collection at the end of the Laws of Court[23] – these triads occur in all the manuscripts containing the Laws of Court.[24] This cluster of triads might well prove to be significant and is discussed more fully below. There are seven triads in the laws of women (15–21), two in the suretyship tractate (22–3), four in land law (24–7) and three in the value of limbs section (33–5). The section on children, the Three Columns of Law and the value of wild and tame have one triad each (28, 31 and 32 respectively). The additions in Iorwerth *B* are a pair of triads, 29–30, on the king and queen's *sarhaed*, placed in a section discussing *sarhaed*.[25] These occur only in Iorwerth *B* and are variant versions of the two triads in the Laws of Court, but the wording is strikingly similar to the pair of triads found in the Laws of Court in Blegywryd and Cyfnerth, so the pair of triads may have originated in those redactions. It seems that this addition was made by the redactor of Iorwerth *B* but not by the others.

Turning to the omissions, manuscripts Iorwerth *A*, *C* and *E* are missing a pair of triads, 20 and 21, on *tri anghyfarch gwr/gwraig*, 'the three unclaimable things of a man/woman', in the laws of women, although the surrounding text found in other Iorwerth manuscripts is included; the pair of triads is found in Iorwerth *D* and Iorwerth *G*, which suggests they were part of the basic Iorwerth text, as

---

[23] There is a run of eleven triads, nos 3–13 in Table 1, above, but triad 14 is found after the *wyth pynfarch* 'eight packhorses', the following section, and is not part of the collection.

[24] *Llyfr Iorwerth*, §42, §43/8 (ed. Wiliam, 22–3); see also the conspectus of editions, xliii–xliv.

[25] *Llyfr Iorwerth*, §110/6, §110/10 (ed. Wiliam, 73).

they occur in the same position in more than one manuscript. This pair of triads features in only one branch of the textual tradition (so were added at α, or alternatively removed at β in the other branch), and this supports Charles-Edwards's stemma of the laws of country in Iorwerth.[26] According to that stemma we would also expect to see the triads in Iorwerth *Lew*, but that portion of text is missing in Iorwerth *Lew*. These triads also occur in *Colan*, but are combined to create one longer sentence without the triad headings.[27] Iorwerth *E* has also omitted triad 17 in the laws of women, but there is no explanation for this omission; the omissions give Iorwerth *E* a lower total of thirty triads.[28] Iorwerth *D* is one triad short of the total of thirty-three, missing triad 19 in the laws of women.[29] The text on either side of the triad is present, so this may be a deliberate omission (the triad is rather long for it to be eye-skip), although it is difficult to explain why this triad in particular was omitted. The text in Iorwerth *D*, however, does appear to have been tidied up in places.[30] The other Iorwerth manuscripts are not complete.

The fact that all complete Iorwerth manuscripts contain the same triads suggests that these triads cannot be considered to be additions to the text, or 'floating sections', to use Enoch Powell's term.[31] The triads were part of the tractates, not to be separated from the text, and may have been an integral part of the text from an early date. This is probably true of all of the redactions – triads were a recognised and useful form in which to present legal data. The main triad collection, however, was treated in the same way as the other tractates: it could be copied in its entirety, but it was a fixed section of law and the rearranging or omitting of triads, or the moving of them around, did not tend to happen.[32]

Assuming that the triad collection is the main difference, some interesting results appear on comparing the three redactions. Without the triad collection (and disregarding the 'tails' of any texts), Blegywryd manuscripts have forty-three triads at relevant points in their tractates. The Cyfnerth manuscripts are far less uniform, and the texts are far more fluid. The triad-tractate tends to occur at the end of the manuscript, before any additional material forming a tail, such as is found in NLW Peniarth 259B (Owen's *Z*), or *Llyfr Damweiniau*, 'The Book of Eventualities' (NLW Peniarth 37, Owen's *U*);[33] the triad-tractate in each manuscript starts with the same triad and follows a similar order. Cyfnerth *X* and *U* have thirteen triads outside the triad collection (but they are not the same thirteen and the manuscripts are not related); the Bodorgan manuscript (*Mk*, privately owned (Bangor University, MS 21108 is a photostat of it)) has twenty; BL Harleian 4353 (*V*) has eighteen; BL Cotton Cleopatra A xiv (*W*) has sixteen; and Cyfnerth *Z* has eight.

---

[26] *Coleg yr Iesu LVII*, xxi, Fig II.

[27] *Llyfr Colan*, §40, §41 (ed. Jenkins).

[28] *Llyfr Iorwerth*, §51/11 (ed. Wiliam, 29).

[29] *Llyfr Iorwerth*, §53/5 (ed. Wiliam, 30).

[30] See below, p. 162, n.36.

[31] J. E. Powell, 'Floating Sections in the Law of Hywel', *BBCS* 9 (1937–9), 27–34; for discussion of this concept, see Roberts, *Legal Triads*, 11–5.

[32] The exceptions are Manuscript *Q*, and Latin D; see Roberts, *Legal Triads*, 28.

[33] *Llyfr Damweiniau* is a lengthy book often appended to the Iorwerth manuscripts, and which consists of a series of sentences stating 'If it happens that X, then Y'; Charles-Edwards, *The Welsh Laws*, 49–52; a recent study of the Book of Damweiniau is found in Robin Chapman Stacey, 'Legal Writing in Medieval Wales: *Damweiniau I*', in *Wales and the Wider World. Wales in an International Context*, ed. T. M. Charles-Edwards and R. J. W. Evans (Donington, 2010), 57–85.

The same triads do not occur at the same points in all three redactions, but then the texts are too different for this to be the case. However, the tractates which contain triads in Iorwerth also contain triads in Blegywryd and Cyfnerth – and there are some tractates which do not include triads in any redaction. In all the redactions there are two (four in Blegywryd) triads in the king's section in the Laws of Court on *sarhaed*. Several triads occur in the land law section – nine in Blegywryd – and also in the law of women, and there are triads in the surety tractate in each redaction, but a higher number in the Blegywryd and Cyfnerth redactions. It is striking that every one of the Cyfnerth manuscripts has at least one triad within these tractates. Blegywryd has long sections at different points in the manuscripts on the justice and judgements, and these sections have a high number of triads (at least eleven). In contrast, some sections have very few or no triads: the value of wild and tame has one triad in Blegywryd and Cyfnerth (the same triad) and a different triad in Iorwerth; the Laws of Court, at least in the descriptions of the officers, do not include triads; and the Three Columns of Law have no triads in Cyfnerth, one only in Blegywryd (the *tri dygyngoll* 'three dire losses' triad which is found in the triad collection in Cyfnerth but in the family law section in Iorwerth[34]) and Iorwerth has the triad on the unlawful fires which is found in the triad collection in Blegywryd and Cyfnerth.

There are then long sections in the law manuscripts which do not include any triads at all. This suggests that it was more usual to include triads in some tractates and not in others, where perhaps the subject matter was less amenable to triadic arrangement. The Laws of Court is the longest tractate which does not have many triads. The remainder of the Blegywryd and Cyfnerth manuscripts are comprised of the laws of country, but the latter part of Iorwerth texts are divided into the laws of country and the justices' test book.[35] And a striking point is that the tractates which include triads in Iorwerth (excluding the collection of triads at the end of the Laws of Court) are all in the laws of country – the Laws of Court and the justices' test book are sections without many triads, apart from the odd one or two.[36] There are no triads in *cyfar*, joint ploughing or the corn damage section, the value of wild and tame has only one triad, and likewise the Three Columns of Law. This is revealing, and may show that the lawbooks did not originate as one text, but in sections; the Laws of Court may have had a separate origin and so at a later stage in Iorwerth did the justices' test book, and the inclusion of triads (or not) in each section was a habit which was carried through the redactions – no triads were added where they may not have been originally.

This gives us a different picture of Iorwerth. It is not the case that the Iorwerth redaction does not have triads, or has hardly any triads; but rather triads are mainly confined to the laws of country. This is very similar to Cyfnerth, with some triads embedded in the tractates in certain areas of law. The difference between the Cyfnerth and Blegywryd texts on the one hand and the Iorwerth texts on the other is the inclusion of a tractate of triads in the former – the triad collection, which accounts for the high number of triads in Blegywryd and Cyfnerth.

34 S. E. Roberts, 'Tri Dygyngoll Cenedl: The Development of a Triad', *Studia Celtica* 37 (2003), 163–82.
35 *Llyfr Iorwerth* (ed. Wiliam), xxi; Charles-Edwards, *The Welsh Laws*, 27–9.
36 The short Iorwerth triad collection occurs towards the end of the Laws of Court in Iorwerth, but is a separate collection; see below, p. 162.

Iorwerth does not have a long triad collection, but there is a small triad collection, comprised of eleven triads, in the Iorwerth manuscripts. This collection is interesting and deserves separate attention. It is found towards the end of the Laws of Court, preceding a section labelled 'miscellaneous' by Wiliam, in Iorwerth *A*, *B*, and *E*, and towards the end of Iorwerth *D*, before *Llyfr Damweiniau*.[37] It is marked by a heading or introductory sentence in the manuscripts containing the section: *Vchof retraethassam ny o'r suydogyon a perthyn ar e llys a'r rey aruer a'r rey deuaut, ac eu breynt ac eu dylyet; eman e traethun ny o petheu ereyll.*[38] This preface does not mark this as a triad collection, but states that it is material other than that on the officers of the court; but it is still a collection of miscellanea on the laws of court, and the triad collection is followed by other related material, including the *wyth pynfarch*, 'eight packhorses', which has a numerical arrangement. Iorwerth *C* is missing large parts of the Laws of Court, including the end; Iorwerth *G*, *K* and *Col* do not have the Laws of Court at all, so this section occurs in all manuscripts containing the laws of court. In all manuscripts except Iorwerth *D* the triad collection follows the final item in the *swyddogion defod ac arfer*, 'officers by custom and use' list (the washerwoman, in this case).[39] In the Cyfnerth manuscripts the triad-tractate is usually at the end of the main text, but there are two positions for the triad-tractate in Blegywryd, a factor which helps mark out the two Blegywryd groups of manuscripts.[40] Group I manuscripts do not have the Laws of Court in full, and the triad-tractate is found towards the end of the main text of the laws – this is closer to Cyfnerth. Group II manuscripts have a complete copy of the Laws of Court, and the triad-tractate is found towards the beginning of the laws of country, after the Three Columns of Law and following suretyship.[41] The positioning of the triad-tractate in the Group II Blegywryd texts may be older than that in Group I.[42] Neither the Blegywryd or the Cyfnerth redaction has the triad-tractate in the same position as the short collection in the Iorwerth manuscripts (although in Iorwerth *D* the miscellanea is placed after the main text of the laws and before *Llyfr Damweiniau*), but there is an interesting link between the redactions. The small triad collection in Iorwerth matches the first triads in the triad-tractate in the Blegywryd manuscripts, and also in Latin *D*.[43] Although the order is slightly different, with the *anhebcor* 'indispensables' triads beginning the collection rather than the *rhwydi* 'nets' triads, there is too much similarity here for this to be a coincidence. Cyfnerth has similar triads at the beginning of the collection, but the clearest link is between

---

[37] *Llyfr Iorwerth* (ed. Wiliam), xliii (see §51); see triads 3–13 in Table 1, above. In Iorwerth *D* the entire 'miscellaneous' section including the triad collection and the *wyth pynfarch* has been moved to the end of the manuscript, and the preface has been amended to state that what follows the officers is the laws of country.

[38] 'Above we have treated of the officers who belong to the court and those by use and those by custom, and their status and their entitlement. Here we treat of other things': *Llyfr Iorwerth*, §42 (ed. Wiliam, 22–3).

[39] The officers by custom and use were part of the court but were not counted among the twenty-four officers, and they were independent heads of their own crafts; D. Jenkins, 'Proglomena to the Laws of Court' in *The Welsh King and His Court*, ed. T. M. Charles-Edwards, M. E. Owen and P. Russell (Cardiff, 2000), 15–28, at 22.

[40] *Coleg yr Iesu LVII* (ed. Richards), xvi.

[41] Roberts, *Legal Triads*, 17. For an example of this positioning see *Coleg yr Iesu LVII*, 33 (ed. Richards).

[42] Roberts, *Legal Triads*, 18; this is supported by the Latin D evidence, *ibid.*, 26–7, 29.

[43] *Ibid.*, Fig 2, 35.

Latin D/Blegywryd and Iorwerth. Latin D has the same triads in the same order. Blegywryd is very similar but has an additional triad as the eighth triad.[44] The eleven triads are the same ones, and it would appear that the triad collection in Iorwerth derives from the same exemplar or basis as the start of the triad collection in Latin D and Blegywryd. Another factor to note is that all the triads are on similar subjects; they discuss the king and his rights (with 'matching' triads in two cases for the nobleman and the bondman) and matters pertaining to the king and his court. Locating these eleven triads after the Laws of Court was therefore a logical step. The positioning of the triad collection in Group II Blegywryd and Latin D may be based on that same logic if not the same textual model, but Group I Blegywryd texts may follow Cyfnerth in putting the triad collection at the end of the manuscript.

The next step is to attempt to explain why there are only eleven triads in the Iorwerth collection, but over a hundred in the Blegywryd/Latin D collections. There are three possibilities. First, there may have been a collection of only eleven triads available in Iorwerth's exemplar for this section, and only eleven were copied; at a later date but still early in the textual history, this list of eleven triads was seen as a group to which more triads could be added, thus creating the lengthy collections in Blegywryd and Latin D.

The second possibility is that there was a triad-tractate in Iorwerth's exemplar, but only certain triads (those connected to the king and his court) were copied, since there was some blank space at the end of the Laws of Court.[45] It is more difficult, however, to explain why the remainder of the triads were not used as 'fillers' in the same way in other tractates, and this theory seems unlikely. Since the triads are all on the same subject it makes sense that they were included here, and they are followed by the *wyth pynfarch*, 'eight packhorses', on the king's rights. Another problem with the use of the triads to fill gaps at the end of quires is that they are in the Laws of Court in all Iorwerth manuscripts; there may be evidence of quire filling in *A* but since the manuscripts do not all derive from Iorwerth *A* the positioning of the triads must pre-date Iorwerth *A*.[46] Quire filling may have happened in the archetype, but this would be difficult to prove. One point in favour of selecting triads on the king and his court is that the next triad in Blegywryd and Latin D is *tri phedwar yssyd*, 'there are three fours', a lengthy triad on various topics but not on the king and his court. That triad is different in form and style from all of the other triads in the collection.

The third possibility is that the triads were not in a collection in the exemplar for the Iorwerth redaction, but were brought together from another source. That source may be the Laws of Court. If we consider the evidence in the Latin manuscripts, Latin A has a triad-tractate which begins with the same eleven triads found in Iorwerth, and may be linked to the Cyfnerth redaction, although it is located following the *mechniaeth*, 'suretyship' section rather than at the end of the Laws of Court.[47] Latin B and Latin E have a different form of the triad-tractate, and the eleven triads forming the collection in Iorwerth are present but

---

44   The eighth triad in Blegywryd is *Tair cyflafan: ibid.*, 124–5.

45   *Ibid.*, 13. There may be evidence for quire-filling activity in Iorwerth *A*, but *A* is not the basis for the other manuscripts in the Iorwerth redaction.

46   *Ibid.*, 13.

47   Latin A's triad collection begins with the triad on *dirwy*, as does the collection in most Cyfnerth manuscripts; see *ibid.*, 421–2; Emanuel, *Latin Texts*, 126–9.

at various points in the Laws of Court tractate, embedded within non-triadic text, and not together as a collection.[48] The surviving fragments of Latin C suggest that the triads were located at relevant points in the Laws of Court, rather than as a short collection, although there is not enough of that manuscript surviving to be able to tell for certain. This may point to the possibility that these triads were originally located at various locations in the Laws of Court tractate, but at some point were taken out of the tractate and put together at the end of the Laws of Court, as in Iorwerth, forming a thematic collection of triads. These same triads then became the basis for the larger triad-tractate. The important detail to consider in all of this is that the triads in each case – in the Laws of Court tractate in Latin B and Latin E, in a collection in Iorwerth, and at the beginning of the triad-tractate in Blegywryd, Latin A and Latin D – are the same eleven triads, and are found in the same order. The short collection of triads in the Iorwerth manuscripts coupled with the evidence from the Latin texts may tell us a great deal about how the triad-tractate developed, and the Iorwerth triads may well tell us what was happening in the early stages of the tradition.

Thomas Charles-Edwards has joked that Iorwerth preferred *damweiniau*, 'eventualities', to triads. This appears to be true of *Colan*, as some of the Iorwerth triads appear as *damweiniau* in that text; but triads do occur in the Iorwerth redaction, and there is a collection. In other words, there does not seem to be an attempt to get rid of the triads in preference to *damweiniau* in the Iorwerth texts. Triads are an important feature of the law-texts, and this is true in Iorwerth as well as in Blegywryd and Cyfnerth.

---

[48] Roberts, *Legal Triads*, 423–4; Emanuel, *Latin Texts*, 242–4 and 199–205.

15

THE RECOVERY OF STOLEN PROPERTY:
NOTES ON LEGAL PROCEDURE IN GAELIC IRELAND,
SCOTLAND AND THE ISLE OF MAN

Fergus Kelly

A good deal of general information on the law relating to theft is to be found in the surviving Old Irish legal material from the seventh to the ninth centuries AD.[1] The main law text on this topic is *Bretha im Gatta* 'judgements about thefts', though it is incomplete, owing to the loss of a page in the manuscript.[2] Material on theft is also present in a number of other Old Irish law texts, such as *Críth Gablach*,[3] *Bechbretha*[4] and *Bretha Cairdi*.[5]

The earlier material in Irish contains little specific information on the legal mechanisms for the recovery of stolen property. However, this aspect of the law of theft is touched on in more detail in a Treatise by Giolla na Naomh Mac Aodhagáin,[6] chief judge of Connacht (*ardollamh Connacht*), whose death in 1309 is recorded in the annals.[7] One passage which deals with the tracking of stolen cattle has been edited and translated by W. N. Osborough in an article entitled 'The Irish Custom of Tracts', published in the *Irish Jurist*.[8] The general principle is that if the cattle can be tracked – presumably by the owner accompanied by witnesses – to a particular place, the inhabitants of that place must pay for the theft (*íoc na gaide*), unless they can show that the track continues in another direction, i.e. 'to put the track of the theft from them' (*lorg na gaide do*

---

[1] This article originated from a paper delivered on 20 March 1997 as part of the centenary celebrations of the Department of Celtic Languages and Literatures at Harvard University. I am most grateful for the various helpful comments made on that occasion.

[2] *CIH* II.477.31–479.22. It has been edited and translated by Vernam Hull, '*Bretha im Gatta*', *ZCP* 25 (1956), 211–25.

[3] D. A. Binchy, ed., *Críth Gablach*, Mediaeval and Modern Irish Series 11 (Dublin, 1941; repr. 1970), ll. 123–4 (p. 5), 217–19 (p. 9) (= *CIH* III.779.6, 780.27–8).

[4] Thomas Charles-Edwards and Fergus Kelly, ed. and trans., *Bechbretha: An Old Irish Law-tract on Bee-keeping*, Early Irish Law Series 1 (Dublin, 1983; repr. with additional material 2008), 85–9 (§§50–4) = *CIH* II.455.31–456.29.

[5] E.g. *CIH* I.116.3–15; III.791.5–6. For discussion of the fragmentary text *Bretha Cairdi* 'treaty judgements', see *CCIH* 302–3; *GEIL* 279 (§62).

[6] The Treatise is printed at *CIH* II.691.1–699.4. I hope to provide an edition and translation within a few years in the Early Irish Law Series.

[7] A. Martin Freeman, ed., *Annála Connacht: The Annals of Connacht, A.D. 1224–1544* (Dublin, 1944), 218 s. a. 1309 §2.

[8] W. N. Osborough, 'The Irish Custom of Tracts', *The Irish Jurist* 32 [new series] (1997), 439–58 (repr. in W. N. Osborough, *Studies in Irish Legal History* (Dublin, 1999), 64–80); in the title 'tracts' means 'tracks'.

chur díobh).[9] If the cattle are tracked along a common cattle-road (*bóthar coitchionn ceathra*), where there would be many other cattle-tracks, the case against the suspected cattle-thieves must be substantiated by putting the case before the country (*tír*)[10] or through the evidence of witnesses (*teasta*). The same applies if the tracks are followed in a hard dry place (*ionadh cruaidh tirim*), where there would be difficulty in clearly establishing the route of the stolen cattle. The text is not explicit, but it is likely that, if the stolen cattle are still alive, they are immediately restored to their rightful owner. The culprits must in addition pay the appropriate fines for theft. Throughout the discussion on cattle theft in the Treatise, it is assumed that this crime is carried out by a number of individuals, rather than by a single thief. Obviously, cattle theft is of its nature a crime which requires a number of perpetrators.

Osborough quotes the similar regulations set out in a Latin agreement entered into by Brian Mac Mathghamhna, king of Airghialla, at the behest of Nicholas Mac Maol Íosa, archbishop of Armagh.[11] It is dated 1297, and thus belongs to the same period as Giolla na Naomh's Treatise. Osborough notes that the English authorities in Ireland in the mid-Tudor period gave this native custom the force of law by means of an act of state adopted in late 1552 or early 1553. The Irish council adopted a further act of state regarding the custom of tracts in 1557, whose wording (quoted by Osborough) is comparable to that of the Treatise: 'that iff eny horse, cowe or other cattayll be stollen and the tracte followydd to a certeyn place and the owner or owners inhabitor or inhabitors thereof be before recorde requyred to putt the tracte oute of the grounde to them belonging [cf. *lorg na gaide to chur díobh*] and they shall refuse so to doo, they to answer the goodes'.[12] This act of state was approved in a letter from James I in 1612 and was recognised in 'His Majesty's directions for ordering and settling the courts within his kingdom of Ireland, 1622'.[13] It remained on the statute-book until it was abolished in 1640.

Giolla na Naomh's Treatise goes on to deal with the situation where the cattle have been killed by the thieves and flesh from their carcases discovered on a particular property.[14] If the landowner denies that he has been involved in the crime there are two approaches which the law may adopt. The matter may be put before a jury or an oath of denial (*séana*) may be adequate to exculpate the accused. If the missing cattle have been traced (dead or alive) to a remote area inhabited by 'people without frequenting from them or to them' (*daoine gan tathaighe uatha ná chuca*), all the inhabitants – both those in good legal standing (*ionnraic*) and those not in good legal standing (*eisionnraic*) – are required to swear an oath regarding the fate of the cattle. Unless someone admits to the theft,

---

9   *CIH* II 693.10–13.
10 This would involve putting the case to a jury of neighbours. Giolla na Naomh's Treatise provides clear evidence of the use of the jury system in Gaelic Ireland *c.*1300. The term employed is *finé coitchionn* 'common jury' (*CIH* II.691.9), where *finé* is a borrowing from Anglo-Norman *visné*, *vyny* (Latin *vicinetum* 'neighbourhood'). For a discussion of the etymology of *fin(n)é*, see R. A. Breatnach, '*finné*', *Éigse: A Journal of Irish Studies* 18 (1980–1), 107–9.
11 Osborough, 'The Irish Custom of Tracts', 442.
12 *Ibid.*, 443–4.
13 G. J. Hand and V. W. Treadwell, ed., 'His Majesty's Directions for Ordering and Settling the Courts within his Kingdom of Ireland, 1622', *Analecta Hibernica* 26 (1970), 177–212, at 206.
14 *CIH* II.693.13–17.

it seems that the whole community is held to be liable (*as rith arna lítheachaibh*).[15] It was evidently felt that in such a case it was up to the community itself to establish who was guilty of the offence: because of the remoteness of the location the involvement of external cattle-thieves would have been unlikely.

Later in his Treatise Giolla na Naomh deals with the case where stolen cattle have been driven across the border of a kingdom with which there is no treaty; that is, into enemy territory (*a gcrích easgarad*).[16] Because of the state of enmity between the two territories, the law views the original owner as having lost his ownership of the cattle when they crossed the border. Consequently, if the cattle are subsequently brought back into the original territory – whether by theft, force or purchase – the original owner cannot reassert his ownership of them. If he wishes to regain his cattle he must buy them back from the current owner, who may belong to his territory (*fear tíre*) or to another territory with which there is a treaty (*comhshíocháin*).

There are interesting parallels from Gaelic Scotland regarding the recovery of stolen goods which have been taken away from the home of the owner(s). In his ground-breaking 1985 O'Donnell Lecture 'Celtic Law and Scots Law: Survival and Integration', W. D. H. Sellar assembled a considerable amount of legal and political terminology which is found in both Irish and Scottish sources.[17] Among the terms discussed by him is Gaelic *deòradh* (Scots *dewar*), which corresponds to Old Irish *deorad* (later *deóraidh*). The meanings of *deorad* given in the *DIL* include 'exile, outlaw, alien, pilgrim, servant',[18] and the suggested etymology is **de-fo-rath* 'one excluded from receiving a fief, a person without legal standing'.[19] He is thus the opposite of the *aurrad* (*airrad*, *urrad*), which may be from **air-uss-rath* 'one entitled to receive a fief, a person of legal standing'.

The phrase *deorad Dé* 'exile of God' is frequently used in the Old Irish law texts and other sources of a hermit who has the power to work miracles.[20] Early Irish law treated the *deorad Dé* as a person of special status: the main text on distraint states that even a king cannot overturn the evidence of a *suí* (ecclesias-

---

15 The text has *as reith arna litecaib*; I read *rith*, verbal noun of *reithid* 'runs', used in the sense of 'extension (of a legal liability)'.

16 *CIH* II.694.19–22.

17 W. D. H. Sellar, 'Celtic Law and Scots Law: Survival and Integration', *Scottish Studies* 29 (1989), 1–27.

18 *DIL*, s.v. *deorad*. The meaning 'one immune from legal process' should be added (see n. 43 below), and also Fergus Kelly, *Early Irish Farming: A Study Based Mainly on the Law-texts of the 7th and 8th Centuries AD*, Early Irish Law Series 4 (Dublin, 1997), 528. Note also the use of the derivative adjective *deorata* (*deorada*) 'impartial' (of a judge) at *CIH* III.752.24; IV.1147.17. The judge is evidently regarded as being detached from his ordinary existence when giving a judgement. A person can thus be viewed as *deorad* in the negative sense of 'outlaw, alien', or in the positive sense of one who adjudicates impartially by reason of specialised training and/or supernatural associations.

19 J. Vendryes and P.-Y. Lambert, *Lexique Étymologique de l'Irlandais Ancien: lettre D* (Dublin/ Paris, 1996) D-53 s.v. *deorad*, prefer to take *deorad* as a derivative of *ráth* 'surety'.

20 Colmán Etchingham, *Church Organisation in Ireland AD 650 to 1000* (Maynooth, 1999), 353, raises the possibility that *deorad* is used as synonymous with *deorad Dé* in the Old Irish text entitled 'The Monastery of Tallaght' (E. J. Gwynn and W. J. Purton, ed., *PRIA* 29 C (1911), 162.15 §85). This paragraph deals with the case of a *deorad* who is appointed as abbot of Clonmacnois by Saint Adamnán. Gwynn and Purton provide the translation 'stranger', but he may be a hermit or *deorad Dé* imposed on the monastery to resolve the disputed succession.

tical scholar), bishop or *deorad Dé*.[21] In a passage on ecclesiastical rank[22] it is stated that a *deorad Dé* is a miracle-worker who is of equal rank (*comdíre*) with a bishop, though he is not in holy orders. He is distinguished from the *aíbellteóir* – also a miracle-worker – by his possession of ecclesiastical learning (*légend*).[23] According to the law text *Coibnes Uisce Thairidne* 'kinship of conducted water', the *deorad Dé* is obliged to enforce a contract for which the men of heaven and the gospel of Christ (*fir nime 7 soscéla Críst*) have been invoked as sureties.[24]

We have no information on how the *deorad Dé* fulfilled the duty of enforcing a contract in practice. Indeed, it would seem that a hermit who had renounced the world and was living a contemplative existence – sometimes in a remote spot – was ill-equipped to get involved in the enforcement of any contract.[25] However, there are Scottish parallels which indicate the process whereby the holder of this ecclesiastical office acquired responsibilities of law enforcement in the wider community. The Scottish *deòradh* was a keeper of relics and maintained by a regular levy on the local people. Sellar quotes the example of a hereditary *deòradh* who had charge of the crozier of Saint Fillan.[26] In 1428 an inquest of fifteen persons before John Spens, bailie of the crown lands of Glendochart, found Finlay Dewart (= *deòradh*) to be keeper of the relic. The inquest noted that if any goods or cattle were stolen from an inhabitant of Glendochart who did not care to pursue the thief, he could send for the *deòradh* of the relic along with four pennies or a pair of shoes and food for one night: the *deòradh* was bound to pursue the goods wherever they might be found in the kingdom of Scotland. The Scottish *deòradh* thus shares two features with the *deorad Dé* of early Irish law: an ecclesiastical role and public responsibility for law enforcement in certain circumstances. The crozier of Saint Fillan was called the *Coigreach* and it was the custom that it should be carried by the *deòradh*.[27] *Coigreach* (*coigrigheach*) means 'foreigner, alien',[28] and stems ultimately from *com-* 'co-' + *crích* 'border', i.e. a person from an adjacent territory.[29] Its meaning therefore approximates

---

21   *CIH* II.357.25–7 (= *ALI* I.78.20–1).

22   *CIH* II.686.31–7. Liam Breatnach describes the material from *CIH* II.684.22–687.36 as 'a status-text closely related to the commentary on *Uraicecht Becc*' (*CCIH* 30).

23   See discussion on the *deorad Dé* and *aíbellteóir* by Etchingham, *Church Organisation in Ireland*, 329–30; see also 79, 226 and 353.

24   *CIH* II.460.1–2 (= D. A. Binchy, ed., '*Coibnes Uisce Thairidne*', *Ériu* 17 (1955), 66 §7); also discussed by Rudolf Thurneysen, *Die Bürgschaft im irischen Recht*, Abhandlungen der preussischen Akademie der Wissenschaften, Jahrgang 1928. Phil.-Hist. Klasse. Nr. 2 (Berlin, 1928), 59.

25   But compare Legal Heptad 1, which refers to a *deorad Dé* suing on behalf of a church which has not been properly administered by its *airchinnech* 'monastic superior, church head' (*CIH* 1.3.33 = *ALI* V.118.11); see Thomas Charles-Edwards, 'The Social Background to Irish *Peregrinatio*', *Celtica* 11 (1976), 43–59, at 53–4.

26   Sellar, 'Celtic Law and Scots Law', 8–9; see also S. Taylor, 'The Cult of St Fillan in Scotland', in *The North Sea World in the Middle Ages*, ed. T. R. Liszka and L. E. M. Walker (Dublin, 2001), 175–210, esp. 186–7.

27   *lator ipsius reliquiae de Coygerach qui Jore vulgariter dicitur* 'the carrier of that relic of *Coigreach* who is in the common language called a *deòradh*': Sellar, 'Celtic Law and Scots Law', 8–9 (my translation). For further discussion relating to this crozier (also spelled *quegrith*, *quigrich*, etc.), see William Reeves, *The Life of Columba, Founder of Hy: Written by Adomnan* (Dublin, 1857), 366–7, footnote v.

28   Edward Dwelly, *Faclair Gaidhlig gu Beurla le dealbhan: the Illustrated Gaelic–English Dictionary* (Glasgow, 1901–11), s.vv. *coigreach, coigrigheach*.

29   *DIL*, s.v. *coicrich*.

to that of *deòradh*. In his *History of the Celtic Place-names of Scotland*, W. J. Watson quotes a reference from 1497 to the staff of Saint Munn called *Deowray* in Gaelic (*Scotice*) and suggests 'it may be that the term *deòradh* was in all cases originally applied to the relic and that its application to the custodian is an instance of transference'.[30] The Irish evidence, however, indicates that *deòradh* was originally applied to the custodian.

Sellar refers also to another *deòradh*, the keeper of the *Bachull Mór* or great crozier of Saint Moluag of Lismore. This crozier was held by a hereditary 'Baron of Bachuill' who was on this account allocated a small estate on the island of Lismore. As well as the care of the *Bachull* his duties included that of almoner of the cathedral and collector of the tithes and other dues of the church. On these occasions Saint Moluag's crozier was carried by the Baron.[31] One can compare the many records of the carrying of a relic in association with the collection of church dues in early Irish sources.[32] Income for the church also derived from the promulgation of the laws or ordinances (*cánai*) of various saints, which were in some instances explicitly associated with the carrying of relics.[33] For example, the Annals of Ulster record that, in the year 727, *Adomnani reliquiae transferuntur in Hiberniam 7 lex renouatur*.[34]

Discussion of the role of the Scottish *deòradh* (*dewar*) inevitably leads on to a consideration of the difficult term *toschederach*, widely attested in Scots and Latin statutes and charters of the fourteenth and fifteenth centuries. This term has been discussed by a number of eminent scholars, including W. F. Skene, W. Croft Dickinson, Basil Megaw, W. D. H. Sellar and William Gillies.[35] It is beyond my competence to enter into the debate on the origins of the various forms of this term, which have been expertly analysed by Gillies. He has collected no less than fifty-six examples, including spellings with *-derach* (e.g. *toschederach*), *-dorach* (e.g. *tosheadorach*), *-dera* (e.g. *tosachdera*), *-deora* (e.g. *thoshachdeora*), *-dore* (e.g. *tosichdore*), *-dor* (e.g. *tosachisdor*) and other variants.[36] Gillies quotes the definition in Sir John Skene's *De Verborum Significatione*:[37]

> Some alleagis [it] to be ane office pertaining to execution of summonds ... sik as ane quha summondis, attachis, or arreistis ane uther, to compeir before ony judge, ... uthers understandis the same to be ane crowner. ... Last, summe understandis it to be ane searchour and taker of thieves and limmers ...

---

30 William J. Watson, *The History of the Celtic Place-Names of Scotland* (Edinburgh, 1926), 264–6.

31 See Alexander Carmichael, 'The Barons of Bachuill', *The Celtic Review* 5/20 (April 1909), 356–75, and a comment on this article by Niall D. Campbell, *The Celtic Review* 6/22 (October 1909), 190–2. Carmichael notes (p. 363) that the keeper of the *Bachull* is termed in Gaelic *An Deor* 'the Almoner'. This form shows apocope of the final *-adh* of *deòradh*.

32 See Etchingham, *Church Organisation*, 270–1; Charles Plummer, ed., *Vitae Sanctorum Hiberniae*, 2 vols (Oxford, 1910) I. Introduction, cxxviii–cxxix.

33 Etchingham, *Church Organisation*, 199.

34 'the relics of Adomnán are brought over to Ireland and the law is promulgated anew': AU^2 726 (recte 727) §5; there are similar entries for the years 734, 811, and 836.

35 William F. Skene, *Celtic Scotland: A History of Ancient Alban*, 3 vols (2nd edn, Edinburgh, 1886–90), III.278–81, 300–2; W. Croft Dickinson, 'The Toschederach', *Juridical Review* 53 (1941), 85–109; Basil Megaw, 'Norseman and Native in the Kingdom of the Isles', *Scottish Studies* 20 (1976), 1–44, at 24; Sellar, 'Celtic Law and Scots Law', 9–11; William Gillies, 'Some Thoughts on the Toschederach', *Scottish Gaelic Studies* 17 (1996), 128–42.

36 Gillies, 'Some thoughts', 131–3.

37 John Skene, *De Verborum Significatione* (Edinburgh, 1597), f. S4 verso, s.v. *Toscheoderache*.

All of these functions relate to public law enforcement, and the last of them, 'ane searchour and taker of thieves and limmers [= robbers]', is of particular relevance in relation to the duties of Finlay Dewart, mentioned above.

Is the *toschederach* therefore simply a term for an elevated category of *dewar*, a chief *dewar*?[38] (In the list compiled by Gillies, ten instances do not have the initial *tosach-*.) Basil Megaw notes that the Manx equivalent *toshiagh jioarey* was the coroner of a steading and an official of superior status to the *mair*.[39] In Cregeen's *Dictionary of the Manks Language* the *toshiagh jioarey* is defined as 'a coroner or sheriff, a man sworn under the crown or king to cite before judges, hold inquests, execute writs, executions, &c. ...'.[40] In Kelly's *Fockleyr Manninagh as Baarlagh* of 1866 the relevant entry reads: '*Toshiaght-Joarrey, s.pl. Toshee-Yoaree*, an officer in the Island, corresponding partly to the English coroner, and partly to the sheriff. The word itself defines his office, which is to take cognisance of strangers. *Deoradh* in Gaelic is "an alien, fugitive, stranger, outlaw".' Gillies suggests in relation to the *toshiagh jioarey* that 'his name should once have signified something like "chief (officer) of strangers", where "strangers" might have meant "foreigners" ... or perhaps "fugitives from justice" or similar'.[41] While it is of course true that the primary meaning of *deorad, deòradh, joaree* in the three Gaelic languages is 'stranger, foreigner', might we here have another example of the secondary meaning 'law-enforcement officer'? The Manx *toshiagh jioarey* would thus be the equivalent of the chief *dewar* or *toschederach* of Scottish documents.

In his study Skene sought to distinguish two terms: *toshachdor* associated with the Western Highlands and the Isle of Man, and *toshachdera* associated with the eastern thanages outside the Highland area. Gillies points out, however, that the attested forms do not compel one to make a simple territorial split between them.[42] He goes on to raise the possibility of an original *tóiseach daor-raith* 'lord of base fief', which 'became contaminated by *deòradh* in areas where Gaelic remained as a spoken language into the fifteenth century (or thereby)'.[43] I would

---

38 Alexander Grant, 'The construction of the Early Scottish State', in *The Medieval State: Essays Presented to James Campbell*, ed. J. R. Maddicott and D. M. Palliser (London, 2000), 47–72, at 55, emphasises that the *toiseachdeor* was the custodian of a relic: 'Oath-swearing was involved, and each province had at least one *toiseachdeor* to look after a holy object used for judicial purposes.'

39 Megaw, 'Norseman and Native', 24.

40 Archibald Cregeen, *A Dictionary of the Manks Language* (Douglas, 1835), s.v. *toshiagh jioarey*.

41 Gillies, 'Some Thoughts', 129.

42 *Ibid.*, 130.

43 *Ibid.*, 139–40. He refers to the legal gloss *is deoruid adon daorrath* in support of his case (*ibid.*, 142, note 28). I find the glosses on this passage on distraint exceptionally difficult to interpret. The Old Irish text has *ATHGABAIL RAITH DONA URBIAT(H)AR* 'the distraint of a fief for which food-rent is not paid (by the client)'. It occurs in two manuscripts: London, British Library, Harley 432, 14c (*CIH* II.399.9–11 (= *ALI* I.218.31–3) and Dublin, Trinity College, 1336 (H 3. 17), col. 83 (= *CIH* V.1701.36–7). The former has more extensive glossing: *ATHGABAIL RAITH .i. dærraith DONA URBIATAR .i. athgabail flatha ratha cetgiallna 7 uasal for isel nosbeir for treisi .i. aithgin in bid fil sund for uin, no 's dear–* [= *deoruid*] 'distraint of a fief, i.e. of a base fief, for which no food-rent is paid, i.e. distraint of the fief of a primary lord, and a "high-ranking person against a low-ranking person" brings it to a period of three days, i.e. the restitution of the food which is here (= in this case) has a stay of one day, or it is *deoruid*'. The H. 3. 17 version (as read by O'Donovan and Binchy) has *ATHGABAIL RAITH DONA URBIATHAR .i. athgabail in bid fil sunn for uin, no is deoruid, adon daorrath* 'distraint of a fief for which no food-rent is paid .i. distraint of the food which is here has a stay of one day, or it is *deoruid*, that is base fief'. In the

argue, on the contrary, that all the forms listed by him (*toschederach, -dorach, -dera, -deora, -dore, -dor,* etc.) derive solely from *tóiseach deòradh.* All the various functions ascribed to the *toschederach* seem to relate to the administration or enforcement of the law, corresponding to such offices as coroner, sheriff or serjeant. None relates directly to the *daor-rath* (Old Irish *dóer-rath*), the base fief granted by a lord to his client.[44] But I do not deny that the semantic journey which I propose – from Old Irish *deorad Dé* 'hermit' to Scots *dewar* and on to *toschederach* 'chief law-enforcement officer' – is somewhat tortuous!

---

manuscript of H 3. 17 'adon daorrath' is written on a separate line to '*no* is deoruid', and seems more likely to be a gloss on RAITH, as in the Harley 432 version. The meanings 'alien, outlaw' do not seem to make sense in this gloss, and I suspect that *deoruid* here means that the defaulting base client may in some circumstances be immune from distraint in spite of his failure to supply food-rent. For the meaning 'immune from legal process' of *deorad* (*deoruid*), see Kelly, *Early Irish Farming,* 521–32 (esp. p. 528), where the various restrictions on the distraint of livestock are discussed.

44 Binchy, *Críth Gablach,* 96–8, s.v. *gíallnae.* I would go along with Gillies's identification of *dereth* in the Dunfermline Abbey grant of *c.*1300 with *daor-rath* ('Some thoughts', 137); for the text, see C. Innes, ed., *Registrum de Dunfermelyn* (Edinburgh, 1842), 226–7.

16

CONTENTIOUS KINSHIP: THE PENUMBRA OF ESTABLISHED KINSHIP IN MEDIEVAL IRISH LAW

Bronagh Ní Chonaill

The medieval Irish legal tradition placed a high value on the presence and social function of the child within the community, understanding the practice of child-rearing to be undertaken for the well-being (*socamail*) of the household.[1] For social stability, a child ought to be the product of a union sanctioned by both affected kin-groups and preferably from parents within a common social bracket. And in all likelihood, this was the norm. A person's legal worth and status at birth could determine not only the manner of upbringing, but also ultimately a person's legal standing and the nature and extent of any involvement within the community. In a society like early Ireland, however, where a variety of sexual relationships were either permitted, acknowledged or refuted, legal concern centred on what impact various unions and separations might bring to bear on the kin-groups involved.[2] Sexual relationships (whether by choice or circumstance) involving people of different social status, and with the possibility of procreation as an outcome, certainly piqued the interest of the medieval legal scholar. Ill-made contracts could be altered, rebalanced or rescinded;[3] was a child a different matter? The modest aim of this contribution, therefore, is to venture into what Thomas Charles-Edwards has described as the 'penumbra' that surrounded established kinship in order to probe core legal impediments to kin-affiliation, while seeking to consider what path the medieval Irish legal commentators might advocate to resolve the fundamental issue of establishing a person's place within a kin and the community in turn.[4] Legal discourse will form the basis of this exploration, supplemented with narrative instances to unpack and illustrate the key points under review.

Permission and acknowledgement

For legal accord, a girl of marriageable age should be gifted by her kin to her future husband and his kin within the context of dialogue and the fulfilment of

---

[1]   C. Eska, ed., *Cáin Lánamna: An Old Irish Tract on Marriage and Divorce Law* (Leiden, 2010), §8, 132; *CIH* II.502.29–519.35; *CCIH* 289; *GEIL* 269.
[2]   *Cáin Lánamna*, §§36–8 (ed. Eska); R. Thurneysen, 'Cáin Lánamna', in *SEIL* 1–80.
[3]   For contracts see N. McLeod, *Early Irish Contract Law* (Sydney, 1995), chapters 2–3, pp. 32–91.
[4]   *EIWK* 75–6.

the contractual process for the establishment of a recognised union.[5] Within the medieval narrative tradition this can be relayed in fine laconic fashion with a simple statement, *do-breth dó*, as in the case of Monchae, daughter of Tríath of the Crecraige, upon her bestowal to Éogan Mór in the Old Irish tale *Scéla Éogain in so 7 Cormaic*.[6] A girl might redirect her suitor's advances to her guardian[7] or exhibit such dutiful behaviour as that displayed by Áchtan, daughter of Olc Aiche, who, when her father aired the possibility of a union between her and Art, responded '*acht bith fó lat-so*'.[8] It is often the situation where permission is not sought or a sexual prohibition flaunted that concerns the legal scribe, however. This can be presented from the legal viewpoint of the maternal kin as a collective, as in an entry in *Cethairslicht Athgabálae*, 'The four divisions of distraint', where it is noted that a child was conceived *tar sarugu ł i nainfis fine maithre*,[9] or from the viewpoint of the woman's immediate guardian, as in the *Heptads*, *mac donithar ri hingin tar apu nathar*.[10] It would appear that the man in question (and his kin by extension) either chose to ignore an explicit directive that a sexual relationship was prohibited or simply entered into a sexual relationship without seeking permission from the woman's kin in the first instance.

This highlights the wider issue of legal dependency and in general how any person (male or female) in such a dependent position (for example, a daughter, the 'son of a living father', a bondwoman or a male slave) could not consent to a sexual relationship without recourse to a guardian (the closest living male relative, head of kin or lord).[11] Where a sexual encounter occurred without permission, the person within the couple who was either legally independent or carried the higher social status could bear sole, life-long responsibility for any offspring conceived. In this case the paternity of the child is not in doubt. However, the vital matter of legal affiliation and recognition of a child by *both* the maternal and paternal kin-groups, as would be the expected norm, may not in fact occur owing to the circumstances surrounding conception. Implicit in much of the legal writings is that both the paternal and maternal kin-groups are important throughout the course of a person's life. The removal of one or the other altered an established system of balancing legal rights and responsibilities on a range of matters, including education, fosterage and the payment and reception of fines – an unequal distribution, it should be noted, where in general the paternal kin-

---

5   D. Ó Corráin, 'Marriage in Early Ireland', in *Marriage in Ireland*, ed. A. Cosgrove (Dublin, 1985), 5–24; *GEIL* 70–5.
6   'she was given to him': T. Ó Cathasaigh, ed., *The Heroic Biography of Cormac Mac Airt* (Dublin, 1977), 119, line 3. All translations are my own unless otherwise indicated.
7   W. Stokes, ed., 'Esnada Tige Buchet', *Revue Celtique* 25 (1904), 18–38; §§11–12, 28–31; D. Greene, ed., 'Esnada Tige Buchet', in *Fingal Rónáin and other stories* (Dublin, 1955), 30, lines 525–6.
8   'if you but approve': Ó Cathasaigh, *Heroic Biography*, 120, line 41.
9   'in defiance of or without the knowledge of the maternal kin': *CIH* II.355.2–3; *CCIH* 286–7; *GEIL* 279.
10 'a child begotten on a daughter in violation of her father's position': *CIH* I.20.29. For the *Sechtae* (Heptads) see *CIH* I.1.1–64.5; V.1881.9–1896.22; II.537.16–549.18; V.1821.28–1854.36; *CCIH* 291–2; *GEIL* 266.
11 *CIH* I.22.1: *do mac beoathar tar apad a athar* 'to the 'son of living father in violation of his father's position'; 20.28: *do cumail i tothlu sech flaith* 'to a female slave secretly in disregard of the lord'; 21.27–8: *do mug i tothla sech a flaith* 'to a slave secretly in disregard of his lord'.

group bears the majority share.[12] Dependency solely on one side of the kindred was simply not ideal in the mechanics of medieval Irish society.

In probing this issue of permission the Irish jurists also focus on the matter of adultery and on established marital unions (as opposed to the more transitory nature of the couplings noted above). The crux of the matter is approached and couched in consistent fashion: *mac dognither re cetmuintir tar apad a .c.muintiri*.[13] Any child conceived in these circumstances was considered to belong to the cuckolded husband until 'fully purchased' from him by the biological father, which entailed the payment of a substantial fine (including body-price, honour-price, and, if appropriate, the full expenditure of child-rearing for the period in question, including the restitution of any payments incurred for the misbehaviour of the child).[14] That a husband's permission, or lack of permission, was central to the manner of resolution (i.e. purchasing the child together with compensation) is further illustrated by the jurists' comments that, although a husband and wife may have been in a state of marital discord at the time of the extra-marital encounter, the nature of their relationship in no way altered the outcome. This would include, for example, a husband who had technically 'put aside', *léicid*, his wife and forbade anyone to engage in sexual intercourse with her while she was in this socially liminal state, or for that matter a couple who were experiencing a lesser degree of recognised discord and were deemed 'in disagreement', *for deabaid*, with one another; the husband and his kin remain the aggrieved party and ultimately should not shoulder the responsibility for any child conceived by his wife with another man.[15]

A terse reference within the later commentary to *Cáin Lánamna* appears to indicate that either party within a marital union could, with permission of the respective spouse, engage in an extra-marital relationship, and this we might expect would increase the complexity in arrangements for any children born of these sanctioned encounters.[16] Nothing further is noted on this, however, in relation to children. The very presence and the nature of legal discourse in the area of permission, and by extension consent to and acknowledgement of a physical relationship, would first and foremost ensure a degree of legal protection for a given kin-group from having to assume any responsibility for a child where permission was neither granted nor sought. Such legal clarity would also firmly establish the primary care-giver for the child in question.

---

[12] For the position and responsibility of the kin-groups see *GEIL* 12–15; *EIWK* 21–88.

[13] 'a child begotten on a *cétmuinter*-wife in violation of her *cétmuinter*-husband' *CIH* I.21.11; cf. also I.21.14.

[14] *CIH* I.294.13–16; *co ndergelltar*, glossed, *co ro-derb-cennaigter* 'until fully/wholly purchased'; for the range of fines noted, *coirpdire, eneclann, laniarraid, aithgin*, see *GEIL* glossary s.v.; *EIWK* 315.

[15] For *léicid* see, *CIH* I.21.18–19; 48.5; 'to put aside', *AFM* 1365.8; 1452.4; E. Knott (ed.), *Togail Bruidne Da Derga* (Dublin, 1963), pp. 2–3, lines 63–7. This practice was discouraged by the church: see L. Bieler, *The Irish Penitentials* (Dublin, 1975), 41; *for deabaid, CIH* I.21.20; *SEIL* 194.

[16] *Cáin Lánamna*, §35 (ed. Eska, 272–3).

Timing

In addition to the matter of permission and dependency, a particular temporal consideration arises when the affiliation of a person to a kin-group is in question. Within *Bretha Éitgid*, 'Judgements of Inadvertence',[17] the situation is presented in which a once-freeman of the community has undergone serious demotion in his social standing to that of a *deorad*, an 'outsider'.[18] What is of particular interest to the legal commentator is the possibility that he may continue to bear children within the community. It should be noted that in this situation neither kin consent nor permission are of explicit concern, only the timing of his fall from social grace, and therefore the critical social and legal imbalance that this introduces within the couple. We may note the crucial chronological distinction: *in mac dorine ria ndenum deoraid frecair di, is a bith amal cach nduine ndligthech don fine*; however, *in mac dorine iar ndenum deoraid recair de, a cin for fine a mathar*.[19] Depending on the timing of conception in relation to his altered legal status, his offspring could experience quite different support networks throughout the course of their lives – some under the presence and influence of both the paternal *and* the maternal kin, with others simply within the domain of the latter for all aspects of life and standing within the community. What might also be a factor in this situation is whether the woman in question was cognisant of his altered circumstances and still engaged in a sexual relationship.

And it is the woman's informed and active role in this situation that finds emphasis in the *Heptads*, where a similar outcome is noted. In this entry, however, the man's altered status is owing to his entry into clerical orders. A woman who engages in sexual intercourse with a cleric, whether of priestly or episcopal standing,[20] is to assume responsibility for any offspring for, as the jurist notes, *rofitir-si in ngradh*.[21] The commentary intimates that prior to his entry into the church the couple concerned were husband and wife, and we may surmise that restraint and better judgement were expected on her part.[22] For his part, the *Penitential of Vinnian* muses: *sciat se ruina maxima cecidisse et exsurgere debere*,[23] and so repent and re-enter the church. Upon repentance, the woman and the maternal kin become the sole sphere of influence over any children conceived in these circumstances.

---

[17] *CIH* I.250.1–337.36; *CCIH* 176–82; *GEIL* 272.

[18] See *DIL*, s.v. *deorad*: this term can denote a range of meanings, including an outlaw, an exile, a pilgrim, an alien; *GEIL* 5–6; see also Fergus Kelly's discussion of this term in this volume, pp. 165–71.

[19] 'the son whom he has fathered before he becomes [lit. made] a *deorad* is like every other lawful member of the [paternal] kin. The son whom he has fathered after he becomes a *deorad*, his liability is on the maternal kin ...': *CIH* I.307.26–28. *Cid dogni deorad do urrad*, I.307.12–308.4; *SEIL* 131.

[20] *CIH* I.5.15, *fear grad .i. in sacart l int espug*, 'a man in orders, that is, the priest or the bishop'; cf, also V.1823.35; for the practice of concubinage and clerical wives within the Church see K. Simms, 'The Legal Position of Irish Women in the Later Middle Ages', *The Irish Jurist* 10 (1975), 96–111, at 101–2 and cf. also Swift above, pp. 33–5.

[21] 'she knows the grade' (i.e. his clerical standing): *CIH* I.22.18; 5.16.

[22] *CIH* V.1895.2, *in sacart dō .i. fer oenbe ta sond* 'he is a priest i.e. this is a man of one wife'; a previously established sexual relationship is also noted in *Irish Penitentials*, Vinnian, no. 27 (ed. Bieler, 83).

[23] 'let him know that he has fallen to the depths of ruin and ought to rise', *Irish Penitentials*, Vinnian, no. 27 (ed. and trans. Bieler, 82–3).

A path to resolution

The foregoing examples reflect the desire within the legal domain to define parameters in the decision-making process in relation to kin-affiliation. Alongside such strictures, however, a degree of flexibility is also in evidence should the two kindreds seek a common resolution to an illicit sexual union. Within the medieval Irish tradition the terminology reflects the very nature of the union involved – *foxal*, 'abduction', becoming *lánamnas foxail*, 'union of abduction', with the woman referred to as a *cétmuinter foxail* or *adaltrach foxail* depending upon the man's marital state.[24] These circumstances are broadly played out in the tenth-century Leinster tale *Esnada Tige Buchet*. Ethne, the daughter of Catháir Mór (King of Ireland), while in fosterage with Buchet is taken by Cormac *ar écin*, 'by force'. She escapes after one night, but she is already with child. After the birth, and through negotiation, Ethne is ultimately accepted as Cormac's queen.[25] Within this episode the important role played by the maternal kin once Ethne escapes should not be overlooked: formal assurances from her kin are required for Cormac and the men of Leinster to be satisfied with the arrangement. Although the precise nature of the assurances is left undisclosed, we can surmise that they centred on the understood paternity of the child and by inference Ethne's sexual history after her escape. We may speculate that such assurances lay within the domain of a woman's family or guardian by virtue of living in close proximity to one another, together with the legal responsibility for the wellbeing and activity of a female in one's charge.[26]

This move to formalise and recognise a union retrospectively in the context of abduction, which involved the initial consent of the woman, could also present a solution in those instances where a woman had willingly entered into a clandestine sexual relationship. In the early-ninth-century tale *Longes Chonaill Chuirc*, 'The Exile of Conall Corc', the (un-named) daughter of Feradach Findfechtnach, king of Scotland, without seeking her father's permission, engages in a relationship with Conall and a pregnancy results. Feradach, who had stated his intention not to agree to this match, is given voice to express a hint of displeasure while moving to resolve the situation by ultimately recognising the union: '*is tu no·tógfaimmís di cia no·bemís ica thogu*'.[27] The first step in Feradach's recognition, however, is the official acceptance of the child (his grandson) within the maternal kin. In fact, within the dialogue it is made explicit by the child's father, Conall, that he himself would not officially recognise the child as his own son until Feradach had first done so; this illustrates Charles-Edwards's observation that, for a child to gain the complete benefit of acceptance within the paternal kin, there appears to have been some need for the maternal kin officially to recognise the child in the first instance.[28] By the end of this short scene Feradach refers to

---

24 *Cáin Lánamna*, §36 (ed. Eska, 274); see N. Power, 'Classes of Women Described in the *Senchus Már*', in *SEIL* 81–108.

25 'Esnada Tige Buchet', §§12–13 (ed. Stokes, 30); lines 539–40 (ed. Greene, 30).

26 This is also the case in medieval Welsh law: see *Llyfr Iorwerth* §55.3 (ed. Wiliam, 30).

27 V. Hull, ed., 'The Exile of Conall Corc', *Proceedings of the Modern Languages Association of America* 56/4 (1941), 937–50; text, 941; 'It is you whom we would have chosen for her, if we had had a choice'; cf. C. Downey, 'Medieval Literature about Conall Corc', *Journal of the Cork Historical and Archaeological Society* 110 (2005), 21–32.

28 *EIWK* 314.

his daughter as a wife; a family unit has been established through formal recognition by all parties; and the contention present in the circumstances leading up to this scene has dissipated.

A legal declaration

In two particular circumstances the extant legal discourse implies that the affiliation of a child could be a relatively straightforward process. In the first circumstance, weight is given to a woman's declaration on the issue of paternity (and by extension probable affiliation) when she was close to, or in, child-birth (*fri huathne*).[29] We may surmise that, given the possibility that a woman would not survive childbirth and/or post-partum complications, her declaration at this moment was tantamount to that of a man facing the gallows, or a death-bed declaration, and therefore likely to be true.[30] The second circumstance noted is found within the Old Irish tract on status, *Críth Gablach*, 'The Branched Purchase', *c.* A.D. 700. Within a section relating to behaviour unbecoming of a king it states *ar ní córus do ríg imthect a óenur: is ed láa insin fortoi[n]gg ben a óenur a mmacc for ríg.*[31] This terse statement appears to function as a warning that a woman's act of swearing, *for-toing*, might carry the day on the issue of paternity, or at the very least, the weight of proof and denial would shift onto the man.[32] It is a cautionary tale for a king not to leave himself open to such a charge where he could not produce witnesses to refute her claim.

The possible weight given to a woman's voice on this matter finds literary illustration, as in the case of the tenth-century *Life of Cumaine Fota*, where Fiachna of the Éoganacht Chaisil begot a child on his own daughter while inebriated, and afterwards 'put her on her word' as regards the paternity of the child she conceived that night.[33] Her response remained unchallenged and accepted. Within the hagiographical genre, the intercession of a local saint could be called upon to resolve such a situation and in particular to salvage the reputation of a cleric. In the ninth-century *Bethu Brigte* we discover Brigit entering into an on-going discussion at Tailtiu regarding Brón, a bishop of Patrick's household who had such a paternity charge laid against him. The woman who made this public charge is asked by Brigit to identify the father and *senais Brigit a gnuis coro-raith at a cend furi cum lingua.*[34] Not finished with her miraculous powers, Brigit, by asking who his father was, compels the very young infant in question to speak in order correctly to identify his biological father. The child informs his audience that his father is none other than '*sed quidam homo qui in extrema*

---

[29] *CIH* VI.2037.15 (*Do tabairt mic i n-orba ann sō síos*); *CIH* II.387.30 (*Cethairślicht Athgabálae*); K. Meyer, ed., *The Triads of Ireland* (Dublin, 1906) no. 165; see 'Female oath', *GEIL* 202.

[30] *Triads of Ireland* (ed. Meyer, 22), no. 165.

[31] 'for it is not proper for a king to travel by himself: it is on that day that a woman swears their child on the king': D. A. Binchy, ed., *Críth Gablach* (Dublin, 1979), lines 533–5 (= *CIH* II.569.24–5); *CCIH* 241–4; *GEIL* 267.

[32] *Críth Gablach* (ed. Binchy), glossary, 99–100; see *DIL*, s.v. *for-toing* 'overswears, proves; fastens liability'.

[33] G. Mac Eoin, 'A life of Cumaine Fota', *Béaloidas* 39–41 (1971–3), 192–205, at 196, *co-ros-cuibsigestar.*

[34] 'Brigit made the sign of the cross over her face, so that her head *and tongue* swelled up': D. Ó hAodha, ed., *Bethu Brigte* (Dublin, 1978), line 485 (p. 31).

partœ concili sedet velut ultimus deformisque' and, therefore, in all respects the antithesis of Bishop Brón.[35]

This miraculous motif is also found within the late-eighth-century *Miracles of St Nynia, The Bishop* (of Whithorn) and 'how he freed a priest of his from the accusation of unchastity through the speech of a new-born child'.[36] Whereas the king in *Críth Gablach* is reproached for being solely in his own company, the hagiographer can utilise a saint to give voice to an infant, where without witnesses or proof to refute such an allegation only the mother's voice would appear to have sounded in the legal arena. As with royal behaviour, a didactic tone for both cleric and audience is apparent (while enhancing the reputation of a given saint). The sources do indicate a measure of unease regarding the possible recognition given to a woman's oath in this capacity, as is evident in the fragmentary text *Immathchor nAilella 7 Airt*, 'the affiliation of Ailill and Art', *c.* A.D. 700, in which the Ollam comments that '*Ní dil cinath cen dagdillse/le lúth-basa ban ní coir comarbsa*'.[37] In this quotation the warning reflects the possible strength a woman possesses when making a declaration of paternity, one that could eventually impact quite dramatically upon a kin-group in relation to land, inheritance and life-long legal and financial obligations.

The physicality of procedure

The tract *Di Astud Chirt 7 Dligid*, 'On the establishment of right and entitle-ment', compiled in the eighth century, notes how offspring of particularly low-grade women cannot be accepted into a kin *cen tocuirid*, 'without invitation',[38] an indication of the control a kin-group might exert when the woman in ques-tion was not of good standing within the community. The general stance taken in relation to the social position of the *meirdrech* or *baitsech* 'prostitute, harlot' was that any child born to her would be the responsibility of the maternal kin.[39] All is not completely lost, however, as there still appear to have been a few, though restricted, legal avenues open to her should she wish to attempt to ulti-mately affiliate a child. It should be noted that the medieval Irish evidence on the mechanics of this case is extremely fragmentary.

The first step in the proceedings centred on her character and whether she was deemed *indraic*, 'reputable, worthy', or *eisinnraic*, 'disreputable'. The second was whether the man in question acknowledges a *comrag*, 'a physical/sexual encounter', with her. This is not to imply that he was necessarily acknowl-edging the actual pregnancy, only that a sexual relationship did occur. If she was considered of reputable standing *and* the man admits to the encounter she was to take the legal path which involves the *fir testda* – the provision of a

---

[35] 'a certain low and ill-shaped man who is sitting in the outermost part of the assembly': *ibid.*, lines 490–1.

[36] T. O. Clancy, ed., *The Triumph Tree* (Edinburgh, 1998), 130–1; 'I'm forced to judge my father's case' (G. Márkus (trans.); for the text see K. Strecker, ed., *Poetae Latini Aevi Carolini*, MGH (Berlin, 1923), 4.6.

[37] 'a great number of bold oaths gives no satisfaction for the guilt of the womb; the right of inheritance does not belong to unsteady women': J. Corthals, 'Affiliation of Children: *Immathchor nAilella 7 Airt*', *Peritia* 9 (1995), 92–124 (text 109; trans. 110).

[38] *CIH* I.233.21; *CCIH* 293–4; *GEIL* 266, *SEIL* 198.

[39] *SEIL* 199.

range of oath helpers, including the weight of her own oath, in order to support her case.[40] If the woman was deemed disreputable she was required to follow the path of an *arra cuir*, necessitating a greater number of oath-helpers with a different composition.[41] If the required oath-helpers are produced, whichever path is deemed appropriate, *Bretha for Macslechtaib*, 'Judgements on Categories of Sons' considers this sufficient proof.[42]

The commentary within a number of texts, *Di Astud Chirt 7 Dligid*, *Bretha for Macslechtaib* and *Do tabairt mic i n-orba*, 'On the bringing of a son into patrimony', introduces a further complication presenting the case of a woman *iter dis a naimsir comperta*.[43] What follows in the pre-DNA world is the recommendation of an *anad* – a legal stay or waiting period for the evidence of *fineguth 7 finecruth 7 finebes*, 'the voice of the kin and the shape of the kin and the mannerisms of the kin', to come upon the child.[44] In the interim, it appears that the child is to remain in its mother's care for the duration of a legal waiting period of three years, at which point the matter is determined.[45] Unfortunately, we are not provided with any information regarding the manner of assessment: however, *ma tait a triur ann, geibid greim lanfira*.[46]

Ambiguous kinship coupled with physical similarity is creatively employed across the medieval narrative traditions as a trope for enhancing intrigue and plot-development. In the ninth-century *Life of Cumaine Fota* an audience witnessing a father and son dialogue (though none present are aware of the biological relationship) is given the line, '"*isib dis iss cosmaile hind Eirinn*"', whereupon the father–son relationship is recognised and acknowledged.[47] In somewhat similar fashion, though with apparent maternal dominance at play, we read within Norse tradition in *Laxdæla Saga* of Óláfr Hoskuldsson (grandson of King Myrkjartan) returning to Ireland to claim his inheritance, and of Myrkjartan, upon conversing with him, stating, '*en fyrir engan mun eru þær ómerkiligri, er þú hefir svá mikit ættarbragð af móður þinni, at vel má þik þar af kenna*'.[48] Not to leave out the most literary flight of fancy in this regard in the figure of Lugaid Reo nDerg

---

40 *CIH* I.232.18.
41 *Ibid.*
42 *CIH* I.107.19–20, *CCIH* 300–1; *GEIL* 270; for oath-helpers see *CIH* VI.2037.1–12.
43 Trans: 'between two [men] at the time of conception'; *CIH* I.232.19–20, *Di Astud Chirt 7 Dligid*; I.107.9, III.981.22, *Bretha for Macslechtaib*; VI.2037.18, *Do tabairt mic i n-orba ann sō síos*; *CCIH* 82.
44 *CIH* I.232.20–21; I.107.11; III.980.20; 981.25; VI.2036.38–9.
45 *CIH* VI.2036.37; III.981.23. Note, in *The Exile of Conall Corc*, a one-year period is given for the three characteristics to develop: R. I. Best *et al.*, ed., *The Book of Leinster Formerly Lebar na Núachongbála*, 6 vols (Dublin, 1954–83), V.37045–6.
46 'if the three [features] are present, it has the force of full-oath/truth': *CIH* III.981.25–7; I.107.12; VI.2036.39. For a reference to a passage within early modern context, see, Nollaig Ó Muraíle, ed., *The Great Book of Irish Genealogies: Leabhar Mór na nGenealach Compiled by Dubhaltach Mac Fhirbhisigh* I (Dublin, 2003), 180. For usage in twentieth-century Munster Irish see D. A. Binchy, 'Fionna-chruth', *Éigse* 15 (1974), 319–22.
47 'you two are the two most alike in Ireland': G. S. Mac Eoin, 'A Life of Cumaine Fota', *Béaloideas* 39–41 (1971–3), line 46 (p. 199); see also T. O. Clancy, 'Saint and Fool: The Image and Function of Cummíne Fota and Comgán Mac Da Cherda in Early Irish Literature' (unpubl. PhD dissertation, Edinburgh, 1991), 92–118.
48 'and it is made all the more remarkable by the fact that you bear so close a family resemblance to your mother that one could easily recognise you from that alone': Einar Sveinsson, ed., *Laxdæla Saga*, Íslenzk Fornrit V (Reykjavík, 1934), 57–8; Magnus Magnusson and Hermann Pálsson, trans., *Laxdæla Saga* (London, 1969), Chapter 21, 88–95.

('Red Stripe'), the product of incest between Clothra and three brothers, each of whom contribute one-third to Lugaid's physique, separated by a red stripe.[49] From the fabulous to the contentious, the physical body was utilised as evidence and incorporated within procedure and proof in the literary and legal worlds.

Within the legal commentary the man in a paternity case has a trump card yet to play in his defence, and that is *cach uair urtoingeas in fer a meamar is lais imdenam.*[50] This symbolic act and oath appears to carry significant legal weight, for the commentators note that the only remaining step a woman could take to counter this move was to choose to undergo an ordeal.[51] We have progressed from a situation whereby the woman might attempt to affiliate her child through oath-helpers and the support of people from within her community, succinctly encapsulated in the term the *fír daine*, 'the truth of men', to having to turn to a radically different concept and procedure to indicate substance and proof, through the *fír dé*, 'the truth of God'. The very inclusion of this step, together with the scattered and terse references within the legal material to the possible range of ordeals (by cauldron, hot-iron, consumption of liquid, lot-casting),[52] indicates the inherent difficulty in the production of proof relating to sexual matters. And yet physical evidence and action are required; from the touch and presence of relics within procedure, the physiological development of the child, an oath on a penis, a hand in a cauldron of hot water, to the prophetic healing or infectious processes that follow such ordeals – the performative and symbolic are striking features within legal procedure.[53]

Conclusion

In the late seventh century *Cáin Adomnáin* stipulates the payment of a fine *mad imdherccad dagmná ... im séna a clainne.*[54] On initial reading, the social reddening of this insult might appear quite individual to the 'good woman'. However, the longer-term ramifications of such a rejection, if the case stood, altered not simply the numerical shape of a particular kin-group but also the range and extent of legal and financial obligations towards a member of this unit.

---

49 S. Arbuthnot, ed., *Cóir Anmann, Part 1*, Irish Texts Society 59 (London, 2005), 139; *eadem*, ed., *Cóir Anmann, Part 2*, Irish Texts Society 60 (London, 2007), 106.

50 'every time a man swears on his member (penis) it is proof with him': *CIH* I.232.26–27.

51 *CIH* I.232.27–8.

52 *CIH* I.233.22; 238.17–18; II.393.35; IV.1495.11; V.1569.4; VI.1990.3–21. For a range of twelve ordeals mentioned in medieval Irish narrative see W. Stokes and E. Windisch, ed., 'The Irish Ordeals, Cormac's Adventure in the Land of Promise and the Decision as to Cormac's Sword', *Irische Texte* 1 (Leipzig, 1891), 183–229; *GEIL* 210–11.

53 See R. Stacey, *Dark Speech: The Performance of Law in Early Ireland* (Philadelphia, PA, 2007); A. T. Lucas, 'The Social Role of Relics and Reliquaries in Ancient Ireland', *JRSAI* 116 (1986), 5–37; C. Doherty, 'The Use of Relics in Early Ireland', in *Irland und Europa: die Kirche im Frühmittelalter*, eds. P. Ní Chatháin and M. Richter (Stuttgart, 1984), 89–104.

54 P. P. Ó Neill and D. N. Dumville, ed., *Cáin Adomnáin and Canones Adomnani* II (Cambridge, 2003), §51; Márkus: 'if it is making a good woman blush ... by denying her children's paternity ...'; G. Márkus, *Adomnán's 'Law of the Innocents'* (Glasgow, 1997). For a discussion of this text see M. Ní Dhonnchadha, 'The *Lex Innocentium*: Adomnán's Law for Women, Clerics and Youths, 697 A.D.', in *Chattel, Servant or Citizen: Women's Status in Church, State and Society*, ed. M. O'Dowd and S. Wichert (Belfast, 1995), 58–69; T. O'Loughlin, ed., *Adomnán at Birr, AD 697: Essays in Commemoration of the Law of the Innocents* (Dublin, 2001).

With much at stake it is no surprise that this area is of considerable concern to the medieval jurist. On certain legal grounds surrounding the circumstances of conception (permission, consent, timing of action) there is clarity as to which kin has sole responsibility for any offspring. A further resolution could stem from the retrospective recognition of a sexual union by all parties involved. Where such an *entente* was not possible, an official move to affiliate or accept a person into a kin-group could be particularly contentious and is deemed one of the seven fraught issues in law.[55] For a woman seeking to press a case, the available legal avenues very much depended on her social status within the community and in this regard we can paint a picture of extremes, from the irrefutable oath to the undertaking of an ordeal. Yet between such extremes we observe the legal mind grappling with situations that challenge mainstream procedure, where the evidence and witnesses normally present to support a case simply do not feature. However, complex legal processes are required and a resolution is necessary. And so the child or person in question, strikingly labelled by one commentator as *iter doirche 7 soirche*, 'between darkness and light',[56] on matters of kin-affiliation and inheritance, remains only temporarily suspended in judicial limbo before either returning to Charles-Edwards' penumbra or entering into the full glare of kin-membership.

[55] *CIH* I.49.36 (Heptad 55, *re fechaiter*).
[56] *CIH* IV.1296.27–8.

17

MARRIAGE BY PURCHASE IN EARLY IRISH LAW

Charlene M. Eska

In a short tract on the Milesian Invasion there is a curious passage in which the Sons of Míl arrive in Ireland only to find the island inhabited by a group of Hebrew maidens. The maidens will not give up their land without receiving a payment (*tindscra*) for their 'friendship' (*cairdes*):[1] *'Is de at fir crendai mnai i n-Eri co brath ar im·chrenad lanamnai isin doman oilcheanai.'*[2] Rudolf Thurneysen has discussed this passage in relation to the notion of marriage by bride-purchase and states that this passage represents the older procedure whereby a man simply buys a wife without expecting a dowry in return.[3] In this essay the extant sources for this practice are re-examined and it is argued that the concept of the husband purchasing his wife may be more a linguistic and terminological artefact than a reflection of reality.[4]

A second instance of this usage occurs in the mythological text *Tochmarc Étaíne* 'the wooing of Étaín'. In his analysis of this text Thomas Charles-Edwards discusses, among other matters, the possible significance of the use of the verbs *renaid* 'sells' and *crenaid* 'buys' in relation to the marriage of Étaín and Midir.[5]

---

1   Rudolf Thurneysen, 'Heirat', in *SEIL* 109–28, at 113.
2   '"Hence it is the men who always buy the women in Ireland, for in the rest of the world the couples mutually purchase each other"': Vernam Hull, ed. and trans., 'The Milesian Invasion of Ireland', *ZCP* 19 (1933), 155–60, at 157 (text) and 159 (translation).
3   Thurneysen, 'Heirat', 112–13: 'Das altertümliche Verfahren, dass der Mann die Frau immer einfach kauft, ohne das seine Gegenleistung (eine Mitgift) von ihrer Familie erwartet wird, findet sich deutlich nur in dem Exzerpt aus dem Heft (*cīn*) von Druimm Snechta, das im Buch von Leinster (Faks. 190c) nur noch teilweise lesbar, aber im Buch von Lecan (fol. 181v, S. 366a) voll erhalten ist.' 'The ancient procedure, that the man always simply bought the woman, without expecting a counter payment (a dowry) from her family, is only found clearly in an excerpt from the Book (*cīn*) of Druimm Snechta, which is only however partially legible in the Book of Leinster (facsimile 190c), but is completely preserved in the Book of Lecan (folio 181v, page 366a).' Thurneysen suggests that the language of the text dates to the first half of the eighth century in Thurneysen, *Die irische Helden- und Königsage bis zum 17.Jahrhundert* (Halle, 1921, repr. 1980), 16, and 'Heirat', 113.
4   This small offering is made with great gratitude for guidance and advice to Thomas Charles-Edwards in recognition of his work in the area of early Irish law.
5   T. M. Charles-Edwards, '*Tochmarc Étaíne*: A Literal Interpretation', in *Ogma: Essays in Celtic Studies in Honour of Próinséas Ní Chatháin*, ed. Michael Richter and Jean-Michel Picard (Dublin, 2002), 165–81, at 171, 176 and 178–9. For an edition and translation of the tale see Osborn Bergin and R. I. Best, ed. and trans., '*Tochmarc Étaíne*', *Ériu* 12 (1934–8), 137–96. All references are to this edition, but I have lightly modernised their translation. Rudolf Thurneysen has dated the text to the ninth century on the basis of linguistic evidence in Thurneysen, *Die irische Helden- und Königsaga*, 598.

Specifically, he discusses the type of marriage Óengus arranges for his foster-father, Midir, and Midir's later acquisition of Étaín from her husband, Eochaid Airem. In the former marriage arrangement Óengus effectively purchases Étaín from her father, Ailill, who, according to Charles-Edwards's interpretation, might thereby forfeit all of his rights to compensation should any injury be done to his daughter. He comments that, if his interpretation of this scenario as marriage by bride-purchase is correct, 'this passage offers important evidence on early Irish marriage'.[6]

Tochmarc Étaine (*TE*) has been divided into three parts by its editors and, for the sake of clarity, I shall follow Charles-Edwards's designation of these parts as *TE* I, II and III respectively. *TE* I begins with the story of Óengus's conception. The Dagda, a king of the mythological race of gods known as the Tuatha Dé Danann, desired a tryst with Eithne (otherwise known as Boand), the wife of Elcmar. To conceal his deception, the Dagda sent Elcmar on a journey that lasted nine months, although it felt like only a day and night to him.[7] Meanwhile Óengus was born, but, before Elcmar returned home, he was sent by his father, the Dagda, to be fostered at his friend Midir's house. All was well until, one day, Óengus got into an argument with one of the boys on the playing field and was taunted for having parents who were unknown. Upset by being shamed thus, Óengus ran to Midir for an explanation. Midir took him to the Dagda to be acknowledged as his son and to be given land in accordance with his true status. The Dagda devised a ruse whereby Óengus received Elcmar's land;[8] the Dagda then gave Cleitech[9] to Elcmar as consolation. So far, so good, until Midir, while visiting Óengus, had one of his eyes poked out while separating a fight among some of the youths in the Brug. Despite being healed by the physician Dían Cécht, Midir refused to remain with Óengus until he had compensation for the injury done to him. Along with a chariot and mantle, he asked for the 'fairest maiden in Ireland'. So began Óengus's quest to acquire Étaín from her father, Ailill.[10]

Ailill initially refused Óengus's request, stating:

'Nis tiber deit,' ol Ailill, 'dáigh ní rochaim bá fort ar suiri do cheniul, ar med do cumachtai 7 cumachta th'athar. Cach a dénai frim ingin do meboil ni rochar fort itir.'[11]

To which Óengus replied: '*Níba hedh ón,*' ol an Mac Oc, '*nois ciursa a díttso fó chetoir.*'[12] After he fulfilled a series of tasks and paid her weight in gold and silver, Óengus finally obtained Étaín for Midir.[13]

The second part of *Tochmarc Étaine* (*TE* II) is concerned with Midir's quest to win back Étaín. He lost her after his wife, Fuamnach, a sorceress, changed

---

6 Charles-Edwards, '*Tochmarc Étaine*', 171.
7 *TE* I, §1, 142 (text) and 143 (translation).
8 The land he got from Elcmar is Brug na Bóinne. The area includes such Neolithic passage tombs as Newgrange and Knowth, and is important in the mythological landscape of Ireland.
9 A mound in the Boyne river valley south of Newgrange.
10 *TE* I, §§2–11, 142, 144, 146, 148 (text) and 143, 145, 147, 149 (translation).
11 '"I will not give her to you," said Ailill, "because I could not profit from you, on account of the nobility of your family, and the greatness of your power and the power of your father. Any shame you may do to my daughter, nothing could be exacted from you at all"': *TE* I, §12, 148 and 150.
12 '"It will not be so," said the Mac Óc. "I will buy her from you at once"': *TE* I, §12, 150.
13 *TE* I, §14, 150 (text) and 151 (translation).

Étaín into a pool of water with her magic rod. After a lapse of centuries (and a few transformations) Étaín was born again. When the story continues we find Étaín married to Eochaid Airem. She had no memory of her previous life with Midir and, not surprisingly, she refused to return to him.[14] Midir, however, was nothing if not persistent.

In the final part of the tale (*TE* III) Midir returned and proceeded to play a series of *fidchell* games with Eochaid. Eochaid played only for stakes, and Midir lost the first two games; he paid Eochaid fifty horses after the first game and performed a series of tasks after the second. For the third game they did not state the stakes until the game, which Midir won, was over. He asked to be able to put his arms around Étaín and receive a kiss from her. Eochaid told him to come back in a month.[15]

Eochaid probably suspected a trick, as he had all of his best warriors gathered at his dwelling at the appointed time. When Midir arrived there he shared an interesting exchange with Étaín, stating that he had been a year seeking her with gifts and that he had not taken her without Eochaid's permission. Étaín replied:

> 'Atrubartsa fritso,' ol si, 'conom riré Eochaid nít rís. Atometha lat ár mó chuit fén dianom riri Eochaid.'[16]

> 'Nid ririubsa immurgu,' for Eochaid, 'acht tabard a di laim umut for lár an tighi amal ro gabais.'[17]

Midir put his arm around her and they flew away in the form of two swans.

In his discussion of Óengus's exchange with Ailill in *TE* I Charles-Edwards suggests that their negotiation might be describing a union by bride-purchase. In such a union the wife's family would lose all legal rights to protect their daughter because they contribute no wealth to the marriage. It is thus the contribution to the marital household on the part of the bride's family that would entitle them to continue to have a legal interest in her. Because of the fact that there was such a discrepancy in power between the Dagda and Óengus on the one side and Ailill on the other, Ailill would have been powerless to redress any wrongs done to his daughter regardless of whether he had contributed any wealth to the marriage.[18]

Charles-Edwards notes the parallel in *TE* III between Midir's buying of Étaín from Eochaid by performing a series of tasks and paying valuable horses, and Óengus's purchase of her from Ailill. He suggests that

> According to the presuppositions of the text, therefore, a father can sell his daughter to a bridegroom and thereby forfeit rights of protection over her; similarly, a husband may sell his wife to another man, though perhaps only if she were sold to him in the first place.[19]

Charles-Edwards goes on to state that the text is in line with the fact that bride-

---

14 *TE* II, §8, 168, 170, 172 (text) and 169, 171, 173 (translation).
15 *TE* III, §§1–9, 174, 176, 178, 180 (text) and 175, 177, 179, 181 (translation).
16 "'I have told you,' said she, "until Eochaid sells me, I will not go with you. As for me, you may take me if Eochaid sells me"': *TE* III, §14, 184.
17 "'I will not sell you indeed,' said Eochaid, "but let him put his two arms around you in the middle of the house as you are"': *TE* III, §15, 184.
18 Charles-Edwards, '*Tochmarc Étaíne*', 171.
19 Charles-Edwards, '*Tochmarc Étaíne*', 179.

purchase was one of the legally recognised forms of marriage according to early Irish law and that the new information revealed by the text is that the wife's family no longer has a legal right to protect her in this type of union and that a husband can sell his wife.[20]

Other scholars have commented on unions by bride-purchase in early Ireland. As noted at the beginning of this essay, Thurneysen suggests that the passage relating to the Milesian Invasion provides evidence for marriage by bride-purchase. He also discusses a passage found in *Gúbretha Caratniad*, 'the false judgements of Caratnia', where it is stated that the son of a living father (*macc béoathar*) is allowed to buy land and 'buy' a wife without the permission of his father.[21] He suggests that there is the possibility that 'buying' a wife in this passage might be an antiquated manner of speech, and that the writer of *Cáin Lánamna*, 'the law of couples', already viewed unions in which the wife and/or her family contributed little or no wealth (*lánamnas mná for ferthinchur* 'union of a woman on a man's contribution') to the marriage, such as a marriage between different social grades, to be in contrast to the more usual unions where both sides contributed to the new couple's household (*lánamnas comthinchuir* 'union of joint contribution').[22] Why Thurneysen puts more weight on the evidence from the tale than on the law tract is unclear to me. Following his line of reasoning, one could argue that both have the potential to be considered 'antiquated' and that this section of the recounting of the Milesian Invasion serves as a mythological/ pseudo-historical explanation of the Irish marriage custom of a *coibche* being given to the bride's father or legal guardian rather than evidence for an earlier form of marriage arrangement. Citing the passage from *Gúbretha Caratniad*, Fergus Kelly states that 'As in other societies, the husband is felt to purchase his bride from her father – hence the use of the expression "purchasing a wife" (*creic cétmuintire*).'[23] This is the only instance of this phrase that I have been

---

20 *Ibid.*

21 Thurneysen, 'Heirat', 113; *id.*, 'Aus dem irischen Recht III. 4. Die falschen Urteilssprüche Caratnia's', *Zeitschrift für celtische Philologie* 15 (1925), 302–70, §7 at 311; and *CIH*, VI.2193.5–6: *Rucus raith ar macc ṁbeoathar. Ba go. Deithbir ar ba creic cetmuintire 7 fochraic tire.* '"I have judged that surety may be given for the son of a living father." [said Caratnia] "It was false." [said the king] "It was correct [because it was] for purchasing a wife and payment for land." [replied Caratnia]' The fragment found at *CIH*, V.1582.6 reads *fochraic .c.muindteire 7 fochraic tire* 'payment for a primary wife and payment for land'. *Gúbretha Caratniad* is dated by Thurneysen to the eighth century in 'Aus dem irischen Rect III', 304–5.

22 Thurneysen, 'Heirat', 113: '… aber das mag nur eine altertümliche Redeweise sein. Jedenfalls betrachtet schon der Verfasser von *Cáin Lánamna* (Teil i.) eine Ehe, in welche die Frau nichts mit einbringt (*lánamnas mná for ferthinchur* §21) als eine Ehe zweiten Grades, dagegen die Ehe mit beidseitigem Einbringen (*comthinchor*) als das Normale.' '…but that may only be an antiquated manner of speech. In any case, the redactor of *Cáin Lánamna* (part i) already considered a marriage, in which the wife did not contribute anything (*lánamnas mná for ferthinchur* § 21) such as a marriage between [social] grades, as opposed to a marriage with a contribution from both sides (*comthinchor*) as the norm.' For an edition and translation into German of this text see *id.*, 'Cáin Lánamna', in *SEIL* 1–75; for an edition and translation into English see Charlene M. Eska, *Cáin Lánamna: An Old Irish Tract on Marriage and Divorce Law*, Medieval Law and Its Practice 5 (Leiden, 2010). The text has been dated on linguistic evidence to *c.*700 by Eska, *Cáin Lánamna*, 61–2. It should be noted that commentary XVII to §2 of the text states the property contributions that are expected from each spouse in a marriage between social grades. Whichever spouse is of the lower grade is responsible for contributing two-thirds of the marriage goods; see Eska, *Cáin Lánamna*, 100 for text and 101 for translation.

23 *GEIL* 71–2.

able to find in the entire corpus of early Irish law. More recently, in his comparative examination of Irish marriage laws and those on the Continent, Bart Jaski
suggests that it is possible that Ireland was participating in the same trend 'as
in the rest of Christian Europe[.] … first the wife was more or less bought from
her family by the payment of a brideprice, later a bridegift was paid to the bride,
supplemented by the *Morgengabe*, a payment made after the wedding night in
honour of the bride's surrender of her virginity and the acquisition of sexual
rights.'[24] By way of evidence from Irish sources, Jaski cites without elaboration
the sources discussed above, but nothing else.[25]

The main source for marriage law in early Ireland, however, is the law tract
Cáin Lánamna. This text lays out the nine legally recognised (though not always
strictly legal) unions. The overriding concern of the text is how property should
be divided in the event that the couple should separate. The property divisions
were based upon whether either member of the couple gave the other legal
grounds for separation and who contributed what by way of goods at the start of
the marriage. In early Irish law marriages were viewed as contractual in nature,
perhaps the clearest expression of which is to be found in relation to temporary
marriages in which both parties agreed upon a specific length of time for the
union to last. These unions also involved the giving of a *coibche* and fines for
violating the stipulated conditions of the union.[26]

Nowhere in *Cáin Lánamna* does the text specifically mention marriage by
bride-purchase or use the verbs *renaid* or *crenaid* to describe the usual payments
made in marriage arrangements; the term used throughout for the valuables given
by a bridegroom to his future wife's father is *coibche* 'bride-price', a portion of
which was usually given to the bride and provided part of her marriage contribution. Nowhere in the corpus of Irish legal texts have I found any reference to
the 'selling' of a wife or maiden.[27] It should be noted, however, that the terms
used for the wealth given to a bride's family do contain roots that convey a
notion of contractual and/or financial obligation. For example, *coibche*, which
has a range of meanings from simply 'contract' to 'payment' to 'bride-price',[28] is
derived from **com-fiach* (*com-* 'mutual, reciprocal' and *fiach* 'debt').[29] *Tinnscra*
(**to-ind-ess-cren-*)[30] and *tochra*[31] (mainly confined to saga texts) both contain
the root *cren-* 'buy' and, by the time that the texts were written, seem to have
roughly the same meaning as *coibche*.[32] In Welsh law the term for the payment
made to one's lord for permission to marry, *amobr*, derives from **am-(g)obr*

---

24 Bart Jaski, 'Marriage Laws in Ireland and on the Continent in the Early Middle Ages', in *'The Fragility of Her Sex'?: Medieval Irishwomen in their European Context*, ed. Christine Meek and Katharine Simms (Dublin, 1996), 16–42, at 25.

25 *Ibid.*, 25, n. 43.

26 Charlene M. Eska, 'Non-lawful Betrothals in Early Irish Law', *Keltische Forschungen* 3 (2008), 33–43.

27 I have canvassed the entirety of *CIH* and the additional texts found in the appendices to *CCIH* 378–483.

28 Donnchadh Ó Corráin, 'Marriage in Early Ireland', in *Marriage in Ireland*, ed. Art Cosgrove (Dublin, 1985), 5–24, at 15–16, discusses the changing meaning of *coibche* over time. Its meaning as 'bride-price' seems to be a later development from simply 'contract'.

29 J. Vendryes *et al.*, ed., *Lexique Étymologique de l'Irlandais Ancien* (Dublin/Paris, 1959–), C-140.

30 *Ibid.*, T-72.

31 *Ibid.*, T-87–8. *Tochra* is the verbal noun of *do-cren* 'purchase'.

32 *GEIL* 72; and cf. Thurneysen, 'Heirat', 119–25.

(*gobr* 'fee, recompense'),[33] where we also see a notion of payment embedded in the term itself.[34]

We thus have evidence for marriage by bride-purchase from two mythological tales and one law tract, to which I have not been able to add any further sources. Our evidence is thus rather thin on the ground, but, as Thurneysen, Kelly and Jaski have alluded, there are similarities to be found between Irish marriage laws and those on the Continent.

In his study of the early continental Germanic laws on marriage Noël Senn traces the development of the marriage laws from a system of marriage by actual purchase (the evidence for this is attested only fragmentarily in the law codes) through a system whereby the groom no longer purchases his bride, but purchases legal rights over her (essentially buying her family's rights to her) to a system where a payment is given to the bride herself.[35] Two questions raised by the notion of 'buying' a wife in general are what the difference is between buying a wife and buying a slave, for surely both transactions involve buying humans for specific purposes, and how one can buy a person who is already 'free'. The answer to the latter question is that the law codes, for example *Lex Salica*, cap. 39.3, do speak of freemen being sold.[36] Concerning the former question, Senn has discussed the fact that marriage by purchase (as it is referred to in the law codes) is not incompatible with the privileged status of a wife. He suggests that what we see for the most part in the law codes does not represent the actual purchase of a wife;[37] rather, marriage by purchase is so called in the codes because it involves all the formal legal procedures that would be involved in any other type of purchase.[38] In other words, although the groom is not actu-

---

[33] *Geiriadur Prifysgol Cymru*, R. J. Thomas, gen. ed. (Cardiff, 1950–2002), s.v. *amobr*; for the various spellings of these forms see Dafydd Jenkins and Morfydd E. Owen, ed., *The Welsh Law of Women* (Cardiff, 1980), 190.

[34] For the laws relating to marriage in medieval Wales see Jenkins and Owen, ed., *The Welsh Law of Women*.

[35] Noël Senn, *Le contrat de vente de la femme en droit matrimonial germanique* (Porrentruy, 1946), discussed in Jo Ann McNamara and Suzanne Wemple, 'The Power of Women Through the Family in Medieval Europe, 500–1100', in *Women and Power in the Middle Ages*, ed. Mary Erler and Maryanne Kowaleski (Athens, GA 1988), 83–101, at 85–6. It should be borne in mind that the early continental Germanic law codes are a mix of old and new customs.

[36] Senn, *Le contrat*, 3; and Karl August Eckhardt, ed., *Pactus Legis Salicae*, MGH *Leges* IV (Hanover, 1962), 144. This collection of the laws was drawn up in the sixth century; see Katherine Fischer Drew, *The Laws of the Salian Franks* (Philadelphia, PA, 1991), 52–5.

[37] Senn suggests that the ultimate proof for marriage by actual purchase is to be found in *Lex Saxonum*. It must be noted, however, that although the sale of the woman in a marriage by actual purchase was the same as the sale of a slave or any other chattel, the idea of the transaction was not the same; see Senn, *Le contrat*, 31; and cf., for example, Karl Otto von Richthofen and Karl Friedrich von Richthofen, ed., *Leges Saxonum*, MGH *Leges* V (Hanover, 1875–1879), 1–102, at 83, cap. 65: *Lito regis liceat uxorem emere, ubicumque voluerit; sed non liceat ullam feminam vendere* 'A *litus* of the king is allowed to buy a wife wherever he wishes; but he is not allowed to sell a woman.' *Lex Saxonum* was promulgated *c*.802; see Patrick Wormald, *The Making of English Law: King Alfred to the Twelfth Century*, vol. 1, *Legislation and its Limits* (Oxford, 1999), 46 and references cited infra. Although later than some of the other continental law codes, the continental Saxons 'were a conservative people, converted to Christianity late'; see Anne L. Klinck, '"To Have and To Hold": the Bridewealth of Wives and the *Mund* of Widows in Anglo-Saxon England', *Nottingham Medieval Studies* 51 (2007) 231–45, at 237, and Patrick Wormald, '*Lex Scripta* and *Verbum Regis*: Legislation and Germanic Kingship, from Euric to Cnut', in *Early Medieval Kingship*, ed. P. H. Sawyer and I. N. Wood (Leeds, 1977), 105–38, at 112.

[38] Senn, *Le contrat*, 21: '… je crois qeu le vente de la femme ne représentait en aucune façon acte

ally 'buying' his wife, the terms used for the transaction involved are the same as those used for any other situation that involves an exchange of goods (or money) for services (or chattel).

A similar situation exists in the early English law codes. For example, we find in §76 of the Laws of Æthelberht the provision *Gif man mægþ gebigeð ceapi, geceapod sy gif hit unfacne is*[39] and, in §31, *Gif friman wið fries mannes wif geligeþ, his wegilde abicge, 7 oðer wif his scætte begete 7 ðæm oðrum æt þam gebrenge*.[40] We furthermore find in *Maxims* I *Cyning sceal mid ceape cwene gebicgan, bunum ond beagum*,[41] and *Maxims* II states that a woman may resort to alternative means if she wants to choose her own lover instead of having a husband – *Gif heo nelle ... þæt hi man beagum gebicge*.[42] There has been much debate as to whether marriage by actual purchase existed in Anglo-Saxon England in view of the fact that the verbs used to describe the transaction are the same as those used for buying other chattels.[43] It has been pointed out, though, that marriage by actual purchase would seem to contradict what we know of the position of women in Anglo-Saxon society;[44] for example, despite being under the legal guardianship of a male (like their Irish counterparts), they seem to have

---

déshonorable pour elle-même ou pour les siens. Pour comprendre le côté de la question, il faut se rendre compte que le femme n'était pas vendue comme un animal, mais que l'acte du mariage seul mérite le nom de vente parce qu'il se déroule avec tout le formalisme et les dispositions juridiques propres à la vente ordinaire.' 'I believe that the purchase of the woman does not represent in any way a dishonourable act for her or for her family. To understand the point of the question, one must realise that the woman was not bought like an animal, but that the act of marriage only merited the name of purchase because it takes place with the formality and legal arrangements proper to an ordinary purchase.'

39 'If a person buys a maiden with a [bride-]price, let the bargain be [valid], if there is no deception': Lisi Oliver, *The Beginnings of English Law* (Toronto, 2002), 78–9, for text and translation. This text is usually dated to *c.*602/3; see also F. Liebermann *Die Gesetze der Angelsachsen*, 3 vols (Halle, 1903, 1906, 1916; repr. Aalen, 1960), III.2. For the terms used for marriage and betrothal see Andreas Fischer, *Engagement, Wedding and Marriage in Old English* (Heidelberg, 1986). There are many close parallels between the Laws of Æthelberht and the continental Germanic laws.

40 'If a freeman lies with a free man's wife, let him buy [him/her] off [with] his/her *wergild* and obtain another wife [for the husband] [with] his own money and bring her to the other man at home': Oliver, *The Beginnings*, 68–9 for edition and translation and 109–10 for discussion.

41 'The king shall pay with a price for a queen, with goblets and rings': George Krapp and Elliot Dobbie, ed., *The Exeter Book*, The Anglo-Saxon Poetic Records III (New York, 1936), 159, lines 81–2; text and translation cited from Oliver, *The Beginnings*, 106. Although the manuscript dates to the late tenth century Klinck states in '"To Have and To Hold"', 236, that the content of these gnomic poems 'is highly traditional'.

42 '... if she does not wish ... that one should pay for her with rings': Elliot Dobbie, ed. *The Anglo-Saxon Minor Poems*, The Anglo-Saxon Poetic Records VI (New York, 1942), 56–7, lines 44b–5a; text and translation cited from Oliver, *The Beginnings*, 106; and see Anne L. Klinck, 'Anglo-Saxon Women and the Law', *Journal of Medieval History* 8 (1982), 107–21, at 109. *Maxims II* is found in the mid-eleventh-century manuscript BL Cotton Tiberius B.i; see Dobbie, *Anglo-Saxon Minor Poems*, lx and lxvi–vii. Cf. the comments by Klinck in the previous note.

43 Oliver, *The Beginnings*, 106–7.

44 *Ibid.* Representative of this view are Christine Fell, *Women in Anglo-Saxon England and the Impact of 1066* (Bloomington, IN, 1984); Mary P. Richards and B. Jane Stanfield, 'Concepts of Anglo-Saxon Women in the Laws', in *New Readings on Women in Old English Literature*, ed. Helen Damico and Alexandra Hennessey Olsen (Bloomington, IN 1990), pp. 89–99, especially 93–5; and Carole Hough, 'Women and the Law in Seventh-Century England', *Nottingham Medieval Studies* 51 (2007), 207–30; and cf. Klinck, 'Anglo-Saxon women', 109; and *eadem* '"To Have and To Hold"'. For marriage in Anglo-Saxon law being viewed as both gift and purchase see T.M. Charles-Edwards, *Early Irish and Welsh Kinship* (Oxford, 1993), 463–4.

had some say in the choice of their marriage partners, although the evidence for this is found in later texts.[45]

All of the above rests upon the assumption that such a notion as actual 'marriage by purchase' even existed. Mezger, in an examination of the Icelandic family sagas, came to the conclusion that there is no evidence from these texts that marriage by purchase existed. In fact, Mezger argues in reference to Germanic law that 'the theory of marriage by purchase has as its mainstay the words having "to buy" and "to sell"; as a matter of fact, it appears that it came into being on the basis of these words'.[46] While Mezger's etymology of Germanic *kaupon* is highly problematic, there is something to be said for the argument that we have Germanic concepts being rendered into their closest Latin approximations in the continental law codes. Thus, terms which might not have strictly meant 'purchase' or 'sell' might have been rendered into Latin using words which only mean 'purchase' or 'sell'.[47] One could even argue that we have a similar situation with English translations of the Irish material.[48] McAll has suggested, in relation to the passage cited above from *Gúbretha Caratniad*, that 'It would be wrong to read too much into the expression "purchase" here in what is essentially a highly respectable form of gift exchange, but one cannot altogether ignore the commercial implications.'[49]

It is probably the case that, in the Anglo-Saxon material, as in some of the early continental Germanic law codes, the terms used for obtaining a wife refer not to the actual purchase of a wife but to the legal act involved. I would like to suggest, based on the comparative evidence of the use of these types of verbs in other law codes, that the same situation pertains in the early Irish sources as well, and that in both Anglo-Saxon and early medieval Irish law we have no direct evidence of the actual purchase of a wife, as we might have in *Lex Saxonum*.

What we find in the Irish sources cited above is not marriage by actual purchase, but the 'purchase' of the legal rights to protect the wife and receive compensation for injury done to her. In fact, in any marriage where the husband pays a *coibche*, he is entitled to receive compensation for any injury done to her.[50] As suggested by Charles-Edwards in his discussion of the use of the verbs *renaid* and *crenaid* in *Tochmarc Étaíne*, it is probably the case, particularly in

---

[45] Richards and Stanfield, 'Concepts of Anglo-Saxon Women', 97; and cf. *Be Wifmannes Beweddunge*, in Liebermann, *Die Gesetze*, I.442–5. At least that is the ideal presented in this late-tenth-/early eleventh-century text. The Laws of Cnut (reigned 1016–35) forbid any woman to be forced to marry a man she does not like. It also forbids any money being given for her unless her future spouse chooses to give her a gift of his own free will; II Cnut §74 (Liebermann, *Die Gesetze*, I.360), *And ne nyde man næfre naðor ne wif ne mæden to ðam, Þe hire sylfre mislicige, ne wið sceatte ne sylle, buton he hwæt agenes ðances gyfan wille* 'And neither a widow nor a maiden is ever to be forced to marry a man whom she herself dislikes, nor to be given for money, unless he chooses to give anything of his own freewill': Dorothy Whitelock, ed., *English Historical Documents: c. 500–1042*, vol. 1, 2nd edn (London, 1979), 466.

[46] F. Mezger, 'Did the Institution of Marriage by Purchase Exist in Old Germanic Law?' *Speculum* 18 (1943), 369–71, at 369.

[47] Mezger, 'Did the Institution of Marriage by Purchase Exist in Old Germanic Law?', 371.

[48] I owe this suggestion to Paul Russell.

[49] Christopher McAll, 'The Normal Paradigms of a Woman's Life in the Irish and Welsh Texts', in *Welsh Law of Women*, ed. Jenkins and Owen, 7–22, at 11.

[50] D. A. Binchy, ed., *Críth Gablach* (Dublin, 1941), lines 121–7, and Eska, *Cáin Lánamna*, §35, 272 (text) and 273 (translation). In a marriage where the wife contributes all or most of the marital goods the wife receives compensation for any injury done to him; see Eska, *Cáin Lánamna*, §31, 240 (text) and 241 (translation).

light of the development of the continental laws, that if the wife's family did not contribute any goods to the marriage they forfeited their rights of protection over their daughter. This is not to say that women in this type of union would have fewer legal rights in the event of a divorce than their counterparts in unions where both families contributed to the new household. They would, however, receive a smaller amount of the profits associated from labour since the labour portion is based upon initial contribution to the household.[51] It should be noted that the property and/or goods each spouse contributed to the marriage remained the property of that spouse. Thus, if a wife contributed no goods to the marriage initially, she would not be entitled to a portion of her husband's property, but only to a portion of the profits associated with labour if the couple should separate. If a man acquired his wife through this type of union it is entirely possible that he would be able to give her to another man in the same way, though, one hopes, with his wife's consent.

---

[51] Eska, *Cáin Lánamna*, §30, 236 and 238 (text) and 237 and 239 (translation).

18

KINGSHIP MADE REAL? POWER AND THE PUBLIC WORLD IN *LONGES MAC nUISLENN*

Elva Johnston

Interpreting Longes Mac nUislenn

> She's young. She's beautiful. She's Irish. So she's dead meat: at least in opera, where box office and body count go hand in hand.[1]

This review of Healy Willan's opera *Deirdre*, a distant descendant of the early Irish tale *Longes Mac nUislenn*,[2] is in a long interpretative tradition, even if indirectly. Of course, the twentieth-century opera is at many removes from the medieval narrative, separated by time and language, by substance and genre.[3] Nevertheless, it reflects an assumption that this saga of broken bonds between men, of fraternal exile, of sex and death, pivots around its central female character, Deirdre. She is simultaneously catalyst and victim, helpless to save her lover Noísiu, and Noísiu's brothers, from deathly betrayal. This is no surprise: the Gaelic Irish themselves recalibrated the story. It was reinvented in the fourteenth or fifteenth century as *Oidheadh Chloinne Uisnigh* – still a tale of shattered male loyalties but now acted against a more emotive narrative of doomed love.[4] This appealingly affective aesthetic underlies nearly all subsequent versions of what

---

[1] Warren Wilson, 'Deirdre', *The Globe and Mail* (Monday October 27, 1997). For many years Professor Thomas Charles-Edwards was the external examiner for early Irish history in UCD. On one of his visits to Dublin we discussed this tale, which I was then using as a text for my third-year BA module, and he suggested that I develop my ideas further. This essay is the result and I offer it partly by way of thanks to Thomas. I value his encouragement and kindness towards me dating back to my time as a DPhil student in Oxford. It is also an attempt to apply his fundamental contribution to our understanding of the working of law in early Irish society to one of that society's literary products.

[2] Vernam Hull, ed. and trans., *Longes Mac n-Uislenn: The Exile of the Sons of Uisliu* (New York, 1949) is the standard edition. I will refer to this edition in the footnotes as *LMU* followed by the section and line numbers.

[3] This and other operatic treatments of the Deirdre story are considered by Axel Klein, 'Stage-Irish, or the National in Irish Opera, 1780–1925', *The Opera Quarterly*, 21/1 (2005), 27–67. See also Elva Johnston, 'Deirdre (Derdriu)', in *The Dictionary of Irish Biography*, ed. James McGuire and James Quinn, 9 vols (Dublin, 2009) <http://dib.cambridge.org/viewReadPage.do?articleId=a2501>.

[4] Caoimhín Mac Giolla Léith, ed. and trans., *Oidheadh Chloinne hUisneach: The Violent Death of the Children of Uisneach*, Irish Texts Society 56 (London, 1993). Caoimhín Breatnach provides a detailed review of the edition in '*Léirmheas*', *Éigse* 28 (1994–5), 200–18.

was increasingly seen as Deirdre's story, including those in English.[5] Significantly, even Keating's retelling of the tale in *Foras Feasa ar Éirinn*, one largely based on *Longes Mac nUislenn* rather than *Oidheadh Chloinne Uisnigh*, did not displace the latter.[6] Instead, subsequent redactions of the narrative attempted to harmonise the accounts, ultimately leaving the main substance of *Oidheadh Chloinne Uisnigh* intact.[7] In the process Deirdre's identification as a suitably tragic Irish woman became predominant.

Indeed, the sheer longevity of what could be termed the 'Deirdre tradition' presents peculiar problems. The central issue touches on *Oidheadh Chloinne Uisnigh*'s narrative choices: it retained the core of the earlier tale while offering a compelling reinterpretation through the addition of substantial new material. *Oidheadh Chloinne Uisnigh* is not a redaction of *Longes Mac nUislenn* but a separate story which treats its characters accordingly. Nonetheless, most resemble their earlier counterparts with the exception of Fergus mac Róich[8] and Deirdre herself. She is painted as a romantic heroine, something at odds with her unromantic and rather negative depiction in *Longes Mac nUislenn*.[9] Perhaps the clearest example is found at the story's end. In *Longes Mac nUislenn* Deirdre outlives Noísiu by a year, serving as Conchobor's distraught but compliant sexual companion.[10] In contrast, *Oidheadh Chloinne Uisnigh* describes how Deirdre dies of grief shortly after her lover's death.[11] It makes perfect sense for a tale emphasising ill-fated love in a world of conflicting duties. The narrative strengthens this emphasis by omitting the ominous circumstances surrounding Deirdre, even before birth, in the earlier saga.[12] This new Deirdre gives the text a different dynamic. In particular, her Cassandra-like prophecies, which have no parallel in *Longes Mac nUislenn*, make her a constant focus of the action and a figure of tragedy.[13] Arguably, this series of developments influenced scholarly bias as well as popular perception, for the more obviously tragic Deirdre of

---

5   Useful considerations include E. G. Quin, '*Longas Macc n-Uisnig*', in *Irish Sagas*, ed. Myles Dillon (Cork, 1968), 53–66; Caoimhín Mac Giolla Léith, 'From Saga to Folktale: "The Deirdre Story" in Gaelic Tradition', in *Bryght Lanternis: Essays on the Literature of Medieval and Renaissance Scotland*, ed. J. D. McClure and M. Spiller (Aberdeen, 1989), 405–19; *idem*, '*Oidheadh Chloinne hUisneach*: The Transmission of a Gaelic Romance', in *Texte und Zeittiefe*, ed. Hildegard L. C. Tristram, ScriptOralia 58 (Tübingen, 1994), 439–54.

6   Geoffrey Keating, *Foras Feasa ar Éirinn: The History of Ireland*, ed. D. Comyn and P. S. Dineen, Irish Texts Society 4, 8–9, 15, 4 vols (London, 1902–14), II.190–6 (§32). Keating's context is explored in Bernadette Cunningham, *The World of Geoffrey Keating: History, Myth and Religion in Seventeenth-Century Ireland* (Dublin, 2000).

7   Discussed in detail by Mac Giolla Léith, '*Oidheadh Chloinne hUisneach*: The Transmission', 442–4. See also the comments of Caoimhín Breatnach, '*Oidheadh Chloinne Uisnigh*', *Ériu* 45 (1994), 99–112, at 111–12.

8   Breatnach, '*Oidheadh Chloinne Uisnigh*', 100–12, suggests that Fergus is chosen by Conchobor as an inherently unreliable surety, allowing the king to manipulate events more effectively.

9   Muireann Ní Bhrolcháin, '*Re Tóin Mná*: In Pursuit of Troublesome Women', in *Ulidia: Proceedings of the First International Conference on the Ulster Cycle of Tales*, ed. J. P. Mallory and Gerard Stockman (Belfast, 1994), 115–21, emphasises the criticism aimed at Deirdre.

10   *LMU* §§17–19.

11   There is some variation, but Mac Giolla Léith, *Oidheadh Chloinne hUisneach*, 16, points out that in the 'vast majority' of manuscript copies of the tale, Deirdre recites an elegy and promptly dies.

12   For an alternative suggestion, emphasising the importance of Fergus mac Róich, see Breatnach, '*Oidheadh Chloinne Uisnigh*', 99–112, esp. 100. Versions of *Oidheadh Chloinne Uisnigh*, written after *Foras Feasa*, include the *Longes Mac nUislenn*-derived material in an attempt to reconcile the two story traditions.

13   In contrast, her one piece of advice in *Longes Mac nUislenn* is heeded: see *LMU* §13.158–60.

Oidheadh Chloinne Uisnigh seems to have leaked into readings of *Longes Mac nUislenn*.[14] This is not to deny that our appreciation of the tale has been greatly enhanced by nuanced interpretations. The importance of the social bonds which join and then divide the male characters has received effective treatment.[15] Nonetheless, Deirdre has proved to be the analytical lodestone. Greater understandings of the role of gender have further highlighted her centrality. Whether Deirdre is seen as a lustful woman, implicitly condemned by Christian writers,[16] or as an incarnation of sovereignty,[17] the storyline revolves around her. It is not too far-fetched here to see the pervasive influence of her retooling by Gaelic tradition; sometimes it is very difficult not to read *Longes Mac nUislenn* in the shadow of its more accessible successors.

The first step in escaping this shadow is to locate *Longes Mac nUislenn* within its own societal reality. Like other early Irish sagas it is rooted in a specific cultural environment. True, the Deirdre story is trans-historical but each iteration can only be understood within the parameters of its own particular origins. There is some debate about the exact date of the extant tale, but scholarly consensus places it in the eighth or ninth centuries.[18] The saga itself is unusual in that two of its main *dramatis personae*, Deirdre and Noísiu, do not feature in the familiar cast from other Ulster Cycle tales.[19] Nevertheless, their fate is centrally important to the structure of the Cycle because Fergus mac Róich, Dubthach Dóeltenga and Cormac Cond Longas act as sureties for the sons of Uisliu. The death of Noísiu and his brothers through Conchobor's treachery and in violation of these sureties is offered as the reason for their exile from Ulster. As a result, they participate in the events of *Táin Bó Cúailnge* on Medb and Aillil's side.[20] In this way *Longes Mac nUislenn* is accounted a *rémscél* or fore-tale of the *Táin*

---

14 Quin, '*Longas Macc n-Uisnig*', 66. Maria Tymoczko, 'Animal Imagery in *Loinges Mac nUislenn*', *Studia Celtica* 20/1 (1985–6), 145–66, at 160, sees Deirdre as the character who engages the audience's sympathy and interest. Cornelius Buttimer, '*Longes Mac nUislenn* Reconsidered', *Éigse* 28 (1994–5), 1–41, reads the tale as centring around Deirdre from birth to tragic death.

15 For example, Máire Herbert, 'The Universe of Male and Female: A Reading of the Deirdre Story', in *Celtic Languages and Celtic Peoples: Proceedings of the Second North American Congress of Celtic Studies held in Halifax, August 16–19, 1989*, ed. Cyril J. Byrne, Margaret Harry and Pádraig Ó Siadhail (Halifax, 1992), 53–64, emphasises the functionality of the tale as a form of social drama.

16 Lisa Bitel, *Land of Women: Tales of Sex and Gender from Early Ireland* (Ithaca, NY, 1996), 52–3; Herbert, 'The Universe of Male and Female', 61–2; Ní Bhrolcháin, '*Re Tóin Mná*', 115–21.

17 Proinsias Mac Cana, 'Women in Irish Mythology', *The Crane Bag* 4 (1980), 7–11, at 10; Tymoczko, 'Animal Imagery', 145–66; Mark Scowcroft, 'Abstract Narrative in Ireland', *Ériu* 46 (1995), 121–58, at 136, n. 63. Note Herbert's sensible critique in 'The Universe of Male and Female', 56.

18 Hull, *Longes Mac n-Uislenn*, 29–32, argued that an Old Irish original was revised around A.D. 1000. Quin, '*Longas Macc n-Uisnig*', 57, suggested the verse was older than the prose, while Tymoczko, 'Animal Imagery', 149, analyses the *rosc* passages as the fossilised survival of an older stratum, inherited by the author of the prose narrative. Herbert, 'The Universe of Male and Female', 53, 59–60, on the other hand, argues persuasively that the 'thoroughgoing *mélange*' of Old and Middle Irish forms throughout suggests a unitary text, and this includes the *roscada*.

19 James Carney, *Studies in Irish Literature and History* (Dublin, 1955), 234–7.

20 The fragmentary narrative *Fochonn Loingse Fergusa Meic Róich* appears to be an independent account of the reasons for Fergus' exile. It is edited by Vernam Hull: ed. and trans., 'The Cause of the Death and Exile of Fergus Mac Roig', *ZCP* 18 (1930), 293–8. Its relationship with *Longes Mac nUislenn* is uncertain. Carney, *Studies*, 234, argued that it contains the original explanation for the exile of Fergus and was subsequently replaced by the more literary *Longes Mac nUislenn*.

and fits neatly into the wider tradition.[21] Yet this neat fit is misleading. It is even possible, as James Carney suggested, that Deirdre, Noísiu, Arddán and Aindle were crafted specifically for the tale, making *Longes Mac nUislenn* a new literary creation poured into an older shared pool of legendary material.[22] This speculation aside, however, the narrative is an example of the dynamism with which traditional material could be treated by early medieval Irish authors. Tellingly, for instance, its positive portrayal of Fergus is at odds with more ambiguous depictions elsewhere.[23] Here, *Longes Mac nUislenn* is in dialogue with the shared events and characters of the Ulster Cycle but feels free to innovate. Moreover, its combination of tight structure and sophisticated thematic approach contrasts with the looser more episodic style of a great deal of the early vernacular narrative corpus.[24] These structural aspects greatly enhance the sense that the tale is composed around a definite message while, at the same time, not being entirely bound by the tradition to which it so richly contributed.

This message can be best decoded within the cultural matrix inhabited by the tale. Earlier, this essay referred to the growing sensitivity to gender in analyses of early Irish sagas. This sensitivity has tended to focus on the role of the female.[25] Historiographically, as well as historically, that focus has pulled women from the margins of scholarly discourse. However, it needs to be balanced by an appreciation of the central functions of men and masculinity in early medieval Irish literature.[26] This is not at all the same as identifying in men dominant historical actors; instead it involves a recognition of how correct male behaviour, as a key articulation of cultural and social ideology, was constructed by the early

---

21 For a discussion of the function of the *rémscéla* see Tom Chadwin, 'The *Rémscéla Tána Bó Cualngi*', *CMCS* 34 (Winter, 1997), 67–75.

22 James Carney, 'Early Irish Literature: The State of Research', in *Proceedings of the Sixth International Congress of Celtic Studies*, ed. G. Mac Eoin, A. Ahlqvist and D. Ó hAodha (Dublin, 1983), 113–30, at 125–7.

23 Suggested briefly by Carney, *Studies*, 155. The negative portrayal of Fergus is explored in detail by Ruairí Ó hUiginn, 'Fergus, Russ and Rudraige: A Brief Biography of Fergus Mac Róich', *Emania* 11 (1993), 31–40, esp. 34–5.

24 The episodic nature of these tales is usually interpreted as diagnostic of their oral origin and/ or performance: Proinisias Mac Cana, 'Narrative Openers and Progress Markers in Irish', in *A Celtic Florilegium: Studies in Memory of Brendan O'Hehir*, ed. K. A. Klar, E. S. Sweetser and C. Thomas (Andover, MA, 1996), 104–19. Donnchadh Ó Corráin, 'Historical Need and Literary Narrative', in *Proceedings of the Seventh International Congress of Celtic Studies*, ed. D. Ellis Evans, John G. Griffith and E. M. Jope (Oxford, 1986), 141–58, suggested that this format was related to the propagandistic function of the tales. Their primacy as literary texts is emphasised by Tomás Ó Cathasaigh, 'Pagan Survivals: The Evidence of Early Irish Narrative', in *Irland und Europa: Die Kirche im Frühmittelalter*, ed. Próinséas Ní Chatháin and Michael Richter (Stuttgart, 1984), 291–307.

25 Examples are numerous and include Muireann Ní Bhrolcháin, 'Women in Early Irish Myths and Sagas', *The Crane Bag* 14 (1980), 12–19; *eadem*, '*Re Tóin Mná*'; Lisa Bitel, '"Conceived in Sins, Born in Delights": Stories of Procreation from Early Ireland', *Journal of the History of Sexuality* 3/2 (October, 1992), 181–202; *eadem*, *Land of Women*; Joanne Findon, *A Woman's Words: Emer and Female Speech in the Ulster Cycle* (Toronto, 1997). It informs readings of *Longes Mac nUislenn*, specifically in Tymoczko, 'Animal Imagery', esp. 152–4. Herbert, 'The Universe of Male and Female', effectively balances male and female roles in the tale.

26 The distinction here is between maleness as biology and masculinity as a psychological and sociological function. Useful introductions to the importance of both in early Christian thought are Peter Brown, *The Body and Society: Men, Women and Sexual Renunciation in Early Christianity* (New York, 1980), esp. 1–19; Joyce E. Salisbury, 'Gendered Sexuality', in *A Handbook of Medieval Sexuality*, ed. Vern. L. Bullough and James Brundage (New York, 2000), 81–98.

Irish learned classes. This complex construction was inscribed through idealised patterns of behaviour associated with the concept of *fír* 'truth' and embodied by the most masculine of men, warriors and kings.[27] It was also expressed in more prosaic environments. Men were vital to public life and the ordering of society. After all, the legal reality of that society was vested in them.[28] Further-more, women were very often defined in relationship to what was proper to men: examples include mental, physical and legal competencies.[29] In all of these, men were explicitly counted superior, although women were necessary as a form of functional contrast and had irreplaceable roles in kindred relations and reproduc-tive strategies.[30] Even the pervasive sovereignty mythos, which conceptualises a kingship incarnated by women but possessed by men,[31] is calculated as an act of sexual dominance in which a man (the king) possesses a woman (sover-eignty). The transaction is a metaphor for male empowerment, culminating in the appropriation of the female body and kingdom. It is not an ideal of bilateral gender complementarity. Indeed, one of the oddities of some analyses of *Longes Mac nUislenn* is the assumption that the tale overwrites primordial beliefs in an active and independent sovereignty goddess, one who is constrained by the author of the tale into a straitjacket of Christian patriarchy.[32] This seems roman-ticised; the survival of a great deal of native social theory through the law tracts reveals a society, hierarchical and male-dominated, which surely had little to learn from Christianity in the practice of patriarchy.[33] Thus, it is Irish society's understanding of the active role of men within communal and political structures which informs *Longes Mac nUislenn*; it is the relationship between the male

---

27 The importance of *fír* has received numerous treatments, including D. A. Binchy, *Celtic and Anglo-Saxon Kingship* (Oxford, 1970); Calvert Watkins, '*Is tre Fhír Flathemon*: Marginalia to *Audacht Morainn*', *Ériu* 30 (1979), 181–98; Tomás Ó Cathasaigh, 'The Concept of the Hero in Irish Mythology', in *The Irish Mind*, ed. Richard Kearney (Dublin, 1985), 79–90; Philip O'Leary, '*Fír Fer*: An Internalized Ethical Concept in Early Irish Literature?', *Éigse* 22 (1987) 1–14; Charles Doherty, 'Kingship in Early Ireland', in *The Kingship and Landscape of Tara*, ed. E. Bhreathnach (Dublin, 2005), 3–31, esp. 25–7.

28 This was embodied in the idea of honour price. A good introduction to the general principles is *GEIL* esp. 7–16, 75.

29 The rights of women were severely circumscribed as described in *GEIL* 68–79. Women were accounted *báeth*, or legally incompetent, a term which also implied mental deficiency.

30 *EIWK* esp. 87.

31 The literature is substantial. Contributions include R. A. Breatnach, 'The Lady and the King: A Theme of Irish Literature', *Studies* 42 (1953), 321–36; Proinsias Mac Cana, 'Aspects of the Theme of King and Goddess in Irish Literature', *Études Celtiques* 7 (1955–7), 76–104; 8 (1958), 59–65. Kim McCone, *Pagan Past and Christian Present in Early Irish Literature* (Maynooth, 1990), 138–60; Máire Herbert, 'Goddess and King: The Sacred Marriage in Early Ireland', in *Women and Sovereignty*, ed. L. O. Fradenburg (Edinburgh, 1992), 264–75; Scowcroft, 'Abstract Narrative', esp. 130–7; Máire Ní Mhaonaigh, 'Tales of Three Gormlaiths in Medieval Irish Literature', *Ériu* 52 (2002), 1–24; John Carey, 'Tara and the Supernatural', in *The Kingship and Landscape of Tara*, ed. Bhreathnach, 32–48.

32 The position, in relationship to early Irish literature in general, is articulated in Ní Bhrolcháin, '*Re Tóin Mná*', 115–21. It is applied to *Longes Mac nUislenn*, in particular, by Tymoczko, 'Animal Imagery', 159, and Herbert, 'The Universe of Male and Female', 58–61.

33 There has been some debate about the Christian authorship of the vernacular law tracts; see, for example, Donnchadh Ó Corráin, Liam Breatnach and Aidan Breen, 'The Laws of the Irish', *Peritia* 3 (1984), 382–438. The scholarly consensus is that they are of Christian authorship but draw inspiration from native custom. As Thomas Charles-Edwards points out ('Early Irish Law', in *A New History of Ireland 1: Prehistoric and Early Ireland*, ed. Dáibhí Ó Cróinín (Oxford, 2005), 331–70, at 331–2), the Irish themselves saw the system as of native origin.

protagonists and antagonists that drives the narrative and decides Deirdre's fate; it is the dangerous disjunction between legal ideals and the practical exercise of power which shapes the narrative's bloody *dénouement*.

Beyond cosmology: situating the tale within society

Longes Mac nUislenn is chronologically anchored in the life of a woman, Deirdre, from ill-fated cry in the womb to suicide; the actions of the saga are, with few exceptions, precipitated or performed by men. The most important of these exceptions is Deirdre's elopement with Noísiu.[34] Even this could be plausibly interpreted as the direct result of the king's decision to rear her apart from the court. These contexts of male action have been highlighted in Máire Herbert's perceptive discussion of Conchobor's narrative significance.[35] Each major section of the tale is set in motion by the king. He saves the unborn Deirdre, itself the underlying cause of all the trouble, has the sons of Uisliu treacherously killed and is the catalyst for Deirdre's suicide. In fact, it is Conchobor's role which makes a direct identification of Deirdre with the sovereignty goddess so problematic, even though there can be little doubt that the associations of that figure form a notable component of the tale's imagery.[36] However, Conchobor's possession of the kingship does not rely on her; he is king before her birth and remains so after her death.[37] This is despite the fact that his behaviour is far from kingly and includes those serious violations of *fír* which, in other tales, presage the end of a man's rule.[38] Conchobor delivers bad judgements and behaves treacherously,[39] but does not fall from power.[40] Obviously, the historicised structure of the Ulster Cycle demanded Conchobor's survival: it is a known event in its shared world. Yet, it still remains to be explained as to why the king should be presented so negatively and counter to his usually more positive depiction.[41]

Heretofore, most answers have focused on sovereignty and on Deirdre's relationship to it. For example, Maria Tymoczko has suggested that the tale is rooted in a clash for kingship. Noísiu, she argues, has the makings of a king;

[34] *LMU* §9, where Deirdre takes the leading role.

[35] Herbert, 'The Universe of Male and Female', 55–6.

[36] Tymoczko, 'Animal Imagery', 147–53.

[37] Herbert, 'The Universe of Male and Female', 56.

[38] The replacement of Mac Con by Cormac mac Airt in the saga *Cath Maige Mucrama* is a classic instance and is analysed by Tomás Ó Cathasaigh, 'The Theme of *Lommrad* in *Cath Maige Mucrama*', *Éigse* 18 (1981), 211–24.

[39] *LMU* §6.81–3 (Conchobor's decision to take Deirdre and rear her apart), §11.135 (Conchobor's underhand pursuit of the sons of Uisliu), §§14–5 (the tricking of Fergus, violation of the sureties and killing of the sons of Uisliu). See also Philip O'Leary, 'Verbal Deceit in the Ulster Cycle', *Éigse* 21 (1986), 16–26; Herbert, 'The Universe of Male and Female', 55.

[40] The later saga *Táin Bó Flidais* seeks to rectify this by having Fergus temporarily seizing the kingship of Ulster in revenge: M. E. Dobbs, ed. and trans., 'On *Táin Bó Flidais*', *Ériu* 8 (1916), 133–49, at 134. Tymoczko, 'Animal Imagery', 158–9, puts forward the interesting, if not altogether convincing, argument that an original *Longes Mac nUislenn* was a tale about the end of the heroic age.

[41] For example, by the eighth century it was believed that Conchobor had received a baptism of blood which insured his salvation long before Patrick came to Ireland. The idea first occurs in his death tale, *Aided Conchobuir*, and is discussed by J. Corthals, 'The *Reitoric* in *Aided Chonchobuir*', *Ériu* 40 (1989), 41–59. Corthals dates the core of the text to the early eighth century.

an aging Conchobor falls short.[42] In particular, Tymoczko has drawn attention to the animal and fertility imagery, with which the tale abounds, and shows the extent to which it is frequently associated with kingship and the sovereignty goddess.[43] Noísiu, the young bull, is linked with peace and plenty, although he dies violently.[44] Conchobor may be the bull of the province but he is old and, it is strongly implied, lacking in virility.[45] The tragedy is that Noísiu, the potential king, is killed while Conchobor clings onto rulership past his prime. Furthermore, Tymoczko notes that the genealogies embedded in *Senchas Síl Ír* include the sons of Uisliu, explicitly giving Noísiu and his brothers a royal pedigree as the grandsons of a king and Conchobor's nephews.[46] In practical terms, this identifies them as members of the ruling kindred and as natural rivals of Conchobor.[47] Yet nothing is made of this possible relationship within the tale, something highly unusual in a society as genealogy-conscious as Ireland. The sons of Uisliu are portrayed as ordinary members of Conchobor's war-band; there is no hint that they are his close relatives. Now it is perfectly possible that they were artificially attached to a pre-existing patriline, a not uncommon feature of the manipulation of genealogies.[48] This may even have happened as a result of the writing of the tale. Significantly, however, although the imagery of sovereignty is skilfully deployed, it is never explicitly stated that Noísiu is the rightful king or is even regarded as *damnae ríg*.[49] He does not gain rulership from Deirdre;[50] rather, he finds exile and death.

At this point it is useful to compare *Longes Mac nUislenn* with another early Irish tale, *Fingal Rónáin*, a text similarly interpreted as a commentary upon sovereignty.[51] This early tenth-century narrative shares several themes with *Longes*

---

42 Tymoczko, 'Animal Imagery', 154–7.

43 *Ibid.*, esp. 147–56. A similar use of gendered animals in the *Táin* is analysed by Patricia Kelly, 'The *Táin* as Literature', in *Aspects of the* Táin, ed. J. P. Mallory (Belfast, 1992), 69–102, at 76–7; the related idea of the *tarbfheis*, 'bull-feast', is considered by Thomas Charles-Edwards, '*Geis*, Prophecy, Omen and Oath', *Celtica* 23 (1999), 38–59, esp. 40–1.

44 *LMU* §8, §15.

45 *Ibid.* §9.111–5.

46 Tymoczko, 'Animal Imagery', 155.

47 Long-standing views of royal succession as being bound by membership of the *derbfhine* were challenged by Donnchadh Ó Corráin, 'Irish Regnal Succession – A Reappraisal', *Studia Hibernica* 11 (1971), 7–39. Bart Jaski, *Early Irish Kingship and Succession* (Dublin, 2000), esp. 277–84, concludes that there was no formal rule of succession but that it was treated flexibly within the overall kindred group.

48 An excellent example is the clearly political manipulation of the Osraige genealogies. F. J. Byrne, 'Derrynavlan: The Historical Context', *JRSAI* 110 (1980), 116–26, at 118, argues that it was probably Cerball Mac Dúnlainge, king of Osraige between 842 and 888, who was ultimately responsible for the reorientation of the Osraige genealogies towards Leinster and away from Munster.

49 A *damnae ríg* literally had the 'material of a king'. The individual so described was regarded as having the potential to be a king but the term did not imply that he was a royal heir; see *EIWK* 107–17 for a full appraisal of the implications of *damnae ríg* and the related term *rígdamnae*.

50 In contrast, *Oidheadh Chloinne Uisnigh* states *agus gurab adhbhar airdríogh Éireann ar ghail agus air ghaisgeadh Naoise Mac Uisneach* ... 'And Naoise son of Uisneach is a potential high-king of Ireland on account of his prowess and valour': Mac Giolla Léith, *Oidheadh Chloinne hUisneach*, 88 (text), 89 (translation).

51 David Greene, ed., *Fingal Rónáin and Other Irish Stories*, Mediaeval and Modern Irish Series 16 (Dublin, 1955), 1–15. The tale has received a great deal of analysis including Thomas Charles-Edwards, 'Honour and Status in Some Welsh and Irish Prose Tales', *Ériu* 29 (1978), 123–41; Tomás Ó Cathasaigh, 'The Rhetoric of *Fingal Rónáin*', *Celtica* 17 (1985), 123–44; Erich Poppe,

Mac nUislenn but treats them differently. Like *Longes Mac nUislenn*, it focuses on the sexual triangle of young man, young woman and old man. In contrast, the young man, Máel Fothartaig, has an explicit familial relationship with the older man, Rónán. The latter is king of Leinster and his father. Furthermore, when Máel Fothartaig rejects the advances of the unnamed young woman, Rónán's new wife, he becomes an exile in order to escape her.[52] He and Noísiu flee their respective royal courts in diametrically opposed circumstances. Thomas Charles-Edwards has pointed out that a contributing factor to the unfolding events is Máel Fothartaig's inability to reject Rónán's wife in public because this would reflect badly on his father's honour.[53] In *Longes Mac nUislenn*, on the other hand, acts of acceptance and rejection are nearly all public, from Conchobor's decision to allow the unborn Deirdre to live to the latter's suicide at Emain Macha.[54] The roles of the women are different as well, even if both kill themselves.[55] In *Fingal Rónáin* the queen engineers the tragedy through her slanderous accusation against Máel Fothartaig, turning father against son. The saga culminates with the death of all three. Rónán loses his life and his kingship because by wrongly condemning his son he sins against *fír*.[56] The end of the saga, disastrous on the personal level for Rónán and his family, is ideologically satisfying. The king who has made a bad judgement dies, essentially validating the early Irish conception of kingship. Thus, the model of a tragic interruption to the fitting replacement of an older king by a more virile successor is much better fulfilled in *Fingal Rónáin* than in *Longes Mac nUislenn*.

This awkward fit has been recognised by Máire Herbert, who suggests an alternative reading of the narrative as an exploration of the tension between culture, represented by men, and nature, symbolised by women.[57] Indeed, there can be little doubt that this tension is a powerful feature of the text. For instance, Noísiu and Deirdre are only safe in the wilderness, apart from human society.[58] Once placed within that society's confines their relationship proves disruptive. However, it is possible to go further. The contrast between culture and nature can also be conceptualised, in more pragmatic terms, as one between a private domesticated space, which is feminine, and a public political space, which is masculine. This is apparent from the outset. Deirdre is at first hidden in the most private living space of all, the womb. Her cry, which reverberates through the feast, an environment of male camaraderie, thrusts her into public and out of hiding.[59] Her future is made plain to the prophetic eyes of the druid Cathbad and becomes part of the communal verbal discourse that joins king and household.[60]

'Deception and Self-Deception in *Fingal Rónáin*', *Ériu* 47 (1996), 137–51; McCone, *Pagan Past*, 135; Sheila Boll, 'Seduction, Vengeance and Frustration in *Fingal Rónáin*: The Role of Foster-Kin in Structuring the Narrative', *CMCS* 47 (Summer, 2004), 1–16.

52 *Fingal Rónáin*, line 55.
53 Charles-Edwards, 'Honour and Status', 137–9.
54 Even Noísiu's elopement with Deirdre could be seen as a public decision: according to *LMU* §9.123–4, Noísiu's singing (an act of fear as well as acceptance) alerts the Ulstermen that something has happened.
55 *Fingal Rónáin*, lines 193–96; *LMU* §19.316–7.
56 Discussed by Poppe, 'Deception and Self-Deception', 143.
57 Herbert, 'The Universe of Male and Female', 57.
58 *LMU* §13.158–61.
59 *Ibid.* §1.6–12.
60 *Ibid.* §§1–6.

Conchobor's effort to have Deirdre raised apart, in a space typologically analogous to the womb, fails spectacularly,[61] and the narrative asserts, throughout, the inescapable primacy of the public world. It is this public space which I wish to address in an effort to simultaneously supplement and problematise our appreciation of what might be termed the cosmic level of Irish ideologies concerning sovereignty and power.

It is necessary to begin with seemingly simple questions. How does a tale such as *Longes Mac nUislenn* relate to the social realities of the early medieval period? How does it, on the level of ideology, intersect with those realities? Irish society, as Thomas Charles-Edwards has shown, was ordered around concepts of status, hierarchy and contract.[62] Kingship formed a central point from which a variety of reciprocal rights and responsibilities flowed.[63] For instance, the important legal tract *Críth Gablach*, a text dated to the early eighth century, offers a meticulously structured communal model where kings and people relate to each other through hierarchy, mutuality and reciprocity.[64] As a text it combines specific legal statements with an overall conception of the role of the king within society.[65] The cosmic attributes of the king are de-emphasised in favour of an institutional focus in a recognisable, although still idealised, social setting. In *Longes Mac nUislenn* this type of setting is arguably the main interest of the tale. Its narrative is underpinned by the imagery of sovereignty but, crucially, is structured around the legal obligations and responsibilities of a king as described in a law tract such as *Críth Gablach*. This performs the very important function of making the kingship described in *Longes Mac nUislenn* seem unusually consonant with the realities of eighth- and ninth- century Ireland. In comparison, the mythological element is relatively weak and, if anything, subverted through the powerlessness of Deirdre in comparison with the practical dominence wielded by Conchobor.

A focus on power and legal obligations, particularly those pertaining to kings, permeates the tale. *Longes Mac nUislenn* is full of kings. Besides Conchobor and the un-named king of Scotland, the tale also features Eógan Mac Durthacht, regional ruler of Fernmag, and Fergus mac Róich who, in the traditional literature, was believed to have been Conchobor's precursor as king of Ulster.[66] Each of these individuals plays a major part and it seems difficult not to conclude that the tale is structured around their actions and reactions. Even the un-identified kings of Ireland, from whom Noísiu expects welcome, have an impact on the narrative. They initially extend *fáesam* 'legal protection' to the sons of Uisliu,[67] but this is undermined by Conchobor's hostility; Deirdre and the sons of Uisliu are forced to flee to Scotland.[68] There, the initial royal favour that they enjoy turns sour

---

61 *Ibid.* §6.85–9. Conchobor's inability to keep out Lebarcham, the *bancháinte*, female satirist, is a foreshadowing of his failure to keep Deirdre from interacting with the outside world.

62 Thomas Charles-Edwards, 'Críth Gablach and the Law of Status', *Peritia* 5 (1986), 53–73; *idem*, 'A Contract between King and People in Early Medieval Ireland? *Críth Gablach* on Kingship', *Peritia* 8 (1994), 107–19; *idem*, 'Early Irish Law'; *idem*, *Early Christian Ireland* (Cambridge, 2000), esp. chapter 3.

63 Charles-Edwards, 'A Contract between King and People'; Jaski, *Early Irish Kingship*, 37–56.

64 D. A. Binchy, ed., *Críth Gablach*, Medieval and Modern Irish Series (Dublin, 1941).

65 Charles-Edwards, 'A Contract between King and People', esp. 111–9.

66 'Fergus mac Roich (Fergus mac Róig)', in *The Dictionary of Irish Biography*, <http://dib.cambridge.org/viewReadPage.do?articleId=a3048>.

67 *LMU* §10.129–30, §11.134.

68 *Ibid.* §11.135.

because of Deirdre's troublesome presence and the fugitives are forced into exile again.[69] They take refuge on an *inis mara* 'an island of the sea'.[70] Significantly, this is the only point in the narrative where Noísiu and Deirdre are free from the power of kings. It is an arresting moment for it is Deirdre's guidance which has brought them to a place outside of the normal public power structures. As such it takes on the characteristics of a private female domain, defined against the male communal environments of the court, warfare and the hunt. Furthermore, islands are frequently associated with women in early Irish literature and are sometimes depicted as places of indolence and sexual pleasure.[71] This is not a fitting place for masculine men, for warriors. This reading is supported by the dramatic reaction of the Ulstermen, heretofore an undifferentiated group whose loyalty to Conchobor has been constant. They ask for the sons of Uisliu to be forgiven and allowed return from exile, making the following point:

> 'Is tróg', a Choncbobuir, ol Ulaid, 'maic Uislenn do thuitim i tírib námad tre chin droch-mná'.[72]

The hostile lands referred to in the passage encompass the island and, by extension, Scotland.[73] However, it is the fugitives' presence on the island itself which is the immediate cause for the Ulstermen's intervention. Deirdre, the bad woman, has taken the warriors away from their correct place in the royal court and among male companions. The reaction of the Ulstermen implicitly attests to the superiority of the public space over the private. This is a narrative crux. The tale returns to the public environment of legal responsibility and remains there for the remainder of its story. Once again, kings are all-important. It is the failure of Fergus, the former king, to fulfil his obligation as *commairge*, 'surety',[74] which allows Conchobor treacherously to arrange the death of the sons of Uisliu at the hands of another king, Eógan Mac Durthacht. The impact of these royal actions strongly suggests that the interplay between kingship, law and power is of utmost importance to the narrative. Moreover, it is Conchobor's ability to retain power, despite the breakdown of the system of legal obligation, which is of key significance.

King and people: the public world of Longes Mac nUislenn

This significance can be teased out by a deeper consideration of the legal and communal milieu of the tale. It defines Conchobor by his relationship with the Ulaid, the Ulstermen. This relationship of king and people was one of considerable

---

69 *Ibid.* §§11–3.
70 *Ibid.* §13.160.
71 Examples include the island of women in texts such as *Immram Brain* and *Immram Maíle Dúin*. See Kuno Meyer, ed. and trans., *The Voyage of Bran son of Febal to the Land of the Living* (London, 1895), §30, §60, §62; Whitley Stokes, ed. and trans., 'The Voyage of Mael Duin', *Revue Celtique* 9 (1888) 452–95; 10 (1889), 50–95, §28.
72 '"Grievous is it, O Conchobor", the Ulstermen said, "for the sons of Uisliu to fall in hostile lands through the crime of a bad woman"': *LMU* §13.162–3 (trans. 65).
73 Although un-named, the enemies mentioned in *LMU* §13.163–5 must be the followers of the king of Scotland.
74 *LMU* §14. Jaski, *Early Irish Kingship*, 91–7, has a useful general discussion of sureties in their broader legal context.

legal importance. *Críth Gablach*, for instance, poses the question as to whether king or people should hold higher status.[75] It suggests that, on one level, they are equal through a balancing of rights and responsibilities; on another level the king is superior because he rules with *cumachtae* 'power'.[76] Ideally, the exercise of *cumachtae* should take place within the ambit of shared obligations. The nature and subversion of these underpins the presentation of Conchobor and the Ulaid in *Longes Mac nUislenn*. Initially, all appears well. The tale's opening scene is of Conchobor accompanied by his *slúag* 'host of warriors', itself diagnostic of royal status.[77] Ruler and followers are united through partaking in a feast. This is emphaised by the *gáir mesca*, the 'drunken shout' of the revellers, as a shout at a feast was one of the three shouts of victory for a king.[78] It is a raucous act of public and group affirmation,[79] and is contrasted with the unborn child's lone scream, one which dramatically interrupts this scene of male solidarity and gives Deirdre her name.[80] Conchobor refuses the advice of his warriors, who wish Deirdre killed, and a potential rift opens between king and followers. Nonetheless, his will dominates, despite misgivings on the part of the Ulaid. This remains the case for most of the narrative. Tellingly, it is the Ulstermen's active support of Conchobor's underhand dealings that drives the sons of Uisliu from Ireland.[81] At only one point does the king appear to give way to the wishes of his people, in his apparent forgiveness and recall of the fugitives.[82] His subsequent act of treachery, the illegal violation of his people's trust as represented by the sureties, results in mayhem, death and exile.[83] However, a year later Conchobor is still politically strong enough to hold an *óenach*, 'royal assembly', an institution which was one of the most important public enactments of the bond joining king and people in early medieval Ireland.[84] But, in holding this assembly, Conchobor is empowered by *cumachtae* rather than by reciprocity. Furthermore, similarly to the opening of the tale, Deirdre is again presented as the isolated figure acting against group solidarity.

The contrast between power and obligation is nowhere clearer than in the final events of the narrative, the death of the sons of Uisliu, the *óenach* at Emain Macha and the suicide of Deirdre. All occur against the backdrop of highly public spaces. Noísiu and the sons of Uisliu are slaughtered on the *faithche*, the green

---

[75] *Críth Gablach*, line 492. The issue is discussed by Charles-Edwards, 'A Contract between King and People', 108.

[76] *Críth Gablach*, lines 444–5; see Jaski, *Early Irish Kingship*, 277.

[77] Jaski, *Early Irish Kingship*, 98–9.

[78] This is the *gáir im fhleid* and was pointed out by Buttimer, '*Longes Mac nUislenn* Reconsidered', 5. The other two are a shout of victory after battle and a shout of praise; see Tadhg O'Donoghue, ed. and trans., 'Advice to a Prince', *Ériu* 9 (1921–3), 43–54, at 46 (verse 9).

[79] The use of public and private spaces for affirmation and rejection is also important in *Fingal Rónáin*. See Kaarina Hollo, '*Fingal Rónáin*: The Medieval Irish Text as Argumentative Space', in *Cín Chille Cúile: Texts, Saints and Places – Essays in Honour of Pádraig Ó Riain*, ed. John Carey, Máire Herbert and Kevin Murray (Aberystwyth, 2004), 241–9.

[80] Derived from the verb *derdrethar* 'to resound'. See *DIL s.v. derdrethar*. The significance of the contrasting sounds is further considered in Buttimer, '*Longes Mac nUislenn* Reconsidered', 2–16; Ann Dooley, 'The Heroic Word: The Reading of Early Irish Sagas', in *The Celtic Consciousness*, ed. Robert O' Driscoll (Toronto, 1981), 155–9, at 156–7.

[81] *LMU* §11.137.

[82] *Ibid.* §13.166

[83] *Ibid.* §16.

[84] D. A. Binchy, 'The Fair of Tailtiu and the Feast of Tara', *Ériu* 18 (1958), 113–38, is a classic examination; Jaski, *Early Irish Kingship*, 49–56.

before Emain Macha, even though it was illegal to fight on the *faithche* of a royal residence.[85] The illegality of the act is highlighted by the fact that Conchobor has to resort to *amsaig* 'mercenaries' and Eógan Mac Durthacht to do the killing; he cannot rely on his own trusted followers. Moreover, Conchobor has defaulted on his oath to the sons of Uisliu and this should have meant the loss of his honour-price and a concomitant fall from kingship.[86] Yet, remarkably, despite short-term gory consequences, Conchobor's status seems unimpaired. Indeed, the exile of great warriors such as Fergus is partially counterbalanced by Conchobor's reconciliation with a previously troublesome sub-king, Eógan Mac Durthacht.[87] This dynamic is acted out at the *óenach* with which the narrative concludes and it is worth considering it in some detail.[88] *Óenaige* were complex institutions which combined the legal, political and economic.[89] In vernacular law, the *óenach* features as a major ingredient in the glue holding Irish society together. *Críth Gablach* describes it as one of the three exactions of the king.[90] Another Old Irish legal tract, *Cáin Fhuithirbe*, emphasises its centrality by condemning those who do not accompany their lord to an *óenach* so that he is publicly shamed by having only a few followers.[91] The *óenach* is presented as being of equal importance to both king and people. It dramatised their unity and was conceptualised by the Irish literate elite as a mirror for the perfect society. Within its own space it encapsulated social and hierarchical principles. It is this idealisation of the *óenach* which makes the final act of *Longes Mac nUislenn* so shocking. In reality, of course, *óenaige* were not necessarily peaceful events and frequently served to exacerbate political tensions as much as defuse them. The annals report several examples of contention and violence at historical *óenaige*. For example, the community of Tallaght prevented the holding of *Óenach Tailten* during 811 in revenge for the violation of their sanctuary. In 827 *Óenach Colmáin* was disturbed by an internal dispute among the Leinstermen.[92] Nevertheless, the exemplary *óenach* held a powerful charge and the events at the *óenach* of Emain should be considered in its light. Two aspects stand out: Conchobor's ability to hold an *óenach* at all, something which has already been considered, and, secondly, Deirdre's suicide.

The latter, unsurprisingly given its dramatic nature, has received the most attention, but the two are inextricably bound. Generally, commentators have tried to unpick the meaning of Deirdre's death. Some view it an act of independence: Deirdre refuses Conchobor's manipulation and his treatment of her as a sexual commodity to be shared with Eógan. Simultaneously, she upholds her honour

---

85   See *DIL*, *s.v. faithche*. This is the second time that the sons of Uisliu face danger on a *faithche*. By *LMU* §11.142–3, they had set up their homes on the *faithche* of the king of Scotland but the discovery of Deirdre put them in mortal danger. Tymoczko, 'Animal Imagery', 147–8, has also noted striking typological similarities to the killing of the calf earlier in the tale.

86   *GEIL* 19.

87   *LMU* §14.176–9.

88   *Ibid.* §19.

89   Charles Doherty, 'Exchange and Trade in Early Medieval Ireland', *JRSAI* 110 (1980), 67–89.

90   *Críth Gablach*, lines 502–5; discussed by Charles-Edwards, 'Contract between King and People', 112.

91   The relevant passage is edited and translated by Liam Breatnach, 'The Ecclesiastical Element in the Old-Irish Legal Tract *Cáin Fhuithirbe*', *Peritia* 5 (1986), 36–52, at 39–40 (= *CIH* II.763.8–4.17).

92   AU 811, 827. Kuno Meyer, ed. and trans., *The Triads of Ireland* (Dublin, 1906), §35 contains a reference to *Óenach Colmáin Elo*. The site of this *óenach* is almost certainly to be identified with the important church of Lynally dedicated to Colmán Elo.

through a public and fatal act of defiance.[93] Tymoczko argues that Deirdre does not so much refuse Eógan as refuse to accept the possibility that she should ever again be the source of conflict between two men.[94] Despite differences, these varying interpretations give Deirdre's death a positive valency. However, it must be remembered that her suicide would have been deeply troubling to the Christian audience of the tale. This is acknowledged by Herbert, who goes on to argue that Christian patriarchal attitudes, held by the tale's redactor, obscured an original story which served as a warning against an improper balance between male and female.[95] Interesting as this is, *Longes Mac nUislenn* also suggests explanations of a more practical nature. Suicide was not only condemned by the Church but was classified by legal experts as *fingal* 'kinslaying', one of the most serious of all crimes.[96] Once again, it is worth making a comparison with *Fingal Rónáin*. There, the suicide of the queen is explicitly part of the structure of guilt and revenge with which the tale climaxes.[97] In other words, it has a functional role within the overall narrative and serves to damn the queen in death and after-life. Deirdre's actions have a function as well, but one which is best understood within the context of the relations between king and people. There is little doubt that Deirdre does reject the two men most responsible for her former lover's death and that, furthermore, she chooses to enact this at the *óenach*. Thus, while her rejection of them may be viewed as personal, her actions make it public. But what does this mean for Conchobor's kingship? In the end – very little. Even the violent response of Noísiu's sureties had failed to overthrow Conchobor. The contrast with *Fingal Rónáin* is striking. The warriors' repudiation of Rónán leads directly to his death. If anything, Deirdre's death could be seen as finally, and ironically, fulfilling the will of Conchobor's followers that she die, the wish which the king had refused to accept. By committing suicide she brings the king and people back into harmony for she removes the disruptive element which had led to their initial rift.

There is another factor to be considered. The Ulster Cycle was highly histori-cised and efforts were made by its many redactors to create a sequential structure, particularly around the *Táin*. This structure did not act as a constraint but gave the author of *Longes Mac nUislenn* great freedom. This is because the intertex-tual nature of the Cycle meant that although the narrative ends with exile and death their aftermath could be made echo through other tales. The audience of *Longes Mac nUislenn* knew that in his future, but their past, Conchobor would be validated through victory over the forces of Medb and Ailill; they knew that the Ulster exiles would not fashion his downfall. After all, these events had already occurred. The death of the sons of Uisliu and Deirdre's suicide had no long-term consequences, cosmic or real, for Conchobor. On the other hand, for the author of *Longes Mac nUislenn*, how events happened was just as important as what happened. The tale is clearly concerned with the proper exercise of kingship

93 Philip O'Leary, 'The Honour of Women in Early Irish Literature', *Ériu* 38 (1987), 27–44, at 42–3, argues that Deirdre's death is a way for her to uphold her honour in a public setting. See also *idem*, 'Jeers and Judgments: Laughter in Early Irish Literature', *CMCS* 22 (Winter, 1991), 15–29, at 27–9; Herbert, 'The Universe of Male and Female', 58–61.

94 Tymoczko, 'Animal Imagery', 152–3.

95 Herbert, 'The Universe of Male and Female', 58–61.

96 *GEIL* 127, n. 17.

97 *Fingal Rónáin*, lines 193–6. It is examined as part of a sequence of carefully structured acts of vengeance by Boll, 'Seduction, Vengeance and Frustration', 10–15.

within a clearly defined public space. It does not offer an exemplary myth of rulership, however, and portrays a king who successfully holds onto sovereignty through military means. Moreover, he is willing to violate basic legal obligations in pursuit of his own personal aims.

Charles Doherty has cogently argued that the conceptualisation of early Irish kingship is about imagining utopia, whether cosmological or social.[98] *Longes Mac nUislenn* suggests that this utopia falls from perfection once it is imagined within a real society. The saga brilliantly deploys images normally associated with the discourse of idealised sovereignty and juxtaposes them with a violent world where pragmatic realities take precedence over matters of ideology. Conchobor's alliance with Eógan is a supreme example and one which is instrumental in the final unfolding of events. Furthermore, these realities are very effectively embodied within the legal framework through which the behaviour of the main characters can be understood. The tale portrays a public male domain centred on communal activities such as the feast, warfare and the *óenach*. The private spaces, associated with Deirdre, are rejected in favour of the public world but this world is one where right behaviour is fragile and constantly threatened. The failure of the kings of Ireland and, later, the sureties, to protect the sons of Uisliu is symptomatic. It allows *Longes Mac nUislenn* to point up the worrying disjunction between the right to power and its proper legally bound exercise. Conchobor, as affirmed through much of the Ulster Cycle, is the rightful king. This does not mean, however, that he behaves as a king should or even that he deserves to remain in power. His actions violate fundamental principles of correct rulership. The narrative seems to imply that, like its flawed Conchobor, actual kings are not really the possessors of a supernatural sovereignty; they are not necessarily handsome and brave, virile and just. *Longes Mac nUislenn* painfully deconstructs an imperfect but resilient kingship. The reciprocal bonds joining king and people are twisted from shape. And in the world of eighth- and ninth-century Ireland who could argue?

---

[98] Doherty, 'Kingship', 26.

19

MONGÁN'S METAMORPHOSIS:
COMPERT MONGÁIN OCUS SERC DUIBE LACHA DO MONGÁN, A LATER MONGÁN TALE[1]

Máire Ní Mhaonaigh

Compert Mongáin ocus Serc Duibe Lacha do Mongán (The Birth of Mongán and Mongán's Love for Dub Lacha – or Dub Lacha's Love for Mongán) belongs to the broad category of narrative Alan Bruford termed 'Romantic Tales', encompassing in his view 'all the late medieval and later romances found in Irish manuscripts from the fifteenth to the nineteenth centuries and the related folktales'.[2] The earliest copy is contained in the Book of Fermoy, written for David Mór son of Maurice Roche in the middle of the fifteenth century,[3] and it was in Bruford's view among the best of the Romantic tales produced at a time when 'Irish poets and scribes enjoyed the patronage of a powerful Irish-speaking aristocracy of mixed Norman and Irish descent'.[4] Notwithstanding this, unlike other contemporary compositions which enjoyed widespread popularity in the seventeenth century and later, as far as post-classical transmission is concerned, our tale survives in a solitary copy written in Munster about the year 1811 by Seághan Mac Mathghamhna and entitled *Tóruigheacht Duibhe Lacha Láimhe Ghile* 'The Pursuit of Dub Lacha of the White Hand'.[5] Though somewhat longer, as a result principally of additional poems put into Dub Lacha's mouth and an

---

[1] I offer this short literary piece to Thomas Charles-Edwards, a historian whose sensitive, sophisticated reading of many texts has considerably advanced our understanding of medieval Irish literature.

[2] Alan Bruford, *Gaelic Folk-tales and Mediaeval Romances: A Study of the Early Modern Irish 'Romantic Tales' and their Oral Derivatives* (Dublin, 1969), 1. Gerard Murphy characterises these narratives as 'a group of tales whose main traits are the prevalence of magic and the piling of unbelievable incident on incident': *The Ossianic Lore and Romantic Tales of Medieval Ireland* (Dublin, 1955), 39. For difficulties regarding the application of the term 'romantic tale' to a heterogeneous body of material see, for example, Joseph Falaky Nagy, 'In Defence of Rómánsaíocht', *Ériu* 38 (1987), 9–26, at 12, and Caoimhín Breatnach, 'The Religious Significance of *Oidheadh Chloinne Lir*', *Ériu* 50 (1999), 1–40, at 36.

[3] Kuno Meyer, ed. and trans., *The Voyage of Bran son of Febal to the Land of the Living with an Essay upon the Irish Vision of the Happy Otherworld and the Celtic Doctrine of Rebirth by Alfred Nutt*, 2 vols (London, 1895), I.58–84. A Modern Irish translation of the tale is contained in Tomás Ó Floinn and Proinsias Mac Cana, trans., *Scéalaíocht na Ríthe* (Dublin, 1956), 115–30.

[4] Bruford, *Gaelic Folk-tales*, 46.

[5] Galway, NUI LS de hÍde, 13. This version of the text has been edited by Séamas Ó Duilearga, 'Tóruigheacht Duibhe Lacha Láimh-ghile [*aliter* Serc Duibhe-Lacha do Mhongán]', *ZCP* 17 (1928), 347–70.

expanded ending, Mac Mathghamhna's text reproduces in essence and frequently in wording the earlier version, the main outline of which is as follows:[6]

> While in Lochlainn, Fiachna Finn mac Báetáin, king of the Ulaid, was required to cure the king of that territory. When the king of Lochlainn reneged on his side of the bargain Fiachna was forced to go into battle on his behalf. The Ulaid king and his men, however, were no match for the poisonous sheep they encountered in Lochlainn, where they would have been annihilated were it not for the aid proffered by Manannán mac Lir, who was to be allowed to sleep with Fiachna's wife, disguised as her husband, as a result of which a son, Mongán, was born. On the night of Mongán's birth a son, Mac an Daimh, was also born to Fiachna's attendant and a daughter, Dub Lacha, to his chief rival, Fiachna Dub. When Fiachna Dub slew Mongán's father the youth returned from Tír Tairngire, where he had been in fosterage with Manannán, and initially made peace with the slayer, marrying his daughter, Dub Lacha, in the process, before killing him some time later.
>
> While visiting Leinster, Mongán foolishly entered into a *cairdeas gan éra* (friendship without refusal) with the king of that territory, Brandub mac Echach, which involved him exchanging Dub Lacha for a herd of remarkable white, red-eared cattle. His wife craftily extracted from the Leinster king a promise that he would not sleep with her for a year and the remainder of the tale recounts various attempts by a chaste Mongán, spurred on by his attendant Mac an Daimh, whose wife was taken into Leinster with Dub Lacha, to retrieve his wife. Two foiled attempts were followed by a successful ruse which involved Brandub relinquishing Dub Lacha for a beautiful hag at the marriage feast itself. The Book of Fermoy version is content to have Mongán and Dub Lacha ride off into the sunset, whereas the later scribe describes a retaliatory attack by the Ulaid king on Leinster in the following year.

Such a summary does little justice to the considerable literary skill of the author, who recounts Mongán's adventures in a fast-flowing engaging style and with exquisite humour. His language is Early Modern Irish and there is little by way of earlier forms in the text to suggest that he was drawing on an Old or Middle Irish exemplar. Nonetheless, much material concerning his main hero survives from an earlier period.[7] Furthermore, the title *Serc Duibe Lacha do Mongán* is recorded in both Middle Irish tale-lists,[8] and the union is mentioned in both prose and metrical versions of the twelfth-century compilation the *Banshenchas*, where Dub Lacha is described as *lennán Mongáin* (Mongán's lover) and mother of his two sons.[9] Similar information is contained in the Book of Leinster genealogies of Dál Fiatach.[10] It remains to be seen, therefore, to what extent our author was

---

6 For a longer summary see Nagy, 'In Defence', 15–17.
7 See Nora White, ed., *Compert Mongáin and Three Other Early Mongán Tales: A Critical Edition with Introduction, Translation, Textual Notes, Bibliography and Vocabulary*, Maynooth Medieval Irish Texts 5 (Maynooth, 2006).
8 Proinsias Mac Cana, *The Learned Tales of Medieval Ireland* (Dublin, 1981), 48, 59.
9 Margaret Dobbs, ed. and trans., 'The Ban-shenchus', *Revue celtique* 47 (1930), 283–339, at 307–8, 332; *Revue celtique* 48 (1931), 163–234, at 183, 221–2.
10 M. A. O'Brien, ed., *Corpus Genealogiarum Hiberniae*, vol. 1 (Dublin, 1962), 409, 330d1–3: *Dub-lacha dano ingen Fhiachnai meic Demmáin ocus Cumne Dub ben Mongáin meic Fhiachnai máthair Cholgan ocus Conaill dá mac Mongáin* 'Moreover, Dub Lacha was the daughter of Fiachna mac Demmáin and Cuimne Dub [and] wife of Mongán mac Fiachna, mother of Colgan and Conall, Mongán's two sons' (*contra* Nagy, 'In Defence', 23).

influenced by existing tales and, more significantly, how he utilised the material in hand.[11]

Sources

Compert Mongáin

With regard to the first part of the tale, Mongán's conception and birth, the Early Modern Irish account corresponds in basic outline with the eighth-century tale *Compert Mongáin*.[12] Thus, in both, Mongán's mother is impregnated by Manannán mac Lir as part of a bargain to save the life of his human father, Fiachna, who is at war abroad (depicted as Alba in the earlier composition). However, while it is the woman who takes the initiative in the Old Irish tale, informing her husband of her pact after the event, she functions as a passive, unknowing participant in the later narrative. Manannán, on the other hand, adopts a more active role in the Early Modern Irish text, taking Mongán into fosterage when he was three nights old and returning him to his kinsmen at the age of twelve or sixteen years. Yet this too may be derivative, Manannán's function as tutor being referred to in another eighth-century narrative, *Immram Brain*.[13]

Tomás Ó Broin suggested that this motif parallels Hercules' sojourn on Mount Olympus, as related in the account of that classical hero's birth, which was, in his view, the ultimate source of both versions of Mongán's birth-tale.[14] In general, the correspondences appear too universal to necessitate a direct relationship between the Graeco-Roman myth and the eighth-century *compert*, though they are somewhat more specific, if still less than striking, in the case of the later tale.[15] Thus, in the Early Modern Irish text, Manannán, like Zeus, dons the appearance of the mortal husband, whereas it is as a stranger that he presents himself to Mongán's mother in the early tale. In addition, both otherworldly suitors come bearing a token to stave off suspicion. Furthermore, a case for borrowing is *a priori* more realistic since frequent references to Hercules in Irish literature of the twelfth century and later suggest that his story was relatively well known. Indeed, in the late fifteenth century an industrious Irish scribe, Uilliam Mac an Leagha, produced a vernacular Herculean biography, *Stair Ercuil ocus a Bás*, loosely based on Raoul Lefèvre's *Receuil des histoires de Troyes*.[16] Completed

---

11 Nagy, 'In Defence', 17, claimed that the Early Modern Irish tale 'can virtually serve the modern-day scholar as a gloss on the older narratives'.

12 *Compert Mongáin* (ed. and trans. White, *Compert Mongáin*, 71–2, 78–9).

13 *Immram Brain* (ed. and trans. Séamas Mac Mathúna, *Immram Brain: Bran's Journey to the Land of the Women* (Tübingen, 1985), 42, 55).

14 Tomás Ó Broin, 'Classical Source of the "Conception of Mongán"', *ZCP* 28 (1960/1), 262–71, at 26.

15 Ó Broin's arguments are rejected by Proinsias Mac Cana, 'Mongán mac Fiachna and *Immram Brain*', *Ériu* 23 (1972), 102–42, at 127–30, and by Bianca Ross, despite her admission, 'dass eine enge inhaltliche Übereinstimmung zwischen den Erzählungen von der Zeugung der beiden Helden zu beobachten ist' ('that a close correspondence in content is apparent in the tales concerning the conception of the two heroes'): *Bildungsidol – Ritter – Held: Herkules bei William Caxton and Uilliam Mac an Lega* (Heidelberg, 1989), 73.

16 Gordon Quinn, ed. and trans., *Stair Ercuil ocus a Bás: The Life and Death of Hercules*, Irish Texts Society 38 (Dublin, 1939). For discussion of the texts see also Ross, *Bildungsidol* and Erich Poppe, '*Stair Ercuil ocus a Bás* – Rewriting Hercules in Ireland', in Kevin Murray, ed.,

in 1464, Lefèvre's tract cannot have been known to the author of our text, which appears to have been transcribed some six or seven years earlier into the Book of Fermoy.[17] Nonetheless, we cannot exclude the possibility that another version of the popular classical myth prompted the inclusion of an occasional detail in the birth-tale he was writing, *Compert Mongáin*.

One such detail not occurring in the Irish text is the so-called twin birth, whereby Alcmene begat Hercules and Iphicles, sons of different fathers, on the same night. Ó Broin, however, saw a reflection of this in the coterminous births of Mac an Daimh, Dub Lacha and Mongán in the Early Modern Irish tale.[18] Certainly, both the attendant's son, Mac an Daimh, and his future wife, Dub Lacha, augment Mongán's character in numerous, pivotal ways, yet the occurrence of a relatively commonplace motif such as a simultaneous birth is hardly sufficient to imply dependency upon the classical source.[19] In any event, whatever its ultimate inspiration, the begetting of Mac an Daimh and Dub Lacha on the same night as Mongán serves as the crucial narrative bridge between the two reasonably self-contained sections of the Early Modern Irish tale.

Serc Duibe Lacha do Mongán

Mongán's attempt to redeem Dub Lacha forms the core of the second part of the narrative and, while we may speculate that this is likely to have borne some resemblance to the now lost story entitled *Serc Duibe Lacha do Mongán* in the tale-lists, the nature of the relationship is impossible to ascertain. Significantly, however, Mongán's foolish bartering with the king of Leinster resulting in the loss of his wife echoes his bargaining with Forgoll in the Old Irish tale *Scél asa mberar co mbad hé Find mac Cumaill Mongán* 'A story from which it is inferred that Mongán was Find mac Cumaill'.[20] Here, too, Mongán almost inadvertently offers his wife to the poet in an attempt to stave off satire and feels honour-bound to consent to the exchange when Forgoll accepts. On this occasion Mongán, alias Find, is saved by his foster-son, Caílte, and a lengthy quest is averted. Notwithstanding the difference between the feeble reaction of weeping Bréothigern, Mongán's wife in this tale, and that of the feisty, crafty Dub Lacha in the later composition, it is probable that this episode inspired the creator of the latter (if not the author of the earlier *Serc Duibe Lacha*, upon which he may have drawn).[21]

The main concern of *Scél asa mberar co mbad hé Find mac Cumaill Mongán*, however, is to demonstrate Mongán's superior knowledge, a theme echoed in another short tale of roughly the same date known as 'Why Mongán was deprived

---

Translations from Classical Literature: Imtheachta Æniasa *and* Stair Ercuil ocus a Bás, Irish Texts Society Subsidiary Series 17 (Dublin, 2006), 37–68.

17 The date 1457 occurs in the section of the manuscript in which our text occurs: see Gerard Murphy, Elizabeth Fitzpatrick *et al.*, ed., *Catalogue of the Irish Manuscripts in the Royal Irish Academy*, Fasciculi XXI–XXV (Dublin, 1940), 3093.

18 Ó Broin, 'Classical Source', 266–7.

19 Ó Broin himself acknowledged the difficulty with this part of the argument but concluded that 'they [sc. incidents such as simultaneous births] are not to be ignored as they are supported by contextual evidence': *ibid.*, 267, n. 2.

20 *Scél asa mberar* (ed. and trans. White, *Compert Mongáin*, 73–4, 79–81; see also Meyer, *Voyage of Bran*, I.45–52).

21 See also Nagy, 'In Defence', 19–20.

of Noble Issue'.[22] But, unlike his dispute with Forgoll, in which Mongán eventually got the upper hand, his altercation with Eochaid Rígéices, *ardfhili na hÉrend* 'chief poet of Ireland', as depicted in this tale, has lasting consequences for the youth. In response to Mongán's indirect efforts to undermine Eochaid's scholarly authority the poet ordains that the former shall have none but *echbachlaig* (horseboys) as descendants, a curse which is deemed as having come to pass. We may note, therefore, that these early compositions depict our hero as exceptionally learned but one whose scholarship is undermined by a foolish streak. Significantly, it is Mongán's folly that is highlighted in the Early Modern Irish tale: indeed, the Book of Fermoy version omits any reference to his wisdom, having Mac an Daimh repeatedly assert that his time in Tír Tairngire with Manannán was misspent *ó nach dernais d'fhoghlaim ann acht bíadh do chaithim ocus obhlóireacht*.[23] Moreover, Mongán himself is depicted as being fully aware of his stupidity, remarking with more than a hint of irony as the king of Leinster arrives to claim his prize: *'ní chúalus-sa neach romam do thabairt a mhná amach'*.[24] Similarly, when the Ulaid offer to retrieve Dub Lacha by force, her repentant husband is adamant that, since it was his *ainghlicus* (folly) which led to her loss, *'nach tuitfe mac mná ná fer d'Ulltachaibh impe aga a tabairt amach, noga tucarsa féin lem trém' glicus hí'*.[25]

In the end Mongán's *glicus* does bear fruit, not least because of his impressive shape-changing powers. The first rescue attempt involved his creation of a large river into which he cast Tibraide, the priest of Cell Chamáin, and his companion clerics, whose forms Mongán then caused himself and Mac an Daimh to assume.[26] When this ruse was farcically foiled he later turned his attention to Cuimne *an mhuilind* 'of the mill' and with his wand *tuc buille don chailligh co*

---

22 Eleanor Knott, ed. and trans., 'Why Mongán was Deprived of Noble Issue', *Ériu* 8 (1916), 155–60.

23 'since all you learned there was how to consume food and play trickery': *Compert Mongáin ocus Serc Duibe Lacha* (ed. and trans. Meyer, *Voyage of Bran*, I.63, 80; cf. 66, 79): *Ocus táinic Mac an Daimh cugi ocus adubert ris: 'as fada damh-sa', ar sé 'mo ben do beth am' écmais tré obhlóir mar thusa, ó nach dernus cairdis gan éra re hóclach rígh Laighen'* 'And Mac an Daimh came to him [Mongán] and said to him: "it is a very long time for me to be without my wife because of a trickster like you; I didn't enter into "friendship without refusal" with the king of Leinster's attendant"'. Similar sentiments occur in the later version of the tale, which is also careful, however, to stress Manannán's positive influence: e.g. Ó Duilearga, 'Tóruigheacht', 352: *Chongaibh an leanbh aige go ceann dá bliadhain déag ionnas go raibh múinte i ngach aon ceird ba chóir dá mhacsamhuil d'fhoghlaim* 'He [Manannán] kept the child with him for twelve years to enable him to be taught every craft which somebody of his ilk should learn'; *ní thug Manannán dóibh é nó gur fhorbhair a neart agus nó gur fhoghlaim a chleasa goile agus gaisge agus go raibh comhachtach a gceardaibh diamhra draoidheachta gur ba slán a dhá bhliadhain déag dhó* 'Manannán did not return him to them until his strength increased, until he learned feats of bravery and valour, until he became powerful in magical, mysterious arts, until he had reached the age of twelve years.'

24 '"I never heard of anyone before me giving away his wife"': *Compert Mongáin ocus Serc Duibe Lacha* (ed. and trans. Meyer, *Voyage of Bran*, I.62–3, 75).

25 '"no woman's son or man of the Ulaid will fall rescuing her until I myself bring her out by means of my craftiness"': *Compert Mongáin ocus Serc Duibe Lacha* (ed. and trans. Meyer, *Voyage of Bran*, I.67, 80–1).

26 *Compert Mongáin ocus Serc Duibe Lacha* (ed. and trans. Meyer, *Voyage of Bran*, I. 64, 77).

nderna ingin óic dob fherr delbh ocus dénamh d'inginaibh an betha di .i. Ibhell Grúadhsholas inghin rígh Mumhan,[27] assuming the form of her husband, *Aed álaind mac ríg Connacht* 'beautiful Áed, son of the king of Connacht' in the process. *Bricht serce* 'a love charm' which he implanted in her cheek ensured that Brandub mac Echach would fall hopelessly in love with her, thereby enabling Mongán to retrieve his own bride.[28]

By depicting Mongán as an expert in transmogrification, the author of the Early Modern Irish *Compert* also had recourse to earlier tradition, as reflected in *Immram Brain*, as well as in *Immacaldam Choluim Chille ocus ind Óclaig* 'The Conversation of Colum Cille and the Youth', both of which portray Mongán adopting a variety of animal forms.[29] Admittedly, the metamorphoses of Mongán the sorcerer in the Early Modern Irish narrative are of a very different order to the primordial permutations in the Old Irish tales. Nonetheless, we must assume that it was knowledge of them which prompted a later author to give considerable prominence to his hero's magical prowess in his own composition.[30]

Characterisation

Mongán

In general, however, the basic facets of Mongán's personality as depicted in *Compert Mongáin ocus Serc Duibe Lacha do Mongán* reflect his portrayal in earlier tales. While his folly may be less marked in the earlier material, nonetheless, therein too his stupidity almost costs him his wife. In addition, both early and late manifestations of the figure are masters of metamorphosis, although their powers are presented in very different ways. His magical ability aside, Mongán is an altogether more human figure in the Early Modern Irish text, in which inactivity and weakness are presented as his most dominant traits. It is Manannán mac Lir, in the guise of a *cléirchín ciar círdubh* 'dark, black-haired little cleric', who shames him into avenging his father's death.[31] Furthermore, despite Mongán's

---

27 'he struck the hag and transformed her into a young girl, the best in appearance and shape of all the girls of the world, namely into bright-cheeked Aoibheall, daughter of the king of Munster': *Compert Mongáin ocus Serc Duibe Lacha* (ed. and trans. Meyer, *Voyage of Bran*, I.68, 81–2).

28 *Compert Mongáin ocus Serc Duibe Lacha* (ed. and trans. Meyer, *Voyage of Bran*, I.69–70, 82–4). The Book of Fermoy reads *blicht serce*, which Meyer takes to be an error for *bricht* (82, n. 1); the eighteenth-century copy has *briocht sirce*: Ó Duilearga, 'Tóruigheacht', 365.

29 *Immram Brain* (ed. and trans. Mac Mathúna, 42, 55); *Immacaldam Choluim Chille ocus ind Óclaig*, ed. and trans. John Carey, 'The Lough Foyle Colloquy Texts: *Imacaldam Choluim Chille ocus ind Óclaig oc Carraic Eolairg* and *Immacaldam in Druad Brain ocus inna Banfhátho Febuil ós Loch Fhebuil*', *Ériu* 52 (2002), 53–87, at 60–1. Carey has suggested that the identification of the youth with Mongán was secondary, being first made by the author of the Mongán tales (including *Compert Mongáin* and *Scél asa mberar co mbad hé Find mac Cumaill Mongán*) who was also the author of *Immram Brain*: 'On the Interrelationships of Some Cín Dromma Snechtai Texts', *Ériu* 46 (1995), 71–92, at 82–3.

30 On the metamorphosis motif see Nagy, 'In Defence', 17, in which connection he also draws attention to what he sees as similarities between the later composition and the Old Irish narratives *Tucait Baile Mongáin* and *Scél Mongáin*: 17–19, 20. For the text of these narratives see now White, *Compert Mongáin*, 77, 83; 75–6, 81–2.

31 *Compert Mongáin ocus Serc Duibe Lacha* (ed. and trans. Meyer, *Voyage of Bran*, I.61–2, 74). The *cléireach dochruidh dibhlidh* is not specifically identified as Manannán in the later version of the tale: Ó Duilearga, 'Tóruigheacht', 352.

obvious suffering in the absence of his wife, he undertakes active steps to rescue her only at the incessant urging of his *gilla*, Mac an Daimh.[32] Born on the same night as his lord, as we have seen, Mac an Daimh, in fact, functions as Mongán's *alter ego*, demonstrating intelligence and action where the king exhibits stupidity and indecision. Other deficiencies in the latter's personality are made good by Dub Lacha who, significantly, also shares her husband's birth-date. It is Dub Lacha, for example, who appeals to Mongán's under-active sense of honour in an effort to persuade him to keep his side of his unthinking bargain with the king of Leinster. In addition, it is her quick thinking which wins the couple a year's grace.[33] All of this stands in sharp contrast to her husband's dithering; of his weak nature she complains to Mac an Daimh.[34] For all his faults, however, Mongán is made to come good in the end, tricking his Leinster enemy into sleeping with a loathsome hag. Moreover, in recognition of his newly acquired leadership qualities, Mac an Daimh and Dub Lacha are accorded more subservient roles. The king reigns rightfully; natural order is restored.

Themes

Loyalty and marital fidelity

At its most basic level, therefore, *Compert Mongáin ocus Serc Duibe Lacha do Mongán* may be read as a tale of youthful folly in which an inexperienced ruler is brought to his senses not least by the steadfastness and skill of a trusty advisor and a clever wife. To this end, the virtue of loyalty is underlined, as seen particularly in Mongán's long-suffering *gilla*, Mac an Daimh, as is marital fidelity, a trait espoused in exemplary fashion by Dub Lacha, Mongán's wife. By contrast, Mongán's affections can be farcically misdirected at a herd of albeit remarkable cows; and the king of Leinster is so fickle as to dump Dub Lacha at the altar, so to speak, for what turns out to be no more than a mirage. Moreover, as the efficacy of the tale is no doubt enhanced by the author's careful elaboration of the perceived failings of a long-established literary figure, Mongán, the final episode of the tale also acquires additional force through the skilful subversion of the traditional sovereignty goddess theme. Thus, in a deliberate reversal of the usual procedure, the beautified Cuimne dramatically resumes her hag-like form on sleeping with the duped Brandub, with whose droll comment *trúagh mar tharrla dam-sa cumusc riut-sa, a Chuimna* "'I regret having slept with you, Cuimne'" the Book of Fermoy version of the tale ends.[35]

Clerical inadequacy

As the tale's hilarious climax indicates, humour is a literary device of which the learned author is fully in control. In fact, it is such a prominent feature of the

---

32 *Compert Mongáin ocus Serc Duibe Lacha* (ed. and trans. Meyer, *Voyage of Bran*, I.63, 66, 76, 79–80).

33 *Compert Mongáin ocus Serc Duibe Lacha* (ed. and trans. Meyer, *Voyage of Bran*, I.62, 75–6).

34 '… *ocus is écrúaidh a ndénann Mongán', ar sí. Ocus dochúaidh Mac an Doimh do gresadh Mongáin* "'… and Mongán behaves weakly", she said. And Mac an Daimh went to incite Mongán': *Compert Mongáin ocus Serc Duibe Lacha* (ed. and trans. Meyer, *Voyage of Bran*, I.66, 80).

35 *Compert Mongáin ocus Serc Duibe Lacha* (ed. and trans. Meyer, *Voyage of Bran*, I.70, 84).

composition that Bruford, one of the few scholars to have commented on the story in the past, views it as a 'comic tale'.[36] Far from being introduced simply for its own sake, however, laughter is the means by which some of the narrative's most pertinent points are communicated. This is seen to particularly good effect in the author's constant ridiculing of the Church. Thus, in the account of Mongán's first rescue attempt, the Ulaid king is brought into contact with a bumbling *náemcléirech* 'holy cleric', Tibraide, who, along with a companion, is performing the Divine Office. Since they mumble incomprehensibly, Mongán has to persuade his *gilla* that the churchmen are in fact engaged in *léigend* 'learning', though Mac an Daimh understands no more than the occasional 'amen, amen'. It is this refrain that the attendant himself adopts when Mongán easily outwits the dumb clerics, proceeding to Brandub's court with his *gilla* in their guise. In this way, Mongán contrives to hears Dub Lacha's confession, taking the opportunity to sleep with his wife. The real Tibraide emerges, sparking a delightful exchange among the doorkeepers, who remark in mock-perturbed fashion: *'Ni fhacamair riamh ... bliadhain budh lia Tibraide 'nan bliadhain so. Tibraide astigh agaibh agus Tibraide amuigh'.*[37] Not surprisingly, it is the disguised Tibraide *astigh* who is victorious, persuading the king of Leinster that Tibraide is in fact Mongán in Tibraide's guise. The cleric retreats to Cell Chamáin and is lucky to escape with his life.[38]

The implication is clear: clerics are in reality fools whose *léigend* has a hollow ring. Furthermore, they may well use the confessional for more than hearing the sins of the faithful, as intimated by 'Cleric' Mongán's ability to have intercourse with his wife,[39] and indeed to kill a woman who had witnessed their coupling before administration of the sacrament is deemed complete.[40] In this way, ecclesiastical figures, as presented in the tale, have less in common with the sinister, supernatural figures they represent in many later Romantic tales[41] than they do with the satirised specimens appearing in a number of late Middle Irish tales, including *Aislinge Meic Con Glinne*, whose many bugbears include the cleric as confessor.[42]

Date

The portrayal in the *Aislinge* had particular resonance in the era of reform in which the text came into being, castigating the good old-fashioned ecclesiastic

---

36 Bruford, *Gaelic Folk-tales*, 26. Nora Chadwick termed it 'pure burlesque' and regarded it as 'a story which after all has probably no further object than to satirise and amuse': 'Pictish and Celtic Marriage in Early Literary Tradition', *Scottish Gaelic Studies* 8 (1955–8), 56–115, at 104–5. According to Gearóid Mac Eoin, much of it is 'pure fun and comedy': 'Satire in Middle Irish Literature', in *Celts and Vikings: Proceedings of the Fourth Symposium of Societas Celtologica Nordica*, ed. Folke Josephson, Meijerbergs Arkiv för Svensk Ordforskning 20 (Göteborg, 1997), 9–25, at 20.

37 '"We have never before experienced a year in which Tibraides were so plentiful; you have a Tibraide inside and a Tibraide outside"': *Compert Mongáin ocus Serc Duibe Lacha* (ed. and trans. Meyer, *Voyage of Bran*, I.65–6, 79).

38 *Ibid.*, I.64–5, 77–9.

39 Mac Eoin, 'Satire', 19–20.

40 *Compert Mongáin ocus Serc Duibe Lacha* (ed. and trans. Meyer, *Voyage of Bran*, I.65, 78).

41 For examples see Bruford, *Gaelic Folk-tales*, 25–6.

42 Kenneth Hurlstone Jackson, ed., *Aislinge Meic Con Glinne* (Dublin, 1990).

of the unreformed monastery, as symbolised by Manchín, abbot of Cork.[43] *Serc Duibe Lacha do Mongán*, referred to in the tale-lists, may well have been contemporary with the *Aislinge*, if List X, which lies behind lists A and B and to which a group of *serca*, including our lost tale, was added,[44] is as late as the twelfth century, as Gregory Toner has suggested.[45] If so, it is tempting to speculate that the picture of the Church in the Early Modern Irish composition, as well as its emphasis on marital fidelity perhaps, owes much to a Middle Irish ancestor, albeit one which has left scant linguistic traces in its fifteenth-century descendant. Indeed, it is tempting to speculate that the lost tale's intended target in this regard may have been the ecclesiastical family of Uí Bhraoin, who held a number of offices in Roscommon and Clonmacnoise between the tenth and thirteenth centuries and among whom Tibraide was a popular forename.[46] To return to the extant narrative, however, what we have gleaned concerning its author reveals a mind immersed in earlier tradition yet constantly seeking to revitalise it in new, exciting ways. Hence, it is difficult to believe that our consummate literary artist would have unthinkingly transferred all or part of a transmitted text had it not had some relevance for his own time.

Pursuit of this line of enquiry is hampered by our lack of knowledge concerning the precise circumstances of the composition of our text. All we can say for definite is that it was in existence about the year 1457, when it was copied into the Roche compilation known as the Book of Fermoy. Whatever its exact date, its religious sentiments accord well with fifteenth-century concerns pertaining to the perceived laxity of clergy, both secular and in religious orders, which both Bianca Ross and Caoimhín Breatnach have seen reflected in a number of contemporary compositions. In this context, Tibraide and his companion represent the worst of clerical excesses which the author, like many of his literary colleagues, was seeking to address.[47] Closely connected with this is the emphasis on sin and repentance, which is a feature of a number of texts of the period;[48] in fact, one might see in Mongán a kind of penitent sinner, proof positive that with proper mortal guidance redemption is possible in this life. Moreover, that one of his two counsellors was the virtuous Dub Lacha is in keeping with the high esteem in which ideal Christian women were held in the fifteenth century.[49] Finally, the text's moral overtones may provide an explanation for its inclusion in the Book

---

43 See Máire Ní Mhaonaigh, 'Pagans and Holy Men: Literary Manifestations of Twelfth-century Reform', in Damian Bracken and Dagmar Ó Riain-Raedel, ed., *Ireland and Europe in the Twelfth Century: Reform and Renewal* (Dublin, 2006), 143–61, at 159–61 and references therein.

44 It was Mac Cana's opinion that the *serca* were added to list X in the tenth century: *Learned Tales*, 78.

45 Gregory Toner, 'Reconstructing the Earliest Irish Tale Lists', *Éigse* 32 (2000), 88–120, at 97 and 113.

46 The last representative of this ecclesiastical dynasty died as coarb of St Commán in 1232 and is described as *saoi cléircechta, sencusa ocus breithemhnassa* in his obituary in AFM.

47 See Bianca Ross, 'William Mac an Leagha's Versions of the Story of Mary of Egypt', in Erich Poppe and Bianca Ross, ed., *The Legend of Mary of Egypt in Medieval Insular Hagiography* (Dublin, 1996), 259–78; Breatnach, 'Religious Significance', especially 38–9.

48 Most notably in the Life of Mary of Egypt, to which a sermon on the subject was deliberately prefaced by Uilliam Mac an Leagha in the longer of his two versions of the text: A. Martin Freeman, ed., 'Betha Mhuire Eigiptacdha', *Études celtiques* 1 (1936), 78–113 and Ross, 'Uilliam Mac an Leagha's Versions', 263, 276–7.

49 Breatnach, 'Religious Significance', 39.

of Fermoy, a considerable proportion of which is concerned with religious matter. It may indeed be significant that it is succeeded by another two-pronged narrative in Early Modern Irish, *Eachtra Airt meic Cuinn ocus Tochmarc Delbchaíme ingine Morgain*, in which the subjugation by virtue of sin is very much to the fore and, incidentally, in which the sovereignty motif is also spectacularly subverted.[50]

Much concerning *Compert Mongáin ocus Serc Duibe Lacha do Mongán* remains elusive. What is in no doubt, however, is the masterly touch of its accomplished creator, who drew skilfully on earlier material concerning the well-known literary figure Mongán to compose an early modern tale with resonance and relevance for his own time. To his neglected gem I can only hope to have brought some well-deserved attention.[51]

---

[50] R. I. Best, ed. and trans., 'The adventures of Art son of Conn and the Courtship of Delbchæm', *Ériu* 3 (1907), 149–73.

[51] I am grateful to Dr Meidhbhín Ní Úrdail who read this piece and made a number of helpful suggestions.

A BIBLIOGRAPHY OF THE WRITINGS OF THOMAS CHARLES-EDWARDS

Maredudd ap Huw

1969

'Edryd, edryf, edfryd, edrydd', *BBCS* 23/2 (May), 117–20.

'Welsh diffoddi, difa and Irish do-bádi and do-ba', *BBCS* 23/3 (November), 210–13.

'The Etymologies of diffoddi and differaf/diffryt' [with N. J. A. Williams], *BBCS* 23/3 (November), 213–17.

Review of B. E. Howells (ed.), *A Calendar of Letters Relating to North Wales* (Cardiff, 1967), *THSC*, 159–60.

Review of B. G. Charles, *Calendar of the Records of the Borough of Haverfordwest 1539–1660* (Cardiff, 1967), *THSC*, 160–1.

Review of Hywel D. Emanuel, *The Latin Texts of the Welsh Laws* (Cardiff, 1967), *SH* 9, 178–80.

1970

'The Date of the Four Branches of the Mabinogi', *THSC* 263–98, repr. in *The Mabinogi: A Book of Essays*, ed. C. W. Sullivan III (New York, 1996), 19–58.

1971

Two Mediaeval Welsh Poems. Stori Gwenfrewi a'i Ffynnon. The Story of St Winefride and her Well by Tudur Aled (1480–1526) and Ffynnon Wenfrewi. St Winefride's Well (Llandysul, 1971).

'Some Celtic Kinship Terms', *BBCS* 24/2 (May), 105–22.

'The Seven Bishop-Houses of Dyfed', *BBCS* 24/3 (November), 247–62.

'The Heir-Apparent in Irish and Welsh Law', *Celtica* 9, 180–90.

'Wb. 28c14 and the "Exclusive" Use of the Equative in Old Irish', *Ériu* 22, 188–9.

Obituary: The Reverend William Price, *Pelican* 38/5–6 (July), 118.

1972

'Kinship, Status and the Origins of the Hide', *Past and Present* 56 (August), 3–33.

'Note from Dr Charles-Edwards on Common Farming', in Kathleen Hughes, *Early Christian Ireland: Introduction to The Sources* (London), 61–4.

1973

'The Ivory Tower: A Voice from Inside', *Pelican* 2/2 (Trinity), 36–8.

1974

'Nei, Keifn, and Kefynderw', *BBCS* 25/4 (May), 386–8.

'Native Political Organization in Roman Britain and the Origin of MW *brenhin*', in *Antiquitates Indogermanicae: Studien zur Indogermanischen Altertumskunde und zur Sprach- und Kulturgeschichte der indogermanischen Völker: Gedenkschrift für Hermann Güntert zur 25. Wiederkehr seines Todestages am 23. April 1973*, ed. Manfred Mayrhofer *et al.* (Innsbruck), 35–45.

'The Foundation of Lastingham', *Ryedale Historian* 7, 13–21.

1975

Review of John Bannerman, *Studies in the History of Dalriada* (Edinburgh, 1974), *SH* 15, 194–6.

1976

'Boundaries in Irish Law', in *Medieval Settlement: Continuity and Change*, ed. P. H. Sawyer (London), 83–7.

'The Distinction between Land and Moveable Wealth in Anglo-Saxon England', *ibid.*, 180–7.

'The Social Background to Irish *Peregrinatio*', *Celtica* 11, 43–59, repr. in *The Otherworld Voyage in Early Irish Literature: An Anthology of Criticism*, ed. Jonathan M. Wooding (Dublin, 2000), 94–108.

1978

'The Authenticity of the *Gododdin*: An Historian's View', in *Astudiaethau ar yr Hengerdd: studies in Old Welsh poetry cyflwynedig i Syr Idris Foster*, ed. Rachel Bromwich and R. Brinley Jones (Cardiff), 44–71.

'Honour and Status in Some Irish and Welsh Prose Tales', *Ériu* 29, 123–41.

1980

'Nau Kynywedi Teithiauc', in *The Welsh Law of Women: Studies Presented to Professor Daniel A. Binchy on his Eightieth Birthday 3 June 1980*, ed. Dafydd Jenkins and Morfydd E. Owen (Cardiff), 23–39.

'The *Corpus Iuris Hibernici*' [review of D. A. Binchy, ed., *Corpus Iuris Hibernici* (Dublin, 1978)], *SH* 20, 141–62.

1981

Review of D. A. Binchy, ed., *Corpus Iuris Hibernici*, 6 vols (Dublin, 1978), *The Pelican* [dated 1980–1], 71–5.

1982

'Charles Plummer and Irish Law', *The Pelican* [dated 1981–2], 69–73.

1983

Bechbretha: An Old Irish Law-tract on Bee-keeping, ed. Thomas Charles-Edwards and Fergus Kelly, Early Irish Law Series 1 (Dublin [repr. Dublin, 2008]).

'Bede, the Irish and the Britons', *Celtica* 15, 42–52.

1984

'The Church and Settlement', in *Irland und Europa: die Kirche im Frümittelalter/Ireland and Europe: The Early Church*, ed. Próinséas Ní Chatháin and Michael Richter (Stuttgart), 167–75.

Review of Wendy Davies, *Wales in the Early Middle Ages. Studies in the Early History of Britain* (Leicester, 1982), *CMCS* 7 (Summer), 122–4.

Review of N. Brooks, *Latin and the Vernacular Languages in Early Medieval Britain* (Leicester, 1982), *The Journal of Roman Studies* 74, 252–4.

1985

Obituary: Trevor Henry Aston, *The Pelican* [dated 1984–5], 20–3.

Review of D. B. Walters, *The Comparative Legal Method. Marriage, Divorce and the Spouses' Property Rights in Early Medieval European Law and Cyfraith Hywel*, Pamffledi Cyfraith Hywel/Pamphlets on Welsh Law (Aberystwyth, 1982), *CMCS* 10 (Winter), 87–8.

1986

Lawyers and Laymen: Studies in the History of Law Presented to Professor Dafydd Jenkins on his Seventy-fifth Birthday Gŵyl Ddewi 1986, ed. T. M. Charles-Edwards, Morfydd E. Owen and D. B. Walters (Cardiff). Contributions by TC-E include 'A Note on Terminology' (pp. 10–12), 'The Texts. Introduction' (pp. 117–18), and 'The Iorwerth text, Edited and Translated' (pp. 137–78).

'Cynghawsedd: Counting and Pleading in Medieval Welsh Law', *BBCS* 33, 188–98.
'*Crith Gablach* and the Law of Status', *Peritia* 5, 53–73.

Review of M. Lapidge and D. Dumville, ed., *Gildas. New Approaches*, Studies in Celtic History 5 (Woodbridge, 1984), *CMCS* 12 (Winter), 115–20.
Review of Kathryn Grabowski and David Dumville, *Chronicles and Annals of Medieval Ireland and Wales: The Clonmacnoise Group Texts*, Studies in Celtic History 4 (Woodbridge, 1984), *The Welsh History Review* 13/1 (June), 103–5.
Review of Alexander C. Murray, *Germanic Kinship Structure: Studies in Law and Society in Antiquity and the Early Middle Ages* (Toronto, 1983), *The English Historical Review* 101, 465–6.

1988

Bede's Ecclesiastical History of the English People: a Historical Commentary, Oxford Medieval Texts, by J. M. Wallace-Hadrill [prepared for the press by TC-E] (Oxford).

1989

The Welsh Laws, Writers of Wales (Cardiff).

'Early Medieval Kingships in the British Isles', in *The Origins of Anglo-Saxon Kingdoms*, ed. Steven Bassett (London), 28–39, 245–8.

Obituary: D. A. Binchy, *The Pelican* [dated 1988–9], 68–72.

1990

'Custom in Early Irish Law', in *La Coutume/Custom, Part 2: Europe Occidentale Médiévale et Moderne*, ed. J. Vanderlinden, Recueils de la Société Jean Bodin pour l'Histoire Comparative des Institutions/Transactions of the Jean Bodin Society for Comparative Institutional History 52 (Brussells), 435–43.

1991

'The Arthur of History', in *The Arthur of the Welsh: The Arthurian Legend in Medieval Welsh Literature*, ed. Rachel Bromwich, A. O. H. Jarman and Brynley F. Roberts (Cardiff), pp. 15–32, repr. in *The Celtic World: Critical Concepts in Historical Studies*, Vol 3: Celtic History, ed. Raimund Karl and David Stifter, Critical Concepts in Historical Studies (London, 2007), 205–22.

1992

'The Pastoral Role of the Church in the Early Irish Laws', in *Pastoral Care before the Parish*, ed. John Blair and Richard Sharpe, Studies in the Early History of Britain (Leicester), pp. 63–80.

Review of A. Bammesberger and A. Wollmann, ed., *Britain 400–600: Language and History*, Anglistische Forschungen Heft 205 (Heidelberg, 1990), *Journal of Celtic Linguistics* 1, 145–55.

1993
Early Irish and Welsh Kinship (Oxford).

'The New Edition of Adomnán's Life of Columba', [review of Alan Orr Anderson and Marjorie Ogilvie Anderson (eds.), *Adomnán's Life of Columba*, Oxford Medieval Texts (Oxford, 1991)], *CMCS* 26 (Winter), 65–73.
'Palladius, Prosper, and Leo the Great: Mission and Primatial Authority', in *Saint Patrick, A.D. 493–1993*, ed. David N. Dumville, Studies in Celtic History 13 (Woodbridge), 1–12.

1994
'The Hendregadredd Manuscript and the Orthography and Phonology of Welsh in the Early Fourteenth Century' [with P. Russell], *The National Library of Wales Journal* 28/4 (Winter), 419–62.
'The Continuation of *Brut y Tywysogion* in Peniarth MS. 20' [with G. Charles-Edwards], in *Ysgrifau a Cherddi Cyflwynedig i Daniel Huws/Essays and Poems Presented to Daniel Huws*, ed. Tegwyn Jones and E. B. Fryde (Aberystwyth), 293–305.
'A Contract between King and People in Early Medieval Ireland: *Críth Gablach* on Kingship', *Peritia* 8, 107–19.

Review of Maura Walsh and Dáibhí Ó Cróinín, ed., *Cummian's Letter* De Controversia Paschali, *together with a Related Irish Computistical Tract* De ratione conputandi, Studies and Texts 86 (Toronto, 1988), *Peritia* 8, 216–20.
Review of Harold Mytum, *The Origins of Early Christian Ireland* (London, 1992), *The English Historical Review* 109, 101–2.

1995
'*Mi a Dynghaf Dynghed* and Related Problems', in *Hispano-Gallo-Brittonica: Essays in Honour of Professor D. Ellis Evans on the Occasion of his Sixty-fifth Birthday*, ed. Joseph F. Eska, R. Geraint Gruffydd and Nicolas Jacobs (Cardiff), 1–15.
'The Penitential of Theodore and the *Iudicia Theodori*', in *Archbishop Theodore: Commemorative Studies on his Life and Influence*, ed. Michael Lapidge, Cambridge Studies in Anglo-Saxon England 11 (Cambridge), pp. 141–74.
'Language and Society among the Insular Celts AD 400–1000', in *The Celtic World*, ed. Miranda J. Green (London), 703–36.

1996
'Irish Warfare before 1100', in *A Military History of Ireland*, ed. Thomas Bartlett and Keith Jeffery (Cambridge), 26–51.

Review of John Carey, *The Irish National Origin-Legend. Synthetic Pseudohistory. With a Memoir of Edmund Crosby Quiggin by David N. Dumville*, Quiggin Pamphlets on the Sources of Mediaeval Gaelic History, 1 (Cambridge, 1994), *CMCS* 31 (Summer), 89–90.
Review of Bernhard Bischoff and Michael Lapidge, *Biblical Commentaries from the Canterbury School of Theodore and Hadrian* (Cambridge, 1994), *Albion* 28, 660–1.

1997
'Anglo Saxon Kinship Revisited', in *The Anglo-Saxons from the Migration Period to the Eighth Century: An Ethnographic Perspective*, ed. John Hines, Studies in Archaeoethnology (Woodbridge), 171–210.

'The Penitential of Columbanus', in *Columbanus: Studies on the Latin Writings*, ed. Michael Lapidge, Studies in Celtic History 17 (Woodbridge), 217–39.

Review of N. B. Aitchison, *Armagh and the Royal Centres in Early Medieval Ireland. Monuments, Cosmology, and the Past* (Woodbridge, 1994), *The English Historical Review*, 425–6.

1998

'The Construction of the Hibernensis', *Peritia* 12, 209–37.

'The Context and Uses of Literacy in Early Christian Ireland', in *Literacy in Medieval Celtic Societies*, ed. Huw Pryce, Cambridge Studies in Medieval Literature 33 (Cambridge), 62–82.

'Alliances, Godfathers, Treaties and Boundaries', in *Kings, Currency, and Alliances: History and Coinage of Southern England in the Ninth Century*, ed. Mark A. S. Blackburn and David N. Dumville, Studies in Anglo-Saxon History 9 (Woodbridge), 47–62.

Review of Sioned Davies, *Crefft y Cyfarwydd: Astudiaeth o Dechnegau Naratif yn Y Mabinogion* (Cardiff, 1995), *Folklore* 109, 118.

Review of Dáibhí Ó Cróinín, *Early Medieval Ireland, 400-1200* (London, 1995), *The English Historical Review* 113, 132.

1999

The Early Mediaeval Gaelic Lawyer, Quiggin Pamphlets on the Sources of Mediaeval Gaelic History 4 (Cambridge).

'A Short History of Corpus Christi College', in *Corpus Silver: Patronage and Plate at Corpus Christi College, Oxford*, ed. Clive Ellory, Helen Clifford and Foster Rogers (Barton under Needlewood), 11–45.

'Geis, Prophecy, Omen and Oath', *Celtica* 23, 38–59.

'Britons in Ireland, *c.* 550–800', in *Ildánach Ildírech: A Festschrift for Proinsias Mac Cana*, ed. John Carey, John T. Koch and Pierre-Yves Lambert, Celtic Studies Publications 4 (Andover), 15–26.

Review of Toby Barnard, Dáibhí Ó Cróinín and Katharine Simms, ed., *A Miracle of Learning: Studies in Manuscripts and Irish Learning: Essays in Honour of William O' Sullivan* (Aldershot, 1998), *Peritia* 13, 315–18.

Review of Ailbhe Séamus Mac Shamhráin, *Church and Polity in Pre-Norman Ireland. The Case of Glendalough*, Maynooth Monographs 7 (Maynooth, 1996), *The Journal of Ecclesiastical History* 50 (1999), 343–4.

Review of Douglas Dales, *Light to the Isles. Missionary Theology in Celtic and Early Anglo-Saxon Britain* (Cambridge, 1997), *The English Historical Review* 114, 672.

2000

Early Christian Ireland (Cambridge).

The Welsh King and his Court, ed. T. M. Charles-Edwards, Morfydd E. Owen, and Paul Russell (Cardiff). Contributions by TC-E include '*Breintiau Gwŷr Powys*: The Liberties of the Men of Powys' [with Nerys Ann Jones] (pp. 191–223), and 'Food, Drink and Clothing in the Laws of Court' (pp. 319–37).

'Law in the Western Kingdoms between the Fifth and the Seventh Century', in *The Cambridge Ancient History, 14. Late Antiquity: Empire and Successors, A.D. 425–600*, ed. Averil Cameron, Bryan Ward-Perkins and Michael Whitby (Cambridge), 260–87.

'"The Continuation of Bede", *s.a.* 750: High-kings, Kings of Tara and "Bretwaldas"', in *Seanchas: Studies in Early and Medieval Irish Archaeology, History and Literature in Honour of Francis J. Byrne*, ed. Alfred P. Smyth (Dublin), 137–45.

2001

'The Textual Tradition of Medieval Welsh Prose Tales and the Problem of Dating', in *150 Jahre "Mabinogion" Deutsch-Walisische Kulturbeziehungen*, ed. Bernhard Maier and Stefan Zimmer, Buchreihe der *Zeitschrift für celtische Philologie* Bd. 19 (Tübingen), 23–39.

'Wales and Mercia, 613–918', in *Mercia: An Anglo-Saxon Kingdom in Europe*, ed. Michelle P. Brown and Carol A. Farr, Studies in the Early History of Europe (London), 89–105.

Review of Colmán Etchingham, *Church Organisation in Ireland, AD 650 to 1000* (Maynooth, 1999), *The English Historical Review* 116, 920–1.

2002

'*Érlam*: the Patron-saint of an Irish Church', in *Local Saints and Local Churches in the Early Medieval West*, ed. Alan Thacker and Richard Sharpe (Oxford), 267–90.

'*Tochmarc Étaíne*, a Literal Interpretation', in *Ogma: Essays in Celtic Studies in Honour of Próinséas Ní Chatháin*, ed. Michael Richter and Jean-Michel Picard (Dublin), 165–81.

'The Uí Néill 695–743: the Rise and Fall of Dynasties', *Peritia* 16, 396–418.

2003

After Rome, The Short Oxford History of the British Isles, ed. Thomas Charles-Edwards (Oxford). Contributions by TC-E include 'Introduction' (pp. 1–20), 'Nations and Kingdoms: A View from Above' (pp. 23–58), 'Conversion to Christianity' (pp. 103–39), and 'Conclusion' (pp. 259–70).

'The Northern Lectionary: A Source for the *Codex Salmanticensis*?', in *Celtic Hagiography and Saints' Cults*, ed. Jane Cartwright (Cardiff), 148–60.

'*Dliged*: its Native and Latinate Usages', *Celtica* 24, 65–78.

'Ireland and its invaders, 1166–1186', *Quaestio Insularis* 4, 1–34.

'Views of the Past: Legal and Historical Scholarship of the Twentieth Century', in *Retrospect and Prospect in Celtic Studies: Proceedings of the 11th International Congress of Celtic Studies held in University College, Cork, 25–31 July 1999*, eds. Máire Herbert and Kevin Murray (Dublin), 15–27.

Review of Bart Jaski, *Early Irish Kingship and Succession* (Dublin, 2000), *The English Historical Review* 118, 1026.

2004

H. C. G. Matthew and B. H. Harrison, ed., *Oxford Dictionary of National Biography*, 61 vols (Oxford) (also online at http://www.oxforddnb.com/). Entries on: Áed Allán mac Fergaile (d. 743), Áed Oirdnide mac Néill (d. 819), Áed Uaridnach mac Domnaill (Áed Allán mac Domnaill) (d. 612), Blaímac mac Áeda (Blathmac) (d. 665), Brigit (St Brigit, Brigid) (439/452–524/526), Brochfael Ysgithrog (Brochfael ap Cyngen) (*supp. fl.* 6th cent.), Brynach (St Brynach, Bernachius, Bernacius) (*fl.* 6th cent.), Cadfan (St Cadfan) (*supp. fl.* 6th cent.), Cadog (St Cadog, Cadoc, Cadfael, Cathmáel) (*fl.* 6th cent.), Cadwallon (Cædwalla) ap Cadfan (d. 634), Cellach mac Máele Coba (d. 658), Cenn Fáelad mac Blaímaic (d. 675), Cináed mac Írgalaig (d. 728), Congal Cáech (d. 637), Connacht, Saints of (*act. c.*400–*c.*800), Cybi (St Cybi, Kebi, Mo Chop) (*fl.* 6th cent.), Cyfeilliog (d. 927), Cynidr (St Cynidr, Chenedre, Cinitr) (*fl.* 6th cent.), Dallán Forgaill (Dallan) (*fl.* 597), Deiniol (St Deiniol, Daniel) (d. 584), Diarmait mac Cerbaill (d. 565), Dogfael (St Dogfael, Dogwel, Dygfael, Dogmael) (*fl.* 6th cent.), Domnall mac Áeda (d. 642), Domnall mac Murchada (d. 763), Dubthach maccu Lugair (*supp. fl.* 432), Elfoddw (d. 809), Fínsnechtae Fledach mac Dúnchada (d. 695), Flaithbertach mac Loingsig (d. 765), Forggus mac Muirchertaig (d. *c.*566), Gwallawg (Gwallog) (*fl.* 572–9–585–92), Gwenfrewi (St Gwenfrewi, Winefrith, Winifred) (*fl. c.*650), Gwynllyw (St Gwynllyw, Woolloos) (*fl.* 6th cent.), Iarlaithe (St Iarlaithe, Jarlath) (*supp. d.* 481), Iona, Abbots of (*act.* 563–927), Lucius (*supp. fl.* 185), Máel Sechnaill mac Máele Ruanaid (d. 862), Meath, Saints of (*act. c.*400–*c.*900), Muirchertach mac Muiredaig (Muirchertach mac Ercae, Mac Ercae) (d. 534), Mynyddog Mwynfawr (*supp. fl.* 6th cent.), Niall mac Maíl Shechnaill (d. 1061), Palladius (*fl.* 429–*c.*433), Suibne Menn mac Fiachnai (d. 628), Taliesin (*fl.* 6th cent.), Tuathal Máelgarb mac Cormaic (*fl.* 535–539), Ua Braín, Tigernach (d. 1088), Ua Cerbaill, Máel Suthain (Maolsuthain O'Carroll) (d. 1010), Ulster, Saints of (*act. c.*400–*c.*650), and Vorteporius (*fl. c.*540).

'The Making of Nations in Britain and Ireland in the Early Middle Ages', in *Lordship and Learning: Studies in Memory of Trevor Aston*, ed. Ralph Evans (Woodbridge), 11–37.
'*Gorsedd*, *Dadl*, and *Llys*: Assemblies and Courts in Medieval Wales', in *Assembly Places and Practices in Medieval Europe*, ed. Aliki Pantos and Sarah Semple (Dublin), 95–105.
'Early Irish Saints' Cults and their Constituencies', *Ériu* 54, 79–102.

Review of John Carey, Máire Herbert and Pádraig Ó Riain, eds., *Studies in Irish Hagiography. Saints and Scholars* (Dublin, 2001), *The Journal of Ecclesiastical History* 55, 140–1.

2005
'Medieval Welsh Law', in *Bausteine zum Studium der Keltologie*, ed. Helmut Birkhan (Wien), pp. 409–13.
'Middle Welsh *mae* "is"', in *A Companion in Linguistics: A Festschrift for Anders Ahlqvist on the Occasion of his Sixtieth Birthday*, ed. Bernadette Smelik *et al.* (Nijmegen), pp. 161–70.
'Introduction: Prehistoric and Early Ireland', in *A New History of Ireland 1, Prehistoric and Early Ireland*, ed. Dáibhí Ó Cróinín (Oxford), pp. lvii–lxxxii.
'Early Irish Law', *ibid.*, 331–70.
'Celtic Inscriptions from Gaul and Britain' [review of Pierre-Yves Lambert, *Textes Gallo-Latins sur instrumentum*, Recueil des Inscriptions Gauloises vol. II, fasc. 2. Gallia 45th Supplement (Paris, 2002), and Patrick Sims-Williams, *The Celtic Inscriptions of Britain: Phonology and Chronology, c. 400–1200*, Publications of the Philological Society 37 (Oxford, 2003)], *Antiquity* 79, 961–3.
'Historical Context and Literary Meaning: Another Reading of *Scéla Muicce Meic Da Thó*', *Journal of Celtic Studies* 5, 1–16.
'The Airgialla charter poem: the legal content', in *The Kingship and Landscape of Tara*, ed. Edel Bhreathnach (Dublin), 100–23.

2006
The Chronicle of Ireland, Translated Texts for Historians 44, 2 vols (Liverpool).

J. T. Koch, ed., *Celtic Culture. A Historical Encyclopaedia*, 5 vols (Santa Barbara, CA). Entries on: *Bretha Nemed* (I.247–8); Kinship, Celtic (III.1063–5); Law Texts, Celtic [1] Irish (III.1109–12).

Review of M. T. Flanagan, *Irish Royal Charters: Texts and Contexts* (Oxford), *Irish Social and Economic History* 33, 115–16.
Review of Christopher A. Snyder, *The Britons*, The Peoples of Europe (Malden, Mass., 2003), *Speculum* 81, 606.

2007
Tair Colofn Cyfraith. The Three Columns of Law in Medieval Wales: Homicide, Theft and Fire, ed. Thomas Charles-Edwards and Paul Russell (Bangor). Contributions by TC-E include 'Crime and Tort and The Three Columns of Law' [transl. by TC-E of Dafydd

Jenkins, *Cyfraith Hywel*, 2nd edn (Llandysul, 1976), chapter 6, pp. 60–79] (pp. 1–25), 'The Three Columns of Law: a Comparative Perspective' (pp. 26–59), 'The *Galanas* Tractate in Iorwerth: Texts and Legal Development' (pp. 92–107), 'The Welsh Law of Theft: Iorwerth versus the Rest' (pp. 108–30), and 'The Three Columns of Law from Iorwerth Manuscripts *E* and *B*' (pp. 258–307).

'The Lure of Celtic Languages, 1850–1914', in *The Making of the Middle Ages: Liverpool Essays*, ed. Marios Costambeys, Andrew Hamer and Martin Heale (Liverpool), 15–35.

2008

'Beyond Empire II: Christianities of the Celtic Peoples', in *The Cambridge History of Christianity 3. Early Medieval Christianities, c.600–c.1100*, ed. Thomas F. X. Noble and Julia M. H. Smith (Cambridge), 86–106.

'The Fellows' Library – Restoration and Renewal', *Jesus College Record*, 41–7.

'Saints' cults and the early Irish church', *Clogher Record* 19, 173–84.

'Picts and Scots: a review of Alex Woolf, *From Pictland to Alba, 789–1070*, The New Edinburgh History of Scotland 2 (Edinburgh, 2007)', *Innes Review* 59, 168–88.

Review of Patrick Sims-Williams, *Ancient Celtic Place-Names in Europe and Asia Minor*, Publications of the Philological Society 39 (Oxford, 2006), *Antiquity* 82/315 (March), 228–9.

2009

'Celtic Kings: "Priestly Vegetables"?', in *Early Medieval Studies in Memory of Patrick Wormald*, ed. Stephen Baxter, Catherine Karkov, Janet Nelson and David Pelteret (Farnham), 65–80.

'Guides, Grants and Deeds' [review of Katherine Forsyth, ed., *Studies on the Book of Deer* (Dublin, 2008)], *The Times Literary Supplement* (4 Dec), 22–3.

'Britain and Ireland, c. 500–c. 750: Social Structure', in *A Companion to the Early Middle Ages: Britain and Ireland c. 500–1100*, ed. Pauline Stafford (Oxford), 107–25.

2010

Wales and the Wider World: Welsh History in an International Context, ed. T. M. Charles-Edwards and R. J. W. Evans (Donington). Including a contribution by TC-E on 'Rome and the Britons, 400–664' (pp. 9–27).

'Foreword' to *St. Patrick: The Life and World of Ireland's Saint*, by J. B. Bury (London), ix–xv.

'The Structure and Purpose of Adomnán's *Vita Columba*', in *Adomnán of Iona: Theologian, Lawmaker, Peacemaker*, ed. Jonathan M. Wooding *et al.* (Dublin), 205–18.

'*Prehistoric Annals* and Early Medieval Monasticism: Daniel Wilson, James Young Simpson, and their Cave Sites' [with K. Ahronson], *Antiquaries Journal* 90, 455–66.

'Society and Politics in Pre-Norman Ireland', in *L'Irlanda e gli Irlandesi nell'Alto Medioevo: Spoleto, 16–21 aprile 2009*. Settimane di Studio della Fondazione Centro Italiano di Studi sull'Alto Medioevo 57 (Spoleto), 173–84.

'The Fellows' Library', in *The Jesus College Record 2010*, ed. Armand d'Angour (Oxford), 93–8.

'The Date of *Culhwch ac Olwen*', in *Bile ós Chrannaibh: a Festschrift for William Gillies*, ed. Wilson McLeod, et al. (Ceann Drochaid), 45–56.

The compiler acknowledges assistance received from Anselm Cramer, Elizabeth O'Brien, Huw Pryce, Julian Reid, Paul Russell and Richard Sharpe in the compilation of this bibliography.

INDEX

Traditional counties are listed for Ireland, pre-1974 counties for England and Scotland, and post-1996 counties for Wales.

Page numbers in bold type refer to illustrations and their captions.

TABULA GRATULATORIA

Maredudd ap Huw
Lesley Abrams
Anders Ahlqvist
Kristján Ahronson
Gareth A. Bevan
Edel Bhreathnach
John Blair
Cormac Bourke
Elizabeth Boyle
Dorothy Ann Bray
Liam Breatnach
Dauvit Broun and Nerys Ann Jones
Marc Caball
John Carey
Thomas Owen Clancy
Iestyn Daniel
Luned Mair Davies
Sioned Davies
Wendy Davies
Clare Downham
D.N. Dumville
Fiona Edmonds
Nancy Edwards
Matthias Egeler
Charlene Eska
Dylan Foster Evans
Wyn Evans
Joseph J. Flahive
Marie Therese Flanagan
Roy Flechner
Janet Foot
William Gillies
Angela Grant
Geraint and Luned Gruffydd
Andrew Hawke and Ann Parry Owen
Deborah Hayden
Máire Herbert
Arkady Hodge
Benjamin Hudson
Lowri Angharad Hughes
Daniel Huws

Richard W. Ireland
Randolph Ivy
Nicolas Jacobs
Christine James
Dafydd Johnston
Elva Johnston
Raimund Karl
Fergus Kelly
John T. Koch
Max Lieberman
Michael D. Linkletter
Ceridwen Lloyd-Morgan
Hector MacQueen
Roger McClure
Catherine McKenna
Pat Menzies
Jimmy P. Miller
Kevin Murray
Bronagh Ní Chonaill
Máire Ní Mhaonaigh
Cynthia J. Neville
Michael Newton
Elizabeth O'Brien
Tomás Ó Cathasaigh
Caitríona Ó Dochartaigh
Bernard and Heather O'Donoghue
Jennifer O'Reilly
Katharine Olson
Morfydd E. Owen
Oliver Padel
Geraldine Parsons
John Penney
Erich Poppe
Huw Pryce
Katja Ritari
Euryn Rhys Roberts
Sara Elin Roberts
Paul Russell
Richard Sharpe
Patrick Sims-Williams and Marged
  Haycock

237

Tabula Gratulatoria

Robin Chapman Stacey
Clare Stancliffe
David Stifter
Frederick Suppe
Catherine Swift
Simon Taylor
Gregory Toner
Patrick Wadden

Dafydd Bened Walters
Bryan Ward-Perkins
Niamh Whitfield
Andreas Willi
Jonathan Wooding
Susan Youngs
Stefan Zimmer
Mark Zumbuhl

Cardiff University
Celtic Library, Jesus College, University of Oxford
Centre for Manx Studies, University of Liverpool
Corpus Christi College, University of Oxford
Department of Anglo-Saxon, Norse and Celtic, University of Cambridge
Prehistory and Europe Department, British Museum
Prifysgol Bangor University
St Anne's College, University of Oxford
St Hugh's College, University of Oxford
St Peter's College Library, University of Oxford
Taylor Institution Library, University of Oxford
University of Wales Centre for Advanced Welsh and Celtic Studies